S0-CBY-914

Duquesne Studies

LANGUAGE AND LITERATURE SERIES

VOLUME TWO

GENERAL EDITOR:

Foster Provost, *Department of English, Duquesne University*

EDITORIAL BOARD:

Judith H. Anderson
Donald Cheney
Patrick Cullen
Arthur M. Eastman
French R. Fogle
A. Bartlett Giamatti
A. C. Hamilton
S. K. Heninger, Jr.
A. Kent Hieatt
Robert B. Hinman
William B. Hunter, Jr.
Albert C. Labriola
Waldo F. McNeir
Mother M. Christopher Pecheux, O.S.U.
Herbert H. Petit
Thomas P. Roche, Jr.
John T. Shawcross
James D. Simmonds
Humphrey Tonkin
Robert F. Whitman

MILTON'S POETRY

Thus saith the high and loftie one, that inhabiteth ETERNITIE.

Adam lost ETERNITIE, Christ regained it: to this the Angels invite us from this the devils withdraw us: have a care whether thou followest.

MILTON'S POETRY

ITS DEVELOPMENT
IN TIME

EDWARD W. TAYLER

DUQUESNE UNIVERSITY PRESS

PITTSBURGH

All rights reserved, Published by Duquesne University
Press, Pittsburgh, Pennsylvania 15219. Distributed by
Humanities Press, Inc., Atlantic Highlands, New Jersey
07716.

Library of Congress in Publication Data

Tayler, Edward. William.
  Milton's poetry

  (Duquesne studies: Language and literature series;
v. 2)
  Includes bibliographical references and index.
  1. Milton, John, 1608–1674—Criticism and interpretation.
  2. Time in literature. I. Title. II. Series.
PR3592.T5T3   821'.4   78-12047
ISBN 0-391-00863-3

Manufactured in the United States of America

FIRST EDITION

VKT *and* WRT
CLM

The Frontispiece—

Ralph Winterton, *The Considerations of Drexelius Upon Eternitie*, HEW 30792. Reproduced by permission of *The Huntington Library*, San Marino, California. Engraved by William Marshal (1636).

Christ as a childe, taken as it were from the manger and the cradle, almost quite naked, and without clothes, *stands in the clouds: on his shoulders he beares a crosse: In the clouds* there is this inscription, ETERNITIE: Beneath Christs *feet,* down upon the earth there is the *Sceleton* of a man (the Protoplast) . . .: *in his left hand* he holds a *piece of parchment,* in which these words are written, *Momentaneum quod delectat, That which delighteth is momentanie: In his right hand* he holds up an *Apple.* Neare unto him there stands a *Raven,* pecking a shelfish with this subscription, *Cras, Cras,* To morrow, to morrow. . . . *Christ* coming down from the clouds *Two adore* with bended knees of diverse sex, in the place of all mankinde. *Behind them* is a running *Houreglasse,* or a *Diall* measuring houres by the running of water, called a *Clepsydra;* and a *Book* lying wide open: One one page there is written, *They spend their dayes in mirth, and in a moment go downe to the grave* (JOB). *On the other page, Who shall deliver me from the body of this death* (Romans). *Before* them stand Two heavenly *Angels.* . . . Neare unto the Sceleton of . . . the first man that God made, is the *Ravens* place in the picture, which makes very much for the representation of *Eternitie* to the life.

CONTENTS

Preface   ix

Introduction   1

  I.   Occasional Experiments   18

 II.   *Lycidas* in Christian Time   45

III.   *Paradise Lost:* From Shadows to Truth   60

IV.   *Samson Agonistes:* Found in the Close   105

 V.   The Tempestivity of Time   123

VI.   *Paradise Regained:* Waiting to Stand   148

Some Conclusions   185

Notes   215

Index   267

PREFACE

In this book—part of a larger project—I have tried to be of use by describing an area of thought that shaped Milton's attitude toward life and art. Since this area includes older views of the relation of Time to Eternity, I have felt obliged to explain again, even to document anew, such technical matters as the theory of types and the distinction between *chronos* and *kairos;* and I entertain the usual hope—that my introductory purpose will not entirely exclude the interest of the specialist. I believe that the notions elaborated here have their applicability not only to Milton but also to Spenser, Shakespeare, and a variety of lesser figures: It was Time, with wings and hourglass, who at Cheapside in 1559 led his daughter Truth to the new Queen Elizabeth, and it was Time, wings clipped and hourglass stopped, who appeared at Harefield Place in 1602 during the old Queen's last pageant; and it was Time, exercising *sub specie aeternitatis* his twin but opposed powers (*tempus edax rerum* and *veritas filia temporis*), who continued to hold court through two later reigns and the Interregnum.

Although I feel that I have been anticipated in certain respects by scholars such as Frank Kermode and Barbara K. Lewalski, I can console myself with the reflection that I am a belated fellow-traveler in good company. Recalling my teachers at Amherst and Stanford makes me once again aware, even after many years, of their continuing presence in what I most want to teach and write. To my colleagues and students at Columbia, where I like to suppose that the traffic in ideas moves more briskly than elsewhere, I owe intellectual debts that I hope I have in part repaid; I have a particular debt to my former chairman, Karl Kroeber, who found a way to allow me the time to write my final chapter. Much of my research was done at the Bodleian and the British Museum during a year when I was honored by the John Simon Guggenheim Foundation, which furthers the cause of disciplined scholarship, perhaps in ways uniquely its own, under the exacting direction of Gordon N. Ray; I feel especially grateful to Stephen Schlesinger and San Woodring. The rest of my research and most of my writing was done at The Huntington Library where I was fortunate enough to hold an NEH-Huntington Fellowship; I want to record in this connection my gratitude for the many kindnesses of the late Claude Simpson. The Huntington is for me, as for so many scholars, much more than a first-rate research center; the staff, under the able and amiable direction of James Thorpe, presides over a place of books that nourishes the spirit as well as the mind, and I have had many occasions to be grateful for the friendship and help of Carey Bliss, Mary Isabel Fry, Noelle Jackson, Virginia Renner, Daniel Woodward, Mary Wright, and many more.

Of the many others who have helped me in many ways, I feel particularly grateful to the following, apologizing to them for the listing alphabetical and to others for inadvertent omission: Boyd Berry, Howard Canaan, Jackson Cope, Stuart Curran, Stanley Fish, French Fogle, Jeffrey Ford, S. K. Heninger, Robert Hoopes, Jody Hoy, Barbara Kerrigan, Jenijoy La Belle, Albert C. Labriola, Gregory Lombardo, Mary Irby Oates, James Riddell, Jason Rosenblatt, Lawrence V. Ryan, Florence Sandler, John Shawcross, Hallett Smith, Marlene Spiegler, John M. Steadman, Stanley Stewart, Peggy-Anne Streep, Irene Tayler, and Joseph A. Wittreich, Jr. In preparing the ms. for the press I was thankful for the scrupulous care of Veronica Towers and the cordial efficiency of Foster Provost. The book is dedicated to the memory of those who gave me life and to the presence of the one who makes it worth living.

Those unfamiliar with the distinction between *chronos* and *kairos* may find it helpful to read the chapter entitled "The Tempestivity of Time" immediately after the Introduction and Chapter I. The chapter on *Samson* first appeared as an article in *ELR* (III [1973]), the one on *Lycidas* in *HLQ* (XLI [February, 1978]). I have quoted Milton in most cases from the readily-accessible edition of Merritt Y. Hughes ("Hughes"); on occasion, generally when I needed the Latin, from the Columbia Edition ("Works").

INTRODUCTION

Perhaps Aristotle was right in supposing that human nature reveals
itself ever and everywhere the same, just as fire burns both here
and in Persia. It is at any rate comforting to reflect that human life
exhibits continuities and agreements, by means of which we may
think to know others after the manner in which we hope to know
ourselves. Sir Thomas Browne expressed gratitude to the divine
dispensation that had accorded him "no sinnes that want a name,"
and critics often seem happy enough in contemplating The Universal Values residing in great works of art. Although one can
scarcely quarrel with what is universal, the seductive lure of easy
speech represents only one of the difficulties in the tendency to
assume resemblances where they may not exist. The grand temptation, as nearly everyone knows, invites us to come upon ourselves in
a work of art, finding there our own lineaments of satisfied or
unsatisfied desire mirrored beguilingly. And, up to a point, properly enough. It will always be easier for one generation of the sons
of men to understand the sense in which Holden Caulfield (of *The
Catcher in the Rye*) is a "boy" than to apprehend the force of the
epithet hurled at Coriolanus. But in reading for the sake of experience it seems clear that we must be prepared to accept the discomfort of growth as well as to delight in identification. In art as in life
the alien may excite hostility, indifference, or the reach for em-
pathy. But if it can be granted that the mind requires an apprecia-
tion of differences as well as similarities to persist fully alive, then it
is not perverse to suggest that one of our stronger reasons for
returning to Milton is that he seems, as the writings of Leavis,

1

Pound, Eliot, and others proclaim, so intransigently *other*. Understanding differences is another person's due, because he is human, and it is the act of deference owed to human greatness of the past. Since "books are not absolutely dead things," texts *déjà ecrit* consisting merely of black marks on white pages, but rather "preserve as in a vial" the extract of a "living intellect," the pleasure of reading first involves understanding another "self" in its singularities, which incidentally though not unimportantly affords us new perspectives on ourselves as selves.

Understanding Milton begins properly where he himself had to begin—"in the beginning":

> God created the heaven and the earth. . . . And God said, Let there be light: and there was light. And God saw the light, that it was good: and God divided the light from the darkness . . . . And God said, Let there be a firmament in the midst of the waters, and let it divide the waters from the waters. And God made the firmament, and divided the waters which were under the firmament from the waters which were above the firmament: and it was so . . . . And God said, Let the waters under the heaven be gathered together unto one place, and let the dry land appear: and it was so. . . . And God said, Let there be lights in the firmament of the heaven to divide the day from the night . . . . And to rule over the day and over the night, and to divide the light from the darkness: and God saw that it was good.

It will be apparent that deity delights not only in addition but also in long division, that the divine complacency stems from the propagation of opposites. As Peter Sterry explained in preaching before Parliament after the victories at Drogheda and Wexford on 1 November 1649, "God bringeth forth his Works in contraries; Light and Darkness; Good and Evil; Michael and his Angels; the Dragon and his Angels."[1] And it is so. For even if we doubt that this is the way it all happened, we may be as sure as Milton that this is the way it is.

The world that lies before us "where to choose" frames the dualities that constitute the human predicament, even for those of us who do not have "Providence thir guide." We could neither speak nor think of light without first knowing night, just as we cannot, according to Milton, know good in this fallen world without first knowing evil. Alexander Bain, the great nineteenth-century logician, states the matter squarely and clearly: "The essential Relativity of all knowledge, thought, or consciousness, cannot but show itself in language," for if "everything that we can know is viewed as a transition from something else [ultimately, its opposite], every experience must have two sides; and either every name must have a double meaning, or else for every meaning there must be two names," which helps to explain why the Miltonic pun remains the highest form of wit.[2]

Genesis by dualism inevitably has moral implications as well, for the world is divided not only into heaven and earth, day and night, wet and dry, male and female but also into soul and body, good and evil, free and enslaved, the members of the opposite sex we may touch and those whom we may not. In Marvell's formulation,

> Luxurious Man, to bring his vice in use,
> Did after him the world seduce,

with the consequence that Nature "grew then as double as his mind."[3] Man had once existed in Eden in the state of *integritas*, perfect "oneness" with his own and external Nature so that reason and desire were similarly one—but then fell into duality. "Adam in Eden," notes Wallace Stevens in "A Supreme Fiction," was "the father of Descartes." In the famous declaration from *Areopagitica*, "It was from out the rind of one apple tasted, that the knowledge of good and evil, as two twins cleaving together, leaped forth into the world. And perhaps this is the doom which Adam fell into of knowing good and evil, that is to say, of knowing good by evil." And it is so, for the panoply of polarities both quickens our awareness and makes choice hard and painful: "that which purifies us," says Milton, "is trial, and trial is by what is contrary." In the words of Louis le Roy (echoing Aristotle's *Rhetoric* 3.9.1410a), "In so much that we may say in all cases, that contraries when they are put neere, one to the other, they appeare the more cleerely. . . . So it seemeth that the good cannot be knowen without the evill: and although they be contrarie, yet have they such a conjunction, that in taking of one, both are tane away."[4] Or, to revert again to Milton: "look how much we thus expel of sin, so much we expel of virtue; for the matter of them both is the same; remove that, and ye remove them both alike. This justifies the high providence of God. . . ."[5] The continuing lapse of Luxurious Man into what is "double as his mind" lies "in the beginning," in creation by division.

Lévi-Strauss points out that all myths formulate contraries, then attempt to mediate the extremes. That this process is at least partly true of Genesis has been demonstrated by Edmund Leach in terms of information theory.[6] There is, first, the principle of the "bit" or binary digit, which refers to two alternative messages that may be selected on an arbitrary basis; God in these terms goes about His business by speaking in "bits," creating a binary (solar) system, just as Ovid's god or nature in *Metamorphoses* proceeds by "division" and "subdivision." Second is the principle of redundancy, necessary to the effective communication of messages against the background of noise. And God does indeed repeat himself, not only sentence-by-sentence but also, and most spectacularly, when He comes to create man, first in Genesis 1:

> And God said, Let us make man in our image, after our like-ness. . . . So God created man in his own image, in the image of God created he him; male and female created he them.

Next in Genesis 2:

> And the Lord God formed man of the dust of the ground, and breathed into his nostrils the breath of life; and man became a living soul. . . . And the Lord God caused a deep sleep to fall upon Adam, and he slept: and he took one of his ribs, and closed up the ribs instead thereof; And the rib, which the Lord God had taken from the man, made he a woman, and brought her unto the man.

Although it is doubtless easy enough for the moralist or theologian to reconcile the two accounts, even cursory examination reveals differences that help in understanding the puzzling esthetic prac-tices of many Christian writers, including Milton.[7]

Creation by division in the Bible, though not in Homer, has the theologically inconvenient result of relegating divinity to the "other world" while man remains confined to this world—a situation that provokes the need for mediating elements or oxymora (preemi-nently Christ the God-Man, partaking of both extremes) and, in addition, poses forcibly the problem of communication between the two realms, between Nature and Grace, corporeal and spiritual, Time and Eternity. The problem of linguistic intercourse between heaven and earth becomes especially acute for the Christian poet when he "pursues"

> Things unattempted yet in Prose or Rhyme,

endeavoring to "see and tell"

> Of things invisible to mortal sight;

and we may perceive a kind of model for his predicament in the "redundant" accounts of creation.

The first (Priestly) creation not only implies that Adam and Eve came into being simultaneously without essential difference in the *manner* of their being made; it is also explicitly metaphorical, a mirror creation in which man comes into being as the "image of God." Mirror creation obviously has important consequences for language as well as theology, for by guaranteeing at least a degree of likeness between creator and creature it sanctifies comparison, analogy, as one way to "tell"

Of things invisible to mortal sight.

The second creation offers no such guarantee. Not only has the creation of woman become clearly secondary to that of man, emphasizing difference between "male and female"; but also man himself loses the singular constitution of "man in our image, after our likeness," and instead becomes a composition of contraries, formed from the earth, "from the dust of the ground," only then infused with a divine element as God "breathed into his nostrils the breath of life." The metaphor here cannot be that of the mirror; rather it is, implicitly, that of Pygmalion at patty-cakes, the potter at his wheel. There is in this second creation no guarantee of likeness, congruence, between the creator and creature, any more than there is between potter and pot. The "redundant" creations thus afford a radical parallel for what Browne was later to denominate the "comparative" and "negative" ways for talking about God; that is, either by analogy, by what Milton's angel calls "lik'ning spiritual to corporal forms," or by positing a series of negatives about God, in the manner of the negative theology of the medieval period, where the enumeration of "not this" and "not that" emphasizes that the ways of God are not those of men and that it is impossible in human terms to "delineate" what "surmounts the reach" of "human sense."

Well before Milton started out to "justify the ways of God to men," the opposed assumptions about the relation of man to the divine that underlie the two accounts of the creation appear in the inconsistent theodicy of the Book of Job, which exhibits in the frame story or Prologue-Epilogue a different view of "justice" than is conveyed by the Dialogue itself. In the rather detached prose of the frame, Job is a patriarchal saint who observes scrupulously the sacrificial cultus and never questions the justice of Yahweh. In the

passionate verse of the Dialogue proper Job attacks in his friends
the simple-minded if venerable orthodoxies about divine justice
that the emergent Israel had found in the Wisdom Literature of
Mesopotamia. The story of Job thus exemplifies in its structure the
principle of the "bit," conveying simultaneously two alternative
messages about the nature of man and the justice of God. The
orthodoxy of the friends may be reduced to something like the
proposition that, since God is just and since Job has been punished,
Job must have sinned. The message of the Prologue-Epilogue denies that Job sinned (thus contradicting the friends), but nevertheless manages to reassert precisely the same theodicy from the opposite direction: since Job did not sin, he receives lots more camels
than he had originally; virtue is rewarded, and the Lord who
tempts also distributes justice in ways readily understood by men.
In either case it is assumed that God's justice is the "likeness" of, the
"image" of, human justice.

It is the function of the Dialogue to subvert this message by
providing an alternative view, based on assumptions that may be
related for the sake of analytical convenience to the second account
of creation in Genesis. The Dialogue, evidently (with the possible
exception of the speeches of Elihu) the work of a single poet, shows
Job demolishing the conventional pieties of the friends, railing
against the injustice apparent in the world, and even questioning
God—all the while seeing himself progressively reduced to his origins. Covered with sackcloth and ashes, he has in effect become
"dust of the ground" and scarcely retains the "breath of life." The
theophany, when Elohim speaks to Job from the whirlwind, con-
firms the alternative message:

> Who is this that darkeneth counsel by words without knowledge? . . .
> Where wast thou when I laid the foundations of the earth? declare, if
> thou hast understanding. Who hath laid the measures thereof, if
> thou knowest? or who hath stretched the line upon it? Whereupon
> are the foundations thereof fastened? or who hath laid the corner
> stone thereof? When the morning stars sang together, and all the
> sons of God shouted for joy?

The unanswerable questions continue until Job confesses:

> Behold, I am vile; what shall I answer thee? I will lay mine hand upon
> my mouth. Once I have spoken; but I will not answer: yea, twice; but
> I will proceed no further.

Yet God proceeds, through question after question, until Job has thoroughly learned his origins and true descent: "Wherefore I abhor myself, and repent in dust. . . ." The theophany has most terrifyingly served its purpose, to show that man's idea of justice need not correspond to that of Elohim: "Wilt thou disannul my judgment? wilt thou condemn me, that thou mayst be righteous?" No more, Job discovers, can he do that than he can "draw out leviathan with an hook." There can in this context be no comparison between the pot and the potter, between man and God; no analogy between the justice of men and the justice of God. The rest is silence ("I will lay mine hand upon my mouth"), except to recognize and confess that "I am vile," and "I abhor myself, and repent in dust. . . ."

The two (contrasting) creations in Genesis do not of course explain the baffling theodicy of the Book of Job, nor should they in any sense be taken as the cause of religious tribulation; but they do exemplify clearly, and from the beginning, the predicament of the Christian poet who feels he must attempt to utter the ineffable, must therefore try to fabricate analogies in which one term is by definition undefinable. Troubled by real or apparent dualisms, the Christian seeks the unity of one God; and the language of the Christian poet cannot but betray his awareness of the dangers of his task. To take the venerable example from theology, the Christian must assume that his soul retains its divine essence even when "in" the body, that the "breath of life" remains somehow radically opposed to the "dust of the ground," for on the separateness of the two elements hinges the doctrine of immortality; but of course this necessary dualism embarrasses the Christian who wants to explain how the soul, the "form" of the body, has any control over the flesh it "inherits." In arguing interaction between body and soul, Descartes found himself hoist by his own pineal gland, and Renaissance physiologists were obliged to posit the existence of "spirits," mediating substances progressively rarefied in blood and brain to make the subtle knot that knits us men. This tension—in its largest aspect a tension between dualistic and monistic views of the world—may be apprehended in almost any sophisticated Christian, anyone who is aware, for instance, that Christian soldiers do not always march onward and that the way up may on occasion be the way down.

The habit of dichotomy leads in the Renaissance to all those works that seek to adjudicate the conflicting claims of Body and

Soul, Nature and Grace, Reason and Faith, Time and Eternity—
together with all those other dualisms that everywhere mark the
thought of the period. And it is, of course, the tension between
opposites that produces paradox when the theologian seeks to preserve the doctrine of immortality without sanctioning an absolute
divorce between body and soul, or when the poet asks to be
ravished that he may be chaste; and when Browne, the religious
doctor, dignifies the creature without disparaging the Creator:

> Nor doth the similitude of creatures disparage the variety of nature,
> nor any way confound the workes of God. For even in things alike,
> there is diversitie, and those that doe seeme to accord, doe manifestly
> disagree. And thus is Man like God, for in the same things that wee
> resemble him, wee are utterly different from him.[8]

In Milton the tensions appear to be as acute as in any of the
metaphysical poets, though the typical kinds of paradox—"Dark
with excessive bright thy skirts appear"—occur less frequently in
his work than in, say, that of Donne. Of the great contrasts that
pervade Milton's poetry, often expressed (necessarily) with some
hint of paradox, the most basic and the most difficult for us to
appreciate fully is that between Time and Eternity.

"Time we may comprehend," says Sir Thomas Browne; "'tis but
five days elder then ourselves, and hath the same Horoscope with
the World." Browne is about to speak of the difficulty of understanding Eternity, whereas most of us would be content to agree
with Augustine's famous confession: "What then is time? If no one
asks me, I know: if I wish to explain it to one that asketh, I know
not. . . ."[9] The question of what Wittgenstein calls a "muddle felt as
a problem" is, after all, easier in some ways for us than for Augustine or Milton, for they had not only to try to understand Time:
salvation required that they apprehend as well something of the
way God's eternal Providence works in and through Time. And
of the two, Eternity, ultimately indefinable because a theological
mystery, was the more difficult concept; but Eternity, continues
Browne, "Who can speak of eternitie without a soloecisme, or
thinke thereof without an extasie?"[10]

If we are not philosophers and if we think about Time at all, most
of us tend to imagine something rather like the Idea of Progress—
an ascending line proceeding out of the historical past, passing
through the complicated present, and then disappearing toward
some indeterminate bang or whimper. When Marcus Aurelius, on

the other hand, asserts that the national intellect "stretches out into
the infinitude of time" only to discover that "our children shall see
nothing new, just as our fathers likewise saw nothing more than we,"
the formulation assumes the "cyclical regeneration of all things";
"All things from eternity are of like forms and come round on a circle." This view, the myth of the eternal return, derives from the
Greeks who early had idealized the reign of Kronos, the Golden
Age when the earth, unwounded by the plough, brought forth
spontaneously so that mankind lived free from want and toil. Later
and more sophisticated thinkers retained the nostalgia, transferring
the ideal age to the period of the philosopher kings, Lycurgus and
Solon. But it is of course in the Myth of the Four Ages, as it appears
in the *Republic*, that we encounter the most sophisticated version of
the cyclical view. And yet behind even Plato's subtle elaborations
there lies the simple paradigm: the uniform, circular path of the
sun. After a certain number of hours, days, months, and years,
which may be counted and, as we say, counted upon, the sun might
be relied upon to shine again at a predetermined point. This pattern
of natural recurrence is realized most grandly in yet another
Platonic myth, that of the *magnus annus* or Great Year of the
Timaeus. Variously interpreted, it was usually understood in the
Renaissance after the manner of Pliny: In the "revolution of the
great yeere so much spoken of . . . the stars returne againe to their
first points, and give significations of times and seasons, as at the
beginning withall, that this yeare should begin at high noone that
very day the sun entreth the signe Aries."[11] This cyclical view,
persisting through the Renaissance in a variety of forms, makes it
impossible to accept unreservedly the notion that Christian history
was regarded as a straight line.

The Hebrews, like the Greeks, were of course aware of the cyclic
recurrences in nature, and the Old Testament preserves a number
of indications of their interest in seasonal repetitions, from the
"circuit of the year" in Exodus 34:22 to the cycle of creation in
Jubilees 1:20; but before the transcendent Yahweh these indications of seasonal time recede into the background of the Old
Testament. The Jewish view of history must be thought of as essentially a consequence of the Exodus, which served to demonstrate in
spectacular fashion the way Yahweh shapes events with respect to
those brought up out of Egypt. (After the passage through the Red
Sea Yahweh is before them in a cloud by day, a pillar of fire by
night: it is not too much to say that in a profound sense Yahweh *is*

history.) There are few books of the Old Testament that do not make direct use of Exodus, for everywhere this signal example of divine intervention in the course of history implies that the God of Israel is God of Time, Lord of History; interpretation of the past derives therefore from the study of Yahweh's acts in history, and interpretation of the future proceeds from the study of the words of His prophets. Instead of Plato's theory of progressive degeneration, as in the Myth of the Four Ages, the Hebrews located in Adam's single act of disobedience to a jealous God what may be recognized as a species of instant degeneration; and the possibility of regeneration, no longer cyclical, becomes contingent on the appearance of a king of the House of David, whom Yahweh will endow with wide dominion. The historical reign of David had lent political and geographical content to "Israel," which previously had been mainly a spiritual concept (designating the covenantal unity of the twelve nomadic tribes under Yahweh); but when the Assyrians put an end to the monarchies in 722 and Jerusalem itself fell in 586, the Babylonian exile and the dispersal of the Jews exhausted the secular meanings of "Israel," encouraging the prophets to revert to the original, spiritual signification while broadening and deepening its application. (The concept of the Davidic King persists also in altered form, as the Messiah who will come at long last to seal up time in final judgment.) In the post-exilic prophets the idea of the state of Israel acquires a transcendent as well as an historical character, becoming an ideal creation of the national mind that once existed as a political fact within history and that will be restored in the victory of Yahweh on "that day" of Zechariah 12:14.

In the "latter days" (Jeremiah 23:20, Isaiah 2:2, and elsewhere among the post-exilic prophets as well as in Jewish tradition) God shall establish a new reign on earth, providing His temporal creature with a new time, the time of the Lord, which shall be from "everlasting to everlasting." God's time (*'olam*) signifies not timelessness but vast duration; intensified by the Hebrew writers through doubling and the use of the plural, it is used to point sharp contrasts between the time proper to Yahweh and the time of his creatures, whose flesh is as grass and whose years, in Psalm 90:9, "come to an end like a sigh." For every man God has fixed the "time" or the "end" (Genesis 6:13, Job 6:11); and in similar fashion He has appointed a final moment for the world itself. Natural time or time of the creation endures according to the days and seasons instituted by God (Genesis 1, 8:22): it has a beginning in creation, a fixed end in judgment. But the time of Yahweh remains unlimited, for He *is*—before creation (Psalm 90:2) and shall endure "forever." The coming of the Messiah in the person of Jesus Christ illuminates the entire past (1 Peter 1:10 ff., Acts 17:26), which previously had remained in partial darkness (Galatians 4:22, 8:10, 4:1; 2 Cor. 3:9, 15; Col. 2:8; Romans 5:20, 4:15), and clearly reveals that time contains the series of acts produced by the free election and infinite love of the Deity. The present and past lose much of their importance to the future, since with St. Paul (Phil. 3:13), "forgetting the things which are behind, and reaching forth unto the things which are before," we await fulfilment. The history of the Gentiles (Romans 1:19 ff., 13:1 ff.), along with that of the Old Testament, becomes propaedeutic, educative in the divine plan of salvation. Paul thus initiates a grandiose and all-embracing notion of the sacred meaning of secular history; and where a God of unlimited duration shapes time in this fashion, history tends to be regarded as though it were modeled on the straight line, marked at crucial points by divine interventions but bounded in particular by the surety of past fulfilment (Exodus) and the expectation of future fulfilment (the coming of the Messiah).

It is not surprising, therefore, that Christian history is often represented as a straight line proceeding from the Alpha of Creation through Incarnation toward the Omega of the Day of Judgment; but this expedient merely has the effect of making the Christian view of history resemble our own Idea of Progress as though drawn on the horizontal rather than an ascending plane. It is true enough that the model of the straight line makes Christian history appear very easy to understand, and it is also true that the Idea of Progress derives in part from the Christian view. Insofar as men came to substitute the Baconian vision of a scientific utopia for the Christian vision of heaven, life itself rather than death might be viewed as the gateway to a better existence; and the beguiling prospect of infinite improvement in *this* life through the exploitation of empirical and mathematical science led, during the eighteenth century, to the secularization of Christian history. Bacon's House of Solomon, its Old Testament framework calculated to new ends, marks a convenient turning point; it only remained for the eighteenth-century rationalists to ignore the eternal significance attached by Augustine to the *civitas dei* and then to project the idea of a heavenly city into the earthly future. But to suppose that Christian history during the Renaissance may be fully understood as a variation of its later man-

ifestation as the Idea of Progress does violence to both theories of
time.

It is true enough that Augustine, brooding over the mysterious
nature of time, early rejected the identification of time with the
circular motion of the heavens, saying that the potter might still
turn his wheel, measuring time, though the planets halted in their
careers. And in the *Citie of God* Augustine explicitly attacks those
philosophers who believe in "reuolutions of time," which the com-
mentator Vives glosses: "*Platonisme* holding a continuall progression and succession of causes and effects, and when heauen hath
reuolued it selfe fully, and come to the point whence it moued first,
then is the great yeare perfect, and all shall bee as they were at
first." Thus Augustine explains, or explains away, the dictum of
Ecclesiastes that there is "nothing new vnder the Sunne" as merely
spoken "generally of all transitory creatures":

> But farre bee our faith from beleeuing that these words of *Salomon*
> should meane those reuolutions that they do dispose the worlds
> course and renouation by: as *Plato* the Athenian Philosopher taught
> in the Academy, that in a certaine vnbounded space, yet definite,
> *Plato* himselfe, his Schollers, the City and Schoole, should after infin-
> ite ages meete all in that place againe, and be as they were when he
> taught this. God forbid I say that we should beleeue this. *For Christ
> once dyed for our sinnes; and rising againe, dieth no more, nor hath death any
> future dominion ouer him, and we after our resurrection shall be alwayes
> with the Lord. . . .*

The advent of Christ and the doctrine of eternal life require that
we reject the myth of eternal recurrence. As Augustine concludes:
"The wicked walke in a circuit [Ps. 119?]: not because their life (as
they think) is to runne circularly, but because their false doctrine
runnes round in a circular maze."[12]

But to reject cyclical recurrence need not necessarily involve
either the rejection of the circle as paradigm or the exclusive adoption of the straight line. The men of the Renaissance were educated
to lead a double life, for while breakfast was assuredly an item of
present experience, the languages they learned, the history they
studied, and the literature they came to appreciate were largely the
products of classical antiquity. Existing in sixteenth-century England but imaginatively alive in antiquity, Renaissance writers inherited a feeling for the circular patterns of ancient time and

sought to assimilate them to the basically straight-line configurations of Scripture. For an uneasy moment in history these two apparently antithetical patterns existed together in almost painful intimacy. But then the dream of perfection, idealized in the past as the Golden Age or the Garden of Eden and in Biblical thought transferred to the future when "Earth shall all be Paradise," became identified with the progressive renovation of society that Herbert Spencer and others were pleased to celebrate so unreservedly. Time, no longer bounded by Creation and Apocalypse, remains a straight line but now rises toward an infinity of technological improvements; the doors to the future, avers Bergson, are open, and Hart Crane's buildings simply go up and up. . . . In looking back over the last two millennia it is at best uncertain that there has been significant progress in the art of life, and in any case the Idea of Progress must become, by its own definitions, a victim of planned obsolescence. But even when we reject the vulgar oversimplifications of the Idea of Progress itself, I submit that we tend to accede to the theory of time and history implied by it: history as a kind of straight line, moving in units of event from a more or less clearly-defined past, through a turbulent present, toward an indefinite future containing more advanced medical techniques and superior automobiles. It is for this reason, I suspect, that modern theologians are so ready to argue that Christian history resembles a straight line—not only because they, like Augustine, are eager to dissociate themselves from anything like cyclic recurrence by drawing sharp distinctions between Greek and Hebrew views of time, but also because of a more or less unconscious acquiescence in the implications of the Idea of Progress.[13]

The straight line remains an oversimple model, limited in its usefulness; and not simply because Christian history is bounded by the apocalyptic moment of closure so that the doors of the future are securely bolted. It is also that the end bears more than casual resemblance to the beginning. There is, first of all, the tendency, evident in Isaiah (40–55) and elsewhere, to envisage the (ideal) future in imagery reminiscent of the original state, to see the end as somehow a return to Eden. In the last books of the *Confessions* Augustine forsakes the more-or-less chronological account of his life up to the moment of Conversion and, meditating on Genesis (or the business of "beginning"), he moves gradually to scrutinize Creation and Judgment, the genesis and the eschaton, as reflections of each other: the beginning, he feels, somehow contains the ending, the ending the beginning. There is as well the imaginative prestige of the circle as a form, as emblem of perfection, which was of course very early associated with time. As Cowley notes, a "*Snake with the Tail* in the mouth of it, was the ancient *Hieroglyph* of the year," and the tendency to think of time as in some way circular persists through the Renaissance. The use of the circle as an emblem of God, either directly or in the paradoxical formulation from *The Book of the XXIV Philosophers* as it was employed by Cusa and many others, contributed to the popularity of the circle as an emblem of eternity as well as time. Milton in the peroration that ends *Of Reformation* refers easily to the "datelesse and irrevoluble circle of Eternity," and Cowley instructs us that "there are two sorts of *Eternity*; from the *Present backwards* to *Eternity*, and from the *Present forwards*, called by the Schoolmen *Aeternitas à parte ante*, and *Aeternitas à parte post*. These two make up the whole Circle of Eternity, which the Present Time cuts like a Diameter. . . ."[14] All these influences converged in such a way that Renaissance discussions of Time and Eternity are almost always syncretic and often confused and confusing, but the diversity of possibilities also made it possible for imaginative writers to entertain now one, then the other, of the available notions.

The final difficulty with the model of the straight line is that it implies that Moses lived before Christ and that the Second Coming postdates the Incarnation.[15] There is the obvious sense in which these statements are true, but to think exclusively in this way will not help very much in trying to understand the structure of *Paradise Lost*, which moves straight through history in a circle, or allow us to appreciate the magnificent commonplaces of Sir Thomas Browne: "the world was before the Creation, and at an end before it had a beginning; and thus was I dead before I was alive, though my grave be *England*, my dying place was Paradise, and *Eve* miscarried of me before she conceiv'd of *Cain*." These resonant paradoxes cannot be diagrammed or visualized—no straight line or circle will do—but, like the better seventeenth-century conceits, must be apprehended by the eye of the mind. Caught in what Milton calls this "transient World, the Race of time," men observe that Moses precedes Christ, that the succession of events moves from the past to the future; but in Eternity, where "there is no distinction of Tenses," "what to us is to come, to his Eternitie is present, his whole duration being but one permanent point without succession, parts, flux, or division."[16]

The simple contrast between the time of the creature, which is as grass, and the time of the creator, which endures from "everlasting to everlasting," appears prominently throughout Scripture. But nowhere, with the possible exception of Ecclesiastes 3:11, do the various words translated "eternity" possess the abstract significance found in them by the Fathers. The Hebrew *'olam* simply means vast duration: *aion*, its equivalent in the Septuagint, was used by Homer to denote the period of a man's life, the "span" or "age" allotted to him. But *aion* is also used by Plato to define the highly abstract notion of Eternity in the *Timaeus*. Later Christians, from Augustine through Anselm to Schleiermacher, were tempted in their study of Scripture to lend the concrete terminology of the Testaments the abstract significances acquired from the Platonic tradition: for such writers, though not for Milton, Eternity came to denote not just huge duration but timelessness, as is the case for Dionysius the Areopagite when he contemplates the relation of Time to Eternity in *Divine Names* X.

Plotinus, and the neo-Platonists in general, had avoided Aristotle's definition of time as the measure of motion in favor of formulae that appealed to the early Christians, especially when baptized by Augustine. Boethius' definition of Eternity, in *Consolation* v. 6, as "a perfect possession all together of an endlesse life, which is more manifest by the comparison of temporall things,"[17] had the effect of throwing into bolder relief a distinction present at least implicitly in the Platonic tradition—that between *sempiternitas* or everlasting succession, and *eternitas* or that which has neither beginning nor end and exists without either succession or parts. Plato's model (*Timaeus* 47D) was the heavens, which revolve everlastingly and possess what was later referred to as sempiternity; since the heavens served to distinguish the "numbers of time," the relation for Plato between astronomical movement and time is close, on occasion seemingly an identity. The heavens revolve, always in motion, everlastingly; but the eternal realm of The Ideas remains always at rest, not in succession but "all in one." Although both Time and Eternity are everlasting, and although Time imitates Eternity as its "moving image," there nevertheless exists a radical difference between the two, for Eternity is single and at rest while Time remains in the continual flux that signifies imperfection. When Augustine rejected the close association of Time with astronomical motion, he also found it necessary to de-emphasize the resemblances of the "image" to the Idea in transforming Plato's ontological argument into a religious opposition between Time and Eternity. Augustine records, in *The Confessions*, the influence the neo-Platonists had on his intellectual development, particularly the way their writings offered him a way of dealing with the problem of evil, bedevilled as he was at that time by Manichean dualisms. Augustine rejected, of course, Plotinus' notion, expressed in *Ennead 2*, of an everlasting world with a history of recurrent periods (*circuitus* in later Latin), just as in *De Civitate Dei* he consistently attacks all the cyclical theorists, refuting in 12.10 the idea of the world ages as it appears in *Timaeus,* in 10.30 and 12.20 the proponents of reincarnation, and in 12.13 the recurrences of the *magnus annus*; but from the Platonists he nevertheless takes the distinction between Being and non-Being, which allows him to understand evil as "privation" or "nothing" and which also provides the metaphysical context for his view of Time in relation to Eternity.

For Augustine Time exists as the order of change and becoming, even as the medium in which the soul seeks salvation; but Eternity exists as the realm of God, of true Being that subsists without contingency or change. (Perhaps we may find here the reason, to adopt the equivocation on "to be" that led to the rise of philosophy, why Augustine never actually tells us what time *is*.) The great meditations on Time at the end of *The Confessions* testify again and again to Augustine's fervent desire to steady his gaze by the unchanging light of Eternity. Time, as the (Platonic) moving image of Eternity, retains something of its relation to the divine realm, but insofar as Time moves it necessarily partakes of non-Being and to that degree it must finally be transcended. In 11.11 of *The Confessions* we hear of those who

> try as they may to savour the taste of eternity, their thoughts still twist and turn upon the ebb and flow of things in past and future time. But if only their minds could be seized and held steady, they would be still for a while and, for that short moment, they would glimpse the splendour of eternity which is for ever still. They would contrast it with time, which is never still, and see that it is not comparable. They would see that time derives its length only from a great number of movements constantly following one another into the past, because they cannot all continue at once. But in eternity nothing moves into the past: all is present.[18]

It remained for Boethius to contribute the definitions refined and elaborated by the Scholastics. Cowley sorts these parcels in the learned notes to Book I of the *Davideis*: "*Eternity* is defined by *Boet.*

Lib. 5 de *Consolat. Interminabilis vitae simul & perfecta possessio*. The whole and perfect possession, ever all at once, of a Being without beginning or ending. Which Definition is followed by *Tho. Aquin.* and all the *Schoolmen*; who therefore call *Eternity Nunc stans*, a standing Now, to distinguish it from that *Now*, which is a difference of *time*, and is alwaies *in Fluxu*."[19]

It is in ways such as these that the simple contrast between the time of the creature and that of the creator becomes an opposition, then the Christian paradox or mystery, of Time and Eternity: although, as Augustine says, the two are "not comparable" and are in fact opposed in many of their aspects, there nevertheless exists a connection between the two, for it is Eternity that lends significance to an otherwise meaningless succession of moments. And it is this connection, however much one of God's mysteries, that encourages Augustine to offer the prayer that might serve as blazon for Milton's mature work: "If only men's minds could be seized and held still! They would see how eternity, in which there is neither past nor future, determines both past and future time. Could mine be the hand strong enough to seize the minds of men? Could any words of mine have power to achieve so great a task?"[20] Man, locked in Time, longs for the sweet fruition of Eternity; and even while *in* Time, longs to "glimpse the splendor of eternity." "*The soul* is the *Horizon* of *Time* and *Eternitie*: For, in that it is immortall, it is partaker of *Eternitie*: and, in that it is infused by God into the body, it is partaker of *Time*."[21] In the knowing Christian there resides the timeless self conferred by God—*synteresis* or something of the divine *scintillans*—that may radiate throughout a man's being, lifting him momentarily from the temporal to the eternal so that the articulations of his soul may attain to *totum simul*, the successions of time coalescing to form a foretaste of Eternity.

There were, in the Renaissance, two main ways by which men not given to the raptures of mysticism might grasp something of the splendor of the everlasting. One lies in the distinction, elaborated by theologians and preachers into a commonplace, between *chronos*, or Time as it is ordinarily apprehended, and *kairos*, which is Time comprehended under the aspect of Eternity. The other is figuralism or typology, the exegetical method that offered men some insight into God's eternal ways with time and history. These two ways are in effect one, for the theory of types is essentially a theory of *kairoi*; and Milton employed both the distinction and the method in guiding his life and shaping his art.

CHAPTER I

Occasional Experiments

Milton's early verse may be thought of as occasional, required by academic circumstance or produced in response to events such as the Gunpowder Plot; most often, to death, that of a Marchioness or even a beadle. The young poet experiments in a variety of meters and modes, in Latin, Greek, and English; and he early shows that he had felt the influence of Sylvester's DuBartas (the paraphrase of Psalm CXIV, "done by the Author at fifteen"), of Jonson ("Epitaph on the Marchioness of Winchester," "L'Allegro," "Il Penseroso"), and even of Donne (the two poems on Hobson), as well as Shakespeare, Spenser, and the Spenserians. His imitations, whether Ovidian or Spenserian, have for the most part a beguiling ease. Although the impression is that of a young poet finding his way, the changing voice of literary mimicry everywhere reveals extraordinary control of language, as well as the ability to assimilate to English, especially in the imitations of Italian forms, something of the sweep and dignity of Vergil. Contrasting the "Fair Infant" with *Lycidas* provides an index to the astonishing achievement of these years, and an examination of some of the early religious poems shows Milton, who aspired to emulate the "choicest wits" of antiquity "with this over and above of being a Christian,"[1] moving not only toward his own distinctive way with the details of language but also toward ways of organizing the larger patterns of his poems.

Although "On the Death of a Fair Infant Dying of a Cough" has had its defenders, the poem almost seems calculated to betray what Milton at this point in his career could not do—if we reflect that it, like *Lycidas*, consists of eleven "stanzas," that it, like *Lycidas*, seeks meaning in death and strives to provide comfort after death, and that it, like *Lycidas*, attempts to organize a poetic response to death that includes both classical and Christian modes of consolation. In the earlier poem Milton bears the burden of classical learning rather gracelessly; he affects the diction of the Spenserians in archaisms like "childless eld" and "mortal wight"; he derives from Sylvester's DuBartas such fashionable compounds as "snow-soft" and "icy-pearled"; and he descends to the hackneyed as the occasion arises, climaxing "infamous blot" and "foul reproach" with "black perdition." (As Wallace Stevens allows, "Some of one's earlier things give one the creeps.") But the weaknesses may not be attributed solely to the language, for I think we may imagine many of the same or similar phrases being turned to better use elsewhere, in Spenser himself or even in the mature Milton. It is, ultimately, the organization, the relation or lack of relation, of the materials.

Milton begins with the commonplace conceit of the flower "no sooner blown but blasted" (already familiar by the time Kyd got around to putting it in *The Spanish Tragedy*), then self-indulgently permits the seed of personification in "winter's force" to exfoliate into a Spenserian allegory about "grim Aquilo" and his errant "quest" for the infant's "Virgin Soul." This attempt at classical consolation ends with the alexandrine of the fourth stanza, "Alack, that so to change thee winter had no power." The first line of the next stanza—"Yet can I not persuade me thou art dead"—provides the transition to the treatment of death in Christian terms ("Heav'n," "Soul most surely blest," "golden-winged host"), though there persists some admixture of classical allusion, one of them qualified in the Christian context by the earliest instance of Milton's parenthetical scepticism: "Or in the Elysian fields (if such there were)." These later stanzas consist in a series of questions in which the poet affects to wonder whether the fair infant who died of a cough was "some Star," the "just Maid" Astraea, or one of the "golden-winged host." This poeticizing reaches its end, if not its climax, in the tenth stanza, which poses the question why the infant did not "stay here below" to shield us from "slaughtering pestilence" and the like—until at last Milton produces an answer by explaining in the alexandrine that the infant protects us with greater efficiency because she is now in a better position to act as an intercessory saint: "But thou canst best perform that office where thou art." In the final stanza the poet addresses the bereaved mother directly, instructing her not to "la-

ment" her "false imagin'd loss" and closing with an allusion to
Isaiah's promise to the childless of an "everlasting name." However
correct the doctrine and apt the allusion, the conclusion of the
poem must strike most of us as something callous. It will not help to
explain that classical allusions are part of the convention, which of
course they are; or to point out that Christianity may at times seem
antagonistic to purely human needs, which of course it often is.
The trouble, once again, lies not with the truisms, doctrinal or
other, but with their arrangement, for the poet has not prepared
us, as he does in *Lycidas*, to re-acknowledge the truth that often
stands behind conventional phrasing.

The direct attempts at consolation occur in line seventy ("But
thou canst best perform that office where thou art") and in the lines
of the following, and concluding, stanza. But the earlier parts of
the poem in no way anticipate the abrupt appeal to the putative
efficiency of intercessory saints, which in this case appears to stem
purely from geographic proximity to the divine; nor do the earlier
stanzas ready us for the allusion to Isaiah, which inevitably seems
tacked-on at the last moment, *ex machina*. And yet it is possible to
detect, as the poet confronts the fact of death, more than a hint of
later preoccupations, for it is death, as Northrop Frye has pointed
out, that defines for the Christian the limits of classical learning.
The attempt at classical consolation is present, though viewed scep-
tically and finally abandoned; and the attempt at Christian consolation is assumed to be effectual and final. But in the "Fair Infant"
Milton evidently lacks any useful way of seeing the one kind of
consolation in relation to the other, any useful way of organizing
the two kinds of consolation so that together they provide a meaningful context for the "consolation" of line seventy and the concluding stanza. Although the sections devoted to classical and Christian
matters are approximately equal in length, this "structure" has
meaning only in terms of mathematics; the two parts are not otherwise linked, nor are they directed in concert toward the sentiments of the last lines. The principle is that of enumeration, also
used in constructing a grocery list: "Yet art thou not," "Yet can I
not," "Resolve me then," "Wert thou some Star," "Or wert thou that
just Maid," "Or wert thou. . . ."

Of the poems Milton wrote between the "Fair Infant" and
Lycidas, the three "calendrical" odes, probably composed as part of
a formal program to celebrate the holy days of the liturgical calen-

dar, afford the clearest indications of his poetic development. Milton anticipated the judgment of posterity in placing "On the Morning of Christ's Nativity" in first position in the editions of his poems brought out in 1645 and 1673; he acknowledged the relative success of "Upon the Circumcision" by silently reprinting it; and he confessed the failure of "The Passion" by printing it with the comment that "this Subject the Author finding to be above the years he had, when he wrote it, and nothing satisfied with what was begun, left it unfinisht." But he continued to reprint this "unfinisht" poem with which he was "nothing satisfied," perhaps testifying in this oblique way to the personal importance that these poems must have held for him as he prepared himself for the sacred vocation of poet-priest. Since the poems on the Circumcision and the Passion both refer, in their opening lines, to the Nativity Ode ("Compos'd 1629"), there is some reason, though the dating remains uncertain, to allot the "Circumcision" to January of 1630 and the "Passion" to Easter of the same year; but in any event the three poems resemble each other enough to invite scrutiny as a group. The introduction of the Nativity Ode employs the same stanzaic form as the "Passion"—the dignified rime royal of Baldwin and Buckhurst, modified in the direction of Spenser and the Fletchers by the addition of an alexandrine and first used by Milton in the "Fair Infant." All three— linked by purpose, subject, and self-reference—exhibit the influence of the Italians as well as the Spenserians, and all imply that the poet, having reached the age of majority, possesses an intense awareness of religious vocation. It is a period of choice and transition for the poet-priest, and whatever the reasons for retaining "The Passion," Milton's characteristic gesture of rejection-retention preserves, as if in the laboratory, a provocative series of experiments that may be thought of as a downward arc from major triumph, through limited success, to self-admitted failure.

"Upon the Circumcision" takes its structure from Italy, Milton's immediate model—imitated exactly in the Trinity MS. and modified only slightly for publication—being Petrarch's *canzone* to the Blessed Virgin.[2] The first of the two precisely equal, and symmetrical, sections begins by reminding the angels how they had sung with joy at the birth of Christ, and then, during the course of a disquisition on the "fiery essence" of angels and their probable lack of tears, the poet exhorts, "Now mourn" (1.6)—for Christ "now bleeds to give us ease" (1.11). The second half of the poem medi-

tates on "more exceeding love or law more just," recurring eventually to the "wounding smart" of the Circumcision that "seals obedience" in relation to that other blood-letting on The Cross:

> but Oh! ere long
> Huge pangs and strong
> Will pierce more near his heart.

Even the theologically uninstructed reader will be apt to perceive
that Milton uses the *stanza divisa* of Petrarch's *canzone* to distinguish
between the Old Dispensation ("law more just") associated with
Moses and the New Dispensation ("more exceeding love") inaugurated by Christ; but line eleven, "now bleeds to give us ease," requires special elucidation. When the poet says, "Now mourn...,"
the "now" refers to the time of the Circumcision (1 January) as
distinct from the "erst" of the Nativity (25 December), though it
ought to be taken to apply as well to the time of the poem and to all
those firsts of January repeated throughout the history of the
church. But the "now" of "now bleeds" represents a bolder effort of
the poetic imagination, for we know, logically and chronologically,
that Christ does not bleed "to give us ease" until the moment on
The Cross. Milton, that is, locates the fulfillment in the inception,
the end in the beginning, just as in *Paradise Regained* he locates the
end of Christ's ministry, the return to Eden, in its beginning, the
Temptation in the Wilderness. To state it dramatically, the "now"
of "now bleeds" is the poetic equivalent of Aquinas' *nunc stans*, an
"eternal now" that exists in Time while glancing at Eternity.[3]

Milton's poetic legerdemain derives from Biblical exegesis. In
writing "Upon the Circumcision" the poet has drawn on the particular branch of "allegory" known as typology or the theory of
types. Allegory appears as an instrument of textual criticism in the
work of the scholiasts on Homer, in the exegetical glosses of the
Hebrews, and in the medieval commentaries on Vergil and Ovid.
Allegory as a literary device may be found in the "myths" of Plato,
the parables of Christ, the fables of Aesop, and the writings of
Samuel Beckett, as well as in such elaborate personification allegories as the *Psychomachia* of Prudentius.[4] All such instances may
be included, though not comprehended, under the broad signification that rhetoricians accorded the term: *allegoria est alieniloquium,
aliud enim sonat, aliud intelligitur* (Isidore 1.37.22). In its simplest
(and vaguest) formulation, allegory says one thing and means

another, the fable serving as a vehicle for "deeper" or "hidden" meanings. This mode of allegory may be thought of as "Platonic," for the story, which need be neither "real" nor "true," remains a shadow, and its ulterior significance—its Idea or Form—represents the true reality. Plato's Er, who awoke at dawn on his own funeral pyre after having enjoyed a vision of the afterlife, had no historical existence. The truth of the myth lies in the revelation that the just man is the happiest man—in the next world as in this one; Er is to all intents and purposes a personification, differing in degree but not in kind from Spenser's Excesse or Langland's Kynde Wyt. In personification allegory there is nothing problematic about the agent or his actions, for only rarely can the agent acquire a new name, as does Spenser's Malbecco, who is at last "hight Gelosie" simply to reveal more fully his true nature; and at no crucial point can the agent act in a manner contrary to his name, which functions as a defining label or badge of his fictional existence. Since Kynde Wyt is a fact of pastoral psychology, not a problematic character, he must act out what is implicit in his name; he breathes and moves to exhibit his essence. Such allegory is written to make moral realities more accessible, or to sugar the pill, or in Mark 4:10–12 and elsewhere to preserve pearls from the snouts of swine—or a combination of many such aims. In this area, thus broadly sketched, Bunyan, Christ, and Kafka occupy a certain amount of no-man's land.

The special form of allegory that depends on personification is only intermittently useful in reading Milton (the "allegory" of Sin and Death) or even Dante, though *Paradise Lost* and the *Commedia* are indeed "allegorical." The more relevant species of allegory, typology or figuralism, takes its most evident beginnings from Paul and the Gospels—not so much from the parables of Christ but from Himself and His doings. Developed in other, even opposite, directions by Origen and Augustine, it eventually coalesced, though only in one of its aspects, with the "four-fold method" as codified by Cassian (*Collationes*) and developed by Aquinas.[5] "The author of Holy Scripture," says Aquinas (*Summa Theol.* 1.1.10), "is God, in Whose power it is to signify His meaning, not by words only (as man can also do), but also by things themselves." Not merely a pleasing fiction that veils truth, the Bible is true history written by the divine poet in people and event as well as word. "So, whereas in every other science things are signified by words, this science has the property that the things signified by the words have themselves also a signification." In the historical allegory composed by Eternal Providence, there are four senses—three mystical or spiritual senses derived from "the historical or literal":

> That signification whereby things signified by words have themselves also a signification is called the spiritual sense, which is based on the literal, and presupposes it. Now this spiritual sense has a threefold division. For as the Apostle says (Heb. x.1) the Old Law is a figure of the New Law, and Dionysius says *the New Law itself is a figure of future glory* (Eccles. Hier. v.2). Again, in the New Law, whatever our Head has done is a type of what we ought to do. Therefore, so far as the things of the Old Law signify the things of the New Law, there is the allegorical sense; so far as the things done in Christ, or so far as the things which signify Christ, are signs of what we ought to do, there is the moral sense. But so far as they signify what relates to eternal glory, there is the anagogical.[6]

As Augustine admits (*Civ. Dei* 16.2), speaking for the majority view, not all "historical relations" in Scripture have mystical senses, but God's text of people and things can often support the allegorical, tropological, and anagogical senses. Of the three mystical senses, the allegorical and anagogical were in particular exploited with extraordinary originality by Dante and Milton.

These two senses paralleled and were in part developed from the typological methods employed by the writers of the Gospels, particularly Matthew, who has first position after the Prophets—in violation of chronology—because his account mediates between the two Testaments. Although Matthew identifies the Suffering Servant of Isaiah with Christ, not much is made of it, for Matthew writes to emphasize the coming of The Kingdom and to reassure the Jews that Jesus is "not come to destroy, but to fulfill" the Law and the Prophets (5:17–18). And accordingly there occurs again and again the formula: "That it might be fulfilled which was" spoken and written by the Prophets, expropriating the *midrashic* predictions of the Messiah and assuming their fulfillment in Jesus of Nazareth. According to Luke, it was Jesus Himself who first played the part of the typological exegete, for after His Resurrection His first item of business was to instruct the disciples in the techniques that Paul was to exploit. "And beginning at Moses and all the prophets, he expounded unto them in all the scriptures the things concerning himself." Heinrich Bullinger accordingly explains that

Our Lord Himselfe, when hee went with the two Disciples toward
Emaus ... began at *Moses*, and went thorow all the Prophets, and
opened unto them the old Scriptures, and shewed them, that so it
behoved Christ to suffer, and to enter into his glory. This is the cause
also that the Scriptures of the New Testament hang together, and
referre themselves to the Scriptures of the Old Testament: so that
these cannot be rightly understood without the other, no more than
the glosse without the text. The text is the Law and the Prophets, the
exposition are the Evangelists and the Apostles.[7]

Typology, the method by which the people and events of the Old
Testament "prefigure" their "fulfillments" in the New Testament,
retains its primacy in Christian allegorizing, providing the vital
links between the two Testaments and serving as the basis for the
Christian theory of history and time.

Even among scholars who have written much and well about
typology, there is the tendency to see the method as purely "Christ-
ological," merely a way of predicting, and then confirming, the
identity of Jesus as the Messiah. But the words and events of even
the New Testament anticipate, however obscurely, the happenings
of the end-time, serving as an assurance that Providence continues
to remain busy in ways somehow accessible to inspired understanding. The theory of types functions not only as another way of
signifying the "allegorical sense" of the four-fold method, for
typology has an "anagogical" dimension as well. The Index
Figurarum in Migne's *Patrologia* includes not only *figuras quae spec-
tant ad Christum* but also *quae ad Ecclesiam, quae ad apostolos et justos,
ad Judaeos et Gentiles,* and *ad haereticos et impios*. And the dance of
type into antitype ceases not with the Incarnation but rather with
the Second Advent, when Jesus fills up time so that, in the words of
the poet Greville, "all these types depart." As Thomas puts it in
quoting Dionysius, the "New Law itself is a figure of future glory."
In the interim typology remains a means of prophecy that permits
us to see through a glass darkly that time when we shall see face to
face.

Because the exegetical method has its origins in the Prophets of
the Old Testament who told of the Coming of the Messiah at the
End of Time, it was perhaps inevitable that these examples of what
Daniélou calls "eschatological typology" should finally, even in
Christian thought, have the effect of permitting a typology of Last
Things.[8] Some Protestants actually equated the type with the

anagoge, as when William Whitaker explains that the "realm of
Canaan was a type of the kingdom of heaven" and that we may
form a judgment of it as "type or anagoge."[9] Paradise prefigures
the time when earth shall all be paradise; the Last Supper prefigures not only the Eucharist but the Messianic Banquet at the End
of Time; and the Exodus is not only a figure of Baptism but also of
the *eschaton* (Rev. 15:3). Augustine says as much in the Seventh
Book of *De Civitate Dei*, where the idea lives explicitly in Vives' commentary: "For the Prophecies are not yet at an end: and though the
summe of them all were fulfilled in Christ, yet by him divers things
since are to come to passe which have been particularly intimated
in the prophecies. . . ."[10] Since Christ was crucified at noon, Milton
assumes that Adam fell at noon; and we may, if we are prophets
enough, suppose that Christ shall spread his throne in middle air at
noon of the Last Day. From almost any one of God's interventions
in time, we may attempt to reason back and forth across history to
discern the eternal patterns of things past, passing, and to come.

Although Erich Auerbach had supposed, at least while writing
Mimesis, that typology began to decline during the sixteenth century, the truth is that the exegetical method gained renewed importance among the writers of the Reformation and affected literature
at least as powerfully as in the past.[11] William Tyndale's *Obedience of
a Christian Man* has been taken generally to represent the Protestant rejection of Papist allegorizing in favor of the so-called "literal"
interpretation. And it is of course true that Tyndale declares that
Scripture has "but one sense, which is the literal"—all others the
sophistical coinages of the "chopological" Scholastics. But since for
Tyndale God's "literal" sense is "spiritual," and since for Tyndale
the Old Testament everywhere speaks of Christ, there remains in
theory as well as practice one species of allegory, the typological.
For Luther Christ is the "I" even of the Penitential Psalms, where
He is exhibited in the *sensus litteralis*—the means by which Luther
the Scholastic becomes Luther the Reformation exegete, collapsing
the four senses into one; and Luther, as nearly everyone knows,
accordingly came to attack "allegories" with witty vehemence, comparing the habit—considered to be particularly seductive to the
idle, the harebrained, and the dissolute—to whoring. But since for
Luther, too, the Prophets speak constantly of Christ, it remained
necessary to practice the typological method.[12] Calvin, knowing the
tendency of "Allegorimakers" to "make holy scripture a nose of

waxe," likewise places his emphasis on the primacy of the literal sense; and with greater discipline, if less earthy wit than Luther, shows on many occasions considerable scepticism with regard to the multiplication of types and antitypes.[13] But confronted with St. Paul's use of the method, even Calvin had no recourse but to allow the "legitimate" applications that occupy a long section of the *Institutes*. Milton himself roundly declares in *Christian Doctrine* that Scripture is "plain and perspicuous in all things necessary to salvation, and adapted to the instruction of even the most unlearned," and that "no passage of Scripture is to be interpreted in more than one sense"—but then concedes that "this sense is sometimes a compound of the historical and typical" (*Works,* XIV, 259, 263).

And in practice the Reformers almost invariably proved more flexible than their polemical statements imply. Although it was appropriate, on the theoretical level, to deprecate the four-fold method as Papist chopology and to accept the theory of types as Protestant adherence to literal truth, it became necessary in the actual process of exegesis to lend the *sensus litteralis* a kind of *sensus plenior*, to widen on occasion the literal sense so that, for example, a preacher could shift from the allegorical or typical sense to a moral application, though often the shift could not be justified through recourse to limited theories of typology. (Even Nicholas of Lyra found it expedient to speak of a "double" literal sense.) The Protestant William Whitaker manages to dissociate himself from the chopological Papists, particularly Bellarmine and Stapleton, while embracing a position remarkably similar to that of St. Thomas, maintaining that we concede "such things as allegory, anagoge, and tropology in scripture; but . . . contend that allegories, tropologies, and anagoges are not various senses, but various collections from one sense, or various applications and accommodations of that one meaning."[14] The Reformers in general wanted no "allegories," yet found it hard to live the exegetical life without them.

The "allegory" of the Protestants centers in the theory of types, which comprehends both the "allegorical" and "anagogical" senses of the four-fold method as practiced by the Papists. Although in its medieval and Renaissance elaborations the theory exhibits giddy complications (pagan history was ransacked for "figures" of Christ and sometimes the basis for a "type" was detected in a purely negative "resemblance"), its essentials may content us as well as Samuel Mather:

I shall content my self with the Apostles Definition of it: That *a Type is a Shadow of good things to come*. Hebr. 10.1. *The Law having a Shadow of good things to come*. Col. 2.17. *Which are a Shadow of things to come, but the Body is of Christ.*

There be three things included in this Description.

—There is some outward or sensible thing that represents some other higher thing.

—There is the thing represented thereby, which is *good things to come*, which we call the *Antitype*.

—There is the work of the *Type*, which is to *Shadow forth* or represent these *future good things*.

—There is in a *Type* some outward or sensible thing that represents an higher spiritual thing, which may be called a Sign or a Resemblance, a Pattern or Figure, or the like.

Here is the general Nature of a *Type*; it is a *Shadow*. . . . This we call the Correlate, or the *Antitype*; the other is the Shadow, this is the Substance; the *Type* is the Shell, this the Kernel; the *Type* is the Letter, this the Spirit and Mystery of the *Type*.

You see it comes all to one scope; and indeed all the Descriptions that our Divines have given of it are to this effect, they are all to the same scope with this of the Apostle; *a Shadow of good things to come*.[15]

The theory of types represents in codified form what is in effect a doctrine of time and an interpretation of history, implying a movement of progressive fulfillment from, in Milton's words, "shadowy Types to Truth."[16] Augustine's famous maxim (*Q. in Hept., lib.* 2, q. 73)—*Novum testamentum in Vetere latebat, Vetus nunc in Novo patet*—becomes in the Renaissance a theological commonplace that implies the manner in which God unfolds the scroll of time: "The old Testament is the occultation or hiding of the new, and the new is the manifestation of the old. For what is delivered and taught in figures, types, and prophecies of the old, the same . . . be taught in the new, but much more fully. . . ."[17] Since God is Lord of History, and since history as we know it stems from the irresponsibility of a young Hebrew couple in Mesopotamia, we may follow Thomas Beverley in noting that "the Line of Scripture-Time is either Historical, and applied to Things that were already past, when that Line was subtended to them; Or it is prophetical, and applied to Things that were to come to pass, when that Line was drawn out for, and applied to them, or are yet remaining to come to pass, and to be fulfilled before the End."[18] (In Donne's elegant formulation, "*Prophecy* is but *antidated Gospell*, and *Gospell* but *postdated prophecy*."[19]) Time is bounded: "There is a Line of Time drawn by Scripture from that Point, It calls, *The Beginning*, (*Genes.* 1.1.) to that Point, It calls *The End*, (Dan. 12. *ult.* and oft elsewhere.)." Time is, in a manner, seamless as well as bounded: "There is not a Greater or more sensible Argument for the Being of God, than his declaring the course of Times, and their Events beforehand, in so even and settled a Continuation. . . ."[20] And time is itself rounded out with God's eternity: "time parts Eternity in the midst: there is an Everlasting, from which time issued; there is an Everlasting when time ceases." Since "Eternity is before and after time," we "must looke both waies, as well to the part of Eternity that is before time, as that which is to come; all is one Eternity, onely 'tis parted by Time, which Time in the midst of Eternity, is as a sparke of fire in the midst of the vast Ocean."[21] Time is surrounded by Eternity, and it is marked at crucial moments, such as Exodus or the Incarnation, by intrusions of the Eternal: "*This Seed* [Jesus] propagating it self through all Generations in the fulness of time, when the season is now for Eternity to shine out through the extended shadow of Time, and to break it up into its own clear Light, *springs forth* from the Womb of the *Virgin Mary* into Flesh and Blood. . . ."[22] The moments of fullness are divine events or *kairoi*, antitypes that fulfill the types and shadows used by God to mark out the preliminary course of history. History is necessarily in this view "progressive," because the process of revelation in and through time is itself progressive. As Donne says, "The Jews were as School-boys, always spelling, and putting together Types and Figures," so that the Christian student of Time might "come from school to the University," to the "*Logos* it self, the Word."[23]

Philo, practicing a specialized form of the *midrash* influenced by the exegetical methods of the Greek rhetoricians, sought to deal with the great divisions created "in the beginning" by locating the invisible world, in the Platonic manner, above and behind the visible world, comparing the literal to "body," the allegorical to "soul"; "mere letters" to "shadows of the body"; and the "meanings beneath" to the "things which truly exist." Philo transforms the four rivers of Paradise into the cardinal virtues, and in *On the Life of Moses* the Books of Deuteronomy and Exodus suddenly begin to look as though they had been written by Spenser. St. Paul, on the other hand, centered his thinking in the theological fact of the Incarnation, preserving the historical reality of, say, Adam and Moses while simultaneously assuming that their full "reality" becomes evident only with the coming of Christ. Spatial or "Platonic" analogy appears in Paul, as in Romans 1:20: "For the invisible things of him from the creation of the world are clearly seen, being understood by the things that are made, even his eternal power and Godhead." But even here the references to creation and eternal power carry the implication of providential force working in time through the "things that are made." And there is of course the equally influential 1 Cor. 13:9-12: "For we know in part, and we prophesy in part. But when that which is perfect is come, then that which is in part shall be done away.... For now we see through a glass, darkly; but then face to face: now I know in part; but then shall I know even as also I am known." Here the emphasis lies on time rather than space, and it may be associated with the practice of making analogies in time based on the theory of types: "For as in Adam all die, even so in Christ shall all be made alive" (1 Cor. 15:22).

And as usual there lies an element of contradiction in the temporal similitude, duly noted by commentators like Calvin (later to be exploited in poetry by Milton): "And where as he saith that Adam was a figure of Christ, it is no marveile: for even in things most contrary there appereth some similitud because therefore, as through that sin of Adam we are al lost, so by that righteousness of Christ we are restored: very aptly hath he called Adam a tipe of Christ...."[24] The parallel between the two is asserted across the ages in order to contradict one aspect of the analogy; the passage from "shadowy Types to Truth," in which Time bears witness to Eternity, includes a dimension of contrary fulfillment. Now we "know in part," and through the theory of types, particularly those events "typical" of Christ, we may "prophesy in part" until the Second Coming, when God shall have completed His providential ways with "this transient World, the Race of time." ("Beyond," says Adam to Michael [PL, XII, 555-56], "is all abyss": "Eternity, whose end no eye can reach.") "But we all," avers Paul, "with open face beholding as in a glass the glory of the Lord, are changed into the same image from glory to glory even as by the Spirit of the Lord" (2 Cor. 3:18). Time is dynamic, progressing through a series of contrary fulfillments toward the End, when God shall once again be "all in all."

In this context we must understand much of Christian literature as "allegorical"—the allegory of people and events written by men in imitation of God's eternal ways with time. In De Civitate Dei the theory of types presides over Augustine's tale of two cities, though nowhere does the testimony to Eternal Providence impeach the historical reality of what occurs in Time. And in *The Confessions* we are not to regard Augustine's aeneid from Carthage to Rome as fiction, for it is not "allegorical" in the way (for instance) Fulgentius read Vergil, the action of the epic merely a veil shrouding the education of the virtuous soul. Alypius was, historically, Augustine's student and friend, though a chance remark in class was taken to apply to him, thus revealing that God had spoken through the teacher; and Monica was, historically, the mother of Augustine, though the chance remark of a servant, contrary to her intent, taught Monica continence, thus revealing that God had spoken again. Victorinus was, historically, a famous rhetorician, but his conversion prefigures that of Augustine—just as the conversion of St. Anthony, who suddenly found that the words of Scripture applied to himself, likewise prefigures Augustine's. So, in a moment ordained by God, is the Autolycus-like Jacob converted into the patriarchal Israel; so, in a moment, on the Road to Damascus, does Saul become Paul; and so, in the fullness of time, does the sinner Augustine become the saintly Augustine. Augustine, at the age of thirty-three, re-enacts Christ's Agony in the Garden. Entering his own garden, Augustine becomes totally distracted, "dying a death that would bring me life" and expunging the "deep shadow on the sons of Adam." "I seized the Bible and opened it, and in silence I read the first passage on which my eyes fell: *Not in revelling and drunkeness. . . . Rather, arm yourselves with the Lord Jesus Christ. . . .*" The time is full, it is a moment of ripeness: "I had no wish to read more, and no need to do so. For in an instant, as I came to the end of the sentence . . . all the darkness of doubt was dispelled."[25] St. Paul is both type and explicator: "For as in Adam all die, even so in Christ shall all be made alive." *The Confessions* is historical, autobiographical; and yet it is "allegorical" (providing only one.of Augustine's versions of his conversion), factual and yet typological. The poet who would deal with Eternity as well as Time may have recourse to the theory of types, allowing him in his poetry to imitate the dynamics of Christian time "from shadowy Types to Truth."

The theory quite evidently proceeds from one of the basic impulses of the human mind—not merely to ascribe meaning to the flux of time but also, and more particularly, to anticipate and then to confirm fulfillment. Plutarch in *De Alexandri* records the famous anecdote of Alexander's saying of Homer's verse ("good king and bold warrior") that it honored Agamemnon and prophesied Alex-

ander; and it is not all that long ago that Mr. Frank Meer unbur-
dened himself in the pages of a metropolitan newspaper:

> Manhattan: Summary of a letter I wrote President Kennedy: 'You
> have been chosen by God to lead this nation and the world from
> disaster, because you are a just and righteous man. You are young,
> handsome, tall, pious, and a respected family man. So was Moses.
> God made your family wealthy in order to give you the proper
> education. In World War II you were in charge of a small boat that
> was torpedoed and sunk. You were saved from the water, as Moses
> was. Like Moses, you met your wife in a casual manner. Like Moses'
> wife, yours is beautiful and intellectual, God bless her. Moses made
> his brother a high priest; you made one of yours Attorney General. I
> thought that perhaps this letter would serve notice to the world that
> God is on our side and that of our beloved chosen leader and Presi-
> dent, John F. Kennedy, God bless him.

What in Plutarch is grandly amusing hyperbole, and in Mr. Meer is
comical-tragical error, was in St. Paul and the Fathers a highly
sophisticated doctrine of time and history. That John F. Kennedy
proved to be an imperfect antitype of Moses no more impeaches
the validity of the theory of types than Dante's and Milton's imaginative subtleties document its accuracy. Typology merely formulates, in a vocabulary congenial to Christian readers of the Old
Testament, certain tendencies of the human mind; and then, in
schematic terms and in its technical elaborations, it reflects a theory
of history that allows theologians (and poets) to comprehend certain basic rhythms of Christian time.

It provided Milton with a way to organize the materials of the two
strophes (the two Dispensations) of "Upon the Circumcision," and
it provides as well a rationale for the *nunc stans* or "standing now" of
line eleven. Since the bleeding of the Circumcision—that "seal" of
"exceeding love"—finds its fulfillment only later in time, at the
moment of the Passion, the "now" must be taken to refer simultaneously to both present and future. Using the technical language
of Biblical exegesis, we may observe that Milton is portraying the
Circumcision as a type or figure of the Passion, the Passion as
antitype or fulfillment of the Circumcision. Lancelot Andrewes
puts it this way: "At His Circumcision then, He entered Bond anew
with us; and, in signe that so He did, He shed then a few drops of
His blood ... as a pledge or earnest, that *when the fullnesse of time
came,* He would be ready to shed all the rest; as He did. ...." What

"then at His *Circumcision* He undertook, at His *Passion* He paid even to the full: and having paid it ... cancelled the sentence of the Law...."[26] In this exegetical sense the "now" of "now bleeds to give us ease" prefigures, in the first part of the poem, the reference to the Passion in the second part, and the word therefore means both "now" and "then" as type relates to antitype.

Recognizing the range of the word in this context—the full meaning of which lies outside the pale of customary discourse— affords some inkling of the way Eternal Providence affects the course of temporal affairs. The poetic *nunc stans* teases us out of the certainty with which we accept the system of tenses built into our language, reminding us that in Eternity the past and future are simultaneously comprehended in God's everlasting "now." Milton's method first locates the Circumcision in Time—between the "erst" of the Nativity and the "ere long" of the Passion—and then suggests its eternal significance. The Circumcision is real, an historical fact; and yet its full meaning remains shadowed until the Passion, when men can then perceive that the "seal" prefigured the fulfillment of "obedience" on the Cross in a movement "from shadowy Types to Truth." The Circumcision is not connected "metaphorically" to the Passion, nor is the relation either "logical" or "associationist": it is figural, based on the typological method of exegesis that became for Milton a way of writing figurative discourse in time *sub specie aeternitatis.* The word "now" in "Upon the Circumcision" represents in little a technique that Milton did not employ when he wrote the "Fair Infant" and would not or could not use in writing "The Passion."

It is foolhardy if not simply foolish to speculate on the reasons for a poet's not having finished what he had begun, and "The Passion" provides so little evidence in its present state (of the eight stanzas that Milton completed, all are in one way or another introductory) that some scholars have simply found it expedient to assume that the poet just did not cotton to the idea of the Crucifixion. Yet it remains possible to draw plausible inferences simply by reflecting that Milton approached the theological events of the Circumcision and the Nativity by placing them in Time and relating them to Eternity. Instead of following this method in "The Passion" Milton attempts a variety of other techniques, none of which was to emerge as an important element in his mature style. There are a few Spenserian archaisms, there are reminiscences of the lushness of the Fletchers, and in the last two stanzas the poet short-circuits

himself in a coruscation of "metaphysical" conceits that might have
embarrassed Cleveland. Milton's aim in general appears to have
been the writing of a "meditation" in the sense defined by St. Ignatius and popularized by English Protestants, for the poet, while
tuning his song and setting his harp and invoking the night, seeks
also to describe the scene, to provide the first part of a meditation—
the *compositio loci*: "See, see the Chariot" and "Mine eye hath found."
In his efforts to render the scene, Milton ignores the theological
and eternal significance of the historical event, and either as result
or corollary he never manages to extricate himself from his own
introductory stanzas. (In *Paradise Regained,* to recur to the grand
example, Milton writes not of the Passion, as one would expect
from the title, but of the Temptation, which he transforms into a
type of the Passion, electing as usual to treat the figure rather than
the fulfillment.) If Milton did not fail to complete "The Passion"
because he attempted an Ignatian meditation in verse and could not
get beyond the composition of place, it is at least apparent that he
failed in trying to write a meditation; and it must be allowed some
significance that the poems on the Circumcision and the Nativity
share techniques that have little or nothing to do with meditative
poetry. The Nativity Ode, if it may be said to have a composition of
place, achieves it only in the last stanza ("But see! the Virgin
blest. . . ."), ending where Ignatius practiced to begin.[27]

The true affinities of the poems on the Circumcision and the
Nativity have not been recognized, perhaps because the structure
of the Nativity Ode has been assumed, on the basis of persuasive
reasoning by Arthur Barker, to be tripartite and because the theme
has been taken to be the routing of the pagan deities, which A. S. P.
Woodhouse declared to be the "intellectual core" of the poem.
Barker contends that the "first eight stanzas . . . describe the setting
of the Nativity, the next nine the angelic choir," and the "next nine
the flight of the heathen gods"; and that these "three movements
each present a single modification of the simple contrast, preserved
throughout the poem, between images suggesting light and harmony and images of gloom and discord." The movements are related, according to this line of argument, "not by the repetition of a
structural pattern, but by the variation of a basic pattern of imagery."[28] Although there can be no doubt that the images recur significantly and that the pagan gods receive considerable emphasis, I
think it can be shown that Milton subordinates the so-called "intellectual core" to his main theme, which concerns time, and or-

ganizes the poem on the basis of principles of scriptural exegesis rather then on congeries, associationist or other, of images.

Milton's special handling of his subject becomes evident through comparison with others', Crashaw's for example, on the Nativity. Where Crashaw provides an almost naturalistic depiction of the scene, Milton specifies the relation of this event in time to God's eternal plan. The four introductory stanzas establish the a-temporal patterns that are later elaborated in the Hymn proper. The first two portray the poet on Christmas morn of 1629 as he looks into the past to contemplate that first Christmas when the Son "laid aside" glory and "chose" to dwell on earth. The third stanza seems initially to share this temporal perspective—even though it is cast in present tense as the poet prepares to welcome the Infant in "hymn, or solemn strain"; the "Now" of line nineteen at first appears to indicate the point just before dawn on Christmas of 1629. But the fourth stanza, also in present tense, makes emphatic the "presentness" of the past, first inviting us to "See how" the "Star-led Wizards haste" from the East and then admitting the poet into the theological landscape: "O run, prevent [come before] them with thy humble ode." It is "now" the actual Christmas of the Nativity and not merely its calendrical commemoration in 1629.[29] The temporal asymmetry—two stanzas in past tense, two in present tense—of the opening immediately suggests that Milton may have been less concerned with providing a "composition of place" than with revealing the "eternal" significance of the Nativity. The "Now" of line nineteen resembles the "now" of line eleven of "Upon the Circumcision, for it refers, from the perspective of the first two stanzas, to Christmas of 1629 and, from the temporal orientation of the next two stanzas, to the first Christmas in history. The "Now" of the Nativity Ode may therefore also be considered a poetic *nunc stans*, glancing simultaneously toward present and past and conflating the two events separated in Time as though viewed from the vantage of Eternity. (As Bergson says, Time is that which prevents things from occurring together.) This meaningful "confusion," familiar to readers of the Christian poetry of the Middle Ages and Renaissance, stems from an awareness that the principal events of history occur but once and yet are "repeated"—in the life of each Christian and throughout the holy days of the church calendar. Christ, who died once for our sins, is continually born and crucified, appearing lovely in limbs not his throughout time the "same yesterday, and today, and for ever" (Hebrews 13:8).

The conflation of past with present, economically rendered in the introductory stanzas, may be detected in the Hymn as well. In Stanza I it "was the Winter" as the Infant "lies" in the manger; Nature "had dofft" and it "was no season then for her," and yet (in Stanza II) she "woos the gentle Air." In Stanza III God "sent" Peace who "strikes a universal Peace." In V the night "was" peaceful and Christ "began" as "Birds of Calm sit brooding."[30] Temporal fluctuation occurs even in the disposition of the imagery, as in XVI where the final line refers to the "wakeful trump" of the Last Judgment but the next lines, the first of XVII, abruptly revert to the past:

> With such a horrid clang
> As on mount Sinai rang...

Instead of a simile drawn, say, from Revelation and alluding to future calamity, the poet refers to judgment past, the "thunders and lightnings" in the Mount (Exodus 19) when God delivered the Tables of the Law to Moses.[31] Milton's simile illustrates the future Apocalypse by drawing on past resemblance—the figure or type of which the Last Judgment is the fulfillment or antitype. After the "world's last session," time shall be no more,

> And then at last our bliss
> Full and perfect is....

Instead of the expected future ("will be"), the poet writes in a kind of eternal present, for as Joseph Fletcher says, "God ... needeth not the distinctions of Time"—the notion stated most memorably by Sir Thomas Browne: "in eternity there is no distinction of Tenses"; the "last Trumpe is already sounded, the reprobates in the flame, and the blessed in *Abrahams* bosome"; "what to us is to come, to his Eternitie is present."[32] Since past experience and future expectation *is* God's eternal present, the poet who would intimate as much to his readers must somehow transcend the system of tenses—past, present, future—that dominates our apprehension of time.

The Nativity Ode ought not therefore to be read as a series of contrasting images, with or without an "intellectual core"; nor should it on such reasoning be divided into three parts. Milton, in common with most poets of the period, tends to compose according to what Sidney calls a "foreconceit" or what we often refer to as "theme," which perhaps comes closest to what Renaissance thinkers apparently understood to lie behind Aristotle's emphasis on "action" in the *Poetics*. But the theme of the Ode is not, as Hughes assumes without question in his editorial notes, the rout of the pagan gods; it is "peace," partial and perpetual. That is, Christ's birth has meaning for the poet in the way it coincides with temporary peace on earth, recalling the harmony that obtained at the beginning of time before sin "jarr'd against nature's chime" ("At a Solemn Music") and prefiguring what in the Ode is called the "happier union" at the end of time.

Only the modern preoccupation with imagery and moments of "dramatic climax" can account, I think, for the neglect or misunderstanding of theme in this instance—because Milton explicitly states what he is about and then reiterates the notion again and again. (He had also made it explicit to Diodati in *Elegia Sexta: Paciferum canimus semine regem*.) In the first stanza of the induction Milton distinguishes between the birth of Christ, the beginning of our "great redemption," and the Crucifixion, when "he our deadly forfeit should release"; then uses the alexandrine to emphasize a further distinction between the birth, a comparatively brief time of peace on earth, and the "perpetual peace" that Christ and the Father shall "work us" at the end of time. In Stanza III of the Hymn proper God "sent down the meek-ey'd Peace," who then "strikes a universal Peace through Sea and Land," and in Stanza V the night is "peaceful" when the "reign of peace upon the earth began." Christ's birth, through the mercy of the Father, coincides with the seven-year (i.e., millennial) *pax romana*, which functions in time as a type of the peace that passeth all time and understanding. Although the Augustan *pax* is "universal" in space "through Sea and Land," it is limited in time. It is not the "perpetual peace" of the end-time, when the "meek-ey'd Peace" (Stanza III) shall join the three other daughters of God, "Truth and Justice" and "Mercy" (Stanza XV), to fulfill the Christian promise shadowed in Psalm 85:10: "Mercy and truth are met together; righteousness and peace have kissed each other."

This view of the Nativity, as inaugurating a reign of peace universal in space but limited in time, explains the disposition of the imagery: for the moment, the "Prince of light" disperses the darkness, and the angelic choir, for the time being, produces harmony. Which means that the "intellectual core" appears not as principal theme but as subsidiary motif; although the oracles cease, the "flocking shadows," the gods of darkness, will not flee forever, and Satan's power is not destroyed but only circumscribed:

> for from this happy day
> Th' old Dragon under ground,
> In straiter limits bound,
> Not half so far casts his usurped sway.

Since the Peace of the Nativity is temporary, historically true but limited in time, the flight of the pagan gods attracts attention as no more than the most dramatic illustration of the partial peace that accompanies the birth of Christ. Instead of the future "perpetual peace" we perceive only how "his reign of peace upon the earth began" and embrace only in "fancy" the vision of glory at the end of time. This understanding of the Nativity also affects the overall organization of the poem, dictating its division into two main parts.

In the first half of the Hymn Milton develops the theme of peace in relation to "nature" and time. Stanzas one to seven depict "meek ey'd Peace" ("No War, or Battle's sound") through the conceit of an illicit liaison between "Nature" and the "Sun, her lusty Paramour," which is interrupted by the appearance of the Son; the stars "stand fixt" before "their Lord" (both the Sun and the Son), as the "Sun himself withheld his wonted speed" while waiting to see a "greater Sun appear." (Milton returns to the conceit involving the Renaissance quibble on Sun-Son in Stanza XXVI where the simile of the "Sun in bed" includes both the rising sun and *christus oriens*.) In Stanzas VIII and IX the poet describes the "silly" shepherds who hear and (in X) see the angelic choir. In the remaining stanzas of the first half of the poem Milton places the angelic music in time, first by recalling the harmony of creation "when of old the sons of morning sung" (cf. Job 38:6 ff.), and then, referring to the music of the spheres, looks forward to the end-time when "Truth and Justice" shall be restored, when "Time will run back, and fetch the age of gold." Considered from this point of view, the first fifteen stanzas represent the "peaceful" and "harmonious" effect of the Nativity on Nature (earth, stars, innocent shepherds) in relation to Creation and Judgment.

The eternal meaning of this effect appears precisely defined in Stanza X, in which "Nature"

> Now was almost won
> To think her part was done,

> And that her reign had here its last fulfilling;
> She knew such harmony alone
> Could hold all Heav'n and Earth in happier union.

The "happier union" glances back toward the love-conceit of Nature, who, though accustomed to "wanton with the Sun," yearns for
the "season" at the end of time when she will be married, by implication in "Maiden White," to the Son. The phrase "last fulfilling"
bears its technical sense from the vocabulary of Biblical exegesis. It
makes Milton's aim explicit. As Daniel Featley explains in one of his
sermons (on 2 Cor. 6:2), the "peace" inaugurated by Christ and to
be perfected at the end of time "was shadowed by the *temporall peace*
concluded through all the world by *Augustus*."[33] The poet has represented the "universal peace" and "harmony" of "nature" at the
Nativity as a figure or type of the "perpetual peace" and harmony
that the Son "with his Father" shall "work us" at the end of time.
The "happier union" shall in its "last fulfilling" be the antitype of its
shadowy prefiguring. Meanwhile, the Nativity shadows but does
not fulfil, for Nature's "part" in the race of time is not yet "done."
Eternal Providence ("wisest Fate")

> says no,
> This must not yet be so,
> The Babe lies yet in smiling Infancy. . . .

At the end of time

> our bliss
> Full and perfect is,
> But now begins. . . .

And as in *Paradise Regained*, and elsewhere in the mature Milton,
the beginning shadows the ending.

The Hymn, like the induction, divides not into three but into two
parts, at Stanza XVI ("But wisest Fate says no"), and the following
stanzas, devoted to an explanation of the decree of "wisest Fate"
and the rout of the gods, make the division more emphatic. Their
function is to reveal the exact sense in which the "peace" of Nature
at the Nativity is only temporary, showing how the "old Dragon"
lies in "straiter limits" but is not finally "bound." All the elements of
the poem—the tenses, imagery, structure—seem calculated to effect one end: defining the eternal significance of an occurrence in
time, measuring its meaning in respect to the past and future of

scriptural history, seeing the event as a "shadowy Type" to be fulfilled according to the decree of Eternal Providence. At the end of
the poem the temporal fluctuation of tense and image ceases,
where in the still moment before dawn, as the natural "Sun in bed"
is about to rise, the Son is "laid to rest" in a kind of eternal present
where "Bright-harness'd Angels sit," have sat, will always sit, "Until
their Lord bespake, and bid them go."

When Milton elected to treat the Nativity as an event in time
explicable through the typological method, the choice influenced
even the smaller elements of style. Perhaps the "Sun" of Stanza
VII, hesitating in deference before the "greater Sun," may be explained as nothing more than the usual Renaissance quibble;
perhaps "wisest Fate" and "mighty Pan" are not to be understood as
types of Providence and Christ but merely as instances of the familiar Renaissance habit of classical circumlocution. And yet there is
throughout the number and variety of such examples a common
element, the rhythm of anticipation and fulfillment that charac-
terizes the movement from "shadowy Types to Truth." The references may be more or less explicit, as in a phrase like "last fulfilling"; or the reliance on the typological method may appear only
obliquely, shadowed in an implied comparison:

> Nor all the gods beside,
> Longer dare abide,
>   Nor *Typhon* huge ending in snaky twine:
> Our Babe, to show his Godhead true,
> Can in his swaddling bands control the damned crew.

To call these lines A Classical Allusion (to the story of Hercules'
strangling the serpents that had invaded his cradle) seems to miss
the point, especially when the next step usually is to label the poet A
Classicist and then to forget, as quickly as possible, the whole inci-
dent. But the allusion functions in effect as a comparison or analogy in time—Hercules as type of Christ, Christ as antitype of
Hercules—and in this way the allusion becomes part of the proleptic patterns of foreshadowing and fulfillment that characterize the
entire poem. In technique the allusion to Hercules resembles the
reference to the thunders and lightnings on Mount Sinai as a type
of the Last Judgment, though in the case of Hercules or "mighty
Pan" the exegetical method is removed from the province of biblical history and applied, more daringly, as a means of lending Christian meaning to classical civilization.[34]

Enough has been said to entertain a hypothesis about one aspect of Milton's early development as a poet. It is widely, and rightly, assumed that the poet, given the peculiarities of his temperament and education, had to find some way to deal with the apparent or real contradictions between classical learning and Christian faith. Here lies the supposed antithesis between Milton The Puritan and Milton The Christian Humanist, which has produced a notorious history of special pleading among literary critics, much of it based directly or indirectly on The Schizoid Axiom: the Puritan Moralist unconsciously distrusted the Humanist Artist, with the result that Milton wrote worse than he knew about God and better than he intended about Satan. Although Milton is assuredly a didactic poet, it may be that he was less disturbed by the supposed conflict than his critics think; but there can be no doubt that toward the beginning of his career he was uncertain about the best means to express what he knew and felt, the best means to lend his poems comely and significant shape.

The problem, so considered, is not merely expository. It is at bottom a problem in how to view time, in how to view the course of history, in how to "measure this transient World, the Race of time," in relation to Eternity. The problem seems omnipresent in the early verse, explicitly addressed in "On Time" but susceptible only of a trick solution.

> Fly envious *Time*, till thou run out thy race,
> Call on the lazy leaden-stepping hours,
> Whose speed is but the heavy Plummet's pace;
> And glut thyself with what thy womb devours,
> Which is no more than what is false and vain,
> And merely mortal dross;
> So little is our loss,
> So little is thy gain.
> For when as each thing bad thou hast entomb'd
> And, last of all, thy greedy self consum'd,
> Then long Eternity shall greet our bliss
> With an individual kiss;
> And Joy shall overtake us as a flood,
> When everything that is sincerely good
> And perfectly divine,
> With Truth, and Peace, and Love, shall ever shine
> About the supreme Throne
> Of him, t'whose happy-making sight alone,
> When once our heav'nly-guided soul shall climb,

Then all this Earthy grossness quit,
Attir'd with Stars, we shall for ever sit,
    Triumphing over Death, and Chance, and thee O Time.

The Bodley MS. prescribes "Upon a Clocke Case, or Dyall," the
original Trinity MS. "To be set on a clock case," and the metrical
divisions of the poem, each corresponding to one hour of the day,
fall into twelve segments that R. Darby Williams diagrams in almost
this way:

HOURS	METRICAL SEGMENT	HOURS	METRICAL SEGMENT
I	pentameter (5 11.)	VII	pentameter (1 1.)
II	trimeter (3 11.)	VIII	trimeter (1 1.)
III	pentameter (3 11.)	IX	pentameter (2 11.)
IV	tetrameter (1 1.)	X	tetrameter (1 1.)
V	pentameter (2 11.)	XI	pentameter (1 1.)
VI	trimeter (1 1.)	XII	hexameter (1 1.)

The poem, a little more subtly than the pattern poems of the Greek
Anthology, has by reason of its metrical arrangement become
transformed into an emblem. As Williams observes, "The poem
belongs on a clock case not only because it thematically deals with
time [and eternity], but also because it emblematically describes the
rising and falling of a clock hand during one revolution." And each
of the half-day periods, as the hand first falls to the sixth hour and
then rises to triumph over time, corresponds hour-by-hour to the
calculated shifts in meter (the pentameter of I to the pentameter of
VII, and so on). With a single, and final, exception: "Were the final
line a trimeter," says Williams, "the pattern would be perfect, but it
would also bring the circle full round, and the hand would be in
position to begin another rotation; we would still, that is, be in the
world of clock time."[35] The final hexameter "doubles" the time—a
metrical sleight-of-hand that would have delighted George Herbert—and in this way shifts attention from the earthly dial of "envi-
ous Time" toward "long Eternity." Time has, for a moment "perfectly divine," seemed to "run out" its "race" as the poet emblematically figures the final triumph "over Death, and Chance, and thee
O Time." Although the poem is as witty as anything in Donne or
Herbert, it is also a *tour de force* that will not, at least for Milton, bear
repetition. Playing the numbers racket, that incessant and serious
game of Renaissance poets, leads only incidentally toward a theory
of time and history that affords perspective on the values and tales
of classical civilization.

The question is not, after all, Which has more value—classical or Biblical history? (The answer precedes the question.) But rather, How do the admittedly imperfect values of antiquity find their limited part in the true and universal history of people and events written by God? How, to put the question more technically, does the poet cultivate the art of classical allusion? Is he to litter allusions with decorative abandon? dispose them according to the canons of Aristotelian logic? reveal through their unconscious patternings the more or less private associations of an "inspired" bard? or what? There are, indeed, clusters of images that characterize Milton's verse throughout his career—some traditional, like the opposition between light and dark, some rather more personal, like the opposition between virgin wholeness and dismemberment. And Milton's verse everywhere, even in the "Fair Infant," reveals the rigorous Renaissance training in logic and rhetoric. But the "Fair Infant" betrays the poet's uncertainty about how to relate classical learning to Christian faith. If asked what "grim Aquilo" has to do with the concluding consolations, Milton himself would have been hard pressed, I believe, to reply. Classical "history" of this variety is a pack of lies, irrelevant to Christian truth. And the art of classical allusion becomes mainly a prettifying endeavor, or a method of negative contrast: "Such more delicious than those Gardens feign'd . . ."

But "Upon the Circumcision" and the Nativity Ode show that Milton had ready to hand a method, the typological theory of the relation of the Old Testament to the New, that might be extended to include classical antiquity. And the failure of "The Passion" may be taken to imply that he was not fully aware at this point in his career of how to exploit the literary possibilities of the exegetical method, which may in turn imply uncertainty about how to relate the role of priest to that of poet. As Melville knew, "There is no steady unretracing progress in this life; we do not advance through fixed gradations, and at the last one pause. . . ." But certainly in writing the first book of *Paradise Lost* the poet handles his classical materials with surety and magniloquent ease:

> Men call'd him *Mulciber*; and how he fell
> From Heav'n, they fabl'd, thrown by angry *Jove*
> Sheer o'er the Crystal Battlements: from Morn
> To Noon he fell, from Noon to dewy Eve,
> A Summer's day; and with the setting Sun
> Dropt from the Zenith like a falling star,

On *Lemnos* th' *Aegean* Isle: thus they relate,
Erring. . . .

(740-47)

Although there seems to be, in a passage such as this, more than
enough of the usual Christian scepticism that appears in Milton as
early as the "Fair Infant" (not content to remark that "they fabl'd,"
the poet must emphasize that "they relate,/Erring"), there is no
need to ask what Christ has to do with Apollo (here Mulciber) or to
fuss about a putative conflict between classical and religious truths.[36]
We need only replace the ellipsis, used with such skill by opponents
of the Puritan Milton, with the poet's words:

> thus they relate,
> Erring; for he with his rebellious rout
> Fell long before. . . .

The writers of antiquity erred not in what happened but in when it
happened; their myths stand in a quasi-typological relation to
Christian truth, their fables an imperfect shadow of Christian history. And the poet knows it—no "uneasiness" here. One answer to
the question, What has Christ to do with Apollo? is that Apollo may
be viewed as a type of Christ, which is in effect the role that Apollo
plays in *Lycidas*. And so with the early use of "mighty Pan" and
Hercules in the Nativity Ode. Although the relatively discrete stanzas of the Ode appear almost as loosely connected as those of the
"Fair Infant," the language of the Ode has a resonance lacking in
the earlier poem, and the typological contrast between partial and
"perpetual peace" provides a firmness of structure absent from the
"Fair Infant." Exegesis has proven its relevance to the writing of
poetry.

CHAPTER II

Lycidas *in Christian Time*

The elements of The Grand Style, foreshadowed in the earlier poems on Italian models, appear fully developed in *Lycidas*; and in *Lycidas* Milton exploits fully, though far more subtly, the exegetical techniques first employed in the Nativity Ode and in "Upon the Circumcision." Although Addison protested that "our language sunk under him," Milton has at last found a style answerable to his lifelong concern with Time and Eternity. Since the typological view implies that time and history exhibit a basic rhythm of prefiguration and fulfillment—from shadowy types to substantial truths—Milton had at hand a way of ordering the forward movement of the monody *and* a way of defining his own place in the historical development of the pastoral genre. But since 1910, when James Holly Hanford published his masterly essay on *Lycidas*, we have continued to talk about the pastoral antecedents of the poem pretty much as he did—or not at all. Hanford began by conceding that "not infrequently the pastoral imagery continues to be felt as a defect, attracting attention to its own absurdities," and ended by hoping that we would "find ourselves forgetting that the pastoral imagery is inherently absurd."[1]

But we need not have recourse to esthetic amnesia if we appreciate how Milton drew on more than one tradition of pastoral and how he consciously, and explicitly, subordinated pagan idylls to Christian images. Although it seems absurd to assume that any imagery is inherently absurd, we would still have to question why Milton—not to mention Spenser, Shakespeare, Marvell—consciously

45

elected to speak absurdly. The argument from inherent absurdity proceeds from the assumption that art imitates life directly, as when Dr. Johnson (who of course knew better) objects to the "inherent improbability" of pastoral and quotes the great line, "Battening our flocks with the fresh dews of night," only to observe: "We know they never drove afield, and that they had no flocks to batten. . . ."[2] In other words, the child next door must be inherently absurd for galloping about on a broomstick, though of course we have learned from life, if not from art, that counterfeit coins may produce real packs of cigarettes.

The broomstick "imitates" a horse only imperfectly, but what counts, after all, is not that it be True To Life but that it be useful as a substitute, that it fulfil our desire to ride.[3] In poetry what counts is the availability of the substitutes and our desire to think and feel, to read for the sake of experience. But when a substitute (convention or even genre) loses a part or the whole of its intelligibility, it may come to be regarded as inherently absurd, which explains why Professor Hanford and Dr. Johnson differ not in their view of the essential hobbyhorse but in the intensity of their desire to ride. I am speaking not of the relation of art to life implied by topical allegory of the simpler sort, in which Lycidas "is" Edward King and Camus "is" Cambridge (but "is" Milton the "I" of line 3 in the same sense?), rather of the relation of the genre to our life of the mind and to previous specimens of the genre. To read Lycidas aright, we must not only discriminate among the fugitive ways it glances at the life of historical personages but also recognize the ways in which the poet explicitly engages his predecessors in dialogue (I am not using the word figuratively), the ways in which his art "means" by imitating and "overgoing" previous art.

But if we assume that pastoral imagery is "merely decorative" or "inherently absurd" because it is somehow "unreal," then our only recourse—so runs the implicit argument since Hanford—is to invest the imagery with psychological force; if the pastoral form does not imitate nature, it must at least reflect psychic realities. The most popular version of these attempts to save the appearances represents Edward King (whom Milton, we are told, did not know all that well and who was in any case probably not very prepossessing) as merely the nominal subject; the poem, we learn, is really about John Milton himself (who may then become The Universal Poet or even Everyman), so that the monody claims our attention, if it claims us at all, by the way its admittedly artificial imagery betrays the predicament of the young poet who desires fame but fears the end of the thin-spun life. Since *Lycidas* resembles Vergil's Tenth Eclogue in beginning without the usual narrative frame, the temptation to think biographically must be almost irresistible for most modern readers:

> Yet once more, O ye Laurels, and once more
> Ye Myrtles brown, with Ivy never sere,
> I come to pluck your Berries harsh and crude. . . .

Surely (we think) this must be the young Milton, uncertain of his craft; his "forc'd fingers" are "rude," and he is again reluctant to test his powers before the "season due"—an impression inevitably reinforced by what we know of Milton's life, that he was always awaiting the right moment, the "hour precise." Surely there is more here than the usual pastoral convention that requires the poet to represent himself as a youth lisping in numbers? Since the myrtles and the laurels symbolize immortal poetry, the words "yet once more" must assuredly point toward previous poetic acts: *Comus* perhaps? the Nativity Ode? or even the "Fair Infant Dying of a Cough"? And maybe so. I have no wish to argue that the poem wrote itself, no inclination even to imply that Milton failed to sense a parallel between Edward King, young priest and poet, and himself, young poet-priest.[4]

But since the poet writes in special relation to his predecessors, the artistic—as distinct from the biographical—significance of the opening lines may be ascertained from the uses to which Milton has put the pastoral traditions. The poet in the pamphleteer confesses in the famous digression in *The Reason of Church-Government* that he aspires to do for England "what the greatest and choicest wits" of Greece and Rome as well as "those Hebrews of old did for their country"—"with this over and above," he adds, "of being a Christian."[5] Emphasis on Milton's "classicism" and "humanism" has led to neglect of the Christian pastoral of the Middle Ages as well as two even more important traditions of pastoral: that of "those Hebrews of old" and that which is "over and above" the Hebrew, the pastoral of the New Testament.[6] Canticles, Psalms, the Prophets, and the Gospels are of course all deeply permeated by that "inherently absurd" imagery. The Lord is my shepherd, I shall not want. Ignoring the scriptural models also obscures one (Renaissance) aspect of classical pastoral itself, for medieval and later Christians habitually read the "choicest wits" in their own terms—rejecting in part, modifying in part, or even supposing that Vergil's Fourth Eclogue had prophesied the coming of the Messiah. In the sixteenth century Puttenham had these developments partly in mind when he acknowledged that the eclogue does not attempt merely to "counterfait or represent the rusticall manner of loues and communication: but vnder the vaile of homely persons, and in rude speeches to insinuate and glaunce at greater matters."[7] Theocritus and Vergil in this context take their clearly assigned places within the "greater matters" of Christian history, which means that in an important sense Milton had not one but three "traditions" on which to draw and that their relation each to the other rested on theological premises derived from the language of biblical exegesis: Vergil, obscurely, and "those Hebrews of old," less obscurely, shadowed forth the "chief Shepherd" (1 Peter 5:4) of the New Testament.

And here, in this triple progression from antiquity through the Old Testament to the New, lies part of the artistic significance of the opening lines of the poem: "Yet once more . . . and once more." Probably because she had in mind only a "literary context," Isabel MacCaffrey mistakenly felt that *Lycidas*, "almost alone among Milton's important poems, does not suggest at the beginning how it will end."[8] But if we ignore for the moment the biographical and literary contexts, we are free to attend to the scriptural force of the allusion, which points unmistakably to Hebrews 12:22-28:

> ye are come unto mount Sion, and unto the city of the living God, the heavenly Jerusalem, and to an innumerable company of angels . . . and to the spirits of just men made perfect. . . . See that ye refuse not him that speaketh. . . . Whose voice then shook the earth: . . . Yet once more I shake not the earth only, but also heaven. And this *word*, Yet once more, signifieth the removing of those things that are shaken . . . that those things which cannot be shaken may remain. Wherefore we receiving a kingdom which cannot be moved, let us have grace. . . .

The relevance of these verses to the end as well as to the beginning of *Lycidas* will perhaps be obvious, but to appreciate the full purport of these oracular utterances it helps to consult the exegetes. The commentators understood the Apostle to be distinguishing two kinds of judgment—that under the Old from that under the New Dispensation—and accordingly they explain that he

> commenteth vpon the Testimonie of Haggai, Chap. 2.6. and from this word *Once*, concludeth, That Heaven and Earth shall passe

away. . .: That these chaungeable Heavens and Earth being removed, Hee may make a Newe Heaven and a Newe Earth . . . but *Once
More*, and no oftener, is CHRIST to shake the same. . . . All thinges
made, shall be shaken: but CHRIST's Kingdome, and the Salvation
of His Subjectes, shall never bee shaken.

The reference to Haggai reveals that the Apostle had first in mind
"the terrible quaking of the Earth, and burning of Mount Sinai,"
secondly the way God's wrath "at the Daye of Iudgement, may be
seene in that little Resemblance of Mount Sinai."[9] The mode of
exegesis is typological, moving "from shadowy Types to Truth":
the author of Hebrews finds in the thunders and lightnings upon
Sinai a type of the Last Judgment, just as Milton in the Nativity Ode
saw in the "thunder" of the "trump of doom" the antitype of the
"horrid clang" on "mount Sinai."

All this helps to explain, insofar as explanation may be needed,
why this place in Hebrews is invariably compared with 2 Peter 3
("new heavens and new earth") and with the Book of Revelation,
which heralds the New Jerusalem, "a new heaven and a new earth,"
when God shall "wipe away all tears from their eyes; and there shall
be no more death . . . : for the former things are passed away." (The
conclusion of *Lycidas* draws heavily on Revelation, especially 7:17,
19:9, and 21:4.) The symmetry of the allusions emerges clearly: *Lycidas* begins with "Yet once more . . . and once more"; it proceeds to
the "two-handed engine" (the Last Judgment seen under the aspect
of Old-Testament justice, the antitype of "that little Resemblance of
Mount Sinai"), which "stands ready to smite once, and smite no
more"; and it ends with "ruth" and "joy and love" (Judgment seen
under the aspect of New-Testament mercy), with the "unexpressive
nuptial Song" of Revelation when the shepherds shall "weep no
more . . . weep no more . . . weep no more," and "all the Saints
above" shall "wipe the tears for ever from his eyes." In *Lycidas* the
dread voice shakes the earth yet once more "so that those things
that cannot be shaken may remain," and so that Lycidas himself
may receive "grace" and a "kingdom that cannot be moved": "In
the blest Kingdoms meek of joy and love." The word "more"
sounds and sounds throughout the poem and, as is usual in Milton,
the beginning of the poem prefigures its ending.

The network of allusion does more than connect the parts of the
poem: "yet once more" defines the arrangement of the three main
parts of the poem, for the phrase suggests, to the reader of *Lycidas*
who is also a reader of Hebrews, the *way* in which "those things that

are shaken" may be removed so that "those things which cannot be shaken may remain." And, finally, the allusion may be used to explain Milton's distinctive use of genre, for the three pastoral traditions not only relate specifically to each of the three main parts of the poem but also provide the means by which the poet modulates his singing voice.

The first fourteen lines define the situation and prefigure the major themes: "For *Lycidas* is dead, dead ere his prime." The first of the three main sections (11. 15–84) begins by invoking the muses and reiterates the note of loss—"now thou art gone, and never must return." This lament for the shepherd-as-poet occasions the ineffectual appeal ("Ay me, I fondly dream") to the Nymphs and Calliope, which prompts the appropriate question about the value of strictly meditating the "thankless Muse" and finds the answer in the "perfect witness of all-judging *Jove*" who "pronounces lastly on each deed." The second section (11. 85–131) repeats the pattern, beginning with an invocation and then reiterating the fact of loss: "That sunk so low that sacred head of thine." This lament for the shepherd-as-priest includes the ineffectual questions of Triton and brings up the relevant problem of the good pastor in a corrupt church, locating the answer this time in the "two-handed engine at the door." The third section (11. 132–85) also begins with an invocation and also "dallies" with an ineffectual "surmise" (the flower passage), then repeats the fact of loss—but this time only to reverse it. Lycidas, here the shepherd-as-poet-and-pastor, who was "dead, dead ere his prime," now "is not dead"; and Lycidas, who was no more than "sunk so low," is now "sunk so low, but mounted high." This section likewise ends in judgment, the merciful judgment of the angel who "melts with ruth" and of Him "that walk'd the waves."[10] The last eight lines, invariably referred to as *ottava rima* but perhaps more properly called *strambotto*, conclude the poem. The movement of the three main parts, from death to life, from sinking to mounting, and from despair to consolation, may be easily reduced to the Christian commonplace that we must lose life to gain it. Yet the order and relation of the three movements is so calculated as to compel the reader to re-acknowledge the truth of the truism.

The forward movement of the monody may be viewed in one of its aspects as an exercise in the critical history of literature, for Milton has in the first two sections dealt with classical and Old-Testament "pastorals" in such a way that they find their proper fulfillment in the "pastoral" of the New Testament. I do not mean, of course, that there are no allusions, say, to the New Testament in the second section (there are many, and they preponderate) or that the first section is devoid of Christian implications—only that the solutions to the problems presented in each part must be associated, in turn, with classical consolation, with Old-Testament vengeance, and with New-Testament mercy. It is this tripartite movement, identified in the minds of Milton and his "fit . . . audience" with the rhythm of time "from shadowy Types to Truth," that orders the ongoing momentum of the poem and lends it its distinctive rhythm of anticipation ("yet once more") and fulfillment ("weep no more"). The shepherd is first the (classical) poet whose hope for immortality rests on the fame of his pastoral verses ("that last infirmity of Noble mind"), which at first appears to be lost through premature death, though finally the solution is to understand that true fame is "no plant that grows on mortal soil" but is rather the "praise" of "all-judging Jove": "Of so much fame in Heav'n expect thy meed." This is to anticipate the end but it is not yet the end. The shepherd is next the (biblical) pastor, whose trade is not to meditate the muse but to feed the "hungry Sheep," and whose preoccupation is not with poetic immortality but with eternal salvation or damnation, with the "massy Keys" of heaven and hell ("The Golden opes, the Iron shuts amain"). His practice of the "faithful Herdman's art" is threatened not by the blandishments of Amaryllis in the shade but by the corrupt clergy, whose "lean and flashy" pastorals "grate on their scrannel Pipes of wretched straw." His consolation lies not in the praise of Jove but in his reliance upon Old-Testament justice, the judgment of the iron key:

> But that two-handed engine at the door
> Stands ready to smite once, and smite no more.[11]

This is of course the end, but it is not the entirety of the end; for we know that at the Second Coming Christ shall temper justice with mercy, shall use the golden key of the New Dispensation as well as the iron of the Old. The engine that remains ready to "smite once, and smite no more" in this way becomes part of the greater movement within the poem of "yet once more," which can be perfected only with the third, and last, of the three main sections. Lycidas, finally both the pastor and poet, "receiving a kingdom which cannot be moved," wanders the fields of eternal pastoral, "where other groves, and other streams along," and hears the pastoral verses of eternity as the saints above "sing, and singing in their glory move."[12] Milton has, in effect, recapitulated the history of the pastoral genre.

The "Fair Infant," like *Lycidas*, consists of eleven stanzas; and, like *Lycidas*, the "Fair Infant" sees the fact of death from the twin perspectives of classical and Christian consolation. But the "Fair Infant" fails, not only because the Spenserian diction seems mannered and awkward but also because the poet appears to have discovered no way as yet to integrate the two kinds of consolation. In *Lycidas*, on the other hand, Milton perfectly adjudicates the (potentially) conflicting claims of the two. It is as if the poet had asked himself how classical pastoral, with its implicit concern for immortality through poetic fame, might be related to Christian pastoral, with its concern for immortality through Christ. And the answer proceeds in an order that reflects the characteristic movement of Christian time "from shadowy Types" to the "Truth" of eternity.

Proleptic patterns appear even within sections, as when the "Herald of the Sea" prepares us for the "Pilot of the *Galilean* Lake." Had Milton specified Triton and St. Peter, the relation would vanish, and it is in this sense that the amplitude of The Grand Style may be viewed without contradiction as an instrument of poetic condensation. Although it is true and doubtless important to recognize that *Lycidas* is moist with water imagery (King did indeed die at sea and the poem is appropriately a "melodious tear"), the connection between the classical "Herald of the Sea" and the "Pilot of the *Galilean* Lake" is not merely associative, the result of poetic revery, for there is a qualitative difference between the two, the first being a "little Resemblance" of the other. "Identity," observes Wallace Stevens, "is the vanishing point of resemblance"; and if we argue—it has been argued—that the pilot *is* Christ, then we lose the surge of fulfillment that derives from our seeing how the "Pilot of the *Galilean* Lake" has shadowed the truth of "him that walk'd the waves." Identity, rather than "little Resemblance," would mean that the poem had in a basic way "finished," completed its design, before the third section. (Similarly, if we take "all-judging Jove" simply as Renaissance shorthand for "God," the poem is in the same way completed before the second section.) But *Lycidas* must be allowed its distinctive temporal dimension, as the poet assimilates without rejecting the kinds of judgment appropriate to classical "immortality" and Old-Testament vengeance. Phoebus Apollo may adumbrate the Son but cannot provide a place for the virtuous heathen in a classical "heaven"; the god of the sun and of song can guarantee only an everlasting meed of praise. And the justice of the Old Testament remains imperfect until fulfilled by the mercy of the Son. The movement is dynamic, from the shadows of Time to the truths of Eternity.

More important is the *use* to which the poet puts the pastoral genre in relation to the Christian end he contemplates for Edward King. Lycidas, who was *dead* and *sunk*, becomes Lycidas who "is not dead," "Sunk though he be beneath the wat'ry floor." Lycidas is "sunk low, but mounted high," and it is this oscillation between low and high that defines the manner in which the pastoral singer modulates his voice.

The allusion to Vergil's Fourth or Messianic Eclogue in the third line of the opening invocation—

> Begin then, Sisters of the sacred well,
> That from beneath the seat of *Jove* doth spring,
> Begin, and somewhat loudly sweep the string—

advertises Milton's intention to imitate the Latin poet in rising above the low style, supposed (purely by convention) to be appropriate to pastoral, and to sing of greater matters.[13] Milton accordingly somewhat loudly sweeps the string, rising to consider the blind Fury and the witness of Jove. Imitating the imitation (Vergil's) of one of the "choicest wits" of antiquity, Milton uses the norm of (classical) pastoral in order to transcend it. And precisely the same motive governs the invocation that begins the second section:

> O Fountain *Arethuse*, and thou honor'd flood,
> Smooth-sliding *Mincius*; crown'd with vocal reeds,
> That strain I heard was of a higher mood:
> But now my Oat proceeds . . .

Since Arethuse, the spring near the birthplace of Theocritus, points to the Greek pastoral poet, and Mincius, the river near the birthplace of Vergil, alludes to the Latin writer, Milton is conversing across the centuries with the "choicest wits" of Greece and Rome, first to acknowledge that he has in his turn violated the decorum of pastoral ("That strain I heard was of a higher mood") and then to submit that he is once more observing the literary amenities ("now my Oat proceeds"). Yet the poet promptly modulates again, rising to the vision of the pilot of the Galilean lake and the dreaded engine at the door.

The third section repeats the pattern precisely:

> Return *Alpheus*, the dread voice is past,
> That shrunk thy streams; Return Sicilian Muse...

Alpheus, the river of Arcady, alludes to Vergil and corresponds to Mincius in the preceding section; the Muse of Sicily, Theocritus, here takes the place of the earlier "Arethuse"; and the "dread voice" parallels the "higher mood" of the earlier section. And once again Milton maintains decorum (the flower passage) for only a moment, rising from the low style of the oaten pipe and reaching for a strain of higher mood—not this time a voice of greater dread but one of immeasurable mercy, the "great vision of the guarded Mount" and the "dear might of him that walk'd the waves."

From the moment that Milton begins to somewhat loudly sweep the string, he is engaged in a conscious, even self-conscious, dialogue with his illustrious precursors; and the dialogue grows in complexity as he proceeds. Much has been written of the "speakers" and their "dramatic contexts" in *Lycidas*; but the most important speaker is, after all, the pastoral singer himself, and it may be that the most important dramatic situation defines Milton's relation to the "choicest wits" of pagan antiquity. Milton speaks to his predecessors, calling them by name in the language of pastoral allusion; he invokes their presence neither to legitimize, nor to preside over, his present endeavor, but rather to show that their vision of nature, while lovely enough "to interpose a little ease," remains at best a "fond," at worst a "false surmise." Return Alpheus (speak again, Vergil), says Milton, knowing that readers of Ovid had learned how in another sense Alpheus had already "returned."

Alexander Ross retails the geographical facts: "*Alphaeus* is a river of Elis in Arcadia, through secret passages running under the earth & sea, it empties it self in the spring *Arethusa* in *Sicilie*; which though Strabo denyeth it, it cannot be otherwise, seeing so many witnesses confirm that whatsoever is cast into *Alphaeus* is found in *Arethusa*."[14] The river god Alpheus had fallen in love with Arethusa, a woodnymph; she, transformed into a subterranean stream, fled to Ortygia, where she rose as a fountain, but Alpheus, the Arcadian stream, pursued her underground to mingle his waters with hers in Sicily. All of which not only explains Ross's "facts"; it also indicates the complexity of Milton's dialogue with antiquity. As by (mythological) allusion Vergil (Alpheus) pursued the streams of pastoral to its fountain or source in Theocritus (Arethuse),[15] so by (literary) allusion Milton turns to his own fountains or sources, that is, to Theocritus by way of Vergil. This elaborate conversation with antiquity testifies to Milton's attempt to do what the "choicest wits" of Greece and Rome and "those Hebrews of old" had done—but "with this over and above" of being a Christian.

The nature of the dialogue points to the artistic function of pagan pastoral. It is the standard from which the poet varies, the stable medium from which he may rise to "greater matters" and to which he may then return. It is "imitation"—but only in the Renaissance sense of "overgoing"; Theocritus and Vergil are guides, not commanders. Analogous to meter in poetry, the pastoral genre is the norm against which the reader measures variations, the means by which he may grasp the significance of the singer's modulations. This particular norm, with just such variations, must have seemed singularly appropriate to readers before Dr. Johnson: the pastoral genre, as Renaissance critics never tired of repeating, occupies the lowest degree in the hierarchy of literary *kinds,* and Christianity, many still repeat, is the religion of the humble, of the meek who shall inherit the earth. Since the pastoral care of the chief shepherd was not for the proud but the humble, many Christian writers, most notably Augustine, tended to invert not only the pagan hierarchy of social values but also the classical hierarchy of styles.[16] We gain life by losing it and we rise by being "lowly wise," which is one of the better reasons why Milton can use the lowest of the genres to utter the highest truths.

In using the pastoral as a standard from which to depart significantly, Milton reanimates the Christian commonplace that is the consolation for the loss of Lycidas. *Lycidas* is so constructed that as a poem it does exactly what Lycidas himself is described as doing; the pastoral poem sinks in order to mount, just as the pastoral figure sinks in order to mount, with the result that structure reflects theme, structure mirrors meaning. From the beginning ("Yet once more") we have anticipated the end, though we do not arrive there immediately but in three successive waves, the crest of each being "higher" than the one before; we are required to stand and wait two times before fulfillment. Once in the first section Milton somewhat loudly sweeps the string; once more in the second section; and yet once more in the third. The poet, that is, sinks yet once more to rise to the final affirmations: "So Lycidas sunk low, but mounted high." In terms such as these we may see that the poem not only recapitulates the history of pastoral but also, and more significantly, uses that history as a mimetic reinforcement of its main theme. Both *Lycidas* and Lycidas sink in order to mount. By what may be thought of as an almost muscular effort of the verse itself—the successive movements of the three sections—Milton readies us to acknowledge yet once more the truth of the Christian truism, for this pastoral monody owes a large part of its artistic success to its having been constructed in imitation of itself. *Lycidas* endures, triumphantly, as a work of art that *is* what it *says*.

The *commiato* or coda reverts to the pastoral norm with astonishing abruptness: "Thus sang the uncouth Swain . . ." Uncouth indeed! In the introductory epistle to Gabriel Harvey, E. K. applies Chaucer's "uncouthe, unkiste" to "this our new poete" Spenser (and his new pastorals), "who for that he is uncouthe (as said Chaucer) is unkist, and unknown to most men. . . ."[17] But while the word may mean "unknown," there is no way that either a seventeenth- or twentieth-century reader can isolate the connotations of ignorant and rude, and seal them hermetically under a bell jar— which must have afforded the poet some mild amusement. The use of the past tense and the third person, as the "I" of line three suddenly becomes the "uncouth Swain" of line 186, must be allowed to have intensified our sense of shocked surprise; the pastoral singer becomes persona, receives his generic designation, only with the final lines, just as the monody proper receives its generic status as a song within a narrative frame only with the concluding lines. "As the impersonal voice addresses us," says Isabel MacCaffrey, "we become co-listeners, and as the foreground recedes into the middle distance we find ourselves paradoxically in a more intimate relation to it," for "we have heard the same song."[18] It is as though we had been forced to look through the wrong end of the telescope, for first we watch the first-person singer, the "I" of line three, recede suddenly, now an "uncouth Swain," into the pastoral landscape occupied by the "young swain" Lycidas; but then the artistic distance narrows once more, not only because we have heard the same song but also because the coda itself so much resembles the song. The "still morn" goes out with "sandals gray," as if human; the shepherd's pipe has "tender stops," as though sentient. The swain's "lay" is "*Doric*," in allusion to Theocritus; and the sun stretches out the hills, in a line that imitates the last verse of Vergil's First Eclogue. We have heard the same song, and now we share the same landscape.

The opening lines of *Lycidas* establish two resonant parallels: that between the natural circle of the days and of the seasons ("mellowing year") and the circle of human life, though the point is at first to lament that one human life—Lycidas "dead ere his prime"—failed of "season due." And, second, the parallel between the poetic act, the writing of the poem, and the subject of the poem, the death of Lycidas—both of which are assumed, at first, to be premature, "crude" or unripe (*crudus*), though the once-reluctant swain will at last come to sing with "eager thought." The circle of the seasons and of the day somehow resembles the cycle of human life, and in some way resembles the act of poetic creation. But since the resemblances are not identities, there is occasion for discomfort and grief. The natural cycles are at first imperfectly understood; specifically, we presume too much if we suppose that Lycidas did not in some way find his "season due." As Browne says, "Let them not therefore complaine of immaturitie that die about thirty," for there is "some other hand that twines the thread of life than that of nature."[19] Milton's task must be to reveal that the circle of poetic creation in art can only be truly completed through reference to a realm that includes and transcends nature. The task must be to show—poetic and theological resolution require it—that the cycles of nature and time may be truly understood only in relation to the realm of grace and eternity. To think otherwise (with Theocritus and Vergil) is to "fondly dream," is to dally with "false surmise"; the flower passages, the appeal to the nymphs of nature—these represent the norm of the oaten flute, nature as it is depicted in the beautiful but partial truths of Theocritus and Vergil. The analogy between nature and grace, time and eternity, truly exists, but it was hidden in types and shadows until the coming of "him that walk'd the waves." We as readers must at last be enabled to recognize, with Jesus in *Paradise Regained*, that God is "He in whose hand all times and seasons roll." It is what Abdiel tries to tell Satan, whose obduracy blinds him to the vanishing points of resemblance, in *Paradise Lost*: "God and Nature bid the same."

Lycidas is an idyll or picture that lacks one half of its frame. Since the narrative frame appears only with the coda, there is a sense in which the poem itself is at first not ripe, its pastoral singer a shadowy type not yet seen in true perspective—a singer nearly anonymous, piping before his "season due." In time the singer will receive a name, a generic designation consonant with his literary predecessors and his present purpose. But meanwhile we as readers, lacking the artistic distance conferred by the device of the

narrative frame common to so many eclogues, become directly implicated in the movement of the poem, following the "I" of line
three in sweeping the string—once, once more, and yet once more.
Twice the pastoral singer defers the true consolation, then without
transition (because it must carry something of the force and im-
mediacy of revelation) there comes the lyric peripety in the form of
the rhetorical charge to the shepherds, that is, to all of us who are
natural, fallen men, we who must, like Adam and Eve, drop "some
natural tears": "Weep no more, woeful Shepherds weep no more."
With the singer, we have been sinking in order to rise, until finally
we have been readied to experience the true meaning of the circles
of nature:

> So sinks the day-star in the Ocean bed,
> And yet anon repairs his drooping head,
> And tricks his beams, and with new-spangled Ore,
> Flames in the forehead of the morning sky:
> So *Lycidas*, sunk low, but mounted high. . . .

Here is transformed the "Star that rose, at Ev'ning, bright," here is
the true surmise of what occurs "under the opening eyelids of the
morn." Nature, as depicted by Theocritus and Vergil, can only
mourn and can reveal only that Lycidas is sunk beneath the watery
floor; but as the great vision looks homeward with mercy we perceive the true relation of nature to grace. The natural cycle that
had been interrupted within nature and time before the season due
has been perfected in the eternal realm. Three times, following the
efforts of the pastoral singer, we have sought the greatest vision,
each time mounting higher than the time before, until at last we see
the analogy of the sun made good by the Son—no fond dream, no
false surmise. It is the "season due." *Kairos* is come.

"Thus sang the uncouth swain . . ." And the song has moved
from the personal to the impersonal, from the vision bounded by
time to the vision of eternity. The swain, no longer merely unknown and rustic, may now bear as well the other meanings of
"uncouth" that were current at the time: marvelous, uncommon,
strange, wonderful—as in the "uncouth Revelations" of St. Bridgit
(1648; cited OED). And Milton may conclude in accord with the
revelation given those who have heard the same song, shared the
same landscape:

> And now the Sun had stretch't out all the hills,
> And now was dropt into the Western bay;

At last he rose, and twitch't his Mantle blue:
Tomorrow to fresh Woods, and Pastures new.

The swain gets up—though as natural men we legitimately might have expected him to lie down—and firmly secures (twitches) his mantle against the chill of evening. But "Sun" is in fact the (nearest grammatical) antecedent of the "he" in "he rose," and of course we know that the sun drops into the western bay only to arise at last attired in its blue mantle.[20] We may expect that in the evening the swain will lie down and that the sun will do no more than drop into the bay, but in the economy of *this* poem one sinks only to mount yet once more, at long last to the "fresh Woods, and Pastures new" of the Chief Shepherd. The uncouth swain, like Lycidas and the sun and the Son and (hopefully) the reader, sinks in order to rise "at last"; that these parallels "work" seems to imply a rare kind of imaginative integrity in the poet. Milton, with "this over and above of being a Christian," speaks across the years to the "choicest wits" of pagan pastoral and exemplifies what it means to pronounce "yet once more" in the syntax of Christian time.

Chapter III

Paradise Lost: *From Shadows to Truth*

Paradise Lost, to borrow the words of Adam (XII, 554 ff.), "Measur[es] this transient World, the Race of time," in relation to "Eternity, whose end no eye can reach." As Milton had declared, as early as the Seventh Prolusion, "Nothing can be recounted justly among the causes of our happiness, unless in some way it takes into consideration both that eternal (*sempiternam*) life and this temporal life" (*Works*, XII, 255). Beginning *in mediīs rebus* the poet, in Northrop Frye's phrasing, ties a knot in time—from which point the action unravels backward and forward to reveal the form and pressure of God's eternal purposes: "Jesus Christ was the *great design*" of history, which may be likened, says Peter Sterry, to "Dramatick Poems, which have the design laid in some one entire . . . action," where the "continuance is set off, heightened by two eminent parts"; the "*knot tyed fast* in the course of the action; then the *uniting* [typographical error for "untying"] *of this knot*. . . . Thus in this great action of time and eternity, the bringing of the Sons of God to Glory. . . ." Thus in *Paradise Lost*. For the "work of God" in time "from the beginning to the end" is, says Sterry in echoing Augustine, "God's Poem," and the "Works of Poets" are, at their best, "imitations drawn from those Original Poems, the Divine works and contrivances of the eternal Spirit." Such poets move "to the remotest Distances, and most opposed Contrarieties" but "bindeth up all with an harmonious Order into an *exact Unity*" by "opening the beginning in the end, espousing the end to the beginning."

Book VI ends with the Fall, "nine days they fell," of the rebel angels, returning imaginatively to the "nine times the space that measures day and night" of Book I, as Homer in the *Odyssey* and Vergil in the *Aeneid* return to the beginning half-way through their epics; and Book VII of *Paradise Lost,* "half yet remains unsung," begins with Creation, ending with the "Paradise within" and "eternal Paradise of rest" when Jesus brings back long-wandered man. This "untying of the knot," says Sterry, is "that which *Jesus Christ* pointeth at in himself": "*you shall see the Son of Man return there, where he wast at first.*"[1] The circular patterns of six books apiece co-exist, as in Vergil, with three movements of four books each. The first four books focus on Satan, his fall and attempted rise; the second four reach back to the "begetting" of Christ, "on such day" as "Heav'n's great Year brings forth" (V, 582–83), and turn on Him in His dual role as destroyer and creator; the last four center in Adam, his fall and the promise of his ascent, and look toward the future to envisage the moment when earth "shall all be Paradise, far happier place" (XII, 464). Although the epic includes, at least by allusion, the entire "Race of time" from Creation to Apocalypse, Milton's emphasis falls on Eden: the expulsion from Paradise, and the promise of Christ who shall "bring back"

> Through the world's wilderness long wander'd man
> Safe to eternal Paradise of rest;
> (XII, 313–14)

and the Eden of the just man, which may be found, in time, between the original Paradise and the one to come "when this world's dissolution shall be ripe" (XII, 459)—

> then wilt thou not be loath
> To leave this Paradise, but shalt possess
> A paradise within thee, happier far.
> (XII, 585–87)

This movement, from Paradise to "paradise, far happier place," suggests Sterry's insistence on "opening the beginning in the end, espousing the end to the beginning"; and it faithfully reflects the movement of Christian history "from shadowy Types to Truth" (XII, 303).

The "Race of time" may be compared to the sands of an hourglass, to "Golden Sands running between two Eternities,"[2] for "Eternity is before and after time: Time hath a beginning and an end; then comes Eternity againe: by this we see, Eternity is not onely (*in saeculum*) for ever, or everlasting; but we must looke both waies, as well to the part of Eternity that is before time, as that which is to come. . . ."³ And meanwhile Time, through types and shadows, must bear the impress of Eternity. Although the end of Time must come, Browne observes that "to determine the day and yeare of this inevitable time, is not only convincible and statute madnesse, but also manifest impiety; How shall we interpret *Elias* 6000. yeares, or imagine the secret communicated to a Rabbi, which God hath denied unto his Angels?" But we may nevertheless be sure that there is a "secret glome or bottome of our dayes; 'twas his wisdome to determine them, but his perpetuall and waking providence that fulfils and accomplisheth them, wherein the spirits, our selves, and all the creatures of God in a secret and disputed way doe execute his will." "Our ends," admits Browne, "are as obscure as our beginnings, the line of our dayes is drawne by night, and the various effects therein by a pencill that is invisible; wherein though wee confesse our ignorance, I am sure we doe not erre, if wee say, it is the hand of God."⁴ Time, however obscurely, betrays the hand of deity, from shadowy types to truth. *Veritas filia temporis*.

Time reveals through types and *kairoi* because shaped by Eternity. Unlike those, and perhaps they are the majority, who supposed that Eternity may best be defined as a species of "timelessness," Milton evidently believed that Plato's notion of time as the "moving image" of the eternal might be understood as displaying real if limited analogical truth.⁵ Not only do the poet's angels eat (with "real concoctive heat") and make love (just talking about it induces a "rosy" glow), but the angelic habitat experiences "grateful vicissitude" of "our Ev'ning and our Morn" (V, 628); and even Aristotle's sublunary notion of time from the *Physics* has its applicability to the eternal realm:

> For Time, though in Eternity, appli'd
> To motion, measures all things durable
> By present, past, and future. . . .
> (V, 580–82)

Just as man is for Milton the image of God in senses disallowed by most of his contemporaries, so is Time the image of Eternity in more exact analogy than men perhaps suppose. Raphael says that "what surmounts the reach"

> Of human sense, I shall delineate so,
> By lik'ning spiritual to corporal forms,

> As may express them best, though what if Earth
> Be but the shadow of Heav'n, and things therein
> Each to other like, more than on Earth is thought?
>
> (V, 571–75)

Although the poet only partly commits himself, he clearly invites his reader to regard the analogies between the visible and invisible worlds as possessing a greater degree of truth or validity than we might otherwise grant.

Milton's aim—to narrow the gap between Nature and Grace, Time and Eternity—requires us to understand the "shadow" (*skia*) in the phrase "shadow of Heav'n" not only in the dualistic signification of Plato's Allegory of the Cave or The Divided Line but also in the typological sense, as when Milton assumes that the "shadowy Type" of Eden prefigures the time "when Earth shall all be Paradise." Robert Cawdrey's definition of "type" as "shadowe of any thing" obviously leaves a good deal of room for imaginative writers to use *skia* in the "temporal" manner of the exegetes or in Plato's ontological and "spatial" sense.[6] Browne is no more unusual than Milton in lending the word its most inclusive meanings:

> The greatest mystery of Religion is expressed by adumbration, and in the noblest part of Jewish Types, we finde the Cherubims shadowing the Mercyseat: Life it self is but the shadow of death, and souls departed but the shadows of the living. The Sunne it self is but the dark *simulachrum*, and light but the shadow of God.[7]

Browne's contemplations are eclectic, as are those of Milton in *Paradise Lost* if not in *Christian Doctrine*.

It is at any rate clear that the framework devised by Milton to measure the "Race of time" in relation to Eternity is typological:

> Of Man's First Disobedience, and the Fruit
> Of that Forbidden Tree, whose mortal taste
> Brought Death into the World, and all our woe,
> With loss of Eden, till one greater Man
> Restore us, and regain the blissful Seat. . . .

The epic cycle of loss and restoration, the circular movement from Eden to Eden, may be comprehended under the relation of "Man" to "greater Man," which is a typological relation that would have been obscured though not obliterated by the more specific "Adam" and "Christ." So much would be obvious to any instructed reader, who might then be relied upon to catch the exegetical method at

work, to take one convenient example, in the metaphors of "Preve-
nient Grace descending" (XI, 3) on the penitent Adam and Eve.
The Son speaks of the "first fruits" sprung from "implanted Grace"
(22–23),

> Fruits of more pleasing savor from thy seed
> Sown with contrition in his heart, than those
> Which his own hand manuring all the Trees
> Of Paradise could have produc't, ere fall'n
> From innocence.
>
> (XI, 26–30)

This (Protestant) garden is sown within man himself: Eden is its
"type," and it itself is the "antitype," "a paradise within thee, happier far" (XII, 587). Here the typological method (strictly interpreted) begins to open out toward imaginative vistas that reveal its
influence but are not as readily explainable in the language of
exegesis as is the relation of "Man" to "greater Man."

More interesting, and no less significant, than the relation of
"Man" to "greater Man" or of Eve to Mary, "second Eve" (*PL*, V,
387 and X, 183), is the way the typological "rhythm" of promise
and fulfillment permeates the diction, the depiction of character,
and the movement of the epic as a whole. It is this typological
feeling for time that dictates Milton's reliance on the figure of
prolepsis, defined by Puttenham as a "maner of speach purporting at the first blush a defect which afterward is supplied, the
Greeks call him *Prolepsis*, we the Propounder," though perhaps "we
ought rather to call him forestaller."[8] The "Propounder" ties and
unties the workings of the eternal in time, "opening the beginning
in the end, espousing the end to the beginning."

The opening line "propounds" the epic as a whole, an extraordinary instance of Milton's way with enjambement or "the sense," as
the poet says in his note appended to the second edition of *Paradise
Lost*, "variously drawn out from one Verse into another." Enjambement conveniently serves as a part of the poetic economies
derived from the impulse toward contradiction and paradox in a
world where good and evil are "as two twins cleaving together,"
though at times the device savors more of secular trickery than
mystical legerdemain:

> On mee as on thir natural centre light
> Heavy, though in their place.
>
> (X, 740–41)

Other juxtapositions reverberate more profoundly, as when we learn that

> next to Life
> Our Death the Tree of Knowledge,
> (IV, 220-21)

which emphasizes the awesome intimacy of the two great opposites and reminds us that Satan, disguised as a cormorant, sits upon the Tree of Life "devising Death" (IV, 197). The enjambed invocation—

> What in me is dark
> Illumine, what is low raise and support—
> (I, 22-23)

not only makes emphatic the need for inner light but invites something of the luminous presence to shine on "low," allowing the lines to function as part of the pervasive imagery of dark and light, low and high, that interpenetrate each other throughout the epic.[9] The effect of another enjambed invocation—

> Then feed on thoughts, that voluntary move
> Harmonious numbers—
> (III, 37-38)

depends on the shift from intransitive to transitive and has been well described by Donald Davie: "This flicker of hesitation about whether the thoughts move only themselves, or something else, makes us see that the numbers aren't really 'something else' but are the very thoughts themselves, seen under a new aspect...."[10]

The "flicker of hesitation" induced by the first line of the epic "propounds" or "forestalls" Milton's whole design, "espousing the end to the beginning":

> Of Man's First Disobedience, and the Fruit...

Since in the theological and iconological traditions the "fruit of that tree is Christ himselfe,"[11] the enjambement invites us to consider not only the "loss of Eden" of the "Forbidden Tree" but also to "propound" the restoration effected by the "greater Man"; the fruit of Eden leads to expulsion and "all our Woe," but in (typological) time, after the "fruitless hours" (IX, 1188) have elapsed, the fruit shall "restore us, and regain the blissful Seat." The doggerel of John Abbott ("Rivers")—

> I bore a fruit, Iesus my royall Son,
> Who did restore what Adam had undone.
> Growing in Calvarie upon a Crosse,
> He did repaire terrestrial Edens losse—

relates the commonplace that informs the "flicker of hesitation" produced by Milton's subtle enjambement.[12]

Such "thoughts, that voluntary move," imitate the specifically typological rhythm of anticipation and fulfillment that may on occasion involve even the meaning of individual words. Encountering Death,

> Incens't with indignation Satan stood
> Unterrifi'd, and like a Comet burn'd,
> That fires the length of Ophiucus huge....
>
> (II, 706–09)

Although there is no reason, at first, to take "incens't" in other than its modern meaning, the etymological signification, in proximity to "burn'd" and "fires," almost immediately forces its way to the surface: the root meaning (*incendere*, to set afire) of the word emerges in the course of Time, which brings truth to light; and it has, of course, its peculiar relevance to Satan, the Grand Incendiary himself, within whom burns the hot hell . . . [13] The word "Ophiucus" works in similar ways.

It is commonplace to speak of the "degeneration" of Satan, but the word, as Milton's allusion to "Ophiucus" suggests, is a misnomer: Satan, borne by the "serpent-bearer," already resembles the snake he becomes. At the end of Book II Satan approaches "this pendent world," the created universe, and in Book III he stands on the "lower stair" (540) of the "passage down to th' Earth," "Just o'er . . . Paradise" (527–28). From this universal coign of vantage,

> Round he surveys, and well might, where he stood
> So high above the circling Canopy
> Of Night's extended shade; from Eastern Point
> Of Libra to the fleecy Star that bears
> Andromeda far off Atlantic Seas
> Beyond th' Horizon; then from Pole to Pole
> He views in breadth....
>
> (555–61)

As Pliny explains, "Neither is the night anything else but the shade of earth. Now the figure of this shadow resembleth a pyramis, pointed forward, or a top turned upside down ... nor goeth beyond the heights of the moon."[14] Satan, immediately over Eden, stands at the eastern end of Libra, and from this point on the outermost reach of the universe looks down upon the earth, which lies upon its "side" or "from pole to Pole": he sees the "pyramis" of "Night's extended shade" pointing directly up at him, and on the western side of earth he watches Andromeda "beyond th' Horizon," which means that the "fleecy Star" or Aries lies directly opposite him on the other side of the globe. In prelapsarian Eden, as "*Albertus Grotus*," following "*Avicen*, and the elder writers also, ... *Polybius* and *Eratosthenes*," had asserted in "imagining a delicate and most temperate region under the equinoctiall [that] divides the *Zone* in two points, *Aries*, and *Libra*," the equinoctial line coincides with the equator; and it is therefore no mere trope of rhetoric for Milton to observe that "*Spring* and *Autumn* here/Danc'd hand in hand" (V, 394-95). Adam sees "twelve houres day, and twelve night" alternate with perfect regularity, with the sun invariably rising in Aries and the "Car of Night" invariably setting in the zodiacal sign directly opposite, in Libra.[15] It is therefore midnight in Eden as Satan enters the universe; and since the eastern end of Libra contains the head or *serpens caput* of the constellation Anguis (snake), Satan enters the universe through the mouth of the serpent.

In Book IX Satan seeks out the serpent, and "in at his Mouth/ The Devil enter'd" (187-88). In Book X Satan involuntarily becomes the serpent: "down he fell/ A monstrous Serpent on his Belly prone" (513-14). But before this final transformation the poet has taken his astronomical bearings with customary accuracy in describing the advent of Sin and Death:

> And now thir way to Earth they had descri'd,
> To Paradise first tending, when behold
> Satan in likeness of an Angel bright
> Betwixt the Centaur and the Scorpion steering
> His Zenith, while the Sun in Aries rose....
>
> (325-29)

The sun in Aries rises (from the point of view of Sin and Death) toward dawn from the other side of the earth while Satan, precisely halfway between Sagittarius and the Scorpion, "steers" from Eden directly toward the "passage" through which (in Book III) he had entered the universe. It is three o'clock in the morning, and Satan's movements are once more serpentine, for Anguis, the astronomical serpent borne by Ophiucus, has its head in Libra, but extends its tail through Scorpio and the Centaur. The Satan who enters the universe through the head of the serpent departs from its rear. This passage, from Ophiucus to Ophiucus, ought not, I think, to be described as "degeneration," as though one were writing the case history of an alcoholic.

It is instead a process of progressive revelation, revelation in and through time. Although Tacitus took accurate note of the "change" in the character of Tiberius upon becoming emperor, the great historian of men and manners said nothing of psychological degeneration. Rather he assumed that Tiberius had always been that way and that circumstances finally allowed him to be revealed for what he was.[16] The method of explanation more nearly resembles allegory than the modern novel: Julien Sorel and Roderick Hudson remain problematic in senses never to be shared by Spenser's Hellenore or Paridell, and when the *Piers* poet brings in Glutton we do not expect this "character" to begin pinching girls, in which case his name would be Lust—rather we anticipate a bout of eating and drinking, after which the "character" will cough up a caudle in his lap, which he does. Whereas the personages of allegory tend to act out the fate of their names, the characters of novels set out, often enough, to make a name for themselves. At crucial points in the action Glutton must betray his essential nature—not out of "psychological development," nor even at the whim of the author, but because his name is Glutton and because name reveals essence.

There is, similarly, little that can properly be called problematic in Satan, for even during that single second in the entire epic when he stands "stupidly good" we recognize clearly that momentarily he has become his opposite, an accident of time and circumstance that serves to accentuate essential nature. Satan's essence is serpentine; his nature requires that he be borne by the serpent-bearer. Although the poet, in the opening books, depicts Satan as an epic hero, God's laughter at this sacred travesty, together with the astronomical imagery, reminds us of the adversary's true nature. What we witness, then, is not a process of degeneration but rather the stripping away of accident, the outward veil, until the essence appears: he who elected to play the serpent in Book IX must become the serpent in X; he who entered the universe by the mouth of the serpent must leave by the tail. It is progressive revelation, the movement of providential history; and it bears, I think, more than accidental resemblance to the way we read words like "incens't."

When Adam tastes of the fruit "as with new wine intoxicated," the act, in the technical terms of Renaissance psychology, represents the subversion of the Reason by Appetite:

> Against his better knowledge, not deceiv'd,
> But fondly overcome with Female charm.
>
> (IX, 998–99)

As "they swim in mirth," Milton reproduces in Adam's funny-unfunny speech the accents of the lush who is watching his pronunciation:

> Eve, now I see thou art exact of taste,
> And elegant, of Sapience no small part,
> Since to each meaning savor we apply,
> And Palate call judicious. . . .
>
> (1017–21)

The repetitions recapitulate, of course, the psychology of the Fall, saying over and over again that Appetite is lord of Reason; but they also provide a context for the etymological pun on "sapience," which as Patrick Hume noted in 1695 derives from "*Sapere*, Lat. to taste, to distinguish, thence to be wise, to know." The quibble focusses much of the epic within its contrary boundaries, for it concentrates in a single word the confusion of Reason and Appetite that is the cause and effect of the Fall. The contrary meanings of "sapience" were of course there from the beginning, but (as with "incens't") it is the context that allows what may be thought of as the essence of the word to emerge; it is again, though in little, a movement in meaning from shadow to truth.

The meaning of the encounter between Satan and Sin resembles my other examples, for while it is clear enough on its own, it is not fully significant until we read the encounter between Adam and Eve. Sin begins by reminding Satan of her origins:

> All on a sudden miserable pain
> Surpris'd thee, dim thine eyes, and dizzy swum
> In darkness, while thy head flames thick and fast
> Threw forth, till on the left side op'ning wide,
> Likest to thee in shape and count'nance bright,
> Then shining heav'nly fair, a Goddess arm'd
> Out of thy head I sprung: amazement seiz'd
> All th' Host of Heav'n; back they recoil'd afraid
> At first, and call'd me *Sin*, and for a Sign

Portentous held me; but familiar grown,
I pleas'd, and with attractive graces won
The most averse, thee chiefly, who full oft
Thyself in me thy perfect image viewing
Becam'st enamor'd. . . .

(II, 752–65)

The birth of Sin travesties the birth of Athene or Wisdom from the head of Zeus, but Milton exploits more fully the allusions to the "left [sinister] side op'ning wide" and to the myth of Narcissus. In the *Metamorphoses* Ovid wittily links the tales of Narcissus and Echo (Narcissus is to the eye what Echo is to the ear), describing Echo's unavailing pursuit in a series of ingenious echoes, some of which are neatly captured in Sandys' version:

Thrust back; he said, Life shall this breast forsake,
Ere thou, light Nymph, on me thy pleasure take.
On me thy pleasure take, the Nymph replyes
To that disdainefull Boy, who from her flyes. . . .[17]

In Milton the "reciprocal" rhetoric begins with "back they recoil'd" and continues through the lust-chase of Death and Sin: "I fled, and cri'd out *Death* . . . and back resounded *Death*" (787 and 789). We have learned, among other things, that Satan is rather a narcissist; but the incidents are proleptic as well, "propounding" or "forestalling" through the myth of Narcissus a connection with the love-chase of Adam and Eve in Book IV, which likewise begins with echoing rhetoric and "perfect image viewing":

As I bent down to look, just opposite,
A Shape within the wat'ry gleam appear'd
Bending to look on me, I started back,
It started back, but pleas'd I soon return'd,
Pleas'd it return'd as soon. . . .

(460–64)

God, that better guide, saves Eve from the fate of Narcissus but not without first allowing her to play out the role of a different Echo:

Till I espi'd thee, fair indeed and tall,
Under a Platan, yet methought less fair,
Less winning soft, less amiably mild,
Than that smooth wat'ry image; back I turn'd,
Thou following cri'd'st aloud, Return fair Eve. . . .

(477–81)

Not only does the language echo itself in each episode; the later echoes the earlier—with crucial differences—just as both echo Ovid. (As Harding observes, we all know that Eve derives from the sinister side of Adam, but no version of the birth of Pallas Athene specifies the "left side" of Zeus.[18]) Satan's self-love is endless, Eve's is ended; the lust-chase of Death and Sin ends in rape "forcible and foul," the love-chase of Adam and Eve ends when "thy gentle hand/ Seiz'd mine, I yielded." We contrast as well as compare, and the full implications of the first chase are realized only through the second. The pattern is that of anticipation and fulfillment, which is in turn the pattern of providential time from shadowy types to truth.

These patterns emerge most explicitly in the last two books of *Paradise Lost*, books that may be denominated an "untransmuted lump of futurity" (in C. S. Lewis's notorious phrasing) only if we remain ignorant of the proper way to "measure" the "Race of time."[19] Milton had ready to hand a number of methods by which to organize scriptural history, and vestiges of all of them appear in the last two books; but he chose to transmute the vision of futurity in ways largely his own. From Plato he could have drawn the Myth of the Four Ages, or from Daniel the notion of the Four Monarchies (the Fifth to be that of Christ). He could have used the tripartite division—ultimately derived from Joachim de Fiore and Augustine's second disquisition on Ps. 29—of the six thousand years from Creation to the Last Judgment, which Donne formulated for the King, who already knew it, as "the two thousand yeares of Nature, before the Law given by Moses, And the two thousand yeares of Law, before the Gospel given by Christ, And the two thousand of Grace, which are running now...."[20] Milton could have adopted the influential hexameral division that appears, on analogy with the six days of Creation, in the twenty-second book of Augustine's *De Civitate Dei*: Adam to Deluge, Flood to Abraham, Abraham to David, David to Babylonian Captivity, Captivity to Nativity, Nativity to Second Coming.[21] Augustine's schema earned such wide acceptance that many scholars have actually given these divisions priority over Milton's text.

Although it is true that Book XI consists in six "visions" and Book XII in six "narrations," Milton uses all six "visions" to move from Adam to the Deluge (the first of Augustine's divisions); and after that the poet and the theologian continue to part company. Milton nevertheless constructed with great care, almost obsessively attentive to detail. The angelic historian "pauses" twice in the course of the last two books, first at the beginning of Book XII (Book XI closes with an allusion to the Last Judgment):

> As one who in his journey bates at Noon,
> Though bent on speed, so here the Arch-Angel paus'd
> Betwixt the world destroy'd and world restor'd;
>
> (1-3)

and then again after the fourth "narration," which also ends with an allusion to the Last Judgment:

> So spake th' Arch-Angel Michaël, then paus'd,
> As at the World's great period . . .
>
> (466-67)

These two "pauses" effectively divide the twelve "visions" and "narrations" into three great "periods"—the first from Adam to Noah, the second from the Flood to the Crucifixion, and the third from Christ to the Second Advent. In addition, the "pause" that separates the first four "narrations" from the last two has a shadowy counterpart in the "visions" of Book XI, where the last two, both of which deal with Noah, seem to form a unit (though not so strongly marked as in Book XII) that stands slightly apart from the first four "visions." This structure, with its elaborate symmetries, must be seen as almost geometrical in its exactness.[22] And it affords clear evidence that Milton had more in mind than a redaction in verse of scriptural history, especially one based exclusively on the hexameral categories of Augustine.

Instead of merely reverting to the commonplace division into two thousand years of "Nature," two thousand of Mosaic Law, and two thousand of Grace, Milton used his three great periods to urge Apocalypse, to anticipate *regnum Christi* and the return of Eden. Book XI ends not, precisely, with the abatement of the Flood and the Covenant of the Rainbow but with an explicit statement of final destruction and renovation:

> Day and Night
> Seed-time and Harvest, Heat and hoary Frost
> Shall hold their course, till fire purge all things new,
> Both Heav'n and Earth, wherein the just shall dwell.
>
> (898-901)

The fourth "narration" of Book XII closes with allusion to the moment "when this world's dissolution shall be ripe" (459):

> then the Earth
> Shall all be Paradise, far happier place
> Than this of Eden, and far happier days.
>
> (463–65)

So also with the fifth "narration":

> then raise
> From the conflagrant mass, purg'd and refin'd,
> New Heav'ns, new Earth, Ages of endless date
> Founded in righteousness and peace and love,
> To bring forth fruits Joy and eternal Bliss.
>
> (547–51)

And it is the sixth, and final, "narration" that ends, of course, with the promise of reward for the just even before the Last Judgment:

> then wilt thou not be loath
> To leave this Paradise, but shalt possess
> A paradise within thee, happier far.
>
> (585–87)

Through apocalyptic increments the poet reaches a crescendo of promises, shifting the emphasis from the fire of destruction to the restoration of a Paradise "happier far" while taking into "consideration both that eternal life and this temporal life." The way to this end coincides with the manner in which the poet has transmuted the lump of futurity.

Michael explicitly declares that the vision of the future has a pedagogical purpose, so that Adam (and the reader) "thereby" may "learn"

> True patience, and to temper joy with fear
> And pious sorrow, equally inur'd
> By moderation either state to bear,
> Prosperous or adverse: so shalt thou lead
> Safest thy life, and best prepar'd endure
> Thy mortal passage when it comes.
>
> (360–66)

In Book X Adam had already begun to puzzle out the meaning of his "mortal passage" and "when it comes," first asking

> why delays
> His hand to execute what his Decree
> Fix'd on this day?
>
> (771–73)

and then, speculating on this "long day's dying" (965), he concludes that at least it was not "immediate dissolution" that God "meant by Death that day" (1049–50). The question had, of course, similarly agitated the exegetes: "Some thinke, that a day is not herè to be taken, according to mans account of daies, but as it is before God, with whom a thousand yeares are but as a day," and so on, listing theories and authorities, though the most usual was "Hieromes interpretation, that Adam began in the same day to die, not actually, but because he became mortall and subiect to death."[23] Adam, that is, has begun to play at exegesis with the word "death," though this is of course only one of the "mysterious terms" of God's judgment that require *glossa extraordinaria*.

In Book XI Michael, accordingly, uses his first words (251 ff.) to explain Milton's view of the deferred sentence of death on that day. Adam's and Eve's "Prayers are heard, and Death . . ." must now wait "many days." There follow the visions, a series of pageants that may be regarded (particularly the first four) as Michael's contribution to the literature of *ars moriendi*, through which Adam learns "true patience," so that he may "best prepar'd endure/ Thy mortal passage when it comes." Michael teaches through binary oppositions, seeing all sins as permutations of the Fall. In the first vision, Cain's slaying of Abel, Adam receives the "sight of death," and Michael attributes it to Adam's "original lapse"; though Cain has "not sinn'd thy sin, yet from that sin derive . . ." (427). The second vision, on the other hand, derives from "th'inabstinence of Eve" (476); the "many shapes" of "Death" from "diseases dire" are "inductive mainly to the sin of Eve" (519). Having fixed attributions, the angel speaks of "temperance," and Adam, "best prepar'd," begins to find the "true patience" to "endure" his "mortal passage when it comes":

> Henceforth I fly not Death, nor would prolong
> Life much, bent rather how I may be quit
> Fairest and easiest of this cumbrous charge,
> Which I must keep till my appointed day
> Of rend'ring up, and patiently attend
> My dissolution.
>
> (547–52)

"Nor love thy Life, nor hate," corrects the angel.

And then the process of deriving sin from sin continues in the third vision: the women in "wanton dress," descendants of Cain, "light the Nuptial Torch" with the "Men though grave," descended from Seth, with the result that Adam, beguiled by the sight of "Feast and Music," exclaims, "Here Nature seems fulfill'd in all her ends" (602). But the angel, having taught patience before death, continues "to temper joy with fear/ And pious sorrow," pointing out that the scene is only "to Nature *seeming* meet" (604, my emphasis), and that the men, for the sake of the "fair Atheists," shall "yield up all thir virtue, all thir fame" (623). Adam, "of short joy bereft," immediately blames Eve: "Holds on the same, from Woman to begin" (633). And again the angel corrects, replying that "from Man's effeminate slackness it begins" (634). The next vision, of rapine and war, is "the product"

> Of those ill-mated Marriages thou saw'st;
> Where good with bad were matcht....
>
> (683-85)

The "good" men acquiesce in "th'inabstinence" of the "bad" women just as Adam had acquiesced in "th'inabstinence of Eve," so that the result must recapitulate the sin of Cain but "multiply"

> Ten thousandfold the sin of him who slew
> His Brother.
>
> (677-79)

Through permutations of the "original lapse," through "ill-mated Marriages" of "good with bad," the sins of Adam and Eve pollute the "Race of time." This four-part stage in the education of Adam, his exercise of "patience" in the face of death, ends with the "translation" of the One Just Man, Enoch, who is "exempt from Death" (709). The last two "visions" shift the emphasis from the nature of man's sin to the nature of God's judgment.

Adam must now learn to discriminate despair from hope, and accordingly the final "visions" both deal with Noah and the Flood. Adam first sees "the face of things quite chang'd" from War to "luxury and riot," and later he confesses that he "had hope"

> When violence was ceas't, and War on Earth,
> All would have then gone well, peace would have crown'd
> With length of happy days the race of man;
> But I was far deceiv'd; for now I see
> Peace to corrupt no less than War to waste.
>
> (779-84)

But meanwhile the vision of the Deluge has led Adam to despair, to doubt the providential course of history; "better had" he "liv'd ignorant of future" (763–64).

> Let no man seek
> Henceforth to be foretold what shall befall
> Him or his Children, evil he may be sure.
> (771–73)

Although Adam has confessed God's Justice and acquired patience to wait for his own death, he despairs of the future of mankind; but the sight of the sixth vision, in which Noah rides out the Flood and God hangs out the rainbow as token of "Cov'nant new," restores hope,

> Whereat the heart of Adam erst so sad
> Greatly rejoic'd, and thus his joy broke forth,
> (868–69)

so that for the first time he interprets what he sees, "the triple-color'd Bow," with complete accuracy and enjoys, for the first time, the unqualified approbation of his angelic instructor: "Dext'rously ["rightly"] thou aim'st. . . ."

Adam and the reader have been readied for Book XII; the six days or ages of the first "World" have been completed; the Age of Adam is accomplished, "death" comprehended as an aspect of the "original lapse" and as an aspect of God's Justice, so that the poet can now turn his attention, and that of the reader, to God's Mercy, to the "seed" of Mercy implanted in the curse on Adam and Eve and the Serpent.

The opening of Book XII marks the end of the Age of Adam and the beginning of the second "great period":

> As one who in his journey bates at Noon,
> Though bent on speed, so here the Arch-Angel paus'd
> Betwixt the world destroy'd and world restor'd.

But the poet's purpose remains the same—to delineate the consequences of the Fall in human history, though in this book Milton shifts the emphasis to politics while Adam observes "Man as from a second stock proceed" (7). Augustine moves from the Flood to Abraham, but Milton, concerned to show the loss of "true Liberty" "since thy [Adam's] original lapse" (83), devotes the first narration to Nimrod and Babel.[24] Throughout the poet's subject will be the way men come to be tyrants over themselves and over others—a Christian version of Socrates' argument in the *Republic*. "Rational Liberty" cannot exist apart from "right Reason" (82–84), which is in postlapsarian man often "obscur'd, or not obey'd" (86),

> And upstart Passions catch the Government
> From Reason, and to servitude reduce
> Man till then free. Therefore since hee permits
> Within himself unworthy powers to reign
> Over free Reason, God in Judgment just
> Subjects him from without to violent Lords.
>   (88–93)

Throughout the remainder of Book XII Milton will interpret history as the conflict of the "one faithful man" (113) of each age (Abraham, Moses, Joshua, Jacob, David, Solomon, Jesus), who is himself free because obedient to God, with "lawless Tyrants" (173); and as the growth of the "one peculiar Nation" (111) of the Jews in relation to "All Nations" (126), which in turn involves the typological relation of the "earthly Canaan" (315) to *regnum Christi*, of whose "Reign shall be no end" (330). History records the loss of liberty, inner and outer, but its "mysterious terms" hold the promise for the "faithful man" of a "paradise within thee, happier far" (587) and for the faithful "kingdom" of an "eternal Paradise of rest" (314).

In the first narration Michael explains that the "second source of Men" (13) lived "thir days in joys unblam'd" (22) under "paternal rule" (24) until the tyranny of Nimrod. At this destruction of patriarchal government, Adam appropriately shows himself "fatherly displeased" (63). The next narrative deals with Abraham and the "mighty Nation" (124) deriving from him, "that in his Seed/ All Nations shall be blest" (125–26); with the "lawless Tyrant" of Egypt; with Moses and "thir government, and thir great Senate" (225); and, finally, with Jacob whose "descent" shall "Canaan win" (269). The angel begins the third narrative by observing that despite the new laws sin "will reign among them, as of thee [Adam] begot" (286), that again, and as always, "sins/ National" shall "interrupt thir public peace" (316–17); and ends with the "Throne hereditary" and "Reign" (370) of Christ. Fourth, the angel speaks of the coming of Christ, whose "love" can "alone fulfil the Law" (404) so that "all Nations shall be blest" (450). It is the end of the second "great period," the beginning of the third and last; the angel "paus'd,"

As at the World's great period . . .
(467)

The last two narrations both treat, though with different emphases,
the period from the First to the Second Advent: first with men in
general, as the apostles seek to "evangelize the Nations" (499) while
religious and political Nimrods continue to appear:

so shall the World go on,
To good malignant, to bad men benign.
(537–38)

Next and last, with the "one faithful man" in particular who, if he
will but practice charity under providence, will then

not be loath
To leave this Paradise, but shalt possess
A paradise within thee, happier far.
(585–87)

Even this brief outline serves to indicate that the narrations of Book
XII, like the visions of Book XI, are disposed with logical precision, so that the elaborately interwoven themes and motifs, bearing
both the despair and the hope derived from man's first disobedience, are marshalled in symmetrical order, securely based in a series of oppositions: tyranny within and without, one nation and all
nations, paradise within and (at the end of time) without, when
earth shall all be paradise.

Now of course even such deft pedagogy as that displayed by
Michael provides no guarantee of artistic worth, though it testifies
to the meticulous care of the poet and begins to suggest some of the
ways he undertook to transmute the traditional lumps of futurity
that came to him prepackaged by Augustine and others. But it
remains true that readers from Addison through C. S. Lewis have
responded to Michael as though he were the God of Book III, the
"School Divine." The response in both cases is a yawn, which is
precisely what spectators do when they are being instructed but not
engaged. Observing a spectacle (television violence or lions and
Christians dining together) arouses emotion, engenders suspense,
whereas playing the same role at a series of visions or pageants,
especially where the denouement is known, would seem to invite
ennui. Milton must have been aware of just so much, for in under-
taking his account of Christian history he sought to transform his

reader from spectator to participant.[25] That he failed the history of criticism attests, though there are good reasons for supposing that the poet himself is not alone at fault.

To appreciate the artistic techniques of the last books—even, in some cases, to recognize them—we must first recall the way God writes the allegory of human history, for His methods are likewise the methods of Milton's Muse. And even if we finally choose to reject the artistic satisfactions provided by the last books, we may at least find them useful as instruction, sharing the education of Adam and Eve in order to read rightly an epic that Milton wrote throughout in "mysterious terms."

The preview of history offered to Adam remains for the reader a review, but if this were the primary difficulty we would not read the Greek tragedies; knowing the outcome did not affect Sophocles in his choice of subject, nor do we denominate the *Oedipus* an untransmuted lump of paternity. Knowing the outcome simply means that we must forsake suspense for other kinds of artistic involvement, and Milton encourages participation at the most rudimentary level through the basic device of withholding information. When Michael observes that "the sev'nth from thee" has been translated or that a "Reverend Sire" began "to build a Vessel of huge bulk," we are obliged to supply the proper names and are to that extent implicated in the proceedings. The device is, simultaneously, a way of distancing ourselves, for we are being constantly reminded that we know more than Adam and Eve.

The tension between involvement and distance produces in Milton special kinds of irony, as for example the moment when Adam begins to ponder the judgment accorded Eve:

> Pains only in Child-bearing were foretold,
> And bringing forth, soon recompens't with joy,
> Fruit of thy Womb: on me the Curse . . .
>
> (X, 1051–53)

The reader is of course being invited to draw on his knowledge of Hail Marys (and Luke 1:42) to provide the missing term, which will become known to Adam only in the fullness of time: "Fruit of thy Womb—Jesus." The technique, at its simplest in such examples as these, works not only against any tendency to identify too fully with Adam and Eve: it has as well the effect of creating an alliance between the narrator and the reader, for both "know more" than Adam and Eve, both see more in their words and actions. Milton elaborates such ironies with the great subtlety in his treatment of the ways in which Adam and Eve come to understand the full meaning of the "curse" pronounced upon them by the Lord God.

Before the "Vicegerent Son," under the name "Lord God," judges the fallen pair, the Father observes that he sends "Mercy colleague with Justice" (59), and the Son agrees to "temper" divine "Justice with Mercy" (77–78). The colloquy between the Son and Adam, followed by the judgment, foreshadows the first of the "progressive steps in repentance; namely, conviction of sin" (*Works*, XV, 385). In devoting some forty-five lines to the judgments themselves, Milton expands the biblical account so as to emphasize the allegorical implications of the "mysterious terms" (173), seen at first by the fallen pair only under the aspect of God's Justice but apprehended by the narrator, and by the (instructed) reader, as containing also the "seed" of Mercy. As Milton observes in *Christian Doctrine*, "Even before man had ... avowed [his guilt] ingenuously and in the spirit of repentance, God ... in pronouncing the punishment of the serpent ... promised that he would raise up from the seed of the woman one who should bruise the serpent's head, Gen.iii. 15., and thus anticipated the condemnation of mankind by a gratuitous redemption" (*Works*, XV, 253).

But in *Paradise Lost* the poet takes care that the "gratuitous redemption" remains concealed from Adam until the last book of the epic. Adam learns that "in the sweat of thy Face shalt thou eat Bread" (X, 205) and that he is dust "and shalt to dust return" (208). Eve hears that she must "in sorrow" bring forth her children and that she must submit to her "Husband's will" (195). But the Lord God reserves the obscure promise of Mercy for the Judgment on the serpent. In the absence of Satan, God proceeds to judge the "serpent though brute":

> yet God at last
> To Satan first in sin his doom appli'd,
> Though in mysterious terms, judg'd as then best:
> And on the Serpent thus his curse let fall ...
> (171–74)

(Satan was first or pre-eminent in sin as well as the first to sin, so that God judges him first, before He pronounces the curses on Adam and Eve. God applies his "doom" to the Serpent "at last" in the course of this particular poetic argument and at the very last to

Satan on the Day of Doom.) The serpent must henceforth go "upon thy belly," and

> Between Thee and the Woman I will put
> Enmity, and between thine and her Seed;
> Her Seed shall bruise thy head, thou bruise his heel.
>   (179–81)

The commentators on Genesis exhibit a good deal of exegetical ingenuity in explaining the judgment of the Lord God but are nearly unanimous in deriving their arguments from common assumptions about the course of Christian history.

There is a kind of "ABC of the Gospel," for "God reveals not what himself is able to *Reveal*; but . . . what his people are able to *Receive* from time to time." (In Calvin's version of The Doctrine of Accommodation, God used "baby-talk" in communicating with the early Hebrews, then advanced in the Gospels to more sophisticated forms of discourse). The "Promise of mans Recovery" was "obscurely and imperfectly revealed" in the judgment on Adam, Eve, and the Serpent because that is the method of the God who is Lord of History. "When God at First created the world, he proceeded from the most obscure and imperfect . . . to the more clear and perfect." Accordingly, "God Re-Created the lapsed world of mankind, and Revealed this new work of his by Covenant and Promise, not all at once but by degrees. The first degree being darkest: the last clearest of all. As the first model of a building: The first lineaments of a Picture. . . ." Apart from such general considerations, there is, adds David Paraeus, a very particular reason, and that is "for the first parents . . . , whose faith and invocation God would exercise by this obscurity, and stir up in them a more ardent desire of the promised Seed, and diligence in searching out the time and manner of the Redemption to come."[26] It is this last reason that emerges in dramatic form in Milton's verse.

The fallen pair are first in a satanic fix, sharing with their Adversary the inability to comprehend the "mysterious terms" of Scripture. Satan, just before his involuntary transformation into a huge serpent, recounts in triumph his "performance":

> True is, mee also he hath judg'd, or rather
> Mee not, but the brute Serpent in whose shape
> Man I deceiv'd: that which to mee belongs,

> Is enmity, which he will put between
> Mee and Mankind; I am to bruise his heel;
> His Seed, when is not set, shall bruise my head:
> A World who would not purchase with a bruise,
> Or much more grievous pain?
>
> (494–501)

Milton represents Satan here, and in *Paradise Regained*, as a kind of fundamentalist of the imagination who thinks that "bruise" means "bruise"—a would-be exegete lacking the power to discern anything beyond the literal sense. Adam, as yet unexercised by the "obscurity" of the "mysterious terms," begins with satanic questions:

> Did I request thee, Maker, from my Clay
> To mould me Man, did I solicit thee
> From darkness to promote me . . . ?
>
> (743–45)

But then, unlike the fallen angels, who "found no end, in wand'ring mazes lost" (II, 561), Adam reaches on his own the first step in repentance, "conviction of sin":

> Him after all Disputes
> Forc't I absolve: all my evasions vain
> And reasonings, though through Mazes, lead me still
> But to my own conviction. . . .
>
> (828–31)

Although Adam recognizes God's Justice, he remains in one way like Satan, in whom "conscience wakes despair" (IV, 23) so that

> Me miserable! which way shall I fly
> Infinite wrath, and infinite despair?
> Which way I fly is Hell; myself am Hell;
> And in the lowest deep a lower deep
> Still threat'ning to devour me opens wide.
>
> (IV, 73–78)

The language used by Adam again invites us to compare and contrast his plight with that of Satan:

> O Conscience, into what Abyss of fears
> And horrors hast thou driv'n me; out of which
> I find no way, from deep to deeper plung'd!
>
> (842–44)

When Eve proposes sexual abstinence as a means of keeping their "hapless Seed" from Death and even glances at suicide, "then both ourselves and Seed at once to free" (999),[27] Adam replies, "That cuts us off from hope" (1043), and his "more attentive mind" begins to penetrate the "obscurity" of the "mysterious terms":

> Then let us seek
> Some safer resolution, which methinks
> I have in view, calling to mind with heed
> Part of our Sentence, that thy Seed shall bruise
> The Serpent's head; piteous amends, unless
> Be meant, whom I conjecture, our grand Foe. . . .
> (1028-33)

The process of understanding has begun, and it coincides with the second and third steps of repentance—"contrition" and "confession." These facts account for the singular ending of Book X.

Every reader of *Paradise Lost* grows habituated to the intrusive presence of the narrator of the epic: he is everywhere, informing you of what Satan *really* feels or even chastising you for what *you* really felt.[28] But at the end of Book X the narrative voice neither murmurs nor qualifies when Adam asks:

> What better can we do, than to the place
> Repairing where he judg'd us, prostrate fall
> Before him reverent, and there confess
> Humbly our faults, and pardon beg, with tears
> Watering the ground, and with our sighs the Air
> Frequenting, sent from hearts contrite, in sign
> Of sorrow unfeign'd, and humiliation meek.
> (1086-92)

On this occasion the narrator simply repeats:

> So spake our Father penitent, nor Eve
> Felt less remorse: they forthwith to the place
> Repairing where he judg'd them prostrate fell
> Before him reverent, and both confess'd
> Humbly thir faults, and pardon begg'd, with tears
> Watering the ground, and with thir sighs the Air
> Frequenting, sent from hearts contrite, in sign
> Of sorrow unfeign'd, and humiliation meek.
> (1097-1104)

We may, of course, dismiss this instance (the only in Milton) of "epic repetition" as a genuflection to Homer, but even Cowley did "not like *Homers* repeating of long messages just in the same words"—except the "Message coming from *God*, from whose words no creature ought to vary."[29] In Milton the repetition has an artistic as well as a theological function: not only do the narrator's words place a doctrinal seal upon this stage in the process of repentance, they also, for a significant moment, narrow to nothing the artistic gap between, on the one hand, narrator (and reader) and, on the other hand, Adam and Eve. Before we begin the last books, that is, we are permitted a moment of stasis in which we all see things the same way, a situation that will not reoccur until the end of the epic, the last lines of which are calculated to extend the moment of artistic oneness throughout all time. But meanwhile the reader must again take up the burden of his separateness, knowing more than Adam and Eve but unable to help them in their struggle to understand the true meaning of the "mysterious terms."[30]

During the six visions of Book XI the angelic historian takes on the role of narrator, correcting and teaching Adam in much the way the narrator had earlier corrected any "satanic" misunderstandings on the part of the reader. The angel fulfils a similar function in Book XII, though of course he proceeds by narration—not only because he perceives Adam's "mortal sight to fail" (9) but also because you can't teach someone to be a biblical exegete merely by showing him pictures.[31] Before Adam can accurately "measure" the "Race of time," before he can properly appreciate the movement and meaning of Christian history, he must be taught to read the "mysterious terms" of Scripture.

Adam had learned, under angelic tutelage in Book XI, the "mysterious" meanings of "death" and "day," the exegetical sense of God's words as recorded in Genesis: "for in the day that thou eatest thereof thou shalt surely die." And Adam has seen in the "Cov'nant new" with Noah the promise of Mercy "colleague" with Judgment. Having completed the first "great period" and "measured" the first part of the "Race of time," Adam stands at "noon"—the midpoint likewise for Christ and Samson—"betwixt the world destroy'd and world restor'd." Adam's "attentive mind" has been readied to perceive the true meaning of God's "mysterious terms," which he had begun "calling to mind," though not as yet very "dext'rously," toward the end of Book X. Adam had (correctly) "conjectured" that by the serpent is "meant" the "grand Foe," but he construes literally and vengefully:

> Satan, who in the Serpent hath contriv'd
> Against us this deceit: to crush his head
> Would be revenge indeed....
>
> (1134-36)

Similarly, Adam had, on awaking the morning after the Fall, found that

> peace return'd
> Home to my breast, and to my memory
> His promise, that thy Seed shall bruise our Foe;
> Which then not minded in dismay, yet now
> Assures me that the bitterness of death
> Is past, and we shall live. Whence Hail to thee,
> *Eve* rightly call'd, Mother of all Mankind,
> Mother of all things living, since by thee
> Man is to live, and all things live for Man.
>
> (XI, 153-61)

Although Adam has perceived one of the positive aspects of his plight (that the "revenge" can take place only if "man is to live"), he remains the fledgling exegete; in bondage to the literal sense, he can envision only physical life, can only imperfectly understand his own "Hail to thee," which the narrator has explicated, in entirely traditional terms, as early as Book V:

> On whom the Angel *Hail*
> Bestow'd, the holy salutation us'd
> Long after to blest *Mary*, second Eve.
>
> (385-87)

Full understanding must await the revelations of Book XII.

Michael begins his lesson in hermeneutics almost immediately, with Abraham in whose "Seed/ All Nations shall be blest" (125-26):

> This ponder, that all Nations of the Earth
> Shall in his Seed be blessed; by that Seed
> Is meant thy great deliverer, who shall bruise
> The Serpent's head; whereof to thee anon
> Plainlier shall be reveal'd.
>
> (147-51)

Michael explains that when the Twelve Tribes wander the desert God shall

> Ordain them Laws; part such as appertain
> To civil Justice, part religious Rites
> Of sacrifice, informing them, by types
> And shadows, of that destin'd Seed to bruise
> The Serpent, by what means he shall achieve
> Mankind's deliverance.
>
> (230–35)

And the angel continues to employ the technical language of typological exegesis while informing Adam that Moses is a "figure" of Christ (241) and that the blood sacrifices of the Jews are but "shadowy expiations" (291). The Mosaic Law, like Moses himself, represents the workings of history, of Christian Time:

> So Law appears imperfet, and but giv'n
> With purpose to resign them in full time
> Up to a better Cov'nant, disciplin'd
> From shadowy Types to Truth....
>
> (300–03)

Since God from the beginning had written history in "mysterious terms" that "plainlier shall be reveal'd," Adam must acquire the language of shadows and types in order to measure "this transient World, the Race of time."

When Michael completes his first lesson about Abraham, Adam finds his "eyes true op'ning" and his "heart much eased." But when the angel shows how the shadowy types foretell the coming of the "Women's Seed" whose throne "for ever shall endure" (324), Adam is with such joy "surcharg'd" that he believes he fully understands the "mysterious" wording of God's judgment:

> O Prophet of glad tidings, finisher
> Of utmost hope! now clear I understand
> What oft my steadiest thoughts have searcht in vain,
> Why our great expectation should be call'd
> The seed of Woman: Virgin Mother, Hail,
> High in the love of Heav'n, yet from my Loins
> Thou shalt proceed, and from thy Womb the Son
> Of God most High; So God with man unites.
>
> (375–82)

Put succinctly in the language of exegesis, Adam perceives not only that Eve is a type of "blest *Mary*, second Eve" (V, 387) but also that he himself is a type of Christ, the "greater Man" (I, 4) or "second

Adam" (XI, 383). Adam has grasped the essentials of Christian history with respect to himself and Eve, but the meaning of "bruise" remains "mysterious":

> Needs must the Serpent now his capital bruise
> Expect with mortal pain: say where and when
> Thir fight, what stroke shall bruise the Victor's heel.
>
> (383–85)

Michael promptly corrects this literal reading:

> Dream not of thir fight,
> As of a Duel, or the local wounds
> Of head or heel. . . .
>
> (386–88)

The Son shall "recure" man's first disobedience "by fulfilling that which thou didst want,/ Obedience to the Law of God" (396–97), so that it is the "God-like act" upon the Cross that "shall bruise the head of *Satan*" (430), "not by destroying *Satan*, but his works/ In thee and in thy Seed" (394–95), "defeating Sin and Death, his two main arms" (431). Adam has learned to measure the mysteries of the "Race of time" along the divine yardstick of types and antitypes, apprehending something of eternal meaning.

The angel "pauses" for the second time, "as at the World's great period" (466–67) or age of the Second Adam; and Adam, now "replete with joy and wonder," exclaims, "O goodness infinite, goodness immense!" There follows Milton's version of the *felix culpa*—the central paradox of Christian history and of *Paradise Lost*:

> That all this good of evil shall produce,
> And evil turn to good; more wonderful
> Than that which by creation first brought forth
> Light out of darkness! Full of doubt I stand,
> Whether I should repent me now of sin
> By mee done and occasion'd, or rejoice
> Much more, that much more good thereof shall spring
> To God more glory, more good will to Men
> From God, and over wrath grace shall abound.
>
> (470–78)

Although the angel has not completely "measur'd this transient World, the Race of time" (he must first indicate how "shall the World go on" until the Last Judgment and, finally, assure Adam of a "paradise within"), this moment "full of doubt" represents the emotional climax of the developments I have been tracing and in its divided sentiments anticipates the muted conflict of feeling in the last lines of the poem.

Adam's intense reaction derives from his understanding of the "mysterious terms," for he can now see how God's Justice shall be tempered with Mercy during the course of Christian history. Adam has glimpsed in the "mysterious terms" the true relation of Time to Eternity: by asserting eternal Providence, God's ways have been justified to men. The last two books, in short, establish a causal relation between the two clauses of the poet's hope that

> I may assert Eternal Providence
> And justify the ways of God to men.[32]

During the last two books Adam himself moves from the "shadowy Types" concealed in the "mysterious terms" to the "Truth" of Christ:

> The Woman's seed, obscurely then foretold,
> Now amplier known thy Saviour and thy Lord.
> (XII, 543-44)

Which means that Adam's progressive understanding mirrors the progressive revelations of God in history and of Milton in *Paradise Lost*. Once again the poet uses methods of exegesis as literary technique, transmuting futurity through the theory of types, so that the character of Adam's education reflects in little the manner of Milton's Muse and the grand design of God.

It should be obvious that God in shaping history took on the role of the late medieval and Renaissance poet, writing an allegory of things, people, and events. What ought to be equally obvious is that the allegory is governed by a special kind of irony, the kind that we call, usually in a context that at least suggests the example of Sophocles, dramatic irony. Even at its simplest, the technique invites a degree of involvement from the reader, for he must understand more in the words and actions of, say, Oedipus than the character himself understands. From this point of view the Christian deity becomes the Sophoclean dramatist, for He does "that which," according to Peter Sterry, "*Aristotle* in his Discourse of Poetry, commendeth," bringing "things down by the Ministry of the Law" and "in ways *unexpected* by, *uncomprehensible* to Men & Angles, to raise things again by the Gospel to that first *supream*

Glory, which was their *Original Patern in Eternity*."[33] When Moses holds up the brazen serpent in the wilderness or when Abraham perceives the sacrificial ram caught in the brush, neither patriarch understands that these events are types of Christ on the Cross. It is of course given to the prophets to speak, their lips purified by the holy fire of God's Spirit, of the future; but when Isaiah proclaims an Eden in the Wilderness and declares the fortunes of the Man of Sorrows, the prophet speaks (like a bagpipe, Hobbes says) under the inspiration of the Holy Spirit, the full implications of his words—that Jesus, the suffering servant, shall restore man to Eden—being known only to the Lord of History and to be revealed only in the fullness of time. Typological history founds itself in the principle of dramatic irony, a view of time in which things "obscurely then foretold" "plainlier shall be reveal'd"; and when Milton exploits this fact in dealing with "mysterious terms," the poet confers on the knowing reader something of the omniscience of deity.

Where the tale is at least twice-told, as in *Samson* or *Paradise Regained*, suspense of the kind common to the detective novel becomes impossible. Instead, our satisfactions must be derived from the manner in which we are encouraged to await the end. In the last two books Milton completes the process hinted at in the ending of Book X, where the narrative voice and the words of Adam and Eve precisely coincide: the reader, knowing the meaning of the "mysterious terms," watches as Adam's knowledge becomes progressively closer to his own. The process is completed in an intellectual but not in an emotional sense when Adam stands "full of doubt"; the epic cannot end here, but we can see, have always seen, the direction in which we are going. As Aristotle says, in reading or in listening—he could not foresee the detective story—all men "like to descry the end." In the words of an anonymous seventeenth-century translator of the *Rhetoric*, there is a kind of writing (Aristotle had Herodotos in mind) that must be called *"diffus'd, because it has no end of it self, until the matter treated of be brought to a conclusion; which is unpleasant"*—because it just stops. "For all men are willing [i.e., they want] to see a conclusion; as being tired out of breath toward the end of the Goal, or Stage, and are willing [wanting] to turn again. But when they see the end, they are not weary...."[34] If we are not to be wearied by the last two books of *Paradise Lost*, we must learn to descry the end. Which involves a consideration of the last lines of the epic.

Adam's education in Christian Time, in the movement "from shadowy Types to Truth," finds its end in the last lines of the epic:

> The World was all before them, where to choose
> Thir place of rest, and Providence thir guide:
> They hand in hand with wand'ring steps and slow,
> Through Eden took thir solitary way.

Dissatisfaction with the last books must, at least to some degree, extend to the final lines—for the fundamental reason that satisfactory closure of the traditional kind depends in great part upon prior anticipations. Richard Bentley expressed his uneasiness by proposing that notorious emendation in which Adam and Eve, "with HEAVEN'LY COMFORT CHEER'D," vacate Eden with "SOCIAL Steps." Outrageously absurd but instructive in contrast with the original, especially when we inspect the reasons Bentley offers in extenuation. He begins by appealing to the opinion of an "ingenious and celebrated writer" (Addison), who had earlier found fault with Milton's ending; but Bentley engagingly confesses that in his own opinion he can find no justification for excising "these two Verses" entirely; they cannot "possibly be spar'd from the Work" as a whole.

> And yet this distich, as the Gentleman well judges, *falls very much below the Passage foregoing*. It contradicts the Poet's own Scheme; nor is the Diction unexceptionable. He tells us before, That *Adam*, upon hearing *Michael's* Predictions, was even *surcharg'd with Joy*, v. 372; was *replete with Joy and Wonder*, 468; was in doubt, whether he should *repent of,* or *rejoice in his Fall,* 475; was *in great Peace of Thought,* 558: and *Eve* herself *not sad,* but *full of consolation,* 620. Why then does this Distich dismiss our first Parents in Anguish, and the Reader in Melancholy?[35]

The "Poet's own Scheme" comprehends, naturally, the entire epic but more immediately the last two books, most immediately Book XII; and Bentley quotes verse if not chapter to document the manner in which the poet "contradicts" himself. There can be no doubt that Bentley is right—so far as he goes; he has perfectly apprehended half of Milton's design, only half because he has attended only to half of Adam's education in how to read "mysterious terms," which like primal words are double in their import. Zachary Pearce twitted Bentley about the "tautologous" emendation, sensibly observing that "for a plainer proof that the scheme of the poem was to dismiss them not without *sorrow*, the poet in XI.117 puts these words into God's mouth, as his instruction to Michael, 'So send them forth, though sorrowing, yet in peace.' "[36]

But the deeper point at issue concerns the diction, the particular words and their order, of the final lines. Bentley puts the questions, for him rhetorical:

> And how can the expression be justified, *with wand'ring steps and slow?* Why *wand'ring?* Erratic steps? Very improper: when in the line before, they were *guided by Providence.* And why *slow?* When even Eve profess'd her Readiness and Alacrity for the Journey.... And why *their solitary Way?* All Words to represent a sorrowful Parting?

So it is that Bentley presumes "at last to offer a Distich, as close as may be to the Author's Words, and entirely agreeable to his Scheme":

> Then hand in hand with SOCIAL Steps their way
> Through EDEN took, with HEAVEN'LY COMFORT CHEER'D.

A relatively rare specimen of the flat mind, rectilinear in its approach to language, and of course we do not find it hard to rise superior to the emendation; but the example may serve to remind us of the tacit emendations that may take place in our heads while reading the last books of the epic. Bentley is not wrong, after all; it is merely that in his lexicon words possess only single meanings. "Why *wand'ring?* Erratic steps? Very improper..." But Milton's "scheme" requires the counterpoise of contrary emotions, which means that the "diction" must be able to convey double meanings.

If asked, readers may not only be encouraged to speak of the "twilight mood" of Milton's last lines; often they will assert what many obviously feel, that the epic ends in the evening. It is true that Christ comes to judge Adam and Eve in the "Ev'ning cool": "Now was the Sun in Western cadence low/ From Noon" (X, 92ff.), the hot hour of the Fall. And it is likewise true that most of the scriptural commentators supposed the expulsion to have been more or less immediate. It is even true that there might be something decorous in having the fallen pair descend the hill of Paradise as "day declin'd" (X, 99), establishing a parallel between the fall of man and the "cadence" or fall of the sun. But in Milton's "scheme" the fallen pair are permitted one last night in Paradise; and at dawn they see the sun "resalute the World with sacred Light" (XI, 134), so that in the descent there is promise of ascent. Because of the way God has ordered the course of history, the Fall must excite contrary feelings.[37] On the one hand there can be no doubt that the Fall is unfortunate, as the narrator states explicitly in surveying the prelapsarian lovers:

> Sleep on,
> Blest pair; and O yet happiest if ye seek
> No happier state, and know to know no more.
>   (IV, 773-75)

God is equally explicit (the narrator and God always agree):

> Happier, had it suffic'd him to have known
> Good by itself, and Evil not at all.
>   (XI, 88-89)

On the other hand there can be no doubt that the Fall is fortunate: not only shall the good man receive a "paradise within" that is, explicitly, "happier far," but also the entire earth "shall all be Paradise, far happier place."

The paradox is irreducible, one of God's "mysteries." It is an inevitable corollary of the typological view of time and history. Paradise, we must note, remains the type (in all senses) of the best condition; but since it is a figure of the best condition, we must likewise note that the type shall be transcended by antitype in the fullness of time, illuminating the shadows by the gradations of unfolding truth:

> then the Earth
> Shall all be Paradise, far happier place
> Than this of Eden, and far happier days.
>   (XII, 463-65)

God writes history in "mysterious terms," and the poet reflects the fact by speaking in paradox or contraries: his use of the word "wander" illustrates the technique.

The word, surrounded by implicit contraries (choosing but guided, solitary but hand in hand), resonates with eschatological overtones in proximity to "place of rest."[38] The God of the Old Testament swore that the erring "should not enter into my rest" (Ps. 95:11), which is quoted in Hebrews 3:10-11, 18 and made a type in 4:1-11. Milton in his *De Doctrina* (*Works*, XVII, 175) accordingly speaks of the sabbath "as a shadow or type of things to come" (*umbra seu typus rerum futurarum*): "namely, of that sabbatical rest or eternal peace in heaven," as "we are taught Heb. iv. 9, 10." The angelic historian explicitly links wandering and resting in *Paradise Lost*, foretelling that Jesus

> shall quell
> The adversary Serpent, and bring back
> Through the world's wilderness long wander'd man
> Safe to eternal Paradise of rest.
>
> (XII, 311–14)

But Bentley (and many a modern reader) consulted only his own dictionary, in which "to wander" means only "to err."
The word derives from the Anglo-Saxon *windan*, meaning "to turn," whence it encompassed the notion of random turning, of rambling and roaming:

> Yet not the more
> Cease I to wander where the Muses haunt
> Clear Spring, or Shady Grove, or Sunny Hill....
>
> (III, 26–28)

But of course in an age that spoke much of the strait gate and the narrow way, "wander" inevitably possessed dyslogistic connotations as well, connecting it with "to err" and allowing Milton to use the words as synonyms, English-Latin doublets. "To err," from L. *errare* meaning "to wander," was in its early uses contaminated by Old French *errer* meaning "to journey," which survives in the locution "knight errant," one whose wanderings take him on rather than from the paths of chivalry. But even more obviously than "wander," the verb "to err" has its improper senses: "We have erred," we are told in the Book of Common Prayer, "and strayed from thy ways like lost sheep." So the narrator of *Paradise Lost* begs that he may escape, in his own presumptuous flight, the fate of Bellerophon, that unlucky flier:

> Dismounted, on th'Aleian Field I fall
> Erroneous there to wander and forlorn.
>
> (VII, 19–20)

If *Paradise Lost* were the vehicle only of primary connotations, then we should have to accept not only the emendations of a Bentley but also the strictures of Pound and Eliot. If in the epic "to wander" always meant "to err," Milton's great argument would truly be cast in expository bronze, entirely without verbal flex or shimmer—

monumental but unmoving. "Why *wand'ring*? Erratic steps? Very improper."

We know that our preconceptions dictate, at least in part, what we allow ourselves to find in words, and preconceptions derive, at least in part, from the age in which we live. Bacon, in Aphorism LV of the *Novum Organum*, distinguishes "one principal and as it were radical distinction between different minds," some "stronger and apter to mark the differences of things, others to mark their resemblances."

> The steady and acute mind can fix its contemplations and dwell and fasten on the subtlest distinctions: the lofty and discursive mind recognises and puts together the finest and most general resemblances. Both kinds however easily err in excess, by catching the one at gradations and the other at shadows.[39]

When we discover or impose similarities, we are able to "abstract" or put things in boxes and bundles; the more resemblances, the larger the bundles. When, on the other hand, we discover or impose distinctions, we move toward the "concrete," putting things into many, sometimes unique, bundles. If we assume that the rare or unique detracts from the general category, then the movement toward the abstract represents a tendency toward perfection, and we will concur with Dr. Johnson's Imlac that the "business" of the poet is "to examine, not the individual, but the species" and that he "does not number the streaks of the tulip"; we will agree that "in the writings of other poets a character is too often an individual" but in "Shakespeare it is commonly a species."[40] But if, on the other hand, we assume that the unique and the individual possess more significance than genera and species, if we fasten on the differences and lend them a greater measure of meaning, we will agree with the Imagist Manifesto of 1912, in which H. D., Aldington, and Pound proclaim that it is the poet's business to number the "petals on a wet, black bough"; we will agree, with Bergson and other modern readers, "that art always aims at what is individual" and that in consequence Shakespeare's characters are great because they are unique, individual. The centripetal rush toward the concrete must of course end in the object itself ("no ideas but in things"), though it is of course possible to fondle the details and to write in such a way that there is little syntactical integument to shroud the skeletal particularities: The poem should not mean but be. The two processes of thought, separable in aphorism, can scarcely be distinguished in practice: one cannot perceive similarities in order to classify without first recognizing what to dismiss because it is accidental rather than essential; and one cannot hope to particularize without first noting what must be disregarded because its occurrence is general. But the tendencies remain. Pound, objecting to abstraction in Milton, catches "at gradations"; Bentley, wanting abstract consistency in the poet, catches "at shadows."

Since "both kinds . . . easily err in excess," we do well, before *rigor cordis* sets in, to reflect on the antithetical possibilities in a word such as "wander." Wandering may be satanic, as when the Sons of Belial "wander forth"—in Milton's fine phrasing—"flown with insolence and wine" (I, 501–02). Satan himself asks (the question is rhetorical) "who shall tempt with wand'ring feet" (II, 404) the abyss of Chaos? And at the meeting with Sin and Death Milton, with calculated use of sacred irony, has Satan represent his "wand'ring quest" (II, 830) as knight errantry. Wandering, that is, may be satanic in the sense of "solitary," as when the fallen angels

> Disband, and wand'ring, each his several way
> Pursues, as inclination or sad choice
> Leads him perplext. . . .
>
> (II, 523–25)

In this sense "wandering" must be opposed to "hand in hand," which is edenic in its intimate overtones. To God alone belongs the "solitary hand" (VI, 139) of absolute power; to Christ belongs the "right hand" of privileged place, which is likewise the instrument of destruction and creation. But Adam and Eve, since that first moment when his "gentle hand" (IV, 488) caught hers, were espoused, like the spring and autumn of Eden itself, that they might dance "hand in hand" (V, 395). "Thus talking hand in hand" (IV, 689) the prelapsarian pair walk to "thir blissful Bower," and Adam awakes his bride "her hand soft touching" (V, 17). When, just before the Fall, Eve chooses a solitary way, "from her Husband's hand her hand/ Soft she withdrew" (IX, 385–86). (Did she then softly withdraw her soft hand?) It is Eve's solitary and "rash hand" (IX, 780) that reaches for the forbidden fruit in "evil hour," "her hand" (850) that bears the "bough of fairest fruit" to Adam, from whose "slack hand" (892) falls the garland he had wreathed for Eve, "and all the faded Roses shed." It is Eve's "liberal hand" (997) that freely proffers the fruit of servitude; "her hand he seiz'd" (1037) as "in Lust," not love, "they burn." Only in the last lines of the epic do the pair walk yet once more "hand in hand," but then with "wand'ring steps."

Freely to choose ("Reason is but choosing") is all-important to Milton, but free choice depends not only on *ratio recta* or right reason ("Reason He made free"); it involves as well the "better guide" of Sonnet XXII, the same "guide" who appears in the last lines of the epic. Adam, recalling the "Guide" (VIII, 298) of the dream that "lively shadow'd" the reality of entering the Garden, confesses,

> Here had new begun
> My wand'ring, had not hee who was my Guide....
> (311-12)

Without the "two twins cleaving together" of right reason and divine guidance, men may lose themselves in "wand'ring thoughts, and notions vain" (VIII, 187), like the fallen angels who "found no end, in wand'ring mazes lost" (II, 561).

But before the Fall everything finds its proper "end." All things are, to borrow a phrase from *Samson*, "guided . . . aright." Before the Fall the earth "seem'd like to Heav'n" where gods might live "or wander with delight" (VII, 329-30), and the waters of creation "with Serpent error wand'ring, found thir way" (VII, 302). The astonishing reduplication in "Serpent error" makes the poet's aim unmistakable and reminds us forcibly that for Milton the Fall is a lapse in speech. Since prelapsarian man knows only good, language possesses (for the unfallen) only good connotations; "Serpent" and "error" stand together and erect, "wand'ring" innocently in the state of innocence.

Man existed in Eden in the state of *integritas* or "oneness" with inner and outer nature (as Abdiel says in reproving Satan, "God and Nature bid the same"), but Adam fell into duality, which is to say, the habit of quibbling. Adam puns immediately after eating the fruit (on "sapience"), and it doesn't take long for Satan to fall into bad puns, the worst of which appear in his sophomoric bluster to the faithful angels when he is just about to discharge (at the "touch-hole") his cannon:

> Heav'n witness thou anon, while we discharge
> Freely our part: yee who appointed stand
> Do as you have in charge, and briefly touch
> What we propound, and loud that all may hear.
> (VI, 564-67)

Landor, who failed to recognize that the functional pun is the highest form of wit, observed crisply that "it appears then on record that the first overt crime of the refractory angels was *punning*: they fell rapidly after that."[41] In 1900 Sir Walter Raleigh, rather reluctantly and tentatively, hit upon what is surely the proper explanation. Although Raleigh allows that "some of [the] puns are very bad," he points out that "in most of these cases it seems likely that [Milton] believed in an etymological relation between the two words, and so fancied that he was drawing attention to an original unity of meaning." So at least he was in locutions like "Serpent error wand'ring."

Raleigh also observed, half rightly, that "there is a modern idea that a pun is a thing to laugh at. Milton's puns, like Shakespeare's, give no smallest countenance to this theory."[42] But of course we do laugh, though on occasion it may be what Milton himself refers to as "grim laughter"; for the good pun exhibits what Eliot has finely called, in connection with "metaphysical wit," an "alliance of levity with seriousness." It was Milton's theory as well as his practice:

> And although in the serious uncasing of a grand imposture . . . there be mixt here and there such a grim laughter, as may appear at the same time in an austere visage, it cannot be taxt of levity or insolence: for even this veine of laughing (as I could produce out of grave Authors) hath oft-times a strong and sinewy force in teaching and confuting; . . . if it be harmfull to be angry, and withall to cast a lowring smile, when the properest object calls for both, it will be long enough ere any be able to say why those two most rationall faculties of humane intellect anger and laughter were first seated in the breast of man.
>
> (*Works*, III, i, 107–08)

In the tradition of Juvenal, also of Tyndale and Erasmus and More, "grim laughter" proceeds not from the belly but from the "rationall" faculty, as in *Paradise Lost* "smiles from reason flow." Reason is both the source and the guide of feeling, and in its trials it encounters "what is contrary," producing where appropriate a paradoxical response. The scene of savage farce in Book X, in which Satan is greeted with "universal hiss" and thrashes about, a monstrous serpent eating the ash-filled (Sodom) apples, is designed to elicit "grim laughter"; and the lousy puns of the War in Heaven ironically betray without Satan's knowing it the "serious uncasing of a grand imposture." The wit of "Serpent error wand'ring" lies in the double-take it forces on the reader, who is required to see the quibble that is not there—an ironic reminder that he and his words are fallen.

After Satan has toiled through Chaos (unaware that God, observing the flight, has been sharing a kind of "grim laughter" with the Son), he directs "his wandr'ing flight" (III, 631) toward Uriel, who stands guard in the sun. Disguised as a "stripling Cherub," Satan claims that his desire to see the wonders of the new creation has brought him from the heavenly choirs "alone thus wandr'ing" (667). Uriel is deceived, but presumably Bentley, on the basis of his stated principles, would have detected the grand imposture: the cherub is "alone" or without a "guide," and he is "wandr'ing." "Erratic steps? Very improper." Satan speaks the language not of Sidney's "erected wit" but of the "infected will," and we, who are fallen, readily understand. But Uriel has not experienced that "doom," to use Milton's formulation in *Areopagitica*, "which Adam fell into of knowing good and evil, that is to say, of knowing good by evil."[43] Since Uriel is not obliged to know good by evil, language for him is univocal, single in its (good) import. Only later will Sin, "residing through the Race," man's "thoughts, his looks, words, actions all infect" (X, 607–08).

After the Fall Adam and Eve, having lost the innocence of Uriel, possess at first only the satanic meaning of "wander." In the prelapsarian Garden of Book IV the river that

> from his darksome passage now appears,
> And now divided into four main Streams
> Runs diverse, wand'ring many a famous Realm
> And Country whereof here needs no account.
>
> (232–35)

The "account" comes later, in the last books, and with it comes the account of how Adam and Eve understand "good by evil" in the word "wandr'ing." After Adam attributes the Fall to Eve's "desire of wandr'ing this unhappy Morn" (IX, 1136), Eve helps spend the "fruitless hours" in "mutual accusation" (1187–88):

> What words have past thy lips, Adam severe,
> Imput'st thou that to my default, or will
> Of wand'ring, as thou call'st it....
>
> (1144–46)

And Adam renews the attack in the same terms in Book X, arguing that he would have "persisted happy" had it not been for Eve's "wand'ring vanity" (874–75). When Eve learns of the expulsion, she speaks movingly of the Garden and finally falters into despair:

> Thee lastly nuptial Bower, by mee adorn'd
> With what to sight or smell was sweet; from thee
> How shall I part, and whither wander down
> Into a lower World, to this obscure
> And wild. . . .
>
> (280–84)

Seeing God's Justice but not His Mercy, the fallen pair use "wander" in Bentley's satanic sense, as though it meant only to err in darkness—"erratic steps." So Adam despairs on first witnessing the "Visions ill foreseen" of the future, prophesying that even Noah and his family will perish in their wanderings:

> those few escap't
> Famine and Anguish will at last consume
> Wand'ring that wat'ry Desert. . . .
>
> (777–79)

But the Angel promptly counters Adam's despair, revealing that this "wand'ring," guided by God, ends in the renewed covenant of the Rainbow. Adam has begun to see that the meaning of "wand'ring," like that of the "mysterious terms," shall in time "plainlier" be "reveal'd." The Ark of God shall be "wand'ring" (XII, 334) until safely enshrined in the Temple; and Abraham wanders toward Canaan, though the angel carefully explains that he is "not wand'ring poor, but trusting" (133) in God.

It is Adam's oxymoron, the "wat'ry Desert" traversed by Noah, that points in its ironic allusiveness most clearly toward the effects of the last lines of the epic—by referring more or less explicitly to the biblical wandering in the desert.[44] Milton has been glancing in this direction since Book II, when Satan's "wand'ring quest" leads him, "alone, and without guide" but "no Spy," to confront Chaos and old Night: "Wand'ring this darksome Desert . . ." (970–73). The poet, that is, represents Satan's journey through Chaos as a sacred travesty or *analogia antithetica* of the Hebrews' wandering in the desert.

On the east lies the valley of the Arabah, which runs to the Red Sea; on the south the granite cliffs of Sinai. Called the Desert of Paran, its Hebrew name signifies "desert of the wandering." Here the children of Israel spend forty years after the Exodus from

Egypt. Having proceeded as far as Kadesh on the border of Palestine, the Israelites send spies (Satan takes care to say he is "no Spy") to survey Canaan; their reports of men like giants, in whose eyes the Israelites were as grasshoppers, dishearten the chosen people, who then murmur against Moses. For their sins God condemns them to the wandering in the desert—until they should be ready to conquer and retain the Promised Land. After forty years they once more gather at Kadesh and, with the Ark of God before them, march down the valley of the Arabah to take possession of the "earthly Canaan."

A compelling tale, pivotal for the Jewish people and their view of what constitutes history: in Ps. 107:40 God "causeth them to wander in the wilderness, where there is no way," in Job 12:24 He "causeth them to wander in a wilderness where there is no way," and Numbers 32:13 reminds the chosen people that the "Lord's anger was kindled against Israel, and he made them wander in the wilderness forty years." In such contexts the word "wandering" signifies punishment and refers aptly to satanic journeying. But here lies only half the reason why it is the proper word for the departure of Adam and Eve from the Garden into the "world's wilderness" of postlapsarian man, the wilderness that man must wander because of the first disobedience. The "fruit"—in more than one sense—of the forbidden tree is wandering.

Although Exodus provides the locus for most if not all of the pejorative meanings of "wander," it is also the book of the Bible that testifies to God's first intervention in the course of time and history; and it reveals Mercy colleague with Justice. The fallen find "no end, in wand'ring mazes lost," but in the fullness of time it shall be seen that the repentant "with Serpent error wand'ring, found thir way." In Thomas Peyton's uninspired rendering, *Tempus* presides over the terms of God's judgments—

> The Register that vp this order drew
> Was Time it selfe clad all in Azure blew,
> Wing'd like an Angel, shadowed with a vaile,
> And Truth his Daughter bearing vp his traile—

so that the Jews, to take the relevant example, might be led for "forty yeeres" as "Tipe of our Church,"

> Vntill at length with wandring hither, thither,
> Like sheepe dispearst fould all at last togither.[45]

Although the Israelites, like Adam and Eve, have been compelled to wander the wilderness, God guides them in a cloud by day and in a pillar of fire by night. The Lord of Time and History sustains them with manna and finally allows them to enter Canaan, the land of milk and honey that lies at the end of wandering. It is the end but not the end, it is the type of the end. Moses sees Canaan but does not lead his people into the promised rest,[46] for that task, according to the exigencies of typological history, must be reserved for

> *Joshua* whom the Gentiles *Jesus* call,
> His Name and Office bearing, who shall quell
> The adversary Serpent, and bring back
> Through the world's wilderness long wander'd man
> Safe to eternal Paradise of rest.
> Meanwhile they in thir earthly *Canaan*. . . .
>
> (XII, 310–15)

It shall be as God proclaims in Book III:

> And I will place within them as a guide
> My Umpire *Conscience*, whom if they will hear,
> Light after light well us'd they shall attain,
> And to the end persisting, safe arrive.
>
> (194–97)

The "fruit" of the tree of disobedience is wandering—but not a satanic "wand'ring quest" accomplished "alone, and without guide."

It will be apparent that Milton imagined the Expulsion from Eden as an Exodus, more precisely as the "type," insofar as it occurs "before" in time, of Exodus. Wandering is what the Israelites did on the way to the earthly Canaan, and wandering is what all of us must do in the "world's wilderness" on the way to "eternal Paradise of rest." In their exodus from Eden, Adam and Eve anticipate the Exodus from Egypt, which in turn prefigures the return to Eden:

> With loss of *Eden*, till one greater Man
> Restore us, and regain the blissful Seat.

Wandering represents the midpoint of the entire epic cycle as it is envisaged by Milton in *Paradise Lost*. Although the beginning of wandering constitutes the ending of the epic, the word "wandering" evokes yet another ending, when earth "shall all be Paradise," thus closing the implicitly circular pattern from Eden to Eden, from Paradise to "eternal Paradise of rest."

But meanwhile, with Providence for "guide," we must, like Adam and Eve, choose our "place of rest." The dramatic ironies have disappeared, the artistic distance has narrowed to nothing; Adam's and Eve's understanding of the "mysterious terms" now coincides with our own, and we have been prepared to recognize ourselves in the wandering of the fallen pair, compelled to acknowledge the "loss of *Eden*" but encouraged to anticipate the time when we shall "regain the blissful Seat." We are fallen, our estate is double; we wander this "transient World" until "time stand fixt," beyond which lies "Eternity, whose end no eye can reach."

"Why *wand'ring*?" Because it means, in the lexicon of the epic and in Christian history, both to stray and to roam, both wandering to find no end in "mazes lost" and wandering "to the end persisting, safe arrive." Pearce rightly points out that the poet's "scheme" requires that the fallen pair be sent "forth, though sorrowing, yet in peace," yet it is the "diction" of the concluding lines that must, pre-eminently, embody, and then communicate, the contrary emotions of the scheme. The oppositions latent in choosing but guided, and in hand-in-hand but solitary, are brought out and fixed impeccably in the word "wander," which illustrates Reynolds' meditations on the workings of the human intellect: "The mind appears to me of that nature and construction that it requires being employed on two things. . . . If I was to judge from my own experience, the mind always desires to double, to entertain two objects at a time." Although Reynolds' observations arise from a reading of Shakespeare's "tragicomedy," they describe well enough Milton's attitude toward the fortunate-unfortunate Fall; and they suggest the Renaissance esthetic of *discordia concors*, the principle that governs the *coincidentia oppositorum* of the fallen world as an imperfect reflection of the eternal realm of "grateful vicissitude" (*PL*, VI, 8). All is as with the "wand'ring course" (VIII, 126) of the stars in "mazes intricate,"·

> Eccentric, intervolv'd, yet regular
> Then most, when most irregular they seem;
>   (PL, V, 622–24)

and the poet who seeks to render accurately his sense of double vision and duration in a world where the "knowledge of good and evil" resembles "two twins cleaving together" must deal in "mysterious terms," words like "wander" that possess, or are made to possess, double significance, encouraging the mind "to double, to entertain two objects at a time."[47]

The epic ends not in the manner of *Paradise Regained*, in which Jesus, quite simply, "Home to his Mother's house private return'd"; nor of *Samson*, in which the protagonist goes "Home to his Father's house" and the Chorus provides a formal close. *Paradise Regained* lacks the direct and formal termination of the tragedy but nevertheless concludes with greater finality than *Paradise Lost*; although we know that Jesus will not remain "private," that he will soon enter upon His ministry, the poet has unmistakably informed us that this poem and this episode in the life of Jesus are finished. The ending of *Paradise Lost*, on the other hand, must necessarily and deliberately represent the beginning of history as we live it; in the poet's end lies our beginning, ended only when time shall "stand fixt." Milton's last lines invite us to look forward to the final Place of Rest and to look backward to Paradise, as the word "wander" expresses the contrary music, the *discordia concors*, both of final loss and final restoration. The Expulsion is an Exodus, a shadow of good things to come.

The word "wander" resembles such words as "fruit," "hand," and "seed." They are all capable, in varying degrees, of conveying opposed meanings, and they are all "mysterious terms" in the sense that their full resonances "plainlier shall be reveal'd" in the course of time. The way full meaning appears only in the *pleroma* or fullness of time mirrors the progression of Christian history "from shadowy Types to Truth," a series of anticipations and fulfillments. John Donne, that exemplary metaphysical, describes the process in his *Devotions*. Asserting first that his God is a *"direct God"* and a *"literall God,"* Donne adds that his God is "a *figurative*, a *metaphoricall God too*":

> Neither art thou thus a *figurative*, a *metaphoricall God* in thy *word* only, but in thy *workes* too. The *stile* of thy *works*, the *phrase* of thine *actions*, is *metaphoricall*. The *institution* of thy whole *worship* in the *old Law* was a continuall *Allegory*; *types* and *figures* overspread all; and *figures* flowed into *figures*, and powred themselves into *farther figures*; *Circumcision* carried a *figure* of *Baptisme*, and *Baptisme* carries a *figure* of that *purity*, which we shall have in *perfection* in the *new Jerusalem*. Neither didst thou *speake* and *worke* in this language, only in the time of thy *Prophets*; but since thou spokest in thy *Son*, it is so too.[48]

Donne's words may be extended to include *Paradise Lost*, which imitates "the *stile* of [God's] *works,* the *phrase* of [His] *actions."* *Paradise Lost,* its overflowing plasticities of language and liquid plenitude of line and image: "*types* and *figures* overspread all: and *figures* flowed into *figures,* and powred themselves into *farther figures,"* as the poet (to use his own words) draws "the sense variously . . . out from one Verse into another," from one image to another, and from one book into another. God's words in Scripture prefigure, and His actions in history show how "*figures* flowed into *figures."* It is for this flow of meaning and event that the poet has found his "answerable style": it "espouses," in Sterry's words, "the end to the beginning" and allows the mind, in Reynold's words, "to double, to entertain two objects at a time"—the temporal event in its eternal context.

CHAPTER IV

Samson Agonistes: *Found in the Close*

Milton exploits throughout *Samson Agonistes* the peculiar kind of dramatic irony that informs the last books of *Paradise Lost*. Like God's works in time, the drama is, in the final words of the Chorus, "ever best found in the close"; for the world itself, as Ralph Cudworth observes, is that "Truer Poem, and we men Histrionical Acters upon the Stage . . . but God *Almighty*, is that Skilful Dramatist." Since His Providence guarantees meaning but occupies a *"Still and Silent Path,"* His ways remain mysteriously significant, fraught with irony, until they reach their "Satisfactory Close." Meanwhile, those who doubt Providence "are like such Spectators of a *Dramatick Poem*," for they "impatiently cry out against the *Dramatist*, and presently condemn the plot: whereas if they would but expect the winding up of things, and stay till the last Close, they should then see" the true design of the whole.[1] Although the divine dramatist emphasizes the beginning and the close—

> Him, First and Last, we know;
> But more we cannot show[2]—

modern readers, through an accident of literary criticism and cultural conditioning, have found themselves preoccupied with the "middle" of things, so that Milton's Christian use of dramatic irony, and consequently *Samson Agonistes* itself, has been imperfectly understood.

In general we have tried to read the dramatic poem in the "Aristotelian" manner, as though we were confronted with a play that

105

closely resembles Sophocles' *Oedipus Rex*. Or so the history of criticism would seem to imply, at least from the time that Dr. Johnson's notorious strictures on the defective structure of *Samson* provoked what has become the standard interpretation of the play: that the drama is a drama of regeneration, and that the process of regeneration supplies precisely what Johnson found to be missing—an Aristotelian "middle."[3]

> The Poem, therefore, has a beginning and an end which Aristotle himself could not have disapproved; but it must be allowed to want a middle, since nothing passes between the first act and the last, that either hastens or delays the death of Sampson. The whole drama, if its superfluities were cut off, would scarcely fill a single act; yet this is the tragedy which ignorance has admired, and bigotry applauded.[4]

But by implicitly accepting Johnson's assumptions about the nature of drama while disputing his inferences, the theorists of regeneration have left themselves vulnerable to the alternative approach of G. A. Wilkes, which in its own terms seems to be at least equally valid. Before revealing the process in the "middle" by which Samson becomes regenerate, it would be convenient to find some point in the drama where he is portrayed as un-regenerate; and Wilkes, aware that the text of the play resists this kind of argument, fastens resolutely on the crucial moment of choice, the point at which Samson abruptly reverses his earlier decisions and accedes to the demand that he perform at the Feast of Dagon. Instead of a process of inner regeneration we are now confronted with a God who accomplishes all at the final moment through the movement of His irresistible Grace: God rather than His champion becomes the primary focus of the play, the sole foundation of its tragic or other effects.[5]

If we accept Wilkes, the play not only wants a middle but also becomes an austere enactment of Calvinistic determinism, ignoring the possibility of cooperative grace and denying the efficacy of human volition. Man's nature and human time have, in this view, little or no rational connection with divine grace and God's eternity. If, on the other hand, we adopt the theory of regeneration, we supply the Aristotelian middle and preserve Milton's Christian Humanism—but apparently only at the cost of disregarding some of the poet's plainer meanings.

This dilemma bears more than casual resemblance to the oldest dubiety about Samson, whether he was saint or suicide. In the

Hebrew of the Old Testament Samson permits himself to wish that his "soul" may die with the Philistines, an unorthodox sentiment that was of course emended in the Vulgate, though the fact of the original survived to the discomfort of learned commentators.[6] In *Pro Populo Anglico Defensio* Milton himself inquires "whether Samson acted in pursuance of a command from heaven or was prompted by his own valour only. . . ." (*Works,* VII, 218 f.: *sive Dei, sive propriae virtutis instinctu occidit.*) If Samson was "prompted by his own valour only," his impulse stems from free will but may have been presumptuous or even suicidal; if he "acted in pursuance of a command from heaven," he cannot be deemed a suicide, but it is by no means clear that he necessarily exercised free will or in any way exemplified his valour or value as a human being. And this dilemma, however phrased, seems plainly part of still larger considerations, such as whether there are any means to justify in human terms the ways of God to men, or whether it is in fact possible to write specifically *Christian* tragedy at all. The question of free will and determinism remains as crucial for modern criticism as for the Renaissance commentators.

A more adequate answer depends on being able to transcend Dr. Johnson's Aristotelian assumptions about the form of tragedy. Their implications may be remarked in this way: what happens ought to happen in sequence, much as cause is related to effect, "since nothing passes between the first act and the last, that either hastens or delays the death of Sampson"; second, what happens, happens in five boxes of structure called acts, each one of which Johnson, in common with many later critics, carefully delimits in the course of his analysis;[7] third, and most basic, what happens as a whole happens in three main categories designated the beginning, the middle, and the end. Dramatic action thus appears successive in a linear, logical sense, moving resolutely from causes toward effects. There is the beginning, which when looked at in time is time past and when looked at logically resembles the major premise; there is the middle, which when viewed temporally may be thought of as time present and when viewed logically may be understood as the minor premise; and there is the end, which temporally may be taken for time future and logically for the conclusion. This is indeed, though crudely, the Aristotelian mode, the world and the drama of Aristotle as interpreted on this occasion by Dr. Johnson.[8]

In maintaining that an understanding of Milton depends on our being able to stop thinking in this "Aristotelian" manner, I am of

course aware that it may fairly be protested that such a thing is
impossible—for that is the way we think even when we are not
thinking about how we are thinking; the very structure of tenses
employed in language betrays the same movement from past
through present toward future. And Milton himself, though explaining that "division into Act and Scene . . . is here omitted,"
bases much of his prefatory epistle on the authority of Aristotle.
But we also know that there is more than one way of reading the
Poetics; and we know that the man of the Renaissance dreamt of
more than syllogistic philosophy, transcending on occasion the
limitations of tense as well as sense: "the world," intones Sir
Thomas Browne, "was before the Creation, and at an end before it
had a beginning; and thus was I dead before I was alive." In the
Renaissance, Time has become everywhere complicated by the
Christian sense of Eternity. "Time we may comprehend," says
Browne; " 'tis but five days elder then our selves." But Eternity, he
adds: "who can speake of eternity without a soloecisme, or thinke
thereof without an extasie?"[9] The question may be taken to imply
that it *is* possible to talk about Eternity *with* a solecism, as indeed
Browne's own paradoxes demonstrate—a solecism that may appear
in the form of Christian tragedy as well as in the style of Christian
discourse.

Whereas Aristotle concerned himself with beginnings, middles,
and ends, the great Christian thinkers tended to become preoccupied with beginnings and endings, the Alphas and Omegas. To
the eye of man, who tries to measure "this transient World, the
Race of time" (*PL*, XII. 554), events must appear to unfold succes-
sively; but to the eye of God all things are viewed in His eternal
present. As the theologian knew that his beginning is his ending, so
the poet was aware of how the flower sleeps within the bosom of its
causes. Fidelity to this view of the procession of events requires an
understanding of dramatic structure, of tragic form, quite different from that implied by syllogistic logic or the relation of
natural cause to psychological effect. And it must have been just
this difference that Milton had at least partly in mind when in the
prefatory epistle he warned his readers that this drama, never "intended" for the "Stage," has neither scenes nor acts: "it suffices,"
says the poet with more than a trace of the dry mock, "if the whole
Drama be found not produc't beyond the fifth Act." This is to
emphasize the ending, to focus on the denouement, to measure the
"transient World" of the drama against its last judgment—the mo-

ment when those who "impatiently cry out against the *Dramatist*, and presently condemn the plot," finally see that all has been brought to a "Satisfactory Close." The chronological train of events, plot as *chronos*, finally reaches the *kairos* ordained by God.

The example of Sophoclean irony, as Parker has demonstrated, was not lost on Milton;[10] but he transformed it in such a way, "with this over and above of being a Christian,"[11] that to regard the technique as dramatic irony in the classical sense has actually turned out to be misleading. Milton's readers, from Dr. Johnson to our own day, have tended to confuse plot—the sequence of events—with what in *Samson* (and the last books of *Paradise Lost*) may be called "proleptic form," the effect of which must be achieved partly through the traditional devices of dramatic irony but in the end must be distinguished from the technique practiced by Sophocles. Spinning plots may be thought of as a comparatively unsophisticated activity, for the highest artistic pleasure to which it aspires seems to be the kind of suspense that excites surprise. (So the "well-made" play.) It is to art what gossip is to life . . . Did the butler? or, Did she *really*? and then (to compound the suspense), With *him*? Coleridge, lecturing on Shakespeare in 1813, makes the necessary distinction luminously apparent:

> Expectation in preference to surprise. It is like the true reading of the passage;—'God said, Let there be light, and there was *light*;'—not there *was* light. As the feeling with which we startle at a shooting star, compared with that of watching the sunrise at the preestablished moment, such and so low is surprise compared with expectation.[12]

Shakespeare's (and Milton's) drama, unlike the detective story or the usual Broadway play, relies not only upon plot, suspense, but also upon proleptic form, upon the anticipation of a known fulfillment; or what Charles Morgan finely calls "the incompletion of a known completion."[13] In a play like *Oedipus* the story—the main features of the plot—is of course known; suspense leading to the unexpected becomes impossible; and so "expectation in preference to surprise," a process in which the audience is encouraged to await the end, anticipate the close, through words and actions that betray significances beyond the immediate comprehension of the characters. But Milton's dramatic ironies could not be the same as those of Sophocles, even if the proleptic form of *Samson* did not comprehend more than irony—for the simple reason that Milton's

understanding of God's Providence affords a view of time largely
unavailable to the classical writers.

At the beginning of *Samson* the protagonist finds no rest from

> thoughts, that like a deadly swarm
> Of Hornets arm'd, no sooner found alone,
> But rush upon me thronging, and present
> Times past, what once I was, and what am now.
>   (19–22)

Yet the main thrust of the play is not from past to present but rather
toward the future, toward the "Divine Prediction" that Samson
"Should *Israel* from *Philistian* yoke deliver" (39). Where Sophocles
in *Oedipus* emphasizes the way the past converges on the present,[14]
Milton, his ear attuned to the tick of Eternity, brings the past to
bear on the present so that both may be made to converge on the
future, the moment of *kairos* when prophecies are fullfilled: the Biblical fullness of time, when time in travail gives birth to Eternity.

Milton therefore contrives to have the entire tragedy implicit in
its opening line,[15] a stroke of proleptic genius that advertises the
poet's beginning to be his ending, though—as the Chorus says of
God—"ever best found in the close" (1748). Samson, eyeless in
Gaza, toils at the mill except on this one day, given over to the Feast
of Dagon, when he has been permitted to come forth to seek rest:
"A little onward lend thy guiding hand/ To these dark steps, a little
further on" (1–2). Since there are no stage directions, since the
hand is given no body, and since the Chorus has not yet appeared,
we remain free to imagine what we will or to follow the editors,
choosing to envision a small boy or guard, perhaps to recall Antigone leading Oedipus at Colonus, or the guides of Teiresias in
Sophocles and Euripides, or even the "darke steppes" of the King
of Paphlagonia, who wanders without a guide in the *Arcadia*. But
of course the theological reverberations are—or should be—ines-
capable, "guide" and "guiding hand" being the commonest shorthand for God and His Providence. In Spenser it is "God guide
thee, Guyon." In Milton the sonnet to Skinner ends with the "better
guide," the same "guide" who appears in the great letter to
Leonard Philaras, Athenian; the same "guide" who in *Paradise Lost*
brings Adam to the Garden and who saves Eve from the fate of
Narcissus—these guides anticipating the exodus into the world
"with Providence thir guide." On the level of plot, then, we may
imagine a human guide, a small boy or a guard will do—but on the

level of proleptic form we must entertain the idea of Providence, a divine guide to the dark steps of Samson.

The binocular vision required of the reader at the outset—his attention having been drawn simultaneously toward separate but not unconnected lines of possible development—persists throughout, an effect of double vision that derives from Milton's theological understanding of a hero whose "breeding" had been "order'd and prescrib'd/ As of a person separate to God" (30–31). Manoa, the earthly father, had been childless until the appearance of the angel of the heavenly Father: it is to the heavenly Father that Samson must remain a "person separate." As we know from Matthew 23, the chapter that inveighs against "blind guides," "call no man your father upon the earth: for one is your Father, which is in heaven." Samson, who before the opening of the drama had stood separate, in single rebellion, "whose strength, while virtue was her mate,/ Might have subdu'd the Earth" (173–74), had later relinquished his virtue to Dalila, becoming "twain" with her; and it is the anticipation of his renewed singularity, his recovered separation to God, that Milton's proleptic form must hold in abeyance, must preserve, for the moment when it is revealed that Samson is

> Like that self-begott'n bird
> In the *Arabian* woods embost,
> That no second knows nor third.
> (1699–1701)

Milton's language, rather remarkably, everywhere sustains the effect of double vision, an effect that may be illustrated most easily, if most surprisingly, in the characterization of Manoa, who of all the *dramatis personae* would seem to be most nearly "one" with Samson. Despite Manoa's good intentions, often because of them, the earthly father gives rise to the most telling ironies of the drama. It is to Manoa that Milton lends the darkest platitude of all, the fiercely farcical line that goes, "I cannot praise thy marriage choices, Son" (420). The reader knows the marriages to be of divine impulsion, the result of the "intimate impulse" (223) that led Samson first to the woman of Timna, then to Dalila—praiseworthy "choices" indeed, their use and abuse grotesquely sinful. In his very first speech Manoa sadly asks, "Who would be now a Father in my stead?" (355). And we, having attended to the implications of the first line of the tragedy, anticipate the answer that will appear in

the fullness of time: "call no man your father upon the earth: for
one is your Father, which is in heaven." Later Manoa asks:

> who knows
> But God hath set before us, to return thee
> Home to thy country and his sacred house,
> Where thou mayst bring thy off'rings....
>
> (516–19)

Again we are being invited to think ahead to the exact nature of the
offering and to prepare ourselves for Manoa's final speech, near
the close of the drama, when the earthly father vows

> To fetch him hence and solemnly attend
> With silent obsequy and funeral train
> Home to his Father's house....
>
> (1731–33)

Manoa throughout exercises what he calls a "Father's timely care/
To prosecute the means of thy deliverance" (602–03); but since we
are aware that Samson's deliverance lies not in Time but in Eternity, there must always be theological overtones in Manoa's repeated
attempts to "ransom" his son.[16] As Shakespeare knew, there lies
only with the Father our final deliverance, through "the world's
ransom, blessed Mary's son." The reiterated irony reaches its height
just after the catastrophe when Manoa, still ignorant of what has
happened, expresses "hope," announcing, "For his redemption all
my Patrimony" (1482); and we see made explicit what had been implicit all along, that Samson is indeed redeemed but through the
patrimony of the Father "who would be now a Father" in Manoa's
"stead."

The proleptic form of the tragedy, adumbrated in the calculated
ambiguity of the first line and sustained by the dramatic ironies
uttered by characters such as Manoa, appears also in the imagery of
the play.[17] In the beginning Samson is "dark, dark, dark" beneath
the "blaze" of (a metaphorical) "noon" (80); at the end he is "with
inward eyes illuminated" (1689) as, literally, "noon grew high"
(1612). In the beginning Samson complains,

> How could I once look up, or heave the head,
> Who like a foolish Pilot have shipwreck't
> My Vessel trusted to me from above,
> Gloriously rigg'd; and for a word, a tear....
>
> (197–200)

This "head," so "gloriously rigg'd" with the locks that signified Samson's separateness to God, is the "head and hallow'd pledge" (535) that the protagonist laid in the "lascivious lap" (536) of Dalila, who "shore" him like a "tame Wether" (538). This "head" we remember when we read about those "counterfeit" coins that bear "friends" as "Superscription" but then "withdraw thir head" (189–92); we remember it in the common "rout" of "heads without name" (677) and in the "head declin'd" (727) of the "counterfeit" Dalila; we recall it again in the threat to Harapha: "long shall not withhold me from thy head" (1125). We hold in memory the "capital secret" (394), the "fatal harvest of thy head" (1024), until that moment in the plot, that moment in Time, when Samson will no longer "withhold me" (1125): "upon thir heads and on his own he pull'd" (1589). Before this climactic moment at noon (*kairos*) between the pillars Samson had "stood with head a while inclin'd" (1636) but then, triumphantly, "at last with head erect" (1639) "upon thir heads and on his own he pull'd." As witnesses to this proleptic movement, this process of progressive revelation in time, we come to recognize that Samson *could* "once look up" *and* "heave the head."

The same pattern of anticipation and fulfillment, of proleptic form, likewise appears in the simile of the "foolish Pilot" who has "shipwreck't" his "gloriously rigg'd" vessel "for a word." This simile Christopher Ricks, who elsewhere brilliantly justifies Milton's "grand style," includes in his chapter on the "unsuccessful metaphor," quoting with approval Dr. Johnson's perfectly logical and wonderfully witty criticism that here the poet "confounds loquacity with a shipwreck."[18] And true enough, where the criteria of imagery are syllogistic and local, confined to the immediate context. But Milton's methods conform here, in the smaller parts of the design, to the proleptic conception of the whole. Properly considered, the simile functions as a kind of witty conceit, drawing its authority from the Bible and in the larger context of the whole play justifying itself as "expectation in preference to surprise." In 1 Thessalonians 4:4 we learn that it is God's will that a man "should know how to possess his vessel in sanctification and honour," so as to avoid the fornication that in the case of a Samson may forfeit special bonds with the Lord; and in 1 Peter 3:7 we are reminded that woman is the "weaker vessel," unless of course a Samson allows her to become the stronger vessel. In this way the conceit of the pilot with "Vessel trusted . . . from above" anticipates that fine moment, the approach of Dalila, when the Chorus presents us with an either-or alternative (true "freedom is but choosing"): "But who is this, what thing of Sea or Land?" (710). We do not remain long in doubt about the alternatives:

> Female of sex it seems,
> That so bedeckt, ornate, and gay,
> Comes this way sailing
> Like a stately Ship
> Of *Tarsus*, bound for th' Isles
> Of *Javan* or *Gadire*
> With all her bravery on, and tackle trim,
> Sails fill'd, and streamers waving,
> Courted by all the winds that hold them play....
> (711–19)

Samson, having "shipwreck't" his "Vessel," has been replaced by this "stately Ship," which else had been the "weaker vessel." As the Chorus asks,

> What Pilot so expert but needs must wreck
> Embark'd with such a Steers-mate at the Helm?
> (1044–45)

By such means Milton also prepares us for the approach of Harapha, about whom the Chorus again poses an alternative: "But had we best retire, I see a storm?" Here "another kind of tempest brings" not a pleasure ship but a fighting vessel:

> Haughty as is his pile high-built and proud.
> Comes he in peace? what wind hath blown him hither
> I less conjecture than when first I saw
> The sumptuous *Dalila* floating this way....
> (1069–72)

This other "kind of tempest" that brings yet another "pile high-built" fulfils still another aspect of the simile to which Dr. Johnson objected, but the episode with Harapha is itself proleptic; and again we must not "impatiently cry out against the *Dramatist*, and presently condemn the plot." Instead we must learn to "expect the winding up of things, and stay till the last close." Meanwhile, it will be obvious that the imagery of sea and land appropriately distinguishes Samson from his enemies, properly keeps him "separate," for this is the Feast of Dagon, the day on which God's champion shall "challenge Dagon to the test," proving the either-or alternative "whether God be Lord,/ Or *Dagon*" (477–78); and "*Dagon* thir Sea-Idol," which is in *Paradise Lost* "upward Man and downward Fish" (I, 462), must in the "last close" be seen as "Sea Monster," as "thir Sea-Idol," a "thing of Sea" rather than "Land."

Samson rejects the ignoble ease proffered by Dalila, resisting her blandishments just as he had resisted the more well-intentioned comforts offered by the earthly father, Manoa. "Thou and I long since are twain" (929), Samson tells her, having recovered the manhood and the singular "separateness" he had lost to the weaker vessel—a turn that Milton has Dalila acknowledge in the imagery of sea and land:

> I see thou art implacable, more deaf
> To prayers, than winds and seas, yet winds to seas
> Are reconcil'd at length, and Sea to Shore:
> Thy anger, unappeasable, still rages,
> Eternal tempest never to be calm'd.
>
> (960–64)

These words (Samson as the "Eternal tempest" of God, the providential force) prefigure the ironic reversal at the close of the drama when, "with burst of thunder" (1651) and "with the force of winds and waters pent" (1647), he brings down the temple "upon the heads of all who sat beneath" (1652). The force of the "eternal tempest" has in "the winding up of things" overwhelmed the "Sea-Idol" and decided to question "whether God be Lord, Or *Dagon*."

Insofar as *Samson Agonistes* may be said to have a middle, it lies, numerically, in the episode with Dalila, which functions like a fulcrum, or, to use Ben Jonson's words, like a "hinge" on which turns the "entire body or figure" of the action. The episode is also the play in little, microcosm of Milton's methods throughout: anticipation, then fulfillment through ironic reversal. As the Chorus finally recognizes, the motives of Dalila are "discover'd in the end, till now conceal'd" (998). This is Milton's method, as indeed it is the method of God's Providence, "That it might be fulfilled which was spoken": "Fear them not therefore: for there is nothing covered, that shall not be revealed; and hid, that shall not be known" (Matt. 10:26). After Samson becomes "twain" with Dalila (this time to separate himself from her), his singularity, his "separateness" to God, may be confirmed in the encounter with the giant Harapha, who says more than he can know when he asks in disbelief, "Dost thou already single me?" (1092). Samson indeed "defies" him "thrice to single fight," after which Harapha departs, though not without Milton's having allowed the Chorus to risk an outrageous pun in the imagery of sea and land: "His Giantship is gone somewhat crestfall'n" (1244). From the beginning we have been encouraged to "expect the winding up of things" and have anticipated the moment at the close when Samson will be like the Arabian bird "that no second knows nor third."

With such matters as these in mind we may acknowledge that the form of the tragedy remains latent until the end of the play. "A little onward lend thy guiding hand": it is all there, implicit in the opening line, but this is foreshadowing the end and not the end itself. When Samson first goes "a little onward," he proceeds "a little further on/ For yonder bank hath choice of Sun or shade" (2–3). Then the Chorus appears, to surmise that "safest he who stood aloof" when Samson "ran on embattled Armies" (129, 135). At the close of the tragedy "feast and noon grew high" as Samson "his guide requested" (1630) to lead him between the pillars. And the ending recalls the beginning, for there is again "choice of Sun or shade." The Philistine nobility sit shaded under roof, whereas the multitude, including the Messenger, "On banks and scaffolds under Sky might stand" (1610). With such an alternative at the close, one lives, we have known all along, by choosing sun rather than shade; when the Messenger explains, "I among these ["under Sky"] aloof obscurely stood" (1611), we recognize once more what we had known from the beginning, that "safest he who stood aloof."

Aristotle, though not Dr. Johnson, might have approved, for in the *Rhetoric* 1405[b] we learn that "good riddles do, in general, provide us with satisfactory metaphors: for metaphors imply riddles, and therefore a good riddle can furnish a good metaphor."[19] To set mixed or "riddling" images against each other (those vessels and coins are good examples) resembles Milton's homeopathic understanding of Aristotle on tragedy: "Nor is Nature wanting in her own effects to make good his assertion: for so in Physic things of melancholic hue and quality are us'd against melancholy, sour against sour, salt to remove salt humours."[20] Whatever the theory, the language of Samson reveals its power in riddling fashion, always obscurely anticipating in mixed metaphor and then triumphantly revealing. Although Samson himself considers that his "riddling days are past" (1064), the riddling images of the tragedy continue to unravel in time, just as the form of the tragedy works through the time of the plot—all moving toward the moment of noon (*kairos*) between the pillars, when and where proleptic form comes together with the chronological sequence of events.

Milton's ironies are relentless, never relinquished until the close. When the Chorus, near the close, watches Samson depart with the Officer, their words are "Go and the Holy One/ Of *Israel* be thy guide" (1427-28). The Chorus speaks from hope—not from knowledge. It is only the reader who knows that God will a little onward lend his guiding hand to those dark steps, where there will once again be choice of sun or shade. So also with the words of Manoa, who in his last speech asserts that "*Samson* hath quit himself/ Like *Samson,* and heroicly hath finish'd" (1708-10), which as a result has brought "to himself and Father's house eternal fame." Manoa naturally thinks of ordinary heroism, having only an imperfect notion of what it means to "quit himself/ Like *Samson*"—in the perfect singularity of a champion "separate to God." Similarly, Manoa believes that his son has brought eternal fame to *his* house; and on the level of plot this is all quite true. But the reader also knows that our "Father's house" has "many mansions" (John 14), that on the level of proleptic form Samson has brought eternal glory to the home of his Heavenly Father, "for one is your Father, which is in heaven." There are no normative characters in this play: no one, within the drama, comprehends the ironies that, together with the imagery and other elements of design, direct our attention to anticipatory form. Manoa and the Chorus differ from Dalila and Harapha mainly in their intentions rather than in their understanding of the protagonist, who (like the Phoenix) preserves his "oneness"—by being, in an artistic as well as a theological sense, "separate to God." Only with the very last lines of the tragedy, the bastard sonnet that transforms a Euripidean ending, does the knowledge of the Chorus coincide in part with that of the reader; we know more, but we have nothing to add.

Milton's concern has been with the relation of Time (plot) to Eternity (proleptic form), which involves the justification of God's ways and the question of free will and predestination. Since perfect freedom for mankind consists in knowing God's will and then in aligning human will with it, the problem lies in choosing rightly among the "cunning resemblances" of a bewildering array of opposites. "What purifies us is trial," adds Milton in *Areopagitica*, "and trial is by what is contrary." But in a fallen world where good and

evil grow up inseparably, the choosing that means freedom is pain-
fully costly and doubly complicated by the need to make a timely
choice conform to the eternal schedule. Reason (*ratio recta*), choice,
freedom—these form the basic triad for Milton, in a world apparently dominated by either-or alternatives that often seem almost
indistinguishable.

The Chorus addresses itself to just such matters again and again,
but consider in particular the meditation on "just men long op-
prest" by "Tyrannic power,"

> When God into the hands of thir deliverer
> Puts invincible might. . . .

> Hee all thir Ammunition
> And feats of War defeats
> With plain Heroic magnitude of mind
> And celestial vigor arm'd. . . .
> (1270-80)

There follows the application, posed in alternatives:

> But patience is more oft the exercise
> Of Saints, the trial of thir fortitude,
> Making them each his own Deliverer. . . .

> Either of these is in thy lot,
> *Samson*, with might endu'd
> Above the Sons of men; but sight bereav'd
> May chance to number thee with those
> Whom Patience finally must crown.
> (1287-96)

Patience or heroism—"Either of these is in thy lot," though more
likely patience, the "trial of thir fortitude." But the reader, as distinct from the Chorus, knows that "either of these" means "both,"
for he has seen Samson exercise patience in the trial of his fortitude
and anticipates an act of heroism. The Chorus often speaks in just
such disjunct axioms:

> . . . what thing [is this] of Sea or Land?
> (710)

Living or dying thou hast fulfilled. . . .
                            (1661)

Just or unjust, alike seem miserable. . . .
                            (703)

God of our Fathers, what is man!
That thou towards him with hand so various,
Or might I say contrarious,
Temper'st thy providence through his short course.
                            (667–70)

Such possibilities seem mutually exclusive, though they are not always so in fact, for as we know from *Areopagitica* the true "temper" of God's variety (to take the last example) depends entirely on contraries. Milton refers to such propositions in *Art of Logic* as *axioma disjunctum contingens*, which may issue in the kind of irony well described by Anthony Low: "The irony results from the ignorance of the speaker, but differs from unconscious dramatic irony because the unexpected issue is not the working out of the prediction in an opposite sense, but the reconciliation of two apparent contradictions, so that both events occur, contrary to preliminary understanding or expectation."[21]

   This kind of irony appears plainly in the crucial pronouncements of Samson himself, who after refusing the Officer three times suddenly feels mysterious

            rousing motions in me which dispose
        To something extraordinary my thoughts.
        I with this Messenger will go along. . . .
                            (1382–84)

Then adds:

        If there be aught of presage in the mind,
        This day will be remarkable in my life
        By some great act, or of my days the last.
                            (1387–89)

In the classical *Ajax* the messenger informs us that it is on this particular "day" in the present that the issue must be "either death or life" (a matter of exclusive alternatives), but in the Christian poet the issue must be, after a moment of irresolution, a matter of death *and* life. On the level of plot, within the realm of time and human knowledge, there is fatal choice, doubt what alternative the future holds: "some great act, or of my days the last." But on the level of proleptic form there can be no doubt that "or" means "and," that Samson will perform a "great act" on this day of his "days the last." This same sense of mystery in alternative choice reappears in the words of the Messenger, who comes to describe the catastrophe:

> For dire imagination still pursues me.
> But providence or instinct of nature seems,
> Or reason though disturb'd, and scarce consulted,
> To have guided me aright, I know not how.
>
> (1544–47)

Was the Messenger guided by natural instinct and reason or by Providence? was Samson impelled by natural heroism, "plain Heroic magnitude of mind," or was he compelled to act by Eternal Providence through the infusion of irresistible Grace? On the level of plot alone we "know not how." The Fall of Man was among other things a descent into time, into duality, where man must constantly choose either good or evil. "It was from out of the rind of one apple tasted, that the knowledge of good and evil, as two twins cleaving together, leaped forth into the World."[22] But man, unlike Satan, is not doomed to wander without a guide:

> The World was all before them, where to choose
> Thir place of rest, and Providence thir guide."
>
> (*PL*, XII, 646–48).

On the level of plot, in the realm of choice and chance and time, we must doubt whether the Messenger was "guided . . . aright" by "providence or instinct of nature"; yet the level of proleptic form whispers that "or" means "and."

Think in this connection of the crucial moment of the drama, Samson's last, as described by the Messenger. A "guide" leads Samson "a little further on" between the pillars,

> which when *Samson*
> Felt in his arms, with head a while inclin'd,
> And eyes fast fixt he stood, as one who pray'd,
> Or some great matter in his mind revolv'd.
>
> (1635–38)

In the Bible Samson only prays; but through the Messenger, on the level of plot, Milton again offers us the freedom that is choice. Did

Samson pray, that is, did he depend solely on Providence, as it appears that Wilkes would have to argue? (In which case the word "motions" in the "rousing motions" Samson feels just before he chooses to go with the Officer bears one of its common seventeenth-century meanings and refers to the "motion," the operation, of divine grace.[23]) *Or* did Samson exercise free will, revolve in his mind a "greater matter" of "Heroic magnitude"? (In which case the word "motions" bears another of its permissible meanings, that of "emotions.") In Milton's words from *The Defence of the English People*, the question is "whether Samson acted in pursuance of a command from heaven or was prompted by his own valour only"? In the world of Time, on the level of plot, we must doubt, sharing the human indecision of the Messenger. But from the vantage of Eternity, presented to the reader by proleptic form, we may perceive that Samson both prayed *and* chose, that the word "motions" refers both to the infusion of divine grace *and* to the surge of heroic emotion, and that therefore at this moment the will of God and the volition of His champion are one and the same. In the fullness of time the *kairos* has come.

If I am more or less right in my suppositions, we not only skirt the critical impasse but find ourselves in the presence of a very considerable work of art, perhaps the unique example of specifically Christian tragedy; for Samson guided solely by God is not "tragic," as Samson guided solely by himself is not "Christian."

Milton has invested Sophoclean irony with providential force, identified dramatic irony as in *Paradise Lost* with the "guiding hand" of God; just as with the riddling images that anticipate in order to fulfill, the poet manages to mirror the mysterious workings in time of the "unsearchable dispose"—in these ways fulfilling again for himself his early ambition to do for his country what the choicest wits of antiquity had done, "with this over and above of being a Christian." Rather than chopping *Samson* into acts and hunting the elusive middle we may recur to Milton's dry warning that it "suffices if the whole Drama be found not produc't beyond the fifth Act." As Cudworth advises, we must not "presently condemn the plot" but must rather "expect the winding up of things, and stay till the last Close"; our task as readers is to stand and to await the "close," where things will be "found ever best." In Time the plot reaches its end at noon between the pillars in a moment of *kairos,* which is not simply time but the "tempestivity of time." We must in effect attend to two lines of development—the movements

of the plot and the progressive revelation of form, as the latent implications of "a little onward lend thy guiding hand" steadily unfold
in relation to the sequence of events; "for there is nothing covered,
that shall not be revealed." It is only with this species of double
vision that a reader can see how the poet informs his ironies and
anticipations with providential meaning. Dramatic irony always
produces artistic distance, thereby conferring a degree of omniscience on the reader; Milton's irony conveys something of the distance and omniscience of God.[24] Through this device the reader
gains perspective on historical time, searches something of the "unsearchable dispose," shares something of the eternal view. And as
he watches—guided by the shaping pressure of Milton's ironies and
proleptic images—the convergence of form and plot, he sees, or
seems to see, the coincidence of Providence and free will, the "intersection of the timeless with time." It is, I am convinced, from this
convergence of the twain that "though we oft doubt," things are
"ever best found in the close." It seems certain, at least, that unless
we read in something like the way I have tried to describe we are
unlikely to put down the book in "calm of mind, all passion spent,"
for this state of mind depends on our being able to see, or to think
we see, that "or" means "and," that Samson "was prompted by his
own valour" *and* "acted in pursuance of a command from heaven."
Samson has fulfilled, between the pillars at the hour precise of noon,
the hope that Milton, at the age of twenty-three, had held for himself: that if man has "the grace to use it so," "all is" in time "as ever"
in the eye of the eternal task-master, whose "*Still and Silent Path*"
may be searched only in riddling fashion until the "last Close" that
coincides with the "tempestivity of time."

CHAPTER V

The Tempestivity of Time

Corollary to the theory of types, and proceeding from much the same theological and psychological impulses, is the notion of *opportunitas* or "tempestivity of time," which constitutes the theme of *Paradise Regained* and forms the basis for the portrayal of Jesus. The typological method connects the two Testaments and relates Time to Eternity. The Christian idea of "opportunity," taken from the Greeks and Latins as *Aegyptive spolia*, stems from the same need to label and rationalize the points of the intersection of the timeless with time. Fr. Joannes David, in *Occasio. Arrepta. Neglecta*, explains that the Greeks and then the Latins accorded *kairos* or *occasio* divine status, the first as a male deity and the second as a goddess. Posidippus' epigram in the *Greek Anthology* (xvi, 275) on Lysippus' statue of "time" or "opportunity" elicits in question-and-answer form the salient attributes of the classical deity, who stands tiptoe and, possessing winged feet because always on the move, has a razor in one hand to indicate a greater degree of sharpness than other edges, and has a forelock but is bald behind to show that opportunity must be grasped quickly or lost forever. It is this figure to which the Satan of *Paradise Regained* refers ("Occasion's forelock") in trying to tempt Jesus. As David points out, we Christians must reject such superstitious idolatries (*reiecta illa superstitiosa idolotatriae*), but we may expropriate the idea and lend it true (Christian) significance, in which case *occasio* or *kairos* may be properly defined as *opportunitas temporis*, the time that may be used or misused in trying to grasp opportunity (*faciendi aut non faciendi*

123

opportunitatem): we may refer to such moments as "opportunity," "tempestivity," or "occasion" (*opportunitatem, tempestivitatem, & occasionem appellamus*). It is the eternal will or divine grace (*gratiae divinae*) that presides over the conjunction of time and occasion (*Tempori & Occasioni coniunctum*).[1] And if you fail "to take opportunity by the fore-lock," if you "let go Time's opportunity," says John Fox with finality, "you will certainly be ruin'd to all Eternity."[2]

This way of dealing theoretically with the relation of Time to Eternity may be considered in some respects more personal, more closely connected to the life of the individual Christian, than the typological method. The need to preserve his sense of self *intacto* seems to have taken an extreme form in the younger Milton, where it may be glimpsed in the preoccupation with virginity and chastity that erupts in *Comus* and threatens to subvert the main theme of the masque. And this preoccupation appears to be connected to the young Milton's tendency to defer certain kinds of choice and action until the "tempestivity of time"—a tendency that reappears in idealized form in the Jesus of *Paradise Regained*.

Although Milton early became aware that his "style, by certain vital signs it had, was likely to live" and early desired to "leave something so written to aftertimes, as they should not willingly let it die,"[3] it was only late in life that he permitted himself to accomplish his aim of writing an epic that would instruct his nation, and only in the very last year of his life did he allow the epic to assume its final shape. The principle of Milton's poetic being seems to have been delay, deferment of the full release of those powers that, in the parable that haunts his prose and verse, it is death to hide. As he himself confessed toward the end of his life, he had been "long choosing, and beginning late" (*PL*, IX, 26). Not that the young Milton was either feckless or lazy; on the contrary, he pursued his studies with demoniacal energy, arising very early and rarely retiring from his "lucubrations" until midnight or later—practices he continued despite the pain and agitation that accompanied his gradual loss of sight. Some inner principle required delay, required that he spend the fleeting hours in preparing himself, in getting ready, thinking always "to burst out into sudden blaze" but always deferring the moment. A corollary example survives, by his own choice, even in his art, where in the unfinished "Passion" the poet, for stanza after stanza, gets ready again and again to sing the hymn proper—but the moment never arrives.

The John Milton who revered his own father likewise venerated

God the Father to such a degree that he came to deny the Trinity and to subordinate the Son; yet even in his later verse Milton never found the Passion, the ultimate subordination of a son, a congenial subject, though the mature poet-pamphleteer found it easy enough to defend the killing of Charles I, the father of his people and God's vicar on earth. Milton wrote for "fit audience ... though few," knowing fame to be "that last infirmity of noble mind"; but he also took enormous pride in the labors of the pamphlet wars of which "all Europe talks from side to side" (Sonnet XXII) and yearned to write the great epic "doctrinal to a nation." From his early years the poet had harbored the usual number of antithetical impulses and apparently confided his prodigious ambitions only to Diodati, who was half his soul. To others he seemed to be saying, with Rostand's Cyrano, "But inwardly I keep my daintiness." It was this immaculate sense of self that earned him the sobriquet The Lady of Christ's; that produced, in the voice of the inviolable Lady of *Comus,* the impassioned praise of "the sage and serious doctrine of Virginity"; and that, it seems more or less clear, encouraged Milton to think for awhile that he himself might possess the Pauline gift (*charisma*) of virginity, theologically the precondition for the release of special powers.[4] This man married thrice, and endorsed polygamy.

After being deserted by his first wife, the aspiring poet promptly wrote his pamphlets on divorce at the dictate, or so it would seem to most of us, of circumstance; but later, in the *Second Defence* of 1654, it appeared to Milton that he had measured out his life in order and reason.

> When the bishops could no longer resist the multitude of their as-sailants, I had leisure to turn my thoughts to other subjects, to the promotion of real and substantial liberty.... When, therefore, I per-ceived that there were three species of liberty which are essential to the happiness of social life—religious, domestic, and civil; and as I had already written concerning the first, and the magistrates were strenuously active in obtaining the third, I determined to turn my attention to the second, or the domestic species.[5]

Similar rationalizations, also from the *Second Defence,* mask the tur-bulencies that must have lurked beneath the need to defer the writing of the great poem, but in this instance the phrasing betrays Milton's reliance on a very particular form of rationalization—the idea of "tempestivity" or "fit opportunity" as defined by the theologians.

> Who and whence I am, say you, is doubtful. So also was it doubtful, in ancient times, who Homer was, who Demosthenes. The truth is, I had learnt to be long silent, to be able to forbear writing... ; and carried silently in my own breast what if I had chosen then, as well as now, to bring forth, I could long since have gained a name. But I was not eager for fame, who is slow of pace; indeed, if the fit opportunity (*occasione*) had not been given me, even these things would never have seen the light; little concerned, though others were ignorant that I knew what I did. It was not the fame of every thing that I was waiting for, but the opportunity (*non enim famam sed opportunitatem*).
>
> (*Works*, VIII, 113)

In his later years Milton had found it convenient to explain the proliferation of divorce pamphlets as one phase in a deliberate program of national edification in the arts and sciences. And, similarly, he had come to feel that his mute inviolacy, his willingness to "forbear writing," was the result of his being "not eager for fame." But we need not therefore suppose that the younger Milton had regarded either the defection of Mary or the continual postponement of the fulfillment of his poetic ambitions with rational and invariable equanimity.

Edward LeComte has amply, and subtly, documented the poet's problems with dating his own poems, as well as Milton's excessive preoccupation with youth and age. Milton tended to date his early poems rather too early, possibly to ward off invidious judgments or perhaps to insinuate the precocity he felt he had not possessed; his best poems he almost invariably left undated. LeComte shows everywhere the pattern "of not minding being taken for younger but worrying about being older," or "worrying that he has not matured fast enough; and, on the other hand, predating himself in order to assuage his fears and to create sympathy for himself with his audience." LeComte concludes that "Milton, the man and the artist, was obsessed with time. . . . His poems are the bulwarks against it. When he was young he feared he was not ready. When he was older, he pretended to be younger."[6]

In the two drafts of a letter to an unidentified friend, Milton left a record of his attempt to justify his slow maturation in time. In the first Milton confesses that the friend, who had been urging him to leave his studies and enter the priesthood, is a "good watch man to admonish that the howres of the night passe on (for so I call my life as yet obscure & unserviceable to mankind) & that the day is at hand wherein Christ commands all to labour while there is light" (John 9:4); he recalls the "terrible seasure of him that hid his talent" (Matt. 25:14–30); and he acknowledges, "I am somtyme suspicious of my selfe, & doe take notice of a certaine belatednesse in me. . . ." The poet then offers Sonnet VII in extenuation:

> How soone hath Time the suttle theefe of Youth,
>   stolne on his wing my three & twentith yeere—

twenty-three, according to the canons of 1603–04 the earliest age of ordination as deacon, followed the next year by elevation to the priesthood. His "tardie moving" Milton hopes to excuse "according to the praecept of my conscience, which I firmly trust is not without god." In the second draft he revises and amplifies, arguing that it is not "too much love of Learning that is in fault" or a "naturall pronenesse" to inactivity, for

> there is against that a much more potent inclination & inbred which about this tyme of a mans life sollicits most, the desire of house & family of his owne to which nothing is esteemed more helpefull then the early entring into credible employment, & nothing more hindering then this affected solitarinesse and though this were anough yet there is to this another act if not of pure yet of refined nature no lesse available to dissuade prolonged obscurity, a desire of honour & repute & immortal fame. . . .

It must rather be that the "certaine belatednesse" that Milton observes in himself "is not without god," though he remains "somtyme suspicious" of himself; even in the letters he feels that he may be doing "that which I excuse my selfe for not doing preach & not preach," which would be enough to "spoyle all the patience of a Parish."

Milton, ambitious of wiving ("potent inclination," he phrases it in the second draft) and impatient for "immortal fame," has pretty clearly begun to reject the priesthood—though he is not making it entirely explicit, to the friend or, probably at this time, to his father or perhaps even to himself—for the vocation of poet-prophet. A decision to be undertaken not without fear and trembling. Since the impulse to delay could not possibly be the first "infirmity of noble mind," the result of underground psychic perturbations, Milton characteristically seeks the (unimpeachable) source of his "tardie moving" in the will of deity, and consequently he elaborates, in

the second draft, "the solid good flowing from due & timely obedience to that command in the gospell set out by the terrible seasing
of him that hid the talent":

> it is more probable therfore that not the endlesse delight of specula-
> tion but this very consideration of that great commaundment does
> not presse forward as soone as may be to undergoe but keeps off
> with a sacred reverence, & religious advisement how best to under-
> goe not taking thought of beeng late so it give advantage to be more
> fit. . . .[7]

Here the rationale later set forth in the *Second Defence* of 1654 receives its first formulation; a psychic predisposition has been translated into, and sanctified by, the religious vocabulary of the time.
In seeking to justify his "tardie" ways to his "good watch man" and
to God, Milton has recourse to the notion of the "tempestivity of
time," of *kairos* or occasion fit.

There is tick-tock time in the Bible, and the New Testament even
has a name, *chronos*, that usually designates it; but not much is made
of this kind of time. In Hebrew the word usually used for time is
'eth, which as I understand it refers not so much to a given moment
in the chronological continuum as to the nature of that moment in
itself: it designates not what time it is but what the time *is*. Modern
examples survive in such fossilized locutions as His Time Has
Come or Her Time Is Near, where the word "time" has less to do
with clocks than the nature of the event (he is about to die, the child
is about to be born), less to do with when something happens than
with what happens. The Hebrew *'eth*, usually but not invariably
translated *kairos* by the writers of the Septuagint, generally denotes
a divine moment, an event in time significant because of the presence of God *in* it. Like the theory of types, it is a way of relating
Time to Eternity. The prophets remind Israel of the *kairoi* of the
past, those historical events, most notably Exodus, that demonstrate God's power to intervene in natural or chronological time;
and then reveal the *kairoi* to come, the events that will in the historical future once again guarantee that God is Lord of Time.

It is in this context that the virtue of Christian patience assumes
its most profound import. We must endure the time, wait or even
suffer in acquiescent patience for the fullness of time: "It is not for
you," Jesus explains in Acts 1:7, "to know the times or the seasons,"
not for you to know the *kairoi*, "which the Father hath put in his
own power." "Concerning the times [*chronoi*] and the seasons

[*kairoi*]," says Paul in 1 Thess. 5:1, "ye have no need that aught be written unto you. For yourselves know perfectly that the day of the Lord so cometh as a thief in the night"; and he asks in 1 Timothy 6:14–15 that we fight the good battle of faith until the "appearance of our Lord Jesus Christ, which the blessed and only sovereign will show at the appropriate times" (*kairoi*). As William Whately explains (his text is Ephesians 5:16), "Now by Time the Apostle means two things":

> First, the very passing away of houres and minutes.... And secondly, the good occasions or opportunities.... For the word in the originall signifies not alone the very sliding of minutes, but the space considered also with some speciall fitnesse that it hath for some good, which we call the season of it.[8]

It is this distinction between natural and divine time that informs the only use of *kairos* in the Gospel according to John (7:6). Jesus distinguishes between His perception of the divine moment and the natural time of His disciples, saying "My time [to become manifest as the Messiah at the Feast of the Tabernacles] is not yet come; but your time is alway ready," meaning that the *kairos* appointed by God, the moment when Jesus must depart for Jerusalem and death, is not yet "ready," not yet "full." Christ's wisdom is not of this world, neither is his method of (dead) reckoning. Although history takes its uninterrupted course in "continuall fluxe" from the "creation of the world to the dissolution thereof" in hours, days, and years, this "Naturall" and "Civill" time reveals its pattern and "Spirituall" meaning only through the "times" or *kairoi* of deity.[9] To be unaware of the *kairoi* means to be unable to read history, unable to ponder the true weight of events, like those in Matthew (cf. Luke 12:55–56) who remain ignorant of the theological weather: "Ye know how to discern the face of the heaven; but ye cannot discern the signs of the times" (*kairoi*).

Thomas Granger's handbook of logic lucidly defines the traditional distinctions. Acknowledging that in logic there is no "diuision of time," Granger observes that we may nonetheless divide time "according to the things subject thereto." First in order of dignity he remarks "eternal" time, "termed in Latine, *evum*, in Greek, *aeion*," where the meaning is "euer being": "It hath no parts of past, present, and to come, but is euer present, without beginning, succession, end." Then there is "finite" time, which is the "duration of things created, or the application of eternitie to the

world and the things thereof": "the time of the world being as I
may say the point (*to nun*) of an infinite circumference." Within
this second division, Granger finds the traditional subcategories; as
he says, "*Time* finite is taken generally and specially."

> 1. In the general acceptation it is termed in Greeke, *chronos, id est,
> tempus*, so it is said to be time past, present, to come, to haue begin-
> ning, succession, and end, and God speaking to man after the man-
> ner of man attributes this finitenesse to himselfe, Reuel. 1.4 & 4.

> 2. In the speciall acceptation it is termed *kairos*, that is, season,
> seasons, or times, both in respect of the Sunnes yearely motion from
> South to North, which is divided into spring, summer, autumne,
> winter, and in respect of his diurnall, or daily motion, from East to
> West making day, and from West to East making night; but chiefely
> in respect of things done, or happening in time: as a sickely time, a
> warlike, or troublesome time, dinner time, a dire season, a wet sea-
> son, marriage dayes, festivall dayes, &c. Also time rightly applied,
> vsed, and taken, is termed opportunitie, and occasion.[10]

It is *kairos* as "opportunitie, and occasion" that Milton emphasizes
in excusing his "tardie moving" in the second draft of his letter,
that he reverts to again in justifying himself in the *Second Defence,*
and that provides Sonnet VII with much of its force and precision.

"Yet that you may see that I am somtyme suspicious of my selfe,"
says Milton to his "watch man" and friend, "& doe take notice of a
certaine belatednesse in me, I am the bolder to send you some of
my nightward thoughts some while since they come in fitly made
up in a Petrarchian stanza."

> How soone hath Time the suttle theefe of Youth
>   stolne on his wing my three & twentith yeere
>   my hasting days fly on with full careere
>   but my late spring no bud or blossome shew'th
> Perhaps my semblance might deceave the truth
>   that I to manhood am arriv'd so neere
>   & inward ripenesse doth much lesse appeare
>   that some more tymely-happie spirits indu'th. . . .

The poet begins, that is, by exploiting a series of more or less
conventional oppositions—between "hasting days" and his lack of
"bud or blossome," between his youthful "semblance" and his actual closeness to "manhood," and between the way his own "inward
ripenesse" does not much "appeare" and the way in which it clothes

("indu'th") the "more tymely-happie spirits." The poet's dilemma is of course personal, but the thought, feeling, and expression remain linked to the cultural context. Paracelsus, for example, speaks here in the voice of conventional wisdom: "Let man see to it that his fruits be not at all external, like those of the trees in the garden, and let him not waste and squander his time. If he disregards this truth and attempts to grind the wheat before it has been threshed, his whole life will be folly and lies. For before the appointed time God gives no fruit; everything must come in due time. . . . And so in everything else, time must complete its cycle; whether a thing ripens sooner or later depends on God."[11] In the words of one of the commentators on Ecclesiastes, "For every thing there is a time prefined of God," so that "if time be prevented [hindered by anticipatory action], it shall be frustrate. . . . For God doth all in time and season, and will haue them cloathed with his owne circumstances also."[12]

For the Christian of the Renaissance "the space of time is nothing but the continuation and succession of so many minutes and moments one of another; but the season of time, or opportunitie of it, is time apted and fitted, to doe a business." Stephen Marshall continues, pointing the distinction for the members of the House of Commons: "Now these two doe very much differ one from another, the one of them the length, the duration of time, the Greeks calls [sic] χρονος [chronos], but the season, the opportunitie is called καιρος [kairos], which is the *tempus commodum*, the tempestivity of time, the ripenesse of time. . . ." God "hath joyned time and dutie inseparably one to another," so that there is an "appointed time" for everything and "no time, but it hath an appointed dutie." Although "wicked men by a devillish wisedome can take the seeming opportunities, to promote their owne wicked designes" (Shakespeare's Edmund and Richard III), godly men must undertake the hard task of joining the times to the purposes of Eternal Providence; "but to know the opportunities of the things that concerne God and our soules, nothing but a gratious heart [i.e., illuminated by God's grace] enables a man to doe it. . . ."[13]

The sestet of Sonnet VII, in strictest iambic measure even, prays for Marshall's "gratious heart," which alone can finally effect the reconciliation of *chronos* with *kairos*:

> Yet be it lesse or more, or soone or slow
> it shall be still in strictest measure even
> to that same lot however meane or high

toward which Tyme leads me, & the will of heaven
all is if I have grace to use it so
as ever in my great task-maisters eye

The last distinction, between time and the will of heaven, suggests
the context in which Milton writes. As Calvin observes, "It is not
Chronos but *Kairos*" that indicates the "fit time" of Heaven.[14] Troubled by what appears to be "tardie moving" in the "duration of
time," the poet seeks justification in his awareness of double duration, in his conviction that the eternal purposes of God "appoint"
what Marshall and many others call the "*tempus commodum*, the
tempestivity of time, the ripenesse of time." And as it is in *King
Lear*, "The ripeness is all." Marshall alludes to one of Milton's fa-
vorite parables in pointing out that failing to respond at the appointed time incurs the loss of the providential moment: "Opportunities are Gods fitting of time to businesse, & none but God can
thus fit it. . . . So the foolish Virgins came with their Lampes . . . but
the season was past."[15] It is equally sinful to try to "prevent" (come
before) the "time prefined," as Jesus shows us again and again in
Paradise Regained, "enduring" the "time" in "patience" while Satan
tempts Him to anticipate the moment, maintaining with plausible
tongue that Jesus' "years are ripe, and overripe," that He is "now at
full age, fullness of time, thy season." It must be as Paracelsus says:
"In all things do as time commands; time draws you and you must
follow. God teaches you to go whither time leads. . . . Next to God,
[time] is the emperor who commands. . . . Commands that must be
observed eternally are decreed by God, and the emperor must only
see to it that they are fulfilled."[16] But whether the act appears in
time to be "lesse or more, or soone or slow," it shall "be still in
strictest measure even"—if only it is performed in the "*tempus commodum*, the tempestivity of time, the ripenesse of time." Not otherwise.

Matters such as these provide the context for the exact meaning
and resonance of the last two lines of the sonnet, which might
otherwise appear to be a platitude masquerading, in the manner of
William Ernest Henley, as a pious genuflection. Although there has
been a good deal of argument over their meaning, Donald Dorian
must be moving in the right direction in his paraphrase: "All time
is, if I have grace to use it so, as eternity in God's sight."[17] Since
"opportunities are Gods fitting of time to businesse, & none but
God can thus fit it," men require grace to be able to adjust natural

time to the eternal timetable, to be able to conform their acts in time to the "will of heaven." "So in the last place, know," concludes Marshall, *"that no wisedome, no learning, nothing but a gratious heart guided by the Spirit of God, doth know how to take opportunities in time...;* no wisedome but the wisedome of grace, and Gods Spirit guiding the heart, doth ever know to doe businesses in their right seasons."[18] When the moment in time coincides with the eternal will of heaven, then indeed "all is ... as ever," so that we might amend Dorian's paraphrase to read: All I do in time, all "is" in time, as though it were done in eternity—if only I receive the "wisedome of grace" to act in "right seasons," the grace to make my timetable "in strictest measure even" with the eternal one. By his "three & twentith yeere" Milton had, through recourse to the distinction between *chronos* and *kairos*, provided himself with theological justification for delay: what impressed others as "tardie moving" has become in Milton's view the exercise of Christian patience in awaiting the fullness of time, the "tempestivity of time."

I am in sympathy with Scott Elledge's impatient declaration that Milton had no "identity crisis," for it is quite true that "he seems always to have known who he was and what he would do," and it is also true that he sought the realization of his ideals with passionate persistence.[19] Yet there remain two periods of exceptional turmoil in the poet's life, which if they are not "crises" in the fashionable sense of the word are nevertheless circumstances that threaten *integritas*, that require searching self-scrutiny, and that almost inevitably promote readjustment of intellectual principles. Clearly the first must be acknowledged to be the marriage of 1642.

In the summer of 1639 Milton returns from the Continent ambitious to write. Exhilarated by the triumphs of his reception among the literati of his revered Italy, he immediately begins to survey English and Biblical history for suitable subjects, even proposes to himself versions of "Adam unparadised." But then he is drawn by circumstances into the pamphlet wars, taking the side of his respected tutor, Thomas Young, and experiences, though only through the prosaic labors of his "left hand," a sense of useful vocation under God and, doubtless, a new sense of identity as a member of the group that he at first envisaged as the elect company, those who were to constitute the community of saints and found the New Jerusalem in England's green and pleasant land. Milton had not only allowed himself to be committed to action; he had entrusted his sense of self to a public cause and public group, doing precisely what many artists, like Gide, have feared and avoided. Yet when he reluctantly responded (in prose), not having yet completed the "full circle of [his] private studies," to the occasion of the pamphlet wars, his poetic ambitions, suddenly released, ring out above the "noises and hoarse disputes" as Milton again and again "covenants" with his "knowing reader," promising but always deferring, even when there was (as Ernest Sirluck has carefully demonstrated) time and leisure, the poem "doctrinal and exemplary to a nation."[20] By his own account prose is that cool element, agitated only with his "left hand"; he is the would-be but frustrated poet, the reluctant pamphleteer, and his poetic plans continually interrupt even the strident polemics of *Reason of Church Government, Reformation in England, Animadversions,* and *Apology for Smectymnuus.* Then, and at long last, after a year of pamphleteering, he and his conscience are free—to fulfill his "covenant" with the "knowing reader" and return to his destined task. But when action was not reaction in response to circumstance, Milton apparently neglected his reiterated insistence on rational choice ("Reason is but choosing") and allowed himself to be actuated by the "intimate impulse" that motivates the protagonist of *Samson Agonistes.*

Although Milton finally has the leisure to resume his long-deferred poetic labors, he has also come to the conclusion, in the *Apology for Smectymnuus,* that there is, after all, a useful distinction to be made between virginity and chastity (a distinction by no means clear in *Comus* or even in *Christian Doctrine*) and that therefore "marriage must not be called a defilement." In 1642, "about Whitsuntide it was, or a little after," records Edward Phillips (his syntax betraying his amused bemusement at his uncle's uncharacteristic activities), "he took a journey into the country; no body about him certainly knowing the reason, or that it was any more than a journey of recreation; after a month's stay, home he returns a married man that went out a bachelor. . . ." As the anonymous biographer wittily notes, perhaps saying a good deal more than he entirely intended, Milton had acted in accordance with his "practice of not wasting that precious talent."[21] The future poet had committed his sense of self not only to the Presbyterians but also to the daughter of a Royalist.

The equilibrist maintained his balanced contraries, his communal and matrimonial solidarities, for only a moment. He soon discovered that *"New Presbyter* is but *Old Priest* writ Large" and that his helpmeet fit was Dalila, he himself having been forced "to grind in the mill of an undelighted and servil copulation" (*Works*, III, ii, 403). Isolated from his wife, Milton wrote the divorce pamphlets, which in turn left him alienated from the Presbyterians with whom he had just aligned himself. He was once more alone with his sense of secret inviolacy; he had succumbed to the temptation to act, and God's poet could not fail to have wondered whether "all is ... as ever" or how things looked from the eternal vantage of his "great task-maisters eye." His sense of *integritas* threatened, Milton may have begun to question his fitness for the sacred vocation of poet-priest; the success of the Nativity Ode had indicated that the poet's lips could be purified by holy fire, but the failure of "The Passion" had made it equally evident that divine inspiration might be taken as well as given. The tremendous efflorescence of prose during these years obscures two suggestive facts: that Milton wrote no verse that was not in some sense "occasional" (sixteen sonnets, a few occasional pieces, paraphrases of two groups of Psalms) and that he actually had the leisure to write the poetry he professed himself eager to produce. Despite his protestations, the labors of his "left hand" seem to have been only part of the reason for Milton's poetic inactivity. And if Milton had found it necessary to break his "covenant" with the "knowing reader," it may be that he had also found himself breaking a covenant (vow of virginity?) with himself and his God. About "Whitsuntide it was ..."

Painful introspection, perhaps even before Mary's failure to return, must have cruelly disabused Milton of at least two principles he had held and advocated—that the proper life might be achieved through the adoption of the "one right [ecclesiastical] discipline" and through the exercise of natural "reason." The Lady of *Comus*, protected by the "hidden strength" of chastity, had been victorious in the trial of temptation, but the Lady of Christ's had been less fortunate. In *Doctrine and Discipline of Divorce* Milton observes that life with a helpmeet unfit "is less pain to conjecture than to have experience" and explains that even the "soberest and best governed men" may err,

> that for all the wariness can be used, it may yet befall a discreet man to be mistaken in his choice... ; and who knows not that the bashful muteness of a virgin may ofttimes hide all the unliveliness and natural sloth which is really unfit for conversation? ... And lastly, it is not strange though many who have spent their youth chastely are in some things not so quick-sighted, while they haste too eagerly to light the nuptial torch....[22]

Even so. Although the divorce tracts afforded Milton the opportunity to objectify, even to justify, his feelings on the level of principle, God's poet could not have failed to question the meaning of the talent it is death to hide, and it will be a long time before we again hear of a poem "doctrinal and exemplary to a nation."

If only to beg a question or two, we may for the sake of convenience toy with an hypothesis suggested by Edmund Wilson's *The Wound and the Bow*—that the artist, like Sophocles' Philoctetes, possesses in compensation for his incurable wound an invincible talent. To consider two examples, not in the way of proof but of illustration, I think first of *Elegia Quinta: In Adventus Veris*:

> Munere veris adest, iterumque vigescit ab illo
> (Quis putet?) atque aliquod iam sibi poscit opus.

So the poet wittily describes the return, with the return of spring, of his poetic powers in lines alluding to Ovid (*Amores* 3.7), who has been describing a sexual round with his mistress; at first the Latin poet's members, *languidiora rosa*, lie there like languid roses, but then (*quae nunc ecce!*) his sexual vigor returns.[23] But like the return of poetic potency? Or think of *Elegia Prima* (to Diodati), in which the virgin finds herself surprised by the strange fire within; in which maidens dance past, like stars breathing soft flames. The seductive cheeks, the golden nets of waving tresses—all provocative, all Ovidian pleasantries. *Collaque bis vivi Pelopis quae brachia vincant.* These ladies have necks superior to the limbs of Pelops, who lived twice because the gods, as Ovid tells us in *Metamorphoses* VI, reassembled him after his dismemberment; unable to locate all his limbs, they provided the young man with an ivory prosthesis. The young poet wittily says that the necks of the young ladies were as white and beautiful as ivory, but the form of the compliment may be thought to betray the dual regard in which Milton at times, like Samson and Adam at times, held women—creatures simultaneously desirable and dangerous.

It is not for nothing that the poetic exemplar in the early poems is Orpheus, potent singer dismembered by the Maenads, "Down the swift Hebrus to the Lesbian shore." Odysseus must at cost escape being calypsoed in the navel of the sea. As Aeneas dawdles over Dido, Vergil takes care that we observe the building stop on the walls of Carthage, symbolizing the cessation of the activity that must at last engross Aeneas—to found the walls of the New Troy. Shakespeare's Cleopatra unmans Antony even in play as she dresses him in her tiaras and brandishes his sword Phillipan. We do not need Freud to inform us, though Freud tells it eloquently and compellingly, that members of the opposite sex may find opposites in their opposites—fear and desire, *odi et amo*.

One way to avoid loss of limb and to insure poetic potency would be to embrace the gift of Pauline virginity, for in one of its aspects accepting the gift exemplifies an age-old psychological maneuver— the leaden rule of the psyche that specifies that it is better to do first unto oneself what others may do unto one. It may well be that we do not want to assume with Ernest Sirluck that at one point Milton entered into a covenant with his God, vowing celibacy while dedicating himself to the role of poet-prophet, but we must, I believe, agree that there is no mistaking the exceptional, even obsessive, importance of chastity to the young poet and pamphleteer.[24] Charges of having frequented the bordelloes provokes a rhapsodic digression in the pamphleteer, ranging from the high mysteries of Plato and Paul to St. John in Patmos' praise of those, not "defiled" by women, who follow the Lamb.

And much earlier, in 1634 and 1637, Milton's concern with extreme forms of chastity threatens the artistic integrity of *Comus*. It seems pretty clear that the masque started out as a celebration of Christian virtue in general, of the "crown that Virtue gives" to those, like Lady Alice and her two brothers, who long for the "Golden Key" that "opes the Palace of Eternity." As Milton saw Christian virtue at this time, based largely on his reading of Plato in light of the Bible (particularly Paul and James), it included resistance to temptation or "trial by contrary," freedom through obedience, and temperance rather than abstinence; but these elements have been overshadowed for most readers by the speeches on chastity, which in the mouth of the Elder Brother echo Plato in the philosopher's more dualistic moments.[25] Although chastity may be felicitously attributed to the Lady (her parents would hope for no less), the force of the poet's pronouncements must have struck even the Renaissance audience as excessive. At one point (11. 462–63) the Elder Brother even seems to want us to believe that chastity confers "by degrees" immortality on the body.

In the Trinity MS there appears an extraordinary passage that was cut from the Bridgewater MS or stage copy.[26] In part an opulent soliloquy in the manner of Shakespeare, in part what I am tempted to regard as an example of the psychopathology of artistic life:

>   A thousand fantasies
> Begin to throng into my memory,
> Of calling shapes and beck'ning shadows dire,
> And airy tongues that syllable men's names
> On Sands and Shores and desert Wildernesses.

And then:

>   These thoughts may startle well, but not astound
>   The virtuous mind, that ever walks attended
>   By a strong siding champion Conscience.
>   O welcome pure-ey'd Faith, white-handed Hope,
>   Thou hov'ring Angel girt with golden wings,
>   And thou unblemish't form of Chastity,
>   I see ye visibly. . . .

Although Inigo Jones, with the resources of the Court, would have had no difficulty in staging all this, sophisticated "machines," to hover an angel or to fly a countertenor, were doubtless harder to come by at the Lord President's castle in Wales—the poet gives Lawes an option, "I can fly or I can run." And the lines were indeed cut from the first production. But in any case it is difficult to avoid the implication that Milton has, as Joyce would say, befrauded himself, for what may have been impossible to stage in Wales also verges on blasphemy in England. M. M. Ross caustically observes: Faith, Hope and Chastity—and the greatest of these is Chastity![27] Although it is almost impossible to suppose that Milton remained unconscious of the implications of the passage (it elevates a natural virtue to the level of grace, displacing the most important of the three theological virtues), the poet, apparently without reflection and certainly without revision, restored the passage in the quarto of 1637.

And the most significant addition to the quarto—present in neither the original Trinity MS nor the stage copy—lends further credence to the supposition that chastity possessed, for Milton at this time, some overwhelming personal significance. During the debate between Comus and the Lady that provides the intellectual focus for the masque, the argument proceeds, with one crucial exception, in clearly-defined stages. Both parties to the debate assume "Nature" as norm, and Comus begins by maintaining that the Lady ignores the "bounties" of "Nature," so that we should "live like Nature's bastards, not her sons."[28] This, the first stage in the argument, occupies lines 706–36: the adversary's point is that the

Lady practices "lean and sallow Abstinence," which is to say, no use of Nature at all. The second stage (11.737–55) follows logically from the first, and it is, again, entirely traditional. In proper *carpe diem* manner Comus urges the Lady not to be coy, not to "let slip time, like a neglected rose": the adversary's point is that the Lady believes in that empty but "vaunted name Virginity," that is, in no use of (sexual) Nature at all. But the Lady has been trained up in the best schools of deliberative oratory. To the adversary's first point, that in the manner of the Stoic and the Cynic she practices abstinence, the Lady with impeccable propriety opposes the "holy dictate of spare Temperance"; that is, she counters the accusation that she does not use Nature at all by maintaining that she uses Nature rightly. But then her oratorical skills desert her. In 1634 the Lady had no reply to Comus' second point—an oversight in itself sufficiently odd to anyone familiar with Renaissance schooling in logic and rhetoric.

Milton had of course ready to hand the materials for a proper reply to the second taunt, for Renaissance thinkers carefully distinguished chastity from virginity. Spenser's Britomart represents the virtue of Chastity—symbolized, in those pre-Freudian days, by her lance—but her quest is for a man. And chastity, as the speeches of the Elder Brother testify, already made up part of the masque of Christian virtue that Milton had written. It is the logical answer. The Lady had already opposed temperance to abstinence. Now she should, logically, counter virginity, or no use of (sexual) Nature, with chastity, the right use of (sexual) Nature. But she fails to reply, though her creator has her asseverate that she hates (ll. 760–61)

> when vice can bolt her arguments,
> And virtue has no tongue to check her pride.

And when, in 1637, Milton finally gave the Lady leave to reply, he added twenty lines that begin with the "Sun-clad power of Chastity" but advert immediately, without transition or distinction, to the "sage/ And serious doctrine of Virginity," that "sublime notion and high mystery." (To Sabrina, in whom there seems to be an equal admixture of virginity and divine grace, belongs the final allegorical victory.) There can be no mistaking the religious fervor evoked in the poet by the high mystery of virginity; it is sufficiently powerful to disrupt the logical coherence of the debate, and it helps to explain why this masque of Christian virtue has been read as a masque of chastity or even a masque of virginity. The trinity of

Faith, Hope, and Chastity, together with the final stage of the debate, would appear to be slips of the tongue that suggest the possibility of a covenant of celibacy, or at the least point to psychic perturbations of considerable strength. Whatever degree of confusion existed in Milton's mind at the time, the matter is resolved, but only momentarily, when in 1642 he contracted a liaison with Mary Powell and asserted that "marriage must not be called a defilement." Virginity could no longer be a personal ideal; he did not possess the Pauline gift. Did then the failure of the marriage indicate divine disfavor? the loss of the talent it is death to hide? Perhaps not, if only the divorce pamphlets could be used to reconstruct the universe on the basis of a theological blueprint derived from the true interpretation of Scripture...

The second major crisis—total blindness—occurs nearly a decade later, in late 1651 or, more probably, in early 1652—and was accompanied, we must suppose, by some depression. But by 1654 at the latest, as the great letter to Leonard Philaras indicates, Milton had achieved patience—that most difficult and most necessary of Christian virtues—in affliction:

> And so, whatever ray of hope also there may be for me from your famous physician, all the same, as in a case quite incurable, I prepare and compose myself accordingly; and my frequent thought is that, since many days of darkness, as the Wise Man warns us, are destined for every one, my darkness hitherto, by the singular kindness of God, amid rest and studies, and the voices and greetings of friends, has been much easier to bear than that deathly one. [And] what should prevent one from resting likewise in the belief that his eyesight lies not in his eyes alone, but enough for all purposes in God's leading and providence? Verily, while only He looks out for me and provides for me, as He doth, leading me and leading me forth as with His hand through my whole life, I shall willingly, since it has seemed good to Him, have given my eyes their long holiday.
>
> (*Works*, XII, 71)

In the *Second Defence*, also 1654, Milton denies the Royalist charge that God had blinded him for his wickedness, yet even in his righteous anger he confesses, "I have accurately examined my conduct, and scrutinized my soul," before concluding: "I call thee, O God, the searcher of hearts, to witness, that I am not conscious... of having committed any enormity which might deservedly have marked me out as a fit object for such a calamitous visitation."[29]

Although we need not imagine the tortured introspections of a Bunyan, we must suppose that blindness, accompanied by the death of his wife and son, occasioned both pain and painful self-examination. Sonnet XIX records, in great verse, the (theological) form—affliction, despair, patience—of introspection; he had "accurately examined [his] conduct, and scrutinized [his] soul."

Although there have been several attempts to date the sonnet in 1655, I am assuming on internal grounds that it was either written some short while after total blindness or, at the very least, no later than the Letter to Philaras or the *Second Defence*.[30] The sonnet pivots on the biblical allusions of line three (Matthew 25:14-30 is invariably cited, but equally relevant is that other parable of the talents in 18:23-34), line seven (John 9:4), and line eleven (Matthew 11:29-30)—all of which lend additional resonance to the motifs of commerce and light. The sonnet is Petrarchan, the sense breaking across the division between octave and sestet in one of the accepted variations from the usual Italian manner; but the sense is also "variously drawn out from one Verse into another" in the manner peculiar to Milton's mature poetry. The subject of the main clause of the first sentence appears only in line eight:

> When I consider how my light is spent,
>   Ere half my days, in this dark world and wide,
>   And that one Talent which is death to hide,
>   Lodg'd with me useless, though my Soul more bent
> To serve therewith my Maker, and present
>   My true account, lest he returning chide;
>   'Doth God exact day-labor, light denied,'
>   I fondly ask. . . .

This quite extraordinary specimen of syntax, pointing perhaps to the simultaneity of events in the mind of the poet, requires the reader to gather, and "patiently" hold, a series of impressions that culminate in the foolish, almost blasphemous, question. Meaning has been delayed until the proper moment—but then we are told that it is not the proper meaning, even told that what we had awaited patiently may not, after all, have "occurred" in the ordinary way:

>   But patience to prevent
>   That murmur, soon replies, 'God doth not need
>   Either man's work or his own gifts; who best
>   Bear his mild yoke, they serve him best; his State

Is Kingly. Thousands at his bidding speed
And post o'er Land and Ocean without rest:
They also serve who only stand and wait.'

Whether we take "prevent" in its modern sense or in the Latinate
meaning ("come before") preferred by Milton, it will be clear that
"patience" did not in fact manage to "prevent" the "murmur." As
Milton himself allows, "impatience under the divine decrees" constitutes "a temptation to which the Saints themselves are at times
liable" (*Works*, XVII, 69). The foolish murmur, held in suspension
with the account of affliction and near despair, lies in evidence on
the page before us and testifies, eloquently if obliquely, to the inner
conflict undergone by the poet—presented indeed as though he
were just now undergoing it.

Poetic talent (I am assuming that at this time in his life Milton
had poetry mainly though not exclusively in mind) is linked neither
to sexuality in general nor to virginity in particular, as in the early
Milton; but to a kind of light seemingly now denied. And the poem
has for its subject the movement from the active life ("more bent/
To serve") to the "mild yoke" of the contemplative life ("they also
serve"), from murmuring under affliction to the acquiring of
Christian patience, that virtue displayed in the Letter to Philaras
and defined in *Christian Doctrine* as "that whereby we acquiesce in
the promises of God, through a confident reliance on his divine
providence, power, and goodness, and bear inevitable evils with
equanimity, as the dispensation of the supreme Father, and sent
for our good" (*Works,* XVII, 67). Even if we acknowledge that "he
hath led me, and brought me into darkness, but not into light"
(Lamentations 3:2), we may be sustained in the assurance that "the
Lord is good unto them that wait for him, to the soul that seeketh
him. It is good that a man should both hope and quietly wait for the
salvation of the Lord. It is good for a man that he bear the yoke . . ."
(3:25–27). As Granger puts it, in terms of the parable that appears
to have meant the most to Milton, a Christian must exercise patience in order to grasp the "fit opportunity," neither anticipating
the moment nor allowing it to pass, for otherwise "with the vn-
profitable seruant we hid our talent in the ground."[31] Although
Milton proposes for himself the contemplative life, the patient
bearing of the "mild yoke," his phrasing in the last line leaves open
the possibility that God's poet may, like the eyeless Samson, be once
more guided to his true vocation. In Milton "stand" possesses special

resonances, among them that to stand in acquiescent obedience usually involves, as with Abdiel, the active attempt to stand against something else; and "wait" may mean not only to wait dutifully in attendance *on* but also to wait patiently *for* (a sense of renewed calling under God).[32]

That Milton's patience, his waiting *for*, received one of its rewards, seems evident from Sonnet XXII, which assuredly must be dated some three years after the poet became totally blind and (I would argue) some two or three years after Sonnet XIX. XXII lacks the tone of impassioned struggle that informs the earlier sonnet, displaying instead a view of self that may be seen, according to one's temperament and inclination, as righteous pride or self-righteous complacency:

> Cyriack, this three years' day these eyes, though clear
>> To outward view of blemish or of spot,
>> Bereft of light thir seeing have forgot;
>> Nor to their idle orbs doth sight appear
> Of Sun or Moon or Star throughout the year,
>> Or man or woman. Yet I argue not
>> Against heav'n's hand or will, nor bate a jot
>> Of heart or hope; but still bear up and steer
> Right onward. What supports me, dost thou ask?
>> The conscience, Friend, to have lost them overplied
>> In liberty's defense, my noble task,
> Of which all Europe talks from side to side.
>> This thought might lead me through the world's vain mask
>> Content though blind, had I no better guide.

The contrast with XIX would be hard to overemphasize. The earlier sonnet begins in affliction, centers in conflict and rebuke, and ends in acknowledgement of limitations—a qualified resolution achieved by the poet's separating himself from the active saints. XXII, on the other hand, begins with separation, with the conscious juggling of alternatives: "of blemish or of spot . . . of Sun or Moon or Star . . . or man or woman . . . hand or will . . . of heart or hope." It centers in the joining of alternatives ("bear up *and* steer") and moves resolutely toward its two-fold resolution—renewed faith in active virtue sustained by faith in the "better guide." (Psalm 32:8: "I will instruct thee and teach thee in the way which thou shalt go: I will guide thee with mine eye.") In the earlier poem the poet had begun to "argue . . . against heav'n's hand," had begun a foolish question. In XXII it is Skinner who questions, and the answer comes not from a personified "patience" but from the poet, conscious of the fame of his "noble task" and of the favor of the "better guide." "All is . . . as ever." No longer will he merely seek to "bear his mild yoke," he will "bear up" (revised in the MS from "attend"); no longer "stand and wait" but "steer/ Right onward," as though now ready to "post o'er" the "Ocean without rest." Sonnet XXII turns not on the virtue of patience but on another, though related, Christian virtue.

In *Christian Doctrine* Milton distinguishes two virtues that are "exercised in the resistance to, or the endurance of evil"—*fortitudo et patientia*. True patience must be distinguished from the hypocrisy that "voluntarily inflicts upon itself unnecessary evils" and "stoical apathy"; but patience remains, pre-eminently, the delaying virtue, the virtue of waiting *for*. "Patience consists in the *endurance* [my italics; *perferens* is analogous to *patiens*] of misfortunes and injuries." "Fortitude," on the other hand, "is chiefly conspicuous in repelling evil" (*maxime in malis propulsandis*); and so in the sonnet on Cromwell Milton speaks of being "guided by Faith and matchless fortitude." Not only is it the more active virtue: "The great pattern of fortitude is our Savior Jesus Christ, throughout the whole of his life, and in his death" (*Works*, XVII, 246–49). Sonnet XIX explicitly exhibits the virtue of patience, whereas Sonnet XXII implicitly displays the virtue of fortitude. And the problem is to imagine how the poet managed the transition—identical to the one he himself imagined for his hero Samson—from the one to the other of these distinguishable, though related, virtues of the afflicted Christian.

As with the marriage of 1642 and the defection of Mary, the pain and frustration of blindness occasioned self-scrutiny and required the invocation of new principles: Milton needed a rationale, not only to justify himself against Royalist charges but also to provide a basis for future action. The *Second Defence* reveals that Milton had found, during the years of pamphleteering, at least one echo of spirit, one mirror of justification, outside himself—Oliver Cromwell, in whom the future epic poet fancied he detected the lineaments of himself. Cromwell must be defended not only in the interests of the "commonwealth alone, but myself in particular":

> He grew up in the privacy of his own family, and till his age was quite mature and settled, which he also passed in private, was chiefly known for his strict attendance upon the purer worship, and for his

integrity of life. He had cherished his confidence in God, he had nourished his great spirit in silence, for some extraordinary times (*summa . . . tempora*).

(Works, VIII, 213)

Cromwell, that is, had grown up much like Milton—and much like the Jesus of *Paradise Regained*: all awaited the *summa . . . tempora* or moment on the pinnacle. But the full exercise of the talent it is death to hide had to await the freedom that comes through obedience, the freedom derived from the submergence of the poet's identity in that of the Holy Spirit, the Celestial Patroness "who deigns"

> Her nightly visitation unimplor'd
> And dictates to me slumb'ring, or inspires
> Easy my unpremeditated Verse;

for otherwise he may fail and fall with Bellerophon—"If all be mine,"

> Not Hers who brings it nightly to my Ear.

(PL, IX, 21 ff.)

Having decided, a decade earlier, that marriage cannot be considered a defilement, Milton on the occasion of his blindness now examines his conduct and scrutinizes his soul before letting the readers of the *Second Defence* know that the "loss of sight . . . cannot be considered as a judicial punishment." We are to remember Tiresias and Phineus, who though blind nevertheless saw; Timoleon of Corinth, Appius Claudius, Caecilius Metellus—culminating in the myopic figures of Scripture. It is "evident that the patriarch Isaac, than whom no man ever enjoyed more of the divine regard, lived blind for many years; and perhaps also his son Jacob, who was equally an object of the divine benevolence." Blindness, far from being a sign of the "divine displeasure," no longer even requires the exercise of Christian patience or of fortitude. It has become, by an extraordinary inversion, inseparable from divine favor:

> And, indeed, in my blindness, I enjoy in no inconsiderable degree the favor of the Deity, who regards me with more tenderness and compassion in proportion as I am able to behold nothing but himself. Alas! for him who insults me; who maligns me merits public execration! For the divine law not only shields me from injury, but

almost renders me too sacred to attack; not indeed so much from the privation of my sight, as from the overshadowing of those heavenly wings which seem to have occasioned this obscurity. . . .[33]

Out of the paradox (2 Cor. 12:9, Heb. 11:34) that strength resides in weakness Milton develops the doctrine of the inner light. He prefers his blindness, which "keeps from [his] view only the colored surfaces of things," to the intellectual blindness of his adversary. "O! that I may thus be perfected by feebleness, and irradiated by obscurity!" "There is, as the apostle has remarked, a way to strength through weakness. . . . In proportion as I am blind, I shall more clearly see." Like the regenerate Samson, who is with "inward eyes illuminated," Milton himself now possesses "an interior light, more precious and more pure."

He is now one with "those wise and ancient bards whose misfortunes the gods are said to have compensated by superior endowments." And we have arrived with the poetic seer at the invocation to the third book of *Paradise Lost*:

> nor sometimes forget
> Those other two equall'd with me in Fate,
> So were I equall'd with them in renown,
> Blind *Thamyris* and blind *Maeonides*,
> And *Tiresias* and *Phineus* Prophets old.

The artist remains the man with the wound and the bow, his "dismemberment" having been compensated by the superior endowment of poetic talent; but blindness, not virginity, has become the precondition for the use of the talent it is death to hide. It is the mark of Milton's renewed sense of vocation, of the special powers conferred by "supernatural renovation," the mark of those who have fought greatly in the wars of truth and dedicated themselves to the "gathering up limb by limb" of the dismembered body of the "virgin Truth."[34] It is the symbol, once it is translated into a sign and seal of divine favor, that guarantees the full and harmonious release of those powers that issue in a poem doctrinal and exemplary to a nation. He had been long choosing but now he need no longer delay—the divine "opportunity" or "tempestivity of time," so it appeared, had come. An "interior light, more precious and more pure," showed God's poet that "all is . . . as ever."

By his "three & twentith yeere" Milton had translated the psychic tendency to defer action, to prepare for action while postponing action, into the theological vocabulary of *kairos* or "fit opportunity." The relation of "all is" to "as ever," of Time to Eternity, deeply concerned the poet throughout his life. And it became an informing principle of his art, most obviously perhaps in *Paradise Regained*, where the personal rationalization of delay, of awaiting the fullness of Time, becomes the poetic rationale for Christ's puzzling behavior. "What dost thou in this world?" asks the frustrated Satan, as Jesus patiently awaits the "tempestivity of time" on the pinnacle when He will simply do what Adam, "sufficient to have stood, though free to fall," failed to do. In *Paradise Regained* the temptation to act has become precisely that—a temptation; and the greatest heroism, as Jesus demonstrates, is (reversing the order of the last words of Sonnet XIX) to "wait" and "stand."

CHAPTER VI

Paradise Regained: *Waiting to Stand*

There is an important sense in which our problems with *Paradise Regained* lie in us rather than in the poem, for we are the fallen and therefore liable to satanic impatience. Roger Matthew might as well have had in mind the modern reader when in the seventeenth century he complained that there seemed to be no way "to rayne backe the outrunners of time in this luxuriant age of dingthrifts of time." "How many," he asks, "lay about them, as if all their exhibition this way were flong them by talents, and therefore spend it with like profusenesse . . . till they turne starke bankrupt for time and grace."[1] Failing to recognize that all time is "as ever" if one has the "grace to use it so," fallen men likewise fail to discern the sense in which men of talent may "also serve who only stand and wait" for the "tempestivity of time." Even the best of Christians, the Milton of *Animadversions* or the "new-baptiz'd" of *Paradise Regained*, may presume too much in relation to Eternity and may expect the imminent establishment of The Kingdom within Time. The reader of *Paradise Regained* keeps expecting something to happen; and when it doesn't—indeed it does not—he grows as restive as Satan, himself like a "swarm of flies in vintage time" (IV, 15).

Marjorie Hope Nicolson, having threshed her way across acres of scholarly jargon, harvests the central datum and states it with her customary clarity. "Milton faced a basic problem familiar in all classical epic and drama." Since the end of the fable is known, "there is no possibility of [the kind of] suspense" to which "we are accustomed in novel or drama." Milton in *Samson* employed "vari-

148

ous devices inherited from the classics" as substitutes for suspense, but in *Paradise Regained* he produced a "protracted debate, often arid and barren, in which neither disputant shows much emotion." Although Miss Nicolson tries hard to find some "suspense" in the characterizations of Satan and Jesus, she reflects literary opinion current since the late seventeenth century in confessing that she is simply "unsympathetic with much of *Paradise Regained*."[2] According to Phillips, *Paradise Regained* was "generally censured to be much inferior" to *Paradise Lost*, but Milton, who recognized the purest distillate when he had produced it, could not "hear with patience any such thing when related to him."[3] (Dr. Johnson, distorting a trifle for the sake of wit, implies that Milton strongly preferred *Paradise Regained* to *Paradise Lost* and observes that, "however it happened, [Milton] had this prejudice, and had it to himself.") Modern habits of reading, derived mainly from the novel and the drama, make it even more difficult for us to become the "fit audience" of the brief epic; instead we look, vainly, for "action," "tension," "climax," and "suspense."

Given the refractory nature of the materials it is perhaps understandable that scholars should have sought refuge in the Bible, though it seems strange that in an age shadowed by the death of God the Word has been given priority over the poet's words. Although the end of Day I coincides with the end of Book I—establishing balanced structure and adequate sense of closure—the remainder of the brief epic appears to lack comparable symmetries, either in the disposition of its temporal and spatial elements or in the arrangement of the temptations. Bethinking himself of the biblical three temptations, Allan H. Gilbert proposed in 1916 that all but the first and last confrontations ought to be considered a single temptation under the rubric "kingdoms." This proposal, accepted by James Holly Hanford in 1918, has persisted with modifications, most notably perhaps in A. S. P. Woodhouse, who observes that the "first temptation, to distrust, is balanced by the third, to presumption, the extreme of defect balanced by the extreme of excess"; and that within the "second" temptation (the "kingdoms") there are two "contemplative" temptations framing an "active pursuit of glory." Noting that in this scheme the "significant breaks are not at the endings of books," Woodhouse found himself compelled to draw the inference that Milton must have made the four-book arrangement "entirely arbitrary" to avoid the appearance of mechanical symmetry.[4] Gary D. Hamilton, uneasy in the presence of this final *reductio* of Gilbert's argument, has attempted to shift attention from the temptations themselves to the Son's responses, which may then be taken to indicate His "growth" in the virtues that Michael in *Paradise Lost* (XII, 575–87) cites as the basis for the "Paradise within"; in Book I the Son "adds faith, in Book II temperance; in Book III he adds patience, and in Book IV he exhibits 'the sum of wisdom.'" Although I have trouble on occasion in allocating the virtues in this manner to each book, Hamilton's argument at least makes clear the need to extricate the poem from its scriptural sources.[5]

Milton himself might approve the endeavor, for despite the veneration he accorded the Sacred Scriptures, he held unequivocally to the extreme view that "under the Gospel we possess, as it were, a twofold Scripture; one external, which is the written word, and the other internal, which is the Holy Spirit [and] that which is internal, and the peculiar possession of each believer, is far superior . . ." (*Works*, XIV, 273 and 275). The faulty transmission of scriptural texts actually attests to the pre-eminence of the inner light, for "it is difficult to conjecture the purpose of Providence in committing the writings of the New Testament to such uncertain and variable guardianship, unless it were to teach us by this very circumstance that the Spirit which is given to us is a more certain guide than Scripture" (*Works*, XIV, 277 and 279). The biblical sources for *Paradise Regained* must be accounted extremely important, but to de-emphasize the "Spirit which is given" to the poet and to adopt without qualification the three-fold divisions of Matthew and Luke deflects attention from the main problems while substituting our scriptural interpretations for those of Milton. By this sleight-of-hand in source study we find three main temptations in *Paradise Regained*—and then begin to subdivide ingeniously.[6]

It is of course true that Milton deals with the temptation to turn stones into bread; that the temptation of the kingdoms may be thought of as subsuming under one head Parthia, Rome, Athens, as well as Israel; and that the final temptation, on the pinnacle, by this mode of (gospel) reckoning makes up three . . . But it also makes the banquet scene somehow redundant, it finds no secure place for the temptation (to riches) that immediately follows in Book II; it leaves equally anomalous the temptation to glory that opens Book III; and it contradicts explicit statements that *all* the "kingdoms" have been offered before Satan turns to the learning that was Greece—not as a political "kingdom" but as the source of wisdom. Matthew and Luke do indeed provide three of the temptations, John much of the doctrinal ambience. But the context that lends shape and cogency to the characterizations and to the narrative derives rather from a paradox inherent in early Christianity that was intensified for Milton by the events of his personal life and the course of the Puritan Revolution.

The early Christians had inherited from the writers of the Old Testament not only the contrast between the Time of the Lord (*'olam*, generally *aion* in the Septuagint) and the time of the creatures but also the compelling notion of the "two ages." The period between Creation and Judgment, what Milton calls the "Race of time," constitutes "this age" or "the present age." It contrasts with the "coming age," which shall be ushered in by the Messiah. In the New Testament this age-to-come reappears, transmogrified into the "Kingdom of God" associated with Jesus the Christ. Matthew 10 and 11—perhaps interpolations dating from after the destruction of Jerusalem in 70 AD—permit the inference that Jesus supposed divine judgment to be imminent, probably to be expected not too long after the imprisonment of His Forerunner, John the Baptist. The delay of judgment may have encouraged Jesus, who at his Baptism seems already to have begun to think of himself as the Messiah, to identify himself also with the Suffering Servant, the Man of Sorrows, of Second Isaiah. The writers of the Gospels and the later exegetes were sure of it, for it was written that it might be fulfilled. And if John the Baptist were indeed a latter-day Elijah, then the insinuation might well have entered the mind of Jesus—it was at least entertained by those who wrote of Him—that apocalyptic hopes could be fulfilled only by the sacrifice of His life after the death of The Forerunner. In this way Jesus would inaugurate the Kingdom of God by assuming the role of suffering and death assigned the Man of Sorrows by Isaiah.[7] (Jesus might be allowed to adopt the role of Suffering Servant, along with the role of Stricken Shepherd in Zechariah, without necessarily "following" John the Baptist; but Paul evidently felt otherwise.) Amos and Hosea had already expressed doubts about the older rituals when Jeremiah questioned the efficacy of external symbols, even the Tables of the Law; and Isaiah, at least in the eyes of later Jews and early Christians, had abandoned faith in a literal Israel, politically organized and geographically bounded, and had transferred the "national" aspirations, thoroughly idealized, to the future in a kind of spiritual diaspora. In accepting the destiny of the Suffering Servant, Jesus dies in effect, for Luke and others, the death of Jewish Israel itself, which was then to be resurrected triumphantly by the Gospels and Paul as Christianity—the religion of the eternal and universal Kingdom of God.

Since Jesus had established a connection between His coming and the Kingdom of God (Mark 14:62 and elsewhere), the future, the "coming age," becomes in a very specific sense part of the "present age." Those apt to discern the "signs of the times" recognize that for the true believer the future Kingdom of God has been incorporated into the present, permitting the true Christian a taste of what is to come (Hebrews 6:5) while simultaneously acknowledging that the "last days" have already begun (Acts 2:16–17). This complicated state of affairs, in which the Kingdom of God is here and yet to come, engenders more or less logical elaborations in later writers: the kingdom is spiritual, a "paradise within thee, happier far"; the kingdom is the invisible city of God, the *corpus mysticum* of true saints, imperfectly reflected in the society of saints and the visible church; the kingdom is *regnum christi* on earth, the result of radical reform of the church; the kingdom is the millennial reign of Christ on earth; and the kingdom is the eschatological Kingdom of Glory.[8] Yet later rationalizations could never fully remove the element of paradox that stems, ultimately, from the belief of the early Christians that the Second Coming, the true establishment of the Kingdom of God, was imminent and from the recognition, on the part of later Christians as they waited and waited and waited, that the end is not yet.[9] Here lies the fundamental reason for the preeminence of patience as a Christian virtue, the fundamental necessity for enduring the "tempestivity of time." The greater hero knows how to play the waiting game.

To put the same theological complication another way, the Incarnation introduces the time of God into the time of man, not merely by manipulating the course of history as with Exodus but by causing deity to live the life of (human) time. The "present age" contains within it, for the space of thirty-three years, the interplay of eternal significances, for Christ has invaded the natural order of time and defined its true meaning and limits by showing that He exists beyond life and death—precisely by submitting knowingly to the life of mortal suffering in time. God, transcending time yet immanent in time, reveals in the mystery of the Incarnation the intersection of the timeless with time. From God's mysteries flow men's paradoxes. To the spiritual paradox that the Christian lives in the world but not for it (Titus 2:12) must be added the temporal paradox that he lives in a present that is future. Although the "present age" continues (until the end of time), the Incarnation establishes the beginning of the "latter days," which is in turn the inauguration of the Kingdom of God that in the "fullness of time" shall be manifest to all at the Second Coming, when Christ, "once offered to bear the sins of many," shall "unto them that look for him . . . appear the second time without sin unto salvation" (Hebrews 9:28).

The Second Book of *Paradise Regained* begins by rendering this paradox of The Kingdom in the situation of the "new-baptiz'd" who, having witnessed the descent of the Dove, expect the imminent Parousia. Their expectations disappointed, they "began to doubt, and doubted many days," whereas at first they had "rejoic'd."

> Our eyes behold
> Messiah certainly now come, so long
> Expected of our Fathers; we have heard
> His words, his wisdom full of grace and truth;
> Now, now, for sure, deliverance is at hand,
> The Kingdom shall to Israel be restor'd. . . .
> (31–36)

But, "for sure" the time is not "now, now"; and in any case they mistake the true significance of the "The Kingdom" that in the course of time shall indeed be "restor'd." God shall in fact, quite in the manner of Milton the poet, "again prolong/ Our expectation" (41–42). As Calvin explains, "Gods hydinge of the times, is not for that hee executeth not hys iudgements euery minute of an houre: but because hee delayeth and prolongeth them. . . ."[10] The apocalyptic fervor of Milton's "new baptiz'd" runs endemic through Christian history, and it was of course not only the early Christians who suffered the reversal of their hopes. Throughout the Middle Ages and the Renaissance—even today—men and women calculate the days remaining until the Latter Day, climb expectant to the top of a suitable mountain to await the Final Cataclysm, only to descend wearily as the sun comes up—still secure in their convictions but once again the victims of faulty arithmetic. As Norman Cohn has demonstrated, the impulse to anticipate the end was quite extraordinarily widespread.[11] Not merely a psychic oddity confined to fringe elements and to the disenfranchised, the surge and resurgence of millennial hopes contaminated Chris-

tianity from the outset and infected many of the best minds in
England, the New Israel of the seventeenth century. The younger
Milton was not immune.

As passages in the early prose attest, Milton began his antiprelati-
cal labors in alliance with the true architects of the New Israel and
in expectation of the Second Coming. In *Animadversions* he proposes to "recount even here without delay the patience and long
suffering that God hath us'd towards our blindnesse and hardnes
time after time," for He "hath yet ever had this Iland under the
speciall indulgent eye of his providence":

> Come therefore O thou that hast the seven starres in thy right
> hand. . . . Every one can say that now certainly thou hast visited this
> land . . . in a time when men had thought thou wast gone up from us
> to the farthest end of the Heavens. . . .
>
> (*Works*, III, i, 145 and 147)

The Latter Day approaches,

> And he that now for haste snatches up a plain ungarnish't present as
> a thanke-offering to thee, which could not bee deferr'd in regard of
> thy so many late deliverances wrought for us one upon another, may
> then perhaps take up a Harp, and sing thee an elaborate Song to
> Generations. [In his exultant mood Milton hopes to sing as a latter-
> day David and Moses.] In that day it shall no more bee said as in
> scorne, this or that was never held so till this present Age, when men
> have better learnt that the times and seasons passe along under thy
> feet, to goe and come at thy bidding. . . ; so thou canst vouchsafe to
> us (though unworthy) as large a portion of thy spirit as thou pleasest;
> for who shall prejudice thy all-governing will? seeing the power of
> thy grace is not past away with the primitive times, as fond and
> faithless men imagine, but thy Kingdome is now at hand, and thou
> standing at the dore.
>
> (*Works*, III, i, 148)

Although Milton never abandoned the conviction that "times and
seasons . . . goe and come at thy bidding," he soon enough came to
realize that once again he would have to exercise patience under
the divine decrees and that the "elaborate Song to Generations,"
itself "deferr'd in regard of" the pamphlet wars, must finally assume another form: it would not be a hymn of praise to the accomplishment of the reformation of Reformation, to the establishment
of the Kingdom of the Saints in "this Iland under the speciall
indulgent eye of his providence." The Kingdom, it turned out, was

not "now at hand," for either the poet or the "new baptiz'd" of *Paradise Regained*; and when the poet came to write his "elaborate Song," it turned out to be a "brief epic" that inculcated the lesson the pamphleteer had had to learn.

The lesson is that of delay, deferment of hopes and aspirations; and to embody it in epic form required the creation of a new kind of hero. I am thinking not so much of the way the poet revalued, and often subverted, the virtues based on the *comitatus* morality of the older epics,[12] but rather of the hero of the world described by Georges Poulet (following Harnack on Luther), which is inhabited by fallen beings who felt they "lived only from instant to instant and by a miracle." Because of the Reformation, "human existence rested no longer in God-the-creator-and-preserver but in God-the-redeemer," with the consequence that the "just man" feels that the "particular moment is joined to an eternal moment." Time, the source of a terror comparable to that of being devoured (*tempus edax rerum*) or of being drowned, remains paradoxically the source of joy for the faithful. Calvin phrases it decisively and eloquently:

> Each moment of faith becomes the foundation of all existence: I see myself continually flowing away: no moment passes without my seeing myself at the point of being engulfed. But since God sustains his elect in such a way that they never sink and drown, I firmly believe that I shall live despite innumerable storms.[13]

The death of the "stream of lyf," as Chaucer's Reeve—in a mood derived from "hooly writ" —reminds us, begins at birth:

> For sikerly, when I was bore, anon
> Deeth drough the tappe of lyf and leet it gon;
> And ever sithe hath so the tappe yronne
> Til that almoost al empty is the tonne.
> The streem of lyf now droppeth on the chymbe.[14]

And the Reformation appears to have intensified what men of the Renaissance already knew—that at their backs time's winged chariot hurried near. As Marvell puts it elsewhere, in the "Calvinist" imagery of inundation:

> Like the vain Curlings of the Watry maze,
> Which in smooth streams a sinking weight does raise;
> So Man, declining alwayes, disappears
> In the weak Circles of increasing Years;
> And his short Tumults of themselves Compose,
> While flowing Time above his Head does close.[15]

Man drowns in time but hopes to be sustained by eternal mandate. Whatever the terms—*chronos* and *kairos*, drowning and sustaining, time and eternity—men of the Renaissance show themselves everywhere conscious of living in divided and dangerous durations, placing great emphasis on the Redeeming as against the Creating God and on those moments when time-bound man seems to catch glimpses of everlastingness.

So that heroism and villainy assume new dimensions. On the one hand,

> The Phlegmatic and Slowe prolongs his day,
> And on Times Wheel sticks like a *Remora*,

while on the other hand,

> those of growth more sudden, and more bold,
> Are hurried hence, as if already old.
> For, there above, They number not as here,
> But weigh to Man the *Geometrick* yeer.[16]

Marvell's elegy at the death of the young Lord Hastings relies on the usual contrasts—between the long but meaningless and the short but significant life, between the earth-measure of human time (*"Geometrick* yeer") and the eternal time-piece by which "they number not as here." The villain, or at any rate the one who lacks heroism, becomes the "Phlegmatic and Slowe," whom we may in the manner of Puttenham (who did not quite get around to this one) denominate The Stirrer. He appears, significantly without a proper name, in Ben Jonson's great Cary-Morison Ode:

> Here's one out-liv'd his Peeres,
> And told forth fourescore yeares;
> He vexed time, aand busied the whole State;
> Troubled both foes, and friends;
> But ever to no ends:
> What did this Stirrer, but die late?

The presence of The Stirrer throws into virtuous relief the exemplary celerity of Morison, whose "life was of Humanitie the Spheare." Although he died young, he "summ'd" the "circle" of perfection; he is not one of those who could, in the words of Sir Thomas Browne, "complaine of immaturitie that die about thirty," for when "all things [were] compleated in [him], [his] age [was] accomplished."[17] Unlike The Stirrer, Morison in his brief life accomplished "All Offices" in "weight, in measure, number, sound," so that "hee stood . . . to the last right end" and, "possest with holy rage," "hee leap'd the present age."[18] Puttenham might have called him The Fore-Shortener, for he resembles Marvell's Cromwell:

> 'Tis he the force of scatter'd Time contracts,
> And in one Year the work of Ages acts.

When Cromwell's "high Grace" accords with "Heavens will," when "all is . . . as ever," we may hope that in "some happy Hour" (*kairos*)

> Fore-shortned Time its useless Course would stay,
> And soon precipitate the latest Day.[19]

But the highest heroism does not belong to The Fore-Shortener.

Herman Melville, meditating on Plutarch's great essay "On the Letter *E I* at Delphi," reproduces in *Pierre,* aptly subtitled "The Ambiguities," part of a lecture by "Plotinus Plinlimmon," who may serve to point up the problems for the hero acting in time but in accord with the eternal will. Plinlimmon, who is a Carlyle-like approximation of three-parts pedant to one-part rhapsode, speculates that "there is a certain most rare order of human souls, which if carefully carried in the body will almost always and everywhere give Heaven's own Truth, with some small grains of variance."

> For peculiarly coming from God, the sole source of that heavenly truth, and the great Greenwich hill and tower from which the universal meridians are far out into infinity reckoned; such souls seem as London sea chronometers (*Greek*, time-namers) which as the London ship floats past Greenwich down the Thames, are accurately adjusted by Greenwich time, and if heedfully kept, will still give that same time, even though carried to the Azores. . . .
>
> Now in an artificial world like ours, the soul of man is further removed from its God and the Heavenly Truth, than the chronometer carried to China, is from Greenwich. And, as that chronometer, if at all accurate, will pronounce it to be 12 o'clock high-noon, when the China local watches say, perhaps, it is 12 o'clock midnight; so the chronometric soul, if in this world true to its great Greenwich in the other, will always, in its so-called intuitions of right and wrong, be contradicting the mere local standards and watch-makers brains of this earth.
>
> Bacon's brains were mere watch-maker's brains; but Christ was a chronometer; and the most exquisitely adjusted and exact one, and the least affected by all terrestrial jarrings, of any that have ever

come to us. And the reason why his teachings seemed folly to the Jews, was because he carried that Heaven's time in Jerusalem time there. Did he not expressly say—My wisdom (time) is not of this world?[20]

The Satan of *Paradise Regained* has "mere watch-maker's brains"— but Jesus is A Chronometer. The heroism of The Fore-shortener and The Chronometer may be contrasted with the dilatory stirrings and flutterings of The Stirrer or The Horologe. The Christian of the Renaissance was, inevitably, a Horologe—that is the condition of fallen men; yet his soul or form yearned for adjustment according to the perfect celestial mechanism, for the grace to make "all is . . . as ever." But to speak strictly there can only be one chronometrical hero, whose heroism must be regarded, so the poet of *Paradise Regained* informs us in his invocation, as "Above Heroic" (I, 15).

Milton in *Christian Doctrine* was sure that there is "in Christ a mutual hypostatic union of two natures, that is to say, of two essences, of two substances, and consequently of two persons," though the "mode of union is unknown to us; and it is best to be ignorant of what God wills should remain unknown" (XV, 271). Milton seems to have been less sure of the consequences of *kenosis*, the "emptying out by the divine nature [of Christ upon assuming flesh] of that which properly belongs to it as divine." For Milton Jesus is "one Christ" and "very man," but "whether he retains his two-fold will and understanding" was a question much controverted. Milton knew from Scripture that Christ, "after having 'emptied himself' . . . might [nevertheless] 'increase in wisdom,' Luke ii. 52. by means of the understanding which he previously possessed, and might 'know all things,' John xxi.17. namely, through the teaching of the Father, as he himself acknowledged" (XV, 275 and 277). But in *Christian Doctrine* Milton felt that "we are not concerned to inquire" too closely into the matter, whereas the exigencies of portraying Jesus in *Paradise Regained* meant that the poet, if not the theologian, had to commit himself to "the Spirit which is given to us [as] a more certain guide than Scripture." William Perkins provides the relevant commonplaces, explaining that the Papists wrongly assume that "Christ had all fulnesse of spirit in his infancie . . . and did not grow in grace at all." On the contrary, "at his baptisme he receiued a greater measure of the spirit than he had before," for "being inaugurated into his Mediatourship, he receiued such fulnesse of the spirit as was behoouefull for so high an office." Jesus possessed, that is, a "full measure of gifts fit" for each stage in his life, and "he increased therein as his estate and calling did require."[21]

This process of successive revelations—not to be confused with what we now refer to as character development—allowed the poet to represent his perfect hero as gaining "understanding" while preserving steadfast, from the very beginning, His faithful "will." Throughout Jesus, even when famished, is

> fed with better thoughts that feed
> Mee hung'ring more to do my Father's will,
> (II, 258–59)

but when the *kairos* comes for his withdrawal into the wilderness, his "understanding" remains imperfect,

> Musing and much revolving in his breast,
> How best the mighty work he might begin. . . .
> (I, 185–86)

He enters the desert, the "Spirit leading" (Milton avoids the determinism of "driven" in Mark 1:12[22]), where He exercises himself in "holy Meditations" (I, 183–293): He recalls a childhood rather alarmingly similar to Milton's own in its studiousness; He had then aspired, without due measure of Christian patience, to "heroic acts" in the pagan mode ("rescue *Israel* from the *Roman* yoke"); later His Mother had told Him of His divine birth, and He had "again revolv'd" the Law and the Prophets so that He could then understand that the Old Testament spoke of Him in types and shadows; and He remembers that He had awaited the "time prefixt"—until John the Baptist, His Forerunner, "proclaim'd" Him the Messiah, until the Spirit descended, and until He heard His "Father's voice,"

> by which I knew the time
> Now full, that I no more should live obscure,
> But openly begin. . . .   (286–88)

"And now by some strong motion I am led" into the wilderness, there to fast, according to Fuller, *"fourty dayes and nights*, in imitation of *Moses* and *Elias* fasting as long; the one at the institution, the other at the restitution of the Law, as Christ at the beginning of the Gospel."[23] But Jesus still remains unaware of the "intent," secure only in His faith that "what concerns my knowledge God reveals."

Satan approaches, there occurs the first temptation—to turn stones into bread: Jesus, like any good Protestant, interprets it as a temptation to lack of faith ("Why dost thou then suggest to me distrust?" I, 355) and rejects it by citing the Providence that sustained Moses for forty days in the Mount and "forty days *Eliah* without food" (352). Jesus, that is, aligns Himself with His types, those who trusted in the Providence of God, and then penetrates Satan's disguise: "Knowing who I am, as I know who thou art" (356).

The temptation itself has little interest for either Jesus or the poet—it occupies less than twenty lines—except as it serves to broach the theme of faith in Providence, that is, faith in the establishment of The Kingdom in relation to God's Time. The rest of Book One is devoted to a lengthy disquisition on the true nature of telling time, opposing the "oracles, portents, and dreams" by which Satan seeks to direct "future life" (395–96) to the "living Oracle" (460) of Jesus. Satan departs as night falls at the close of Book One, and Jesus, left to himself,

> tracing the Desert wild,
> Sole, but with holiest Meditations fed,
> Into himself descended, and at once
> All his great work to come before him set;
> How to begin, how to accomplish best
> His end of being on Earth, and mission high.
> (II, 109–14)

Since the poet's purpose excludes "drama" and "suspense" (real but relatively unsophisticated satisfactions in a work of art), the matter is as simple as it is represented: Jesus "knows" His antagonist, His "will" hungers to do His "Father's will," and now, at the close of the first day, immediately after Satan leaves Him "vacant," Jesus gains complete "understanding" of His Mission. Any argument for the virtues of dramatic suspense—extraneous values at best—becomes untenable at this point; and the suggestion seems clear that it was no part of the poet's business from the first. In any case, the temptations of the next two days, their nature and purpose, must be understood within the framework established in the first book during the first day.

Jesus' role after descending into Himself is simply to "stand," to be exemplary in a specific way: to endure the time while manifesting the characteristics of the inner or spiritual "kingdom"—the "Paradise within thee, happier far" (*PL*, XII, 587) that typifies the millennial "kingdom," the *regnum christi*, when

the Earth
Shall all be Paradise, far happier place
Than this of Eden, and far happier days.
(*PL*, XII, 463–65)

"They also serve who only stand and wait," and Jesus, pre-eminently, exemplifies the hero "Above Heroic" for whom standing is waiting and waiting standing.

Whether we contemplate the structure of *Paradise Regained* from the point of view of its "spatial" organization into four books or in terms of its temporal movement (number of days elapsed), Milton's purpose appears to be substantially the same—and it seems to have surprisingly little to do with the traditional understanding of the three temptations as they are arranged and defined in Scripture. Day I sets the pattern, for it includes, in addition to the Baptism, the temptation to distrust Providence and instead to trust in satanic "oracles," as well as the responses of the "new-baptiz'd" and of Mary, which reinforce the theme of the "kingdom" in relation to "time." Day II deals with the "kingdoms," Day III with the moment in "time" on the pinnacle. If we consider what happens in each of the four books, without attempting to reduce everything to three temptations, the theme of the "kingdom" and "time" emerges with even greater clarity of focus.

Book I, coinciding with Day I, introduces the theme, defines its nature and scope. The epiphany (18–43) immediately follows the seventeen-line invocation; John the Baptist has proclaimed "Heaven's Kingdom nigh at hand," and the Spirit descends upon Jesus in the "likeness of a Dove." The infernal council (44–105) meets to assess the meaning of the epiphany (whether this "exalted man" is indeed God's "first-begot"); Satan, hoping for "like success" as with Adam, resolves to investigate by means of temptations ("not force, but . . . fraud"), though the narrator (106–29) instantly reminds us that Satan's attempts at destruction inevitably become, through the operation of contraries, part of the divine plan:

> But contrary unweeting he fulfill'd
> The purpos'd Counsel pre-ordain'd and fixt.

The heavenly council (130–67) counterbalances the satanic by truly defining the meaning of the epiphany and allowing the narrator (168–81) to emphasize that the "Father knows the Son." The narrator then focusses on Jesus ("meanwhile the Son of God") as He enters the desert with "holy meditations" (182–95) to marshal His

"multitude of thoughts" and to trace His own history from childhood to the baptism (196–293),

> by which I knew the time
> Now full, that I no more should live obscure,
> But openly begin, as best becomes
> The Authority which I deriv'd from Heaven.

Having offered three perspectives on the significance of the
epiphany, the poet proceeds (294–356) to the first encounter between Satan and Jesus, which includes the rather brief treatment of
the temptation to turn stones into bread. The remainder of Book I
(357–502) consists in the debate about "oracles" that expands the
"distrust" connected with the first temptation into a general discussion of the nature of (providential) time. Satan represents himself
as a prophet to mankind, lending

> Oft my advice by presages and signs,
> And answers, oracles, portents and dreams,
> Whereby they may direct their future life.

Jesus replies that the oracles are "ambiguous and with double sense
deluding," that God, "when his purpose is," shall "declare his Providence," which is "not known" to Satan, and that meanwhile

> God hath now sent his living Oracle
> Into the World to teach his final will,
> And sends his Spirit of Truth henceforth to dwell
> In pious Hearts, an inward Oracle.

Book I and Day I, that is, include the first temptation but only as
part of the larger scheme that deals with the nature of providential
time: the Baptism, the two councils, Jesus' "holiest Meditations," the
debate about "presages and signs"—all these attest that the time is,
in Jesus' words, "now full" and that Satan is right to anticipate the
fulfillment of the curse on the Serpent.

> Long the decrees of Heav'n
> Delay, for longest time to him is short;
> And now too soon for us the circling hours
> This dreaded time have compast, wherein we
> Must bide the stroke of that long threat'n'd wound....
>   (55–59)

The Baptism, which is an epiphany or visible manifestation of Eternity in Time, inaugurates (in a sense yet to be determined), through the "living Oracle" of Christ and through the "inward Oracle" of the Holy Spirit, the *regnum christi* on earth, for the fulness of time has come (Gal. 4:4).

Book II begins by adverting to the themes of Book I, offering yet another perspective on the meaning of the epiphany. After the "new-baptiz'd," at first convinced that the "time is come" when "the Kingdom shall to Israel be restor'd," began "to doubt" but finally resolve to "wait" and trust in "Providence" (1–57), the narrator shifts to Mary, who likewise had "to wait with patience" and therefore "meekly compos'd awaited the fulfilling" (58–108). And Jesus, into "himself descended," determined "at once" upon "all his great work," his "end of being on earth" (109–14). Jesus, the "living Oracle," ignores the "presages and signs" just offered by Satan (at the end of Book I) and through God acquires the means (typological and other) "whereby [he] may direct [his] future life." The "new-baptiz'd," sensing at last that they know neither the true nature of the "Kingdom" nor the time of its restoration, turn not to the "answers, oracles, portents and dreams" of Satan but to the "inward Oracle" of their "pious Hearts" and all their "fears" they "lay on Providence."

The poet has established that the nature of the "Kingdom" is one of God's "mysteries," that the nature of "Time" is itself a "mystery," and that the proper response of men is simply to wait, in hope and with patience, until the plenary moment of the "tempestivity of time."

"Even the Son," argues Milton, "knows not all things absolutely; there being some secret purposes, the knowledge of which the Father has reserved to himself alone. Mark XIII.32 'of that day and that hour knoweth no man, no not the angels which are in heaven, neither the Son, but the Father'; or as it is in Matt. XXIV.36. 'my father only.' Acts I.7. 'the times and the seasons, which the Father hath put in his own power'" (*CD, Works,* XIV, 317 and 319; cf. 227). Milton had himself learned, out of his experience of Reformation in England, that the "times and the seasons" are mysteries that the "Father has reserved to himself alone," and the Jesus of *Paradise Regained* provides the exemplary illustration. Jesus must await the *kairos*, meanwhile doing the something that looks like nothing—waiting to stand.[24]

Having established and then emphasized the framework that

lends meaning to the encounter between Jesus and Satan in the wilderness, the poet describes the second satanic council (II, 115–234), which initiates and immediately precedes the demarcated group of temptations that occupy the remainder of the poem. (The temptation to turn stones into bread, represented as exploratory, had formed part of the effort to establish theme; but now that Satan has "found him, viewed him, tasted him," the temptations proper may begin.) It is the evening of the first day, and the Son first feels hunger; that night He dreams of food, and Satan returns, "not rustic as before," at noon—the hour of the Fall in *Paradise Lost*—of the second day (235–301). The temptations that follow are framed at either end by banquet scenes: the first, a banquet of sense (302–405), allows Jesus, as the allusions make clear ("not Fruits forbidden," the "crude Apple that diverted Eve," their "taste no knowledge works"), to resist the temptation to which Adam and Eve succumbed, in this way to reverse symbolically the original sin that lost Paradise. The second, a celestial banquet (IV, 581–95), symbolizes, as the allusions make clear ("Fruits fetcht from the tree of life"), the regaining of Paradise lost. (The inclusion of the second, celestial banquet constitutes as well a reminder of the *eschaton*.)[25] The remainder of Book II is taken up with the temptation to riches (406–86), Satan proclaiming that "Riches are mine, Fortune is in my hand" and Jesus replying that outer kingdomes are but "Golden in show" and that the true kingdom lies in him "who reigns within himself."

Book III opens with the temptation of "fame and glory" (1–149), in which Satan strives to make Jesus anticipate ("Thy years are ripe, and over-ripe") a time of earthly fame, but the Son of God cites the example of the true fame of "patient Job" and withstands the temptation to which Satan himself, "insatiable of glory," had succumbed.[26] The offer of Israel (150–250) parallels the previous temptation by inviting Jesus to forget that "all things are best fulfill'd in their due time" and to grasp "Occasion's forelock" in gaining an earthly kingdom; but the Son of God knows to wait "without distrust or doubt" because he can "best reign" who "well hath obey'd," and He acknowledges that the "everlasting Kingdom" both begins and ends as the Father "in his purpose hath decreed." Satan then takes Jesus to a mountain top (Niphates?), and the offer of Parthia (267–443) closes Book III: Satan argues that Jesus needs Parthia to secure the earthly kingdom of "David's throne," but again Jesus rejects "much ostentation" and repeats, in his role as

"Israel's true King," that His "time . . . is not yet come," leaving the earthly Israel to God's "due time and providence."

Book IV begins with the offer of Rome (1–153) as an alternative to Parthia and again repeats the themes adumbrated in Book I: secure, says Satan again, the earthly kingdom of "David's throne" as was "prophesi'd," but Jesus retorts that it is not the moment "when my season comes to sit" and that when it does "there shall be no end" to His spiritual kingdom. When Satan next offers all the "Kingdoms of the world" (154–94), Jesus prepares as usual to "endure the time." Satan then proposes the learning that was Greece (195–364) "Till time mature thee to a Kingdom's weight," but Jesus replies that the Prophets "only, with our Law, best form a King." Since Satan is now "quite at a loss, for all his darts were spent," he vents the frustrated question that has occurred to many readers of the brief epic:

> Since neither wealth, nor honor, arms nor arts,
> Kingdom nor Empire pleases thee, nor aught
> By me propos'd in life contemplative,
> Or active, tended on by glory, or fame,
> What dost thou in this World?
>
> (368–72)

Since "all his darts were spent" indeed, Satan then recurs to the theme of "prophetic" time that occupies the last 150 lines or so of Book I and that reappears in each of the temptations. Representing himself as an astrological prophet who reads Jesus' "Fate, by what the Stars" foretell, Satan reiterates the proposition that Jesus is

> Now at full age, fulness of time, thy season,
> When Prophecies of thee are best fulfill'd.
> (381–82)

This entire section (365–498), which includes the night of tempest "to tempt the Son of God with terrors dire," emphasizes that Satan resembles those in Matthew who "cannot discern the signs of the times." Before the night of the tempest Satan sees that

> A Kingdom they [the stars] portend thee, but what Kingdom,
> Real or Allegoric I discern not,
> Nor when, eternal sure, as without end,
> Without beginning; for no date prefixt
> Directs me in the Starry Rubric set.
>
> (389–93)

When Satan returns the next day ("Yet with no new device," the narrator emphasizes again, "they all were spent"), he seeks to interpret the tempest as one of those signs that "fore-signify and threaten ill":

> Did I not tell thee, if thou didst reject
> The perfect season offer'd with my aid,
> (467–68)

that you would have trouble "gaining David's throne"? Everything depends upon

> The time and means: for each act is rightliest done,
> Not when it must, but when it may be best.
> (475–76)

Jesus rejects this "opportunistic" view of time along with the notion that the "prodigies" of the night represent a "sure foregoing sign" (they are "false portents, not sent from God, but thee"), just as He had rejected the "presages and signs" along with the satanic view of time in Book I. The remainder of Book IV is devoted to the moment on the pinnacle. It will be apparent even from this brief rehearsal of what actually occurs in the poem that Milton subordinates the Gospel accounts to a particular interpretation of scriptural history.

The poet simply repeats the same lesson over and over again in each instance: that the true king exercises patience and reigns over his passions, that the eschatological Kingdom is not (as Milton himself had once thought) "now at hand," and that meanwhile the true Kingdom of God must be a "fairer Paradise" (IV, 613) within the individual Christian. By "standing," Jesus

> hast aveng'd
> Supplanted Adam, and by vanquishing
> Temptation, hast regain'd lost Paradise.
> (IV, 606–08)

The Kingdom is here, part of the "present age," and yet it is not here, for it is part of the "coming age." The Kingdom is not to be realized by men in any social or political body, not even in the reformed church or the community of saints. It is, rather, a "paradise within" the regenerate Christian, "happier far"; and it will be realized outwardly only during the millennial reign of Christ on earth at the end of time,

> for then the Earth
> Shall all be Paradise, far happier place
> Than this of Eden, and far happier days.
>   (*PL*, XII, 463–65)

To achieve the kingdom within, the Christian must of course imitate Christ, exercising not only such virtues as temperance and wisdom but also, and most particularly for Milton, patience—the virtue that enables one to "stand" and to "endure the time."

Tertullian, locating the "origin of impatience in the Devil himself" as the "prime source of sin," contemplates the "divine patience" exhibited during the Incarnation:

> In His mother's womb He awaits and after His birth suffers himself to grow into manhood, and, when an adult, shows no eagerness to become known, but bears reproaches and is baptized by His own servant and by His words alone repels the attacks of the Tempter.[27]

This "Christian Patience" represents the highest heroism, for when it is, according to Matthew Poole, "distinguish't from Patience as a meer moral Virtue found among the Heathen," we may see why the Apostle Paul "glories" in it "as men are apt to do in the Heroick Acts of great conquerors, or the Captain of an Army in the valiant Performance of his Soldiers."[28] The Jesus of *Paradise Regained*, for whom waiting is standing and standing waiting, distinguishes *chronos* from *kairos* and embodies the personal ideal—ultimately the highest heroism—of Milton's early sonnet:

> yet be it lesse or more, or soone or slow
>   it shall be still in strictest measure even
>   to that same lot however meane or high
> toward which Tyme leads me, & the will of heaven
>   all is if I have grace to use it so
>   as ever in my great task-maisters eye.

Satan's are "mere watch-maker's brains; but Christ was a chronometer"—the hero "Above Heroic" who refuses to "prevent" or come before the *kairos*.

The Chronometer hears when opportunity knocks but moves to answer only if he has "grace to use it so." When Satan claims that Jesus ought to grasp "Occasion's forelock" (III, 173), the use of the figure betrays The Adversary's reliance on the pagan notion of *kairos*.[29] Accordingly, The Chronometer delays, immobilizing himself in time while awaiting the knell of Eternity, for he recognizes with The Preacher of Ecclesiastes that it is not necessarily "the happier reign the sooner it begins" (17):

> All things are best fulfill'd in their due time,
> And time there is for all things, Truth hath said.
>
> (182-83)

Since the "due time" or *kairos* lies with the Father, "He in whose hand all times and seasons roll" (187), The Chronometer, with exemplary patience, awaits the precise moment of the "tempestivity of time," when Time and Eternity coincide: then indeed "all is . . . as ever."

By his "three & twentith yeere" (Sonnet VII), it will be recalled, Milton had secured a rationale for the psychic tendency to delay, transforming the psychological tendency to defer choice and action into the theological notions of "fit opportunity" and "tempestivity of time" that stem from the venerable distinction between *chronos* and *kairos*. Toward the end of his life the poet exploited the principle of delay to create the Jesus of *Paradise Regained*, that "most perfect Hero" or hero "Above Heroic." And this creation, properly understood, may become the source of a whole range of artistic satisfactions that are entirely real but foreign to the expectations aroused in us by the traditional novel and the conventional play. Readers expecting psychological characterization and dramatic action respond sympathetically to the satanic query: "What dost thou in this world?" But Jesus does not enter the world of time and brief epic to "do" anything. He is there to lay down the "rudiments" of His great warfare by waiting and standing. There can be nothing problematic in His psychology; Jesus is not going to change His mind and fall down to worship Satan. Or dramatic in His actions: on one occasion the Son proffers His usual "sage" and "temperate" reply over His shoulder, while ambling away from Satan . . . But all this need not mean that the brief epic lacks artistic force.

Jesus is The Chronometer, testifying by His patience to the way Time relates to Eternity and incarnating the knowledge that God has written history in the shadowy types that point toward truth. Similarly, Satan is not a "character" so much as an imperfect timepiece; there is nothing problematic about Satan, for he is bound by nature and by natural time, ever uncertain about "Real or Allegoric," yet always active "as a swarm of flies in vintage time" (IV, 15). The "characters" exist, as Aristotle maintained they should, for the sake of the plot, which then becomes significant as a thing in itself. In Eliot's words, it is "only by the form, the pattern" that we may approach the "still point of the turning world" (of *Paradise Regained*). Jesus and Satan move as though masked in some elaborate ritual or dance, their gestures largely symbolic and their words heavy, freighted, with meaning.[30] In the beginning Satan is active, inquisitive, busy about his councils in his permitted domain, that of the middle air; Jesus is private, low, obscure, contemplative. The two shall meet, on three main occasions; but only through a series of highly-stylized gestures and counter-gestures. The Son is "our Morning Star then in his rise" (I, 294), for it had been prophesied that "to the fall and rising he should be/ Of many in Israel" (II, 88–89); and even Satan suspects the answer to the question put by Jesus: "Know'st thou not that my rising is thy fall?" (III, 201) On the first day Satan descends to tempt the Son, then returns to middle air, while Jesus descends into Himself; on the second day the Son ascends "up to a hill" to seek out a place to "rest at noon," and suddenly "in a bottom" Satan "before him stood"; on the third day Satan "Him walking on a Sunny hill he found" and transports the Son to the pinnacle of the Temple, which in the distance appears "like a Mount."[31]

The combatants, that is, move up and down, illustrating in their actions, their physical movements, the imagery of height and depth that pervades the language of the brief epic—until they reach, together and simultaneously, the symbolic midpoint, the moment of symbolic "noon," on the pinnacle. Satan and Jesus are met in the center, the "still point" where waiting is standing and standing waiting. The God of *Paradise Lost* had created Adam "Sufficient to have stood, though free to fall," and the Milton of Sonnet XIX had been sure in his blindness that "they also serve who only stand and wait." And if we have read neither for naturalistic characterization nor for dramatic suspense, the final confrontation in the middle of space and time ought to exert on us its extraordinary effect:

> There on the highest Pinnacle he set
> The Son of God, and added thus in scorn.
> There stand, if thou wilt stand; to stand upright
> Will ask thee skill; I to thy Father's house
> Have brought thee, and highest plac't, highest is best,
> Now show thy Progeny; if not to stand,
> Cast thyself down; safely if Son of God. . . .

To whom thus Jesus. Also it is written,
Tempt not the Lord thy God; he said and stood.
But Satan smitten with amazement fell. . . .

This is the moment we have been enabled to anticipate, as Jesus
and Satan move up and down toward the midpoint in space and
time, the "season due" or *kairos*, where and when we shall observe
the awful poise of Him who "stands." There is a peculiar kind of
suspense involved in all this—not the suspense of the whodunit
where we are surprised by an unforeseen outcome but the exquisite
suspense, to recur to the original meaning of the word, of being
held in anticipation of the close, of exercising the difficult virtue of
patience until the moment of almost cataclysmic release.

At the start of Book III, "Satan stood," being "mute confounded
what to say"; later, and again, "Satan had not to answer, but stood
struck" (146); and finally, at the beginning of Book IV, "troubl'd at
his bad success," the "Tempter stood" once more and for almost
the last time. The crescendo reaches its height on the pinnacle
where the word is reiterated five times, until Satan "fell whence he
stood to see his Victor fall." As Boyd M. Berry points out, "Standing is the perfect verb to represent the puritan mode of heroism."
Although the "creatures do act to shape their ultimate destinies,"
they "do not act transitively and decisively upon an external, mun-
dane environment." Rather, they "testify to their commitment, accept reality, and, as the Son says when he rides out to victory [in
Paradise Lost] on the third day, 'stand still' . . . ."[32] Seymour Chatman's fine analysis of Milton's reliance on participial constructions
affords further perspective on what it means to "stand."

> In a way, the passive past participle conveys as much philosophical as
> historical depth. Ostensibly free characters are constrained by the
> well-placed past participle, its agent not necessarily expressed but
> easily recognizable. It is not surprising that so pregnant a structure
> should be put to powerful stylistic use by a writer concerned with
> basic questions of free will, agency, and sufferance. So much do
> Milton's past participles reiterate God's infinite control at the almost
> subliminal level of grammar that their stylistic power is hard to ig-
> nore. *The Fruit of that Forbidden Tree*—who forbade it? *The chosen
> seed*—who chose it? *Satan lay vanquish't/ Confounded though
> immortal*—who vanquished and confounded him? God, of course.
> The grammar cunningly conceals the obvious question and answer.
> Milton secures acquiescence no less by our elemental acts of com-
> prehending the syntax than by the logical power of his argument.

We are prompted to assent (for the purposes of the poem at least) by grammatical directive, quite simply as a function of making out what is said. God is the implicit agent of many of those participial actions and effects. It is not necessary to mention His name; He is there by grammatical *fiat*. Indeed, only the damned are morally stupid enough to raise the question of agency.[33]

It is remarkable, if not astonishing, how little is *accomplished* by the creatures even in *Paradise Lost*: although the good angels fight the rebels indefatigably for two days, there is on either side no permanent loss or gain and God reserves the judgment of the third day unto the Son; and although the faithful Abdiel receives the ultimate *bene placit* for having journeyed fearlessly across heaven's wide champaign to bring news of the revolt, the all-seeing eye of God has of course already perceived all, compelling us to surmise that Abdiel hears "Servant of God, well done" not because he had actually done anything to affect the outcome but because he alone, "unshak'n, unseduc'd, unterrifi'd," among all the rebel angels had "stood up" (V, 807) to oppose Satan. In *Paradise Regained*, the verb "to stand," as it is applied to Jesus, perfectly represents the proper response of the creature, for it preserves free will in the "Race of time" shaped by eternal mandate. Jesus, like any man, is sufficient to stand, though free to fall; Jesus, unlike Adam, stands, "but Satan smitten with amazement fell," "fell whence he stood to see his Victor fall."

When Jesus "stands," it is a gesture "Above Heroic," involving neither the swords and spears of the old romances, nor even the cannon that embody the epic aspirations of the rebel angels; Jesus stands, after having waited in patience and endured the time, to show by "undoubted proof" that "Son of God" means in this instance "first-begot." It is an epiphany—the theological equivalent, as Northrop Frye somewhere observes, of literary anagnorisis or recognition—that reveals essential meaning, the meaning that Jesus held all along but that had to await the moment of revelation, the moment of the truth that appears only in the fullness of time, on the pinnacle. The pinnacle represents, in Eliot's words, the "intersection of the timeless with time," which means that Jesus' words must be allowed their full weight. The question is not whether Jesus means "Tempt not the Lord thy God" to refer solely to God or to Himself *as* God—but whether the injunction may be taken, to use Milton's phrasing about another yet related matter, in its "compound sense." Although Milton did what he could to remove the logical inconveniences embodied in the doctrine of the Trinity, the hypostatic union itself compelled him toward forms of paradox and double-talk. The Son is very man, "distinct from and clearly inferior to the nature of the Father"; and yet the "nature of the Son is indeed divine" (*CD, Works*, XIV, 337). Since the Son's "two natures [human and divine] constitute one Christ, certain particulars appear to be predicated of him absolutely, which properly apply to [only] one of his natures" (*Works*, XV, 279). The theological mystery produces a "compound sense," together with an element of ambiguity that the unaided human intellect cannot resolve; so that unless Jesus "himself makes a distinction" it necessarily follows as the result of the hypostatic union "that whatever Christ says of himself, he says not as the possessor of either nature separately, but with reference to the whole of his character, and in his entire person" (*Works*, XIV, 229). When Jesus says, "Tempt not the Lord thy God" *and* "stands" He shows by "undoubted proof" not that He *is* God the Father but that He is "indeed divine," that He is "first begot" as well as "perfect man." Satan, "smitten with amazement fell," hearing the Son speak "not as the possessor of either nature separately, but with reference to the whole of his character, and in his entire person," and seeing Him "stand." The revelation of dual nature is not lost on The Adversary.

Here lies the meaning of the second simile that follows the moment on the pinnacle:

> And as that *Theban* Monster that propos'd
> Her riddle, and him who solv'd it not, devour'd,
> That once found out and solv'd, for grief and spite
> Cast herself headlong from th' *Ismenian* steep,
> So struck with dread and anguish fell the Fiend. . . .
>   (IV, 572–76)

Traditionally, as Alexander Ross points out in *Mystagogus Poeticus*, "Satan is the true *Sphinx*," and "there is no way to overcome him, but by hearkening to the counsell of *Minerva*, as *Oedipus* did; that is, by following the counsell of Christ." Therefore, we may say that "sin is the *Sphinx* or monster, that lodgeth within the winding Labyrinth and rock of our hearts, which if with *Oedipus* we master, with *Oedipus* we may expect a kingdome, but far better, and of longer continuance. . . ."[34] Although it is clear that the poet proposes a likeness between the Sphinx and Satan, Oedipus himself, perhaps for reasons of decorum, does not appear explicitly in the simile as a type or even an agent of Jesus, who in any case has represented all along not Oedipus but the "riddle" (*vide* His equivocal replies: "I bid not nor forbid," "Think not but that I know these things; or think/ I know them not") that Satan as a kind of Oedipus must "solve." But the point of the simile, as often in Milton, lies not only in the negative element that complicates, almost reverses, the analogy, but also in what is implied beyond what is stated explicitly. As Oedipus "found out and solv'd" the riddle of the Sphinx by discovering "man," so Satan (the poet implies) finally "found out" in this argument "Above Heroic" that Jesus is "Man-God"; or, alternatively, as the Sphinx fell "for grief and spite" at the word "man," so Satan fell "with dread and anguish," if we compare "small things with the greatest," at the revelation "Man-God." The simile, itself by implication "Above Heroic" and possessing as it does an element of mystery in the way its parts just miss exact proportion and conventional similitude, offers a disturbing idea of "likeness" itself. When Wallace Stevens declares that "identity is the vanishing point of resemblance," he has in mind only one aspect of Milton's way with the simile, which is to insinuate that the resemblance between the natural and divine is complex, shadowy, fugitive—though perhaps finally more nearly alike "than on Earth is thought."

For it is true that the poet strives to express matters not entirely susceptible to formulation in straight-forward terms. The dissatisfaction of the critics with *Paradise Regained* points directly to the primary problems: Jesus' rejection of classical learning appears to mirror the poet's rejection of the devices of language that adorned *Paradise Lost*, and the poet's portrayal of Jesus seems to "praise [the] fugitive and cloistered virtue" that the Milton of *Areopagitica* had denigrated.[35] The artist, according to the anti-Miltonists, has become completely submerged in the preacher, the poet in the moralist; and even Douglas Bush, that most ardent admirer, speaks of his pain in witnessing the older Milton, through the Jesus of *Paradise Regained*, turn his back on classical civilization. Put briefly, the lesson of the brief epic appears to be that there exists for the older Milton an absolute dichotomy between Nature and Grace, body and soul, human learning and divine revelation. In *Paradise Lost*, Abdiel argues that "God and Nature bid the same," an argument that seems to be entirely untenable with respect to the brief epic, especially with respect to the main theme of obedience and patience in time. With Michelangelo in Sonnet 105, Milton seems to be saying that *l'eterno* has nothing to do with *tiempo*. Human notions of time seem to have little or nothing to do with the eternal timetable, for the ritual combatants wear the opposed masks of Time and Eternity.

Plutarch, whom Plotinus Plinlimmon had read (we trust) with profit, meditates on the mutability of man, on the passage that Montaigne made his rite: "Yesterday dieth in this day, and this day will be dead by tomorrow: neither continueth any man alwaies one and the same . . . and if he be not the same, he is not at all. . . ." For true being is

> to be eternal, that is to say, which never had beginning in generation, nor shall have end by corruption; and in which, time never worketh any mutation. For a moveable and mutable thing is time [and] may be compared unto a leaking vessel, containing in it (after a sort) generations and corruptions. And to it properly belong these termes: *Before and after: Hath been, and shall be*: which presently at the very first sight do evidently shew, that time hath no being. . . . God alone is (and that, not according to any measure of time, but respective to eternity) immutable and immovable, not gaged within the compass of time . . . but being one really, by this one *Present* or *Now*, accomplisheth his eternity or being alway.

Does all this mean that for Plutarch, as (apparently) for the Milton of *Paradise Regained*, the One is divorced from the Many, that the "now" of Time has no relation to the "alway" of Eternity, and that Being has no connection with Becoming? Not for Plutarch: Whatever of God "is infused into the World, the same in some sort containeth and confirmeth the substance thereof, maintaining the corporal nature of it, which otherwise by reason of infirmity and weaknesse, tendeth alwaies to corruption," with the consequence that it is in fact "possible for a sensitive nature, to shew an intellectual; and for that which is movable, to express that which is stable and permanent."[36] There remains, that is, some connection between the grand divisions established by divine *fiat* "in the beginning"—some traffic between the realms of Being and non-Being, Eternity and Time; so that the possibility of making analogies and similitudes likewise remains, finally unimpaired though radically qualified.

Plinlimmon also begins with what appears to be an absolute dichotomy:

Now in an artificial world like ours, the soul of man is further removed from its God and the Heavenly Truth, than the chronometer
carried to China, is from Greenwich. . .; so the chronometric soul, if
in this world true to its great Greenwich in the other, will always, in
its so-called intuitions of right and wrong, be contradicting the mere
local standards and watch-maker's brains of the earth.

But this does not mean that the "China watches are at all out of the
way. Precisely the reverse," for "though the earthly wisdom of man
be heavenly folly to God; so also, conversely, is the heavenly wisdom of God an earthly folly to man. Literally speaking, this is so."
"But here one thing," declares Plinlimmon, "is to be especially observed":

Though Christ encountered woe in both the precept and practice of
his chronometricals, yet did he remain throughout entirely without
folly or sin. Whereas, almost invariably, with inferior beings, the
absolute effort to live in this world according to the strict letter of the
chronometricals is, somehow, apt to involve those inferior beings
eventually in strange, *unique* follies and sins, unimagined before. It is
the story of the Ephesian matron, allegorized.

And consequently the "God at the heavenly Greenwich" does not
really "expect common men to keep Greenwich wisdom in this
remote Chinese world of ours." (It would also be a "falsification of
Himself, inasmuch in that case, China time would be identical with
Greenwich time, which would make Greenwich time wrong"!) Man
cannot live by no bread alone, for "literally speaking" there can be
no true correspondence of the two worlds. And does it then follow
that Nature is satanic, totally opposed to Grace? that man is absolutely time-bound, entirely at odds with eternity? Or does Milton,
unlike Plinlimmon, suppose that the ordinary man ought to become The Chronometer, leaving behind the confines of "nature's
bounds"? So it would appear, if God's truth is completely opposed
to the learning that was Greece and Rome. But Plinlimmon, at
least, carefully adds:

But why then does God now and then send a heavenly chronometer
(as a meteoric stone) into the world, uselessly as it would seem, to
give the lie to all the world's time-keepers? Because He is unwilling to
leave man without some occasional testimony to this:—that though
man's Chinese notions of things may answer well enough here, they
are by no means universally applicable, and that the central Greenwich in which He dwells goes by a somewhat different method from

this world. And yet it follows not from this, that God's truth is one thing and man's truth another; but—as above hinted, and as will be further elucidated in subsequent lectures—by their very contradictions they are made to correspond.

All thoughtful men have been struck "with a sort of infidel idea, that whatever other worlds God may be Lord of, He is not the Lord of this":

> But it is not, and can not be so; nor will he who regards this chronometrical conceit aright, ever more be conscious of that horrible idea. For he will then see, or seem to see, that this world's seeming incompatibility with God, absolutely results from its meridional correspondence with Him.

So also Plutarch, contemplating the apparently contradictory meaning of the letter *El* at Delphi: "it seemeth" that the proposition Thou Art stands "somewhat contrary to the precept" Know Thyself, "and yet after a sort it seemeth to accord and agree therewith." It is antithetical accord or, in the phrase Milton uses in *Areopagitica*, "brotherly dissimilitude."

The momentary confusion engendered by the simile of the Theban Monster—as we sort out the terms of the comparison—resembles in little those occurrences in *Paradise Lost* when "expectation stood" or "expectation held/ His look suspense" before resolution is effected, and it also has its analogues elsewhere in *Paradise Regained*. At the final confrontation we are told:

> So Satan fell; and straight a fiery Globe
> Of Angels on full sail of wing flew nigh,
> Who on their plumy Vans receiv'd him soft . . .
> (581–83)

The antecedent of "him" is as clear grammatically as it is blasphemous theologically. Had the confusion continued, had "expectation held," we would watch Satan sit down to the celestial banquet; yet Milton's final meaning is of course unmistakable: the "satanic" expectation, in time, reaches its proper fulfillment in Christ. A similar "flicker of hesitation" likewise accompanies a reading of the simile that precedes the one of the Theban Monster:

> But Satan smitten with amazement fell
> As when Earth's Son *Antaeus* (to compare
> Small things with greatest) in *Irassa* strove

> With *Jove's Alcides*, and oft foil'd still rose,
> Receiving from his mother Earth new strength,
> Fresh from his fall, and fiercer grapple join'd,
> Throttl'd at length in th' Air, expir'd and fell;
> So after many a foil the Tempter proud,
> Renewing fresh assaults, amidst his pride
> Fell whence he stood to see his Victor fall.
> And as that *Theban* monster. . . .
>
> (562–72)

The terms of the simile are entirely conventional, for Hercules was traditionally a type of Christ (as in Milton's own Nativity Ode) and, as Alexander Ross repeats it, "Satan is like Antaeus, for the more hee is beat down by the Herculan strength of Gods Word, the more violent and fierce he groweth; but being squeezed by the brestplate of justice, he loseth his force."[37] And yet, on a first reading, I think we might be forgiven if our "expectation held" a different view of what was happening. After all, the action of the combatants—what actually occurs, what we might be tempted to visualize— would seem to belie the traditional interpretation, for it is *Satan* who resembles Hercules in raising *Jesus* up in the air.[38] In which case we might read,

> As when Earth's Son *Antaeus* (to compare
> Small things with greatest) in *Irassa* strove
> With *Jove's Alcides*, and oft foil'd still rose;

and so reading, half expect that Jesus, the Morning Star, is still in His rise, half expect that Antaeus, held aloft by Jove's Alcides, will somehow turn out to be Christ. And yet our "expectation stood" in the wrong—as clearly wrong as the grammatical antecedent of "him" in line 581.

Since poetic analogies are rarely uncomplicated, it usually requires tact, even a willing suspension of logic, to read with discrimination. Who but John Donne, asks Dr. Johnson, would compare a good man to a telescope? And even we, in comparing our loves to a red, red rose, must rely on them not to think of thorns (or at best to think of paradisial petals *sine spinae*). In the first epic simile in Western literature, Homer compares a crowd of men to a swarm of bees, typifying under the opposed terms of the analogy the conflicting feelings of men at war: the impulse to achieve great deeds, in the world of epic, and the impulse to retreat into peace, into the world of the georgic and the pastoral. Milton's first simile in

Paradise Lost (I, 196 ff.) compares Satan to the Leviathan, though as the poet elaborates the analogy to include the narrative of the "Pilot of some small night-founder'd Skiff" we begin to understand (if we have also read the bestiaries) that Satan in some more exact sense *is* Leviathan, so that as resemblance fades toward identity the simile verges on metaphor. More often, the poet invites us to contemplate the areas in which the process of comparing small things to great becomes suspect as traditional modes of similitude prove inadequate:

> A multitude, like which the populous North
> Pour'd never from her frozen loins....
>
> (I, 351–52)

> His Spear, to equal which the tallest Pine
> Hewn on Norwegian hills, to be the Mast
> Of some great Ammiral, were but a wand....
>
> (I, 292–94)

> There lands the Fiend, a spot like which perhaps
> Astronomer in the Sun's lucent Orb
> Through his glaz'd Optic Tube yet never saw.
>
> (III, 588–90)

Given the nature of Milton's usual subjects, which involve the depiction of "things invisible to mortal sight," it seems inevitable that we should often be made aware of something incommensurable in the simile.[39] The language of theological analogy, which includes the vocabulary of "mysterious terms," relies ultimately on various forms of paradox and catachresis.

Comparing greater matters (an armed horde) to smaller (a swarm of bees) is of course a natural impulse of the human mind, but in Milton's day the habit, hardening into formula, had been codified by literary precedent. Coolidge cites Herodotus ii. 10, Thucydides iv. 36, Cicero, *De Re Publica* iii. 23, 34, Ovid, *Metamorphoses* v. 416–17, Statius, *Silvae*, v. 61–62, Castiglione, *Il Cortegiano* IV, xix, Ben Jonson, "Epigram to the Queene," Pope, "Windsor Forest," 102 ff., Wordsworth, "Miscellaneous Sonnets," II, 21; but readers of medieval and Renaissance literature will have encountered their own examples. Cowley's "Of Wit" seems typical enough:

> In a true piece of *Wit* all things must be,
> Yet all things there *agree*.

> As in the *Ark*, joyn'd without force or strife,
> All *Creatures* dwelt; all *Creatures* that had *life*.
> Or as the *Primitive Forms* of all
> (If we compare great things with small)
> Which without *Discord* or *Confusion* lie
> In that strange *Mirror* of the *Deitie*.[40]

Vergil in *Eclogue I* has already begun to vary from the norm, using the past tense to admit a note of elegiac recognition that the traditional manner of analogy no longer holds: *sic parvis componere magna solebam*—thus I used to compare great things to small. In *Paradise Lost* (and elsewhere) Milton again and again compares great things to small, on several occasions employing what we may think of as the Vergilian formula itself (II, 921–22, VI, 311, X, 306) in order to rise to the "highth of this great Argument" by relegating the "great thing" of former epics to the "small thing" of his own comparison.

But in *Paradise Regained*, where the poet claims that his argument is not only more heroic but "Above Heroic," the formula has itself varied toward the superlative:

> As when Earth's Son *Antaeus* (to compare
> Small things with greatest) in *Irassa* strove. . . .

In all previous instances the poet was content with the comparative degree. Related peculiarities derive from the two allusions, one literary and one theological, that occur in the opening lines of the brief epic. Milton's first line,

> I who erewhile the happy Garden sung,

glancing at the opening line of Spenser's epic ("Lo! I the man, whose Muse whylome. . . ."), alludes to what readers of the Renaissance, submitting to the authority of Donatus and Servius, would recognize as the opening line of the Aeneid: *ille ego, qui quondam gracili modulatus avena*—I who erewhile modulated my [song] on a slender reed. In Vergil and Spenser the opening proclaims that the poet is graduating from the lower genre of pastoral to the higher genre of epic, but Milton seems to be insisting that the elements compared ought to be reversed, for he alludes unmistakably not, say, to *Lycidas* but to *Paradise Lost*. And if we follow out the implications of the analogy, it appears that we are to think of *Paradise Lost* in relation to *Paradise Regained* as pastoral in relation to epic. Yet

Paradise Lost is assuredly epic, though many have argued that *Paradise Regained* does not properly belong to the genre, for among other things it is written not in the high style of epic nor in the traditional twelve books but in the lower style of pastoral or of the four-book georgic. Milton pleads, of course, that his argument "Above Heroic" allows him to regard *Paradise Lost* as the "small thing" in comparison with the "greatest" heroism exhibited in *Paradise Regained*, but again the nature of the analogy, involving as it does an egregious element of contrast, produces a moment of hesitation before matters can be viewed in correct perspective.

The next lines—

> By one man's disobedience lost, now sing
> Recover'd Paradise to all mankind,
> By one man's firm obedience fully tried—

allude to St. Paul (Romans 5:19): "For as by one man's disobedience many were made sinners, so by the obedience of one shall many be made righteous." Since Paul rests his discourse upon the theory of types (Christ as Second Adam), his rhetorical tactics, like Milton's similes, which quite generally begin "as when," have a definable temporal aspect: Paul's simile is an analogy in time, and it involves contrast as well as comparison. As Heinrich Bullinger says, we are to "note this similitude": "And like as our disease began in Paradise by temptation; even so at the temptation in the wildernesse began the Lord our health: And like as the Father of us all did eat the forbidden meat, so did the Lord did not eat the meat that hee might have eaten, but fasted fortie daies and fortie nights. Afterward came he among the people, and began to preach salvation, saying, *the time is fulfilled, and the kingdome of God is at hand....*"[41] Adam's original disobedience is both like and unlike Christ's later obedience; the two must be compared, for they are linked in time through God's eternal wisdom, and yet they must also be contrasted, for the movement from shadowy types to truth inevitably involves, at least in some degree, the negation of what came before.

Although Jesus said that He came not to destroy the Law but to fulfil it, the Jews were under no illusions about what fulfillment might mean in this case. Fulfillment makes obsolete, inexorably, the past, except as the past may be used to interpret and burnish the present and future. Milton says, "Law can discover sin, but not remove," and

> So Law appears imperfet, and but giv'n
> With purpose to resign them in full time
> Up to a better Cov'nant....
>
> *(PL*, XII, 290, 300–02)

In the fullness of time Jesus comes to fulfil, as type fulfils antitype, which has for corollary a view of history that opens towards its end through a series of revelations, a passage from imperfect to more nearly perfect and finally to the perfection of glory. There is an element of mystery inevitably involved in such a temporal process: fulfillment means contrasting fulfillment, fulfillment under a negative as well as a positive aspect. Samuel Mather speaks of such similes in the form of a simile: "As there is a Similitude, a Resemblance and Analogy between the Type and the Antitype in some things: so there is ever a dissimilitude and a disparity between them in other things. It is so in all similitudes. It is a Rule in Reason [i.e., in the art of logic]. There is a mixture of Consentaneity and Dissentaneity; or else instead of Similitude, there would be Identity."[42] But the mystery, the element of paradox that allows us to see that Adam both "is" and "is" not Christ, must be construed as no more and no less than the eternal workings of deity in time.

It is in this sense that Milton's methods of comparison, his ways with simile, reflect with extraordinary fidelity the ultimate nature of reality as he saw it. In the opening line of *Paradise Regained* the poet speaks, in effect, in "mysterious terms," in terms, that is, of contrasting fulfillment. Since *Paradise Regained* is "Above Heroic," Milton may compare the brief epic to *Paradise Lost* as the Christian may compare greatest things to small. And since the comparison, like St. Paul's, derives from the theory of types, it exemplifies Christian paradox: the argument "Above Heroic" is, paradoxically, above because it is below, not only in the depiction of its protagonist but also in its style. Milton, like Augustine, inverts the traditional hierarchy of styles as well as the classical hierarchy of values. St. Paul counts the wisdom of this world folly, and considers it the highest honor to speak simply, eschewing the colors of Greek rhetoric. Where the Ciceronians asserted that the *sermo sublimis* was appropriate to the highest matters, Augustine had argued that the truth of Christianity, because it is the highest truth, might justly be rendered comparatively unadorned in the unaffected manner of the Gospels. Similarly, Milton's epic "Above Heroic" may justly be expressed in the lower style of, say, Vergil's Georgics and may appropriately appear, like the Georgics and the Gospels, in four books: The poet "progresses" backward from epic to bucolic "style"—while moving forward: he must sing of deeds "Above Heroic, though in secret done," of the universal Saviour who shall "enter, and begin to save mankind" while "home to his Mother's house private return'd" (I, 15; IV, 635, 639). As God had said in the First Book, "His weakness shall o'ercome Satanic strength" (161), echoing Adam's resolve, instructed by the example of his "Redeemer ever blest," to rely on God's "providence" and "by small,"

> Accomplishing great things, by things deem'd weak
> Subverting worldly strong, and worldly wise
> By simply meek. . . .
>
> (XII, 564–69)

The last word shall be first and the meek style shall inherit the earth.

The narrator sums up the poet's method, which is itself an imitation of God's ways of working in time, in speaking of Satan:

> But contrary unweeting he fulfill'd
> The purpos'd Counsel pre-ordain'd and fixt.
>
> (I, 126–27)

The "him" (of IV, 581) that we at first take to refer to Satan may be considered a species of contrary fulfillment; and the simile about Hercules and Antaeus works in something of the same way, for in reading Milton's "As when. . . . So after" we half expect that Antaeus corresponds to Christ, Satan to Hercules: in both instances, meaning is threatened (at best logical relations disintegrate, at worst blasphemy appears), but then the confusions, the contraries, are gloriously resolved. Antaeus is fulfilled in Satan (his rise his fall), and Hercules is fulfilled in Christ. The "him," likewise after a contrary moment, finds proper fulfillment in Christ. What was hidden is revealed in the fullness of time, as Milton compares greatest things to small by contrary fulfillment; "by their very contradictions," Plinlimmon says, "they are made to correspond." He "who regards" the "chronometrical conceit" of *Paradise Regained* "aright . . . will then see, or seem to see, that this world's seeming incompatibility with God absolutely results from its meridional correspondence with Him." "God and Nature bid the same," in *Paradise Regained* as in *Paradise Lost*, though the manner of their bidding must finally remain one of God's mysteries; and the poet who would imitate mysteries must use something like the language of paradox or, to recur to Milton's own formulation, the language of "brotherly dissimilitude."

It is for reasons such as these that Milton entitles the brief epic *Paradise Regained* rather than "Christ Tempted." Not only does the poet in this way mirror the basic paradox of the "Kingdom" (that it is here and yet to come); he also declares the handiwork of Christian time—that from the eternal vantage of Him who is Alpha and Omega the beginning contains the ending. (Satan, "compos'd of lies," traces that other circle—as in Herbert's "Sinnes Round"—of imperfection: "From the beginning, and in lies wilt end.") The Baptism and Temptation mark the beginning of Christ's ministry, in something like the way, to adapt Browne, the flower sleeps within the bosom of its causes.

> In the seed of a plant to the eyes of God, and to the understanding of man, there exists, though in an invisible way, the perfect leaves, flowers, and fruit thereof: (for the things that are *in posse* to the sense, are actually existent to the understanding.) Thus God beholds all things, who contemplates as fully his workes in their Epitome, as in their full volume, and beheld as amply the whole world in that little compendium of the sixth day, as in the scattered and dilated pieces of those five before.[43]

God has decreed that Jesus shall in the wilderness "first lay down the rudiments" of the "great warfare" that shall take place at the end of time (I, 157–58), when (as Michael says to Adam, *PL*, XII, 463–65) the earth "Shall all be Paradise, far happier place" than "this of Eden." (Probably it should be emphasized that Milton in his frequent use of "rudiments" relies on the technical vocabulary of exegesis, as in the "rudiments of the world," Col. 2:20, or "bondage under the elements [margin: "rudiments"] of the world," Gal. 4:3, where the word signifies the Old Law, the type or shadow of the good things Christ shall effect.) Meanwhile the poet insists that Jesus by withstanding the temptations in the wilderness "hast regain'd lost Paradise" (IV, 608):

> For though the seat of earthly bliss be fail'd,
> A fairer Paradise is founded now.
>
> (612–13)

The beginning of the ministry shadows the end of the ministry, in the sense that Christ Tempted prefigures Christ Crucified. The poet, in consequence, has been careful to intimate The Passion not only through typological allusions but also by adding to the traditional forty days, without biblical sanction or exegetical precedent, a period of precisely three days, which looks back to the three-day War in Heaven of *Paradise Lost* and forward to the three days of The Passion.[44]

As readers we have been taught to restrain doubt, to wait in patience the moment decreed by God. As Paul says (Romans 8:25), "But if we hope for that we see not, then do we with patience wait for it." Insofar as we have been able, with the poet's help, to "discern the signs of the times," we experience something of the eternal view, as when the God of Book III of *Paradise Lost* looks down

> from his prospect high,
> Wherein past, present, future he beholds....

Witnesses to a delaying action in time, we gain some sense of the eternal schedule that depends neither on "Occasion's forelock" nor on the temporal flux of beginning, middle, and end but rather on those moments (*kairoi*) "pre-ordain'd and fixt" by the Father in whose hands all times and seasons roll. And insofar as we are able, with the poet's help, to glimpse something of the providential nature of time, we may hope to understand with the younger Milton that

> all is if I have grace to use it so
> as ever in my great task-maisters eye.

Some Conclusions

Milton avoided the satanic silliness of self-authorship—as though heedful of Jonson's dictum that he who was "onely taught by himselfe, had a foole to his master"—by apprenticing himself to a variety of predecessors, acquiring a good deal not only from Ovid and Vergil but also, and even, from Sylvester's DuBartas and the Fletchers. Although the turn was ultimately toward the "sage and serious" Spenser, Milton had already caught from Jonson a way of significant enjambement and a feeling for the heft of moral abstractions; from the "metaphysicals" a sensitivity to the intellectual conceit, often wonderfully plausible ("dark with excessive bright" or "blind mouths") but on rare occasions clevelandizing (some parts of the Hobson poems and the last stanza of "The Passion"); and from Shakespeare something of dramatic idiom, of levels of diction, and of the flex of the poetic line—most clearly evident in *A Mask* and *Samson*. He could steal effectively even from Randolph, and it was apparently hard for Milton to lose sound of any lilt or cadence, even in moving from Spenser's Sabrina— "Adowne the rolling river she did poure"—to his own incomparable "Down the swift Hebrus to the Lesbian shore." Auden must be at least half right:

> Art in intention is mimesis
> But, realized, the resemblance ceases.

In any event, the apprenticeship begins to end with the Nativity Ode, moving significantly in the direction of the Italians in "On

185

Time," "At a Solemn Music," and "Upon the Circumcision," where the effort to transmute English into something richly and strangely Vergilian coincides with the effort to shape his poems in accord with patterns of Christian time; these separate but parallel developments reach their height in *Lycidas*, which exhibits complete mastery of the elements of the style now called Miltonic.[1] It is the perfect medium, and it has proven inimitable.

"It comes to this," says Wallace Stevens, "that poetry is part of the structure of reality," which then leads him to advance a subjunctive syllogism that eludes close scrutiny but remains provocative: "If this has been demonstrated, it pretty much amounts to saying that the structure of poetry and the structure of reality are one or, in effect, that poetry and reality are one, or should be."[2] Milton's verse has not only for its subject but also for its structure the "reality" of Time in relation to Eternity. Until around the fifth century B. C. time does not appear to represent an explicit force to be consciously reckoned with by the ancients. It seems to be of little or no explicit concern to Hesiod, though it is of course present by inference in the myth of the four ages; and in Homer, I understand, it never even functions as the subject of a verb. But with the tragedies of the fifth century one must at least entertain the notion that for Aeschylus and Sophocles "time" has become an important component in their view of what constitutes "tragedy." Homer moves freely, ignoring the present while turning to the past with excruciating leisure to apprise us of the history of a well-wrought bow or the origin of an exquisite cheekpiece on a well-crafted bridle—even, as Auerbach has taught us, delaying the moment of anagnorisis with a lengthy account of the origin of the scar of Odysseus. But in the great tragedies the past surges insistently toward the present. Oedipus looks to the past at first with incomprehension but finally with awful understanding—the past bears the pain of knowing. (And this awareness of the power of the past leads also, apparently, to the first histories.) In such a situation, the reader, knowing the outcome, remains tuned into high-pitched expectancies in regard to the way his knowledge of the past is being focussed in successive stages upon the present, so that participation in the crisis, when action finds its meaning in sudden revelation, depends on apprehending the relation of past to present. So too for the Christian, though the structure and rhythm of his activities includes the future as well, and in the manner in which, for the Christian, "prophecy" may be felt to differ from "oracle." Of even greater significance are the complications produced by the need to view Time under the aspect of Eternity.

For the Christian, Time tends to be viewed as an enigmatic series of divinely demarcated events, one event constituting the "beginning" and another the "ending"—history as countless numbers of alphas and omegas that represent smaller parentheses within the larger parenthesis that is "time" itself. *Paradise Regained* has a clearly-defined beginning in time ("Now had the great Proclaimer . . .") and an equally well-defined ending ("Home to his Mother's house private return'd"), but the beginning is in the midst and the ending marks the beginning of Christ's Ministry; and this three-day parenthesis in the life of Jesus resonates backward in the direction of the three-day War in Heaven and forward to the three-day Passion. As omegas succeed alphas, the eternal resonances deepen and widen along the line of time. Considered in relation to the theory of types (or the distinction between *chronos* and *kairos*), Time becomes, almost literally, a series of containers that are filled in the "tempestivity of time" by God, most dramatically during the "season" of the Incarnation: "When the fullness of time was come, God sent forth his Son" (Gal. 4:4). The critical moments or *kairoi*, marked at beginning and end by type and antitype, are accessible in some degree to the inquiring intellect and to prophetic understanding but finally must be reckoned among the divine mysteries, for we know from Mark 13:32 (and elsewhere) that the day and the "hour knoweth no man, . . . not the Son, but the Father." "There are two things known to God the author of Scriptures, but unknown to man," declares Sir Francis Bacon: "namely, the secrets of the heart, and the successions [outcomes] of time."[3] Consequently we must exercise patience, must "waite on the Lord," writes William Perkins in commenting on Galatians, "and be content," "for he is Lord of time, and all seasons are in his hand: and his will or prouidence makes times fit or unfit." The fit time constitutes an instant of fullness, and this *"fullnesse of time, or the full time,"* continues Perkins, arguing in the usual circle, "is called *a full time,* because it was designed and appointed by the will & prouidence of the heauenly father."[4]

As type finds fulfillment in antitype—as figures "powred" out, in Donne's words, into "farther figures"—there occurs moment after moment of fullness, until the end of time itself. "And then (and never till then)," proclaims Lancelot Andrewes, "shall be the *fullnesse* indeed, when God shall be, not (as now He is) somewhat in every one, but *all* in *all* . . . and there shall be neither *time*, nor *season* any more. No *fullnesse* then, but the *fullnesse* of *aeternitie*. . . ." Meanwhile *"Time* receives his *filling* from God." Since in "it selfe, *time* is but an *empty measure*, hath nothing in it," that "which filleth *time*, is some memorable thing of Gods powring into it. . . ." The Lord of History, Who alone knows the *kairoi*, began with types; and with these "He *filled* up certain times of the yeare under Moses, and the Prophets," but the *"measure* was not yet full: filled perhaps to a certain *degree*, but not *full* to the *brimme*. . . ." Only with the "Performance of those promises, the body of those shadowes, the substance of those figures, the fulfilling or filling full of all those prophecies," shall we participate in the "fulnesse of time, truly so called," which is the Incarnation; and yet even this "tempestivity," though truly named, itself shadows the *"fullnesse* of *aeternitie*."[5] In the movement of successive, and progressive, revelation that marks the "Race of time," the doctrines of types and *kairoi* provide a rationale for the intrusions of the Eternal that lend history its comely contours, allowing those with the "grace to use it so" a way of comprehending something of the "unsearchable dispose." By taking the measure of the times of fullness the Christian may aspire to a heightened awareness of the direction of Eternal Providence.

Since for Milton the *logos* was both in the beginning and at the end, Roland Barthes' observations about closure in *lisible* or "readerly" works have special pertinence here: "Writing 'the end' . . . posits everything that has been written as having been a tension which 'naturally' requires resolution" on the basis of a "cultural model," the "same model that has marked Western thinking about the organic (with Hippocrates)" and about the "poetic and the logical (Aristotelian *catharsis* and syllogism)." The classical or "readerly" text comes, like man himself, to what is assumed to be a natural end, and the writer, as well as the reader, is likely to keep that end in view. By acquiescing in "the need to set forth the *end* of every action (conclusion, interruption, closure, dénouement), the readerly [text] declares itself to be historical. In other words, it can be subverted, but not without scandal." Not, in Milton, without scandalizing the name of Christianity, for the cultural model derived from the Renaissance view of Christian history necessarily emphasizes beginnings and endings, lending special significance to the Apocalypse or final unfolding that constitutes The End. The corollary in the classical text is the "flourish below a signature," and any attempt "to deny this final Word (to deny the end as a word)

would in fact scandalously dismiss the *signature* we seek to give each
of our 'messages.' "[6] Meaning is therefore "found in the close,"
which means that as readers we must concur again with Coleridge
on Shakespeare: "Expectation in preference to surprise." In the
Renaissance universe of discourse and act, "expectation" (to quote
Barthes again) becomes "the basic condition of truth: truth, these
narratives tell us, is what is *at the end* of expectation"; to narrate in
this fashion required Milton to adopt an "answerable style," one that
"raises the question as if it were a subject which one delays predicat-
ing; and when the predicate (truth) arrives, the sentence, the narrative, are over, the world is adjectivized (after we had feared it would
not be)"; in effect, "truth predicates an incomplete subject, based
on expectation and desire for its imminent closure" (the younger
Milton, the "new-baptiz'd" of *Paradise Regained*), and this kind of
"hermeneutic narrative" is "dated, linked to the kerygmatic civilization of meaning and truth, appeal and fulfillment."[7]

We read for the sake of experience; we read for the sake of
exercise, exercise in thought and feeling; and only when we feel
defensive need our reading become an art of defensive warfare.
And we obtain our artistic satisfactions (as we do our other satisfactions) where we can, which in our day usually means the novel or
the drama—impertinent models for reading Milton, who offers a
whole range of other but powerful satisfactions that have little or
nothing to do with what we are habituated to find intriguing with
respect to "character" or "suspense" (meaning "surprise"). All
readings doubtless involve misreadings, and literary criticism invariably becomes, to some degree, an act of translation; and yet the
notion of entering another universe of discourse, the idea of trying
to understand a great poet in his own terms, seems worth preserving as an ideal, for our freedom to choose and to grow cannot but
be inhibited by the effort, however well-intentioned, to assimilate
Shakespeare or Milton by a process of temporal acculturation,
translating their densities of locution and their literary conventions
into ones more congenial to present-day habits of response. Good
intentions count for little in this area, because what Plato and Milton knew—that obedience means freedom—remains as true for us
as for Kant: "The light dove, cleaving the air in her free flight, and
feeling its resistance, might [well] imagine that its flight would be
still easier in empty space." (The sail-winged Satan tested the possibility for himself when he plummeted into the "illimitable Void" of
Chaos.) When Waldock maintains that *Paradise Lost* is a pretty bad

"novel" or when Brooks and Hardy contend that *A Mask* is a pretty good "drama," the results are the same though the aims are different; and we are not the richer for it in either case because the irrelevant genres prevent us from appreciating the way in which the poetry is "ever best found in the close."[8]

Between the beginning and the end, between the "question and answer" of the classical narrative, there is, observes Barthes, a "whole dilatory area" of "reticence"—the "rhetorical figure which interrupts the sentence, suspends it, turns it aside (Virgil's *Quos ego . . .*)"; there is "the *snare* (a kind of deliberate evasion of the truth), the *equivocation* (a mixture of truth and snare which frequently, while focussing on the enigma, helps to thicken it), the *partial answer* (an aphasic stoppage of the disclosure), and *jamming* (acknowledgement of insolubility)."[9] These devices, particularly as they involve "expectation in preference to surprise" or the "incompletion of a known completion," Milton exploits in both smaller and larger aspects of his "answerable style," answerable to the reality of Christian Time with its beginning and end in the Word. What Barthes sees as equivocation, partial answer, and enigma Milton knew as paradox or "brotherly dissimilitude" and *crypsis*.

In Chapter XVII of the Second Book of his *Art of Logic* Milton remarks the importance of "method," which must be considered a divine gift that secures "order"—itself a great virtue—in life and art. Method consists in the "disposition of various homogeneous axioms" that permit the intellect to proceed from the universal to the particular, which means for Milton a movement from the "better known, and clearer" to the "more obscure," from a "very general definition" to a "less general," and from the "simple to the composite." This is Vergil's method, not in the *Aeneid* but in the *Georgics*; it is the method of Cicero in his orations where the disposition of *in prooemio, narratione, confirmatione,* and *peroratione* follows the "order of art and nature" (*Works*, XI, 471–83). But there is in addition a "general effect of disposition" called *crypsis* or "concealment" that results from "defect or redundance or inversion of parts" (*Works*, XI, 297), which corresponds to the "triple crypsis of the sorites" in logic, that is, "defect, redundance, and inversion" (*Works*, XI, 469). When the "auditor is to be allured by pleasure or some stronger impulse," as for instance in poetry, which in the famous words from *Of Education* is "more simple, sensuous, and passionate," then a "crypsis of method will usually be employed": certain axioms suppressed, some redundancy in "lingerings on the fact," and "especially the order of things will be inverted" (*Works*, XI, 483–85). Poets may, that is, begin with the more particular and (hence) the more obscure, hinting through some significant "defect" that the reader must stand in expectation of the close, and then end with the more general and (therefore) more clear, as in *Lycidas* and the major poems, where the cryptic "defect . . . of parts" corresponds to Puttenham's version of prolepsis, "purporting at the first blush a defect which afterward is supplied, the Greeks call him *Prolepsis*, we the Propounder." The poem, resembling God's way with history, shadows its closure in its opening—but not without some "crypsis of method."

Of all the great divisions made "in the beginning," that between Time and Eternity seems the most remarkable and the most "cryptic" (in all senses); certainly it possesses the greatest portion of metaphysical grandeur, though it is also, of all the dualisms that trouble the devout Christian, the one most likely to exacerbate manichaean doubts. Although Plato's view of Time as the "moving image" of Eternity may be taken to imply that the two modes of duration resemble each other, the trace of likeness might easily be obscured. Davies of Hereford unhesitatingly declares that "Eternity and Time are opposite."[10] The two are most often opposite when eternity is defined not as infinite duration but as timelessness, which may then produce almost insoluble problems for the truly devout. "What is the Life of Man," asks Samuel Annesley, "but a coming into time, and a going out into Eternity?" You "stand in time, but you should look into Eternity: you stand tottering upon the very brink of time, and when by Death thrust out of time, you must into Eternity. . . ."[11] This "tottering upon the very brink of time" may become intolerable for the inquiring Christian if he happens to conceive of eternity as a timeless realm, for as J. L. Stocks puts it, "If the Divine life is temporal, the analogy of human purpose serves pretty well. God is the great artificer who moulds things to His will, as man, with infinitely less wisdom and power, moulds things to his." But "if the Divine life is timeless, the analogy with human purpose fails."[12] It is the problem implicit in the two creations of Genesis, translated to the metaphysical plane of discourse.

A partial solution may be found in the Incarnation, in the great exemplar, Jesus the Christ, "the *same yesterday, to day,* and *for ever,* standing in the middle-space," according to Peter Sterry, "between Eternity and Time; joining in one, Eternity with all its Glories, and

Time with all its diverse Births and Successions." Since He stands in this world to signify the union of "God and the Creature, of Eternity and Time," His Incarnation may be taken by some to guarantee the possibility of traffic between what would otherwise be the great "opposites." Man himself may participate in double duration. Possessor of an immortal soul, he also inherits flesh; and when, in the "inferior part of the Soul, Motion and Time have their first birth," man himself becomes "mixt of Eviternity and Time."[13]

Such theological considerations channel, and intensify, the feeling for paradox that we share in being human, for as Thomas Jackson says, the Christian knows that "things have a kind of double duration, and run a course of time as it were indented":

> Life, albeit in it self most sweet, yet in us is often charged with ... great measure of sowr occurrences. ... The gluts or gushes of pleasure, may at one time be much greater than another, yet still transient, never consistent. The fruition of them cannot possibly be entire: begotten and dying in every moment; they are, and they are not in a manner, both at once; so that we lose them as we gain them.[14]

This "kind of double duration" remains inaccessible to Aristotelian or natural reason, which in Milton's *Art of Logic* (*Works*, XI, 93) can know only that time is "duration of things past, present, and future"; but the idea of divided durations is open in some measure to "regenerate reason" (*ratio recta*), which is the faculty that chooses, that liberates, and that leads to both virtue and truth. Milton found in his later years that he had, as a young man, placed rather too much confidence in the powers of natural reason—usually called "understanding" in the anti-episcopal tracts—and in the human institutions that supposedly embodied these powers.[15]

Northrop Frye accurately summarizes the most important results of Milton's maturer views:

> The visual emphasis that Milton distrusts as potential idolatry exists in time as well as space. In time it takes the form of an anxiety of continuity, which produces the doctrine of apostolic succession in the Church and the principle of hereditary succession in the state. The belief that all matrimonial contracts have to be treated as unbreakable is a by-product of the same anxiety. Apostolic succession replaces the spiritual succession of those called by God with the mechanical continuity of a human office; hereditary succession similarly destroys the divine principle of the leadership of the elect. The genuine king, like the genuine prophet, emerges when God calls

him. The succession of leaders and prophets is discontinuous in human terms, and no human devices will safeguard it. Thus, according to the opening of the Gospel of Matthew, Jesus was legitimately descended from Abraham and David through his father Joseph, and yet Jesus was not the son of Joseph. Samson was one of a line of heroes called by God when his people turned again to him after a period of apostasy. The calling is represented by a very beautiful annunciation story in the Book of Judges, which ends with the angel returning to heaven in the fire on an altar. This image, twice referred to in *Samson Agonistes*, modulates into the image of the phoenix, the image of divine succession, a unique power of renewal through total self-sacrifice which cannot be programmed, so to speak, by any human institution.[16]

To make use of the vocabulary of *Areopagitica*, Milton has finally come to the realization that in this fallen world there can be no true "continuity"; the Temple of the Lord "cannot be united into a continuity, it can but be contiguous in this world."[17]

The younger Milton had entered the pamphlet wars with chaste hopes and virginal zeal, exhorting his countrymen to shake off the tyranny of custom, to return to the pristine original of the church of Christ, and to adopt the "one right discipline" in ecclesiastical matters that would hasten the establishment of *regnum christi* in England. But his countrymen proved recalcitrant, Milton himself lost faith in the imminence of Millennium, and then "home he returns a married man, that went out a bachelor." In the divorce tracts that follow the estrangement from Mary Powell, Milton comes more and more to emphasize the role of regenerate reason in relation to the rule of charity. The subtitle, "guided by the Rule of Charity," of *Doctrine and Discipline of Divorce*, indicates both the direction and end of Milton's thought: we must not accept "*any* precept" (my stress) in the Bible—particularly, one supposes, Jesus' words forbidding divorce—unless "charity commends it."[18] Out of the experience of the marriage Milton had come to realize that he did not possess the Pauline "gift" of virginity, and we will, indeed, no longer hear about the trinity of Faith, Hope, and Chastity that had sustained The Lady of *A Mask*. Milton had come to conceive what it was "to grind in the mill of a servil copulation," and he had learned not only that the rule of charity must be paramount in judging the deeds of men and the word of God, and not only that even the wisest and the most chaste of men are liable to error because insufficiently protected by natural understanding and the

"one right discipline." He had also come to respect anew the meaning of the great divisions created by God "in the beginning." Even
before the writing of *Areopagitica* he had reached a fresh understanding of sect and schism by meditating in *Doctrine and Discipline*
on the

> "allegorick precepts of beneficence fetcht out of the closet of nature
> to teach us goodnes and compassion in not compelling together un-
> matchable societies, or if they meet through mischance, by all conse-
> quence to dis-joyn them, as God and nature signifies and lectures to
> us not onely by those recited decrees, but ev'n by the first and last
> of all his visible works; when by his divorcing command the world
> first rose out of Chaos, nor can be renewed again out of confusion
> but by the separating of unmeet consorts" (*Works*, III, 419–20).

Distinguishing opposites must precede renewal and unification,
which is to say that dualism necessarily precedes monism.

To bind *Areopagitica* to its occasion—the licensing act of 1643—
contracts the horizons of Milton's vision, which includes in its view a
wide-ranging and often profound meditation on the life of the
intellect, the nature of Truth, and the relation of Good to Evil.
Although Milton wrote to "deliver the press from the restraints
with which it was encumbered,"[19] the question of censorship, ultimately a question of reason in relation to freedom of choice, excited in the future epic poet a variety of moral and political observations that clearly imply an artistic credo. The notorious "misreading" in which Milton appeals not to the "sage and serious" doctrine
of Virginity but to the "sage and serious" example of Spenser reveals much, for Milton seems to remember that Spenser, the "better teacher," brings Guyon "with his palmer through the cave
of Mammon."[20] But since the "better teacher" intends in this instance to demonstrate the strength of Temperance apart from rational "election" (*proairesis*), Spenser takes care to have Guyon enter
alone and without a guide. And since the Palmer represents what in
the *Apology for Smectymnuus* is referred to as "regenerate reason"
(*Works*, III, i, 287), Milton's slip of the pen bypasses Spenser's attempt to show Guyon's reliance on the *habitus* of temperance and
points towards Milton's own emphasis on the active choices of the
"true warfaring Christian," whose "freedom" of "Will" everywhere
depends on *ratio recta* because "Reason also is choice" (*PL*, III, 108).
In *Areopagitica* choice must be exercised constantly in the discrimination of opposites, for we "bring not innocence into the world":
"that which purifies us is trial, and trial is by what is contrary."[21]

And the mature Milton had come to see that rational choice could not in a fallen world be confined to any "one right discipline," for "good and evil . . . grow up together almost inseparably . . . in so many cunning resemblances hardly to be discerned"[22] that "a man may [easily] be a heretic in the truth,"[23] and it is in any case "not impossible that she [Truth] may have more shapes than one" in this world, especially in matters of "things indifferent," where "Truth may be on this side, or on the other, without being unlike herself."[24] When "God gave [man] reason, he gave him freedom to choose, for reason is but choosing";[25] and yet to discern the "cunning resemblances" of the great moral opposites has become vastly more complicted than it was for the inviolate Lady of *A Mask* or, it may be thought, for the Lady of Christ's College, Cambridge.[26]

There is an ethical dilemma here that tends to issue in "contrariety" and paradox, much in the way that the notion of *felix culpa* produces "contradiction" in *Paradise Lost*. God shall bring "goodness immense" out of evil, and since all things finally do the will of God—even the Adversary of *Paradise Regained* "contrary unweeting . . . fulfill'd" the "purpos'd Counsel preordain'd and fixt" (I, 125–26)—Milton's reiterated insistence on freedom consists, in the last analysis, in choosing to do the will of God, which produces paradoxical variations on the psychological truth that obedience is freedom. (As Abdiel tells Satan [*PL*, VI, 181], "Thyself not free, but to thyself enthrall'd.") In *Areopagitica* this newly-won awareness of the "cunning resemblances" of the great opposites has led to disagreement about Milton's position and may be one of the reasons why for the most part other controversialists took care to avoid—or at least found it possible to ignore—the poet's arguments.[27]

Areopagitica conforms faithfully to the traditional structure of the oration.[28] The *partitio* advertises four main points—the last subdivided into three—and Milton follows the plan scrupulously within the larger pattern of the five-part *oratio*; but there are present, nevertheless, alogical elements that imply a struggle to articulate matters that lie beyond the reach of ordinary discourse. Truth herself is specifically a "virgin,"[29] and yet this "virgin Truth," possessing the greatest "ingenuity" (free-born candor and liberality), "opens herself faster than the pace and method of discourse."[30] And the tendency toward paradox appears not only in traditional forms, as when Milton hazards that "we have looked so long upon the blaze that Zwinglius and Calvin hath beaconed up to us, that we are stark blind."[31] It may be felt as well in the eloquent cataracts of mixed metaphors. The English people, about to enter the "ways [and wars] of truth," are serpentine in "casting off the old and wrinkled skin of corruption"; the English nation is a female Samson who shall rouse "herself like a strong man" and shake "her invincible locks"; she is an "eagle,"

> muing her mighty youth, and kindling her undazzled eyes at the full midday beam; purging and unscaling her long-abused sight at the fountain itself of heavenly radiance; while the whole noise of timorous and flocking birds, with those also who love the twilight, flutter about, amazed at what she means, and in their envious gabble would prognosticate a year of sects and schisms.[32]

Although we "boast our light," the "sun itself" may smite "us into darkness."[33] The "body" of the "virgin Truth" is "homogeneal and proportional," a "perfect shape most glorious to look upon," but fallen men have "hewed her lovely form into a thousand pieces." The task of the Reformers, "still closing up truth to truth," therefore seems entirely clear: it is to gather "up limb by limb," and it is the "wicked race of deceivers" who are the "dividers of unity, who neglect and permit not others to unite those dissevered pieces which are yet wanting to the body of Truth."[34] And yet, to approach what in another context might be thought of as contradiction, "we care not to keep truth separate from truth, which is the fiercest rent and disunion of all."[35]

Such examples—and many more might be adduced—betoken neither confusion nor logical contradiction; yet neither may they be explained away solely by attention to individual context or by recourse to certain undeniable complexities in the metaphysical context, as for instance that the oration appeals to postlapsarian men on the basis of a prelapsarian vision of the "homogeneal" nature of the "virgin Truth." What comes close to logical contradiction on the level of the argument as a whole has its counterpart in the cascades of contrary images, and these, at crucially difficult points in the disquisition, precipitate not merely into "neighboring differences"[36] about matters indifferent but into explicit paradoxes about matters significant. Plato (Laws 644) allows the Athenian to propose that we may "conceive each of us living beings to be a puppet of the Gods, either their plaything only, or created with a purpose—which of the two we cannot certainly know." But we "do know, that [our] affections in us are like cords and strings, which

pull us in different and opposite ways, and to opposite actions; and
herein lies the difference between virtue and vice."[37] Although
Milton acknowledges that "herein lies the difference between
virtue and vice," he knew that man had indeed been "created with a
purpose," or purposes, one of which was to exercise precisely that
kind of freedom denied to puppets; "when God gave him reason,
he gave him freedom to choose, for reason is but choosing; he had
been else a mere artificial Adam, such an Adam as he is in the
motions" or puppet shows. It follows that we cannot remove vice by
banishing "all objects of lust" or by practicing the "severest discipline that can be exercised in any hermitage"; "look how much we
thus expel of sin, so much we expel of virtue: for the matter of
them both is the same; remove that, and ye remove them both
alike. This justifies the high Providence of God. . . ." Such "great
care and wisdom is required to the right managing of this point"
that we may not trust ourselves to him who is, perhaps like the
earlier Milton, "but a youngling" in virtue, for "they are not skilful
considerers of human things who imagine to remove sin by remov-
ing the matter of sin"—because "it is a huge heap increasing under
the very act of diminishing."[38]

Contradictions, antithetical images, and powerful antitheses find
expression, at points like these, in paradox, which is man's response
in language to human and divine "mystery." In part by discovering
that even the wisest and most virtuous may err, Milton had come to
count himself among the "skilful considerers of human things"
who recognize that the opposites of good and evil, truth and false-
hood, and virtue and vice are not easily distinguished. Nor can one
opposite be eradicated without destroying the other; "how much
we expel of sin, so much we expel of virtue." Sir Thomas Browne
likewise knew that the wisest men may err, for "every man is his
owne *Atropos*, and lends a hand to cut the thred of his owne dayes";
and therefore Browne reasons that "when vice gaines upon the
major part, vertue, . . . being lost in some, multiplies its goodnesse
in others . . . and persists entire in the general inundation." In
brief, "They that endeavour to abolish vice destroy also vertue, for
contraries, though they destroy one another, are yet the life of one
another."[39] Although this awareness of antinomy in the moral life
seems to have come almost easily to Browne, Milton's hard-won
acceptance of the equivocalities of human experience must have
had its origin in a nature at least unconsciously receptive to contrary alternatives.

Sonnet IX, for example, locates alternative possibilities "at the mid-hour of night":

> Lady that in the prime of earliest youth,
>> Wisely hast shunn'd the broad way and the green,
>> And with those few art eminently seen
>> That labor up the Hill of Heav'nly Truth,
> The better part with *Mary* and with *Ruth*
>> Chosen thou hast; and they that overween,
>> And at thy growing virtues fret their spleen,
>> No anger find in thee, but pity and ruth.
> Thy care is fixt and zealously attends
>> To fill thy odorous Lamp with deeds of light,
>> And Hope that reaps not shame. Therefore be sure
> Thou, when the Bridegroom with his feastful friends
>> Passes to bliss at the mid-hour of night,
> Hast gain'd thy entrance, Virgin wise and pure.

We know that the Lady receives her meed of praise for virtues that Milton had sought for himself—perhaps pre-eminently the virtue of virginity; and yet the syntax of the last few lines may be thought to induce a "flicker of hesitation" with respect to whose entrance is to be gained by whom. Although there can be no doubt that "Thou" must be understood as the subject of the main predication, the length of the subordinate clause allows its grammatical subject, the "Bridegroom," to linger on the periphery of the mind just long enough to provoke a moment of indecision; and it can be demonstrated that the earlier portions of the sonnet anticipate, even reinforce, the latent ambiguity of the final lines. The poem moves, imaginatively, from "prime" to the "mid-hour of night" through what may be thought of as two differing contexts of allusion, one culminating in the Parable of the Wise and Foolish Virgins, who are called at midnight; and the other in the story of Ruth the Moabite, which reaches its climax when Boaz turns in his slumber at the hour of midnight. The young woman of the sonnet, whose historical identity is unknown but whose virtues might cause Milton to identify with her, may be numbered among the virtuous "few" because she has "chosen" the "better part with Mary," which means that the Lady has chosen the "contemplative life" in Christ rather than the "active life" in the world represented by Martha (Luke 10); this allusion anticipates the choice of the five Wise Virgins who "fill" their "odorous Lamp[s]" against the coming at midnight of Christ the Bridegroom.

But the Lady has also "chosen" the "better part with . . . Ruth," who elected to leave her native Moab—her sister chose to remain—with Naomi, her Hebrew mother-in-law, and to go to Jerusalem where she gleans the alien corn. ("If I should say I have hope, if I should say I have an husband tonight. . . .") When Naomi hears that Boaz has looked with favor on Ruth as she follows his reapers, Naomi instructs her to lie at his feet when he sleeps; he turns at the "mid-hour" of night, observes the Moabite and the proprieties, and marries her.[40] This allusion, oddly intensified by the rime riche of line eight, re-surfaces in the "Hope that reaps not shame" of line eleven and anticipates, in its muted appeal for a chaste union with an earthly bridegroom, the hint of ambiguity in the last lines. The poet has indeed praised the virtue of the Lady, but with exquisite tact, conscious or unconscious, he has managed to suspend the future alternatives in a state approaching equilibrium: the Lady may, with Mary and the Wise Virgins, look toward marriage at the "mid-hour" to the Heavenly Bridegroom; and at the "mid-hour of night" she may also, with Ruth, entertain the possibility of a chaste marriage to an earthly bridegroom. The absolute choice between virginity and chastity that had troubled the Lady of Christ's and that has troubled critics of the Lady of *A Mask* need not yet disturb the Lady who lives in the "prime of earliest youth."

But this sense of contrary possibilities, this sense of what Eliot detects in Marvell (an awareness, implicit in every experience, of other and even opposite kinds of experience that are possible), appears most clearly in the greater poems and in *Areopagitica*. In *Areopagitica* it emerges not only in the imagery and in the tendency toward logical contradiction but also in Milton's understanding of the Fall, which is viewed, emphatically, as a lapse from *integritas* or "oneness" into the dualities and oppositions of human life as we know it:

> It was from out the rind of one apple tasted, that the knowledge of good and evil, as two twins cleaving together, leaped forth into the world. And perhaps this is that doom which Adam fell into of knowing good and evil, that is to say, of knowing good by evil.[41]

The "virgin Truth" similarly existed in a state of singular perfection, all her body "homogeneal"; and this understanding of the Fall even, and remarkably, corresponds to Milton's understanding of language in *Paradise Lost*. The Adamic tongue, in which the rivers of Paradise "with Serpent error wand'ring" find their ways, is univocal, exists in a state of *integritas*, whereas the language of the fallen world, as the poet illustrates through etymological quibbles ("sapience"), betrays its lapse into a duality that is as double as the mind of man. The "cunning resemblances" that the great opposites bear to each other receive in the passage of the "one apple tasted" from *Areopagitica* their most profound and compressed formulation. What appears elsewhere as antithetical image or even logical contradiction here approaches Freud's notion of the "primal word." It will be granted, at least initially, that logical contradiction may be recognized, in rhetoric and on a smaller scale, as antithesis; that antithesis, phrased keenly in brief compass, may be considered paradox; that paradox in image or idea, when collapsed into a single locution, may be thought of as oxymoron; and that oxymoron compressed becomes "primal word," as for instance in the word "cleaving." The "two twins," presumably Siamese, of good and evil are "cleaving together" in a marriage of untrue minds, but we also and infallibly know that in the wars of truth, where "that which purifies us is trial, and trial is by what is contrary," our best endeavors must be to discriminate, to cleave the great opposites in twain and to choose freely in accord with right reason and the will of God.

The play of antithetical figures has its basis in venerable analogies between poetry and the world, both of which reveal the patterning of *discordia concors* or what Spenser's "E. K." calls "disorderly order." Vives, commenting on Augustine's use of analogy in *Citie of God* 11.18, makes the matter explicit: "God would never have foreknowne vice in any worke of his, Angell, or Man, but that he knew in like manner, what good use to put it unto; so making the world's course, like a faire poeme, more gratious by *Antithetike* figures." (So Milton's Satan when "contrary unweeting" he "fulfill'd.") "*Antitheta*" are "called in Latine, opposites" and are "the most decent [decorous, comely] figures of all elocution." Vives concludes: "Thus as these contraries opposed doe give the saying an excellent grace, so is the worlds beauty composed of contrarieties, not in figure, but in nature."[42] God's work from and "in the beginning" was, as Edmund Calamy told the members of the House of Lords at Westminster, 25 December 1644, "to bring light out of darknesse, good out of evill, unitie out of division," for "He worketh by contraries." This is "true both in Philosophy and in Divinitie," for the primitive church was "like a pure Virgin" but afterwards she "fell into divisions & lost her Virginity."[43]

And something like this appears to be true not only of philosophy and divinity but also of Freud's findings as well. (Some may like to recall in this context the "uncertainty principle" and the "principle of complementarity" of modern physics.) A decade after the *Traumdeutung* Freud chanced upon the work of the philologist Karl Abel, which clarified a crucial aspect of the dream-work that the master of them who know the unconscious "did not then understand"; and accordingly Freud begins his review of Abel's work by quoting from *The Interpretation of Dreams*.

> The way in which dreams treat the category of contraries and contradictories is highly remarkable. It is simply disregarded. "No" seems not to exist so far as dreams are concerned. They show a particular preference for combining contraries into a unity or for representing them as one and the same thing. Dreams feel themselves at liberty, moreover, to represent an element by its wishful contrary; so that there is no way of deciding at first glance whether any element that admits of a contrary is present in the dream-thoughts as a positive or as a negative.

What excited Fraud was the "astonishing information that the behavior of the dream-work is identical with a peculiarity in the oldest languages known to us"; and Freud quotes a number of passages from Abel, one of which I reproduce here.

> Now in the Egyptian language, this sole relic of a primitive world, there are a fair number of words with two meanings, one of which is the exact opposite of the other. Let us suppose, if such an obvious piece of nonsense can be imagined, that in German the word "strong" meant both "strong" and "weak"; that in Berlin the noun "light" was used to mean both "light" and "darkness"; that one Munich citizen called beer "beer," while another used the same word to speak of water: this is what the astonishing practice amounts to which the ancient Egyptians regularly followed in their language.

Freud observes that the antithetical meanings of primal words, like the dream-work itself, remain altogether inexplicable only insofar as we neglect the fact that all our "concepts owe their existence to comparisons"; and the quotations from Abel are again apposite: "If it were always light we should not be able to distinguish light from dark, and consequently we should not be able to have either the concept of light or the word for it. . . . Since every concept is in this way the twin [Siamese?] of its contrary, how could it be first thought of and how could it be communicated to other people who were trying to conceive it, other than by being measured against its contrary . . . ?" Freud's excitement stemmed ultimately from the discovery that the deeps of the mind might correspond to the depths of language as well as from the way Abel's thinking about opposites clarified his own.[44] A slip of the tongue, specimen of the psychopathology of everyday life, reveals the opposite of what we thought we meant or betrays through opposites what we do mean. These are "cunning resemblances" indeed.

Abel was himself elated to discover that what he thought he had discovered about ancient languages had been predicted, as it were, by the great logician Alexander Bain, whom I have already quoted in my Introduction:

> The essential relativity of all knowledge, thought, or consciousness, cannot but show itself in language. If everything that we can know is viewed as a transition from something else [ultimately its opposite, one supposes], every experience must have two sides; and either every name must have a double meaning, or else for every meaning there must be two names.

When the "higher genus" contains many members, "the contrariety, though no less real, becomes diffused. 'Red' in the universe *colour* is not negatived by any simple colour, but by a plurality of colours"; but when, on the other hand, the universe of discourse more nearly resembles the one created by the discourse of deity "in the beginning" and tends to emphasize the greater divisions, the class consists more exclusively of "two members," such as "straight-bent," "good-evil," and "virtue-vice." In this case the "one is the complete negative of the other." The nuances of our emotional life derive from circumstances like these, for "when an impression is repeated, after an interval, we are affected with a new and peculiar consciousness, the shock or consciousness of agreement in difference." And therefore "all feeling is two-sided," particularly those feelings actuated by the antithetical sense of primal opposites.[45] It is what we feel in a word like "sapience" or in the concluding lines of *Paradise Lost*—a cleaving together of opposed emotions that Milton in *Areopagitica* labels, accurately enough, "brotherly dissimilitudes."

Out of the divorce pamphlets had come a new awareness of the complexities of choice and of the value of sect and schism. In *Areopagitica* this awareness finds its "answerable style" in "antithetical figures," for paradox in its various forms may reflect the difficulty of the freedom that is choosing between the "cunning resemblances" of good and evil. "It was from out the rind of one apple tasted . . ." Milton therefore seems to be speaking of the architecture of his own artistic thought when he describes the edification of the Temple of the Lord:

> Yet these are the men cried out against for schismatics and sectaries; as if, while the temple of the Lord was building, some cutting, some squaring the marble, others hewing the cedars, there should be a sort of irrational men who could not consider there must be many schisms [!] and many dissections made in the quarry and in the timber, ere the house of God can be built. And when every stone is laid artfully together, it cannot be united into a continuity, it can but be contiguous in this world; neither can every piece of the building be of one form; nay rather the perfection consists in this, that out of many moderate varieties and *brotherly dissimilitudes* [my stress] that are not vastly disproportional, arises the goodly and the graceful symmetry that commends the whole pile and structure.[46]

Augustine's *antitheta* resemble Milton's "brotherly dissimilitudes" in that the principle of style includes a view of the world. Milton's similes exhibit difference-in-agreement, and the world described in *Paradise Lost* renews itself out of the opposition of the elements that "in quaternion run, perpetual circle," "rising or falling" like the exhalations to "still advance [the] praise" of creation and creator. In a fallen world we may be edified not with perfect "continuity" but only with "contiguity."[47]

Roman Jakobson had found it convenient to organize his thinking about aphasia in terms of *metaphor*, which stresses analogical "continuity" and moves toward identity (the plow sailed the furrow; Ajax is a dumb ox), and *metonymy*, which depends on juxtaposition or "contiguity" ("pair of ragged claws" for a lacerated psyche, or "skirt" for a female from the American culture of the past). The dyad likewise functions as an analytical tool in Jakobson's excursions into the area of literary criticism.[48] Jakobson's binary system of classification, having affinities on the one hand to information theory and, on the other, to the working distinction between *synchronic* and *diachronic* employed by Ferdinand de·Saussure, has resulted in a proliferation of dichotomies, though the dyad metaphor and metonymy retains its fashionable importance. In *The Savage Mind*, as well as in his later works, Claude Lévi-Strauss has recourse to the dyad in his ethnological studies; and Jacques Lacan has teased the terms through the byzantine by-ways of his studies of the

role of langauge in psychoanalysis.[49] Literary critics have not been
slow to embrace the beguiling dyad; and it is of course true that we
must think in terms of opposites, especially in the beginning,
though as always the necessity produces in criticism, as elsewhere,
its minor anomalies. David Lodge appeals to Jakobson's classic "Two
Aspects of Language and Two Types of Aphasic Disturbances" in
the course of an argument proving that "metaphor is the natural
means of expression" for the "central assertion of the modernist
novel," whereas Charles Altieri, who also makes use of Jakobson,
proves that the modern artist, in ardent "pursuit of metonymy,"
can see "no alternative to metonymic views of art and experience."[50]

Large dichotomies easily eventuate in alternative conclusions,
which may be one of the reasons lurking behind Northrop Frye's
opinion that "structuralism, hermeneutics, phenomenalism, socio-
linguistics, cultural anthropology, and the philosophy of language
have, as I think, made a rather disappointing contribution so far to
the understanding of literature, however relevant the context for it
that they have set up. . . ."[51] In the case of Milton the context may
be thought to have particular relevance because the pairing of
"continuity," which ratifies metaphor, and "contiguity," which implies metonymy, helps to illuminate the poet's complex response to
his postlapsarian world. Howard Nemerov, whom I have already
quoted in the first note of my Introduction, points out with wise
whimsy that "once there are opposites, a mere two tricks make
game. The first is that the opposites will have to bear on one and
the other hand the whole weight of the much and the many of the
world as experienced: every leaf and every star must join one team
or the other. The second is that, since a world of opposites is impossible, intolerable, the opposites must be mediated. . . ." Seamless
"continuity," represented in *Areopagitica* by the homogeneal and
proportional body of the Virgin Truth, existed once in Eden, appeared once more at the First Advent of Christ, and shall reappear
yet once more in "perfect form" at "her Master's second coming."

Meanwhile we confront, through the "allegorick precepts" of *Doctrine and Discipline*, the "contiguous" metonymies of the postlapsarian world that in the beginning "rose out of Chaos" at God's "di-
vorcing command" and that cannot "be renewed again but by the
separating of unmeet consorts," by the separating of the great opposites (to recur to *Areopagitica*) in spite of their many and "cunning
resemblances" produced by their "cleaving together." If "we care

not to keep truth separate from truth," we perpetrate "the fiercest rent and disunion of all"; and yet, to repeat the essential opposite, we must "gather up limb by limb," always "closing up truth to truth" in order to "unite those dissevered pieces which are yet wanting to the body of Truth." This task, as irreducibly double in its import as the paradox of the fortunate fall in *Paradise Lost*, has its corollary in the deployment of poetic images, where the task of likening spiritual to corporal forms and of comparing great things to small may involve a "flicker of hesitation" as "expectation stood" for a moment confounded by what "can but be contiguous" in Time—until "continuity" can be reasserted from the vantage of Eternity. The metonymic aspect of Milton's similes tends finally toward the reassertion of a kind of metaphorical identity, "more than on Earth is thought."

Milton stands at one of the critical junctures of Western history, marked broadly and a little inaccurately by the shift from forms of medieval realism to the kinds of nominalism present in Hobbes. Even in Browne, the author of *Vulgar Errors*, there persists the doctrine of "signatures and markes":

> I hold moreover that there is a Phytognomy, or Physiognomy, not onely of men, but of Plants, and Vegetables; and in every one of them, some outward figures which hang as signes or bushes of their inward formes. The finger of God hath left an inscription upon all his workes, not graphicall or composed of Letters, but of their severall formes, constitutions, parts, and operations, which aptly joyned together doe make one word that doth expresse their natures. By these Letters God cals the Starres by their names, and by this Alphabet *Adam* assigned to every creature a name peculiar to its Nature.[52]

The doctrine of signatures rests on two important assumptions— that each entity has a "form," "essence," "nature," or *quidditas*, which makes it what it *is*, and that the primary object of inquiry lies in the relation of things and words, *res et verba*. In Plato's *Cratylus* the inquiry is both philosophical, depending in part on the Theory of Forms, and philological, concerned with the way etymologies may or may not reveal the true relation of the word to the thing; the dialogue is inconclusive, as is the subsequent history of the debate. (As late as the nineteenth century, to cite the notorious example, it was assumed on the basis of etymology that men could not be "hysterics.") Adam in Eden possessed angelic or "Intuitive"

(*PL,* V, 488) powers of ratiocination, which corresponds to the
Scholastic understanding of Aristotle's *nous* (L. *intueor* or the in-
stantaneous illumination proceeding from unimpaired intellectual
vision); and through this "sudden apprehension" of the forms of
things the first man accorded each animal passing before him the
one right name that signifies essence. But then there occurred the
Fall and the Tower of Babel . . . though the belief in the doctrine of
signatures survives in combination with the effort to recover, directly through philological excavation or indirectly through the
construction of a "real character," the Adamic language. In the
English Renaissance, from Ascham through Bacon, the insistent
conundrums lie in the relation, often an opposition, of words to
things. Since for Bacon "words are but the images of matter," the
advancement of learning depends, quite simply, on our not confusing the two, for "to fall in love with them is all one as to fall in love
with a picture" in "Pygmalion's frenzy."[53]

But for Hobbes words are no longer "signs of the things themselves." They are "signs of our conceptions,"[54] which makes for a
momentous shift because it deflects attention from the doctrine of
signatures as a guarantor of meaning and focusses on the relation
of "Perspicuous Words" to ideas. Instead of attempting to divine
the hidden "forms" of things and then settling on the right word—
"quincunx," say—to describe God's "signature," the effort in
Hobbes, and Locke, is to clear the head of traditional detritus by
forming "exact definitions first snuffed and purged from ambiguity." The relation between the word and thing has been subordinated to the relation of the word and the idea; the thing itself no
longer reveals "continuity, it can but be contiguous in this world";
and *homo philosophicus,* whose little world made cunningly was related by resemblance to the larger world of nature, begins to turn
into Norbert Elias' *homo clausus,* whose interest lies in ideas and
words and whose relation to external nature has become tenuously
ambiguous without the "signatures" that point to the "essences" of
things.[55] Augustine's "I believe, therefore I am" had been loosely
translated into Descartes' *cogito ergo sum,* and Descartes himself
might have isolated himself from nature or "extension" had it not
been for the pineal gland and a residuum of deity; Leibniz found
himself living among "windowless monads" that manage the acts of
individual and social intercourse by metaphysical fiat; and Kant's
"subject" looks out from an aprioristic bathysphere in an attempt to
discern the *ding an sich.* D. H. Lawrence's attack on Ben Franklin

assumes a situation in which it is "me" (the isolated, and belea-
gured, individual) against "them" (and the "dummy standards" of
"their" society); and in such terms we now, anachronistically, read
Sophocles' *Antigone*. In a situation like this we are invited to choose,
though it finally makes little difference under the circumstances,
between Cartesian man, who assumes the Platonic doctrine of in-
nate ideas, and Condillac's Sensitive Statue, who had to begin his
intellectual existence, fortunately enough for him, with a whiff of
jasmine. There were headier scents available, even in the 1740s,
and, as it is, *homo clausus* has little enough air to breathe.

In the older epistemology, as Aristotle makes explicit in the
Nicomachean Ethics, you had to be one to know one; Robert Greville,
whose *Truth* Milton had read with care, simply assumes that "what
good we know, we are: our act of understanding being an act of
union."[56] Milton himself assumes the older epistemology when in
the *Apology* he describes the act of composition as an act of union;
the poet "ought himself to be a true poem, that is, a composition
and pattern of the best and honorablest things."[57] But modern
thinkers require detachment or, as the parlance has it, "objectivity,"
which effectually separates the knower from the thing known. Separation becomes the condition of knowing, and man himself becomes separate from the *polis*. The autonomous self or little world,
once it has been detached from the macrocosm, necessarily retires
into what Keats finely calls the "hushed casket" of the soul, ex-
periencing private joys and agonies apart from the rest of mankind; every man is an island. The thinkers of the Reformation,
shifting the external prohibitions of shame toward the inhibitions
of guilt, emphasize what Milton calls the "umpire Conscience"
within the individual human being, which may in turn produce an
emphasis on the chastity or even the virginity of one who is isolated
in unspotted purity from society; "these are they which are not
defiled with women, for they are virgins: these are they which
follow the Lamb" (*CD, Works,* XVII, 219). For Milton there finally
remains but One Just Man in each age, beginning with the pattern
laid up in Heaven by Abdiel and proceeding in discontinuous and
singular succession through such as Enoch down to Milton himself,
who writes for "fit audience . . . though few" in an unjust age the
third testament to God's Word and who composes his "true poem"
in "brotherly dissimilitudes."

The notion of a "real character" or universal language, in which
the word coincides unambiguously with the thing, represents a

secular version of the Adamic language, as may be detected even in
the phrasing of the historian of the Royal Society, who alludes to
the *"universal Confusion"* of Babel before praising the efforts of the
new natural philosophers "to return back to the primitive purity,
and shortness, when men deliver'd so many things, almost in an
equal number of *words*."[58] The compelling dream of an Adamic
tongue, surviving in altered form even in Thomas Sprat of the
Royal Society, was then succeeded by the equally odd ideal of language as the "perspicuous" or pure precipitate of thought, in which
the basic problem lies not in the relation of words to things but in
the relation of language to thought. The doctrine of signatures,
which had sanctified an "essential" connection between words and
things, encouraged even while it validated the habit of analogical
thinking; discovering "similitudes" and "correspondences" was the
means, as indeed it was one of the primary ends, of knowledge.
Knowing consisted in searching along an endless plane of receding
analogies in an effort to locate the *vestigia* of deity, to come upon
the core of mystery in the allegory of things and events produced
by the divine historian.

But the more sceptical thinkers of the seventeenth century questioned not only the doctrine of correspondences but also the analogy of microcosm and macrocosm—and not always on the basis of
Hobbesian materialism or the empiricism of, say, Robert Boyle,
who was pleased to "consider the frame of the World . . . as a Great,
and, if I may so speak, Pregnant *Automaton*" and "Human Bodies"
as "Hydraulico-pneumaticall Engines."[59] Milton shows considerable scepticism toward the legendary materials he handles in the
History of Britain, but his distrust of language derives not from
scepticism about the validity of the medium but from the Christian
conviction that words may be used truly by the inspired poet and
abused in the glozing terms of Comus or the false oracles of Satan.
The Adamic language, along with the homogeneal and proportional body of Truth, existed once in Eden in univocal splendor
and will return with the Second Advent, but in the fallen world
correspondence and analogy have become suspect, equivocal. The
great similitudes of antiquity, the older ways of comparing small
things to great, require qualification, for they "fable" and "feign"
or even "relate, erring." In this world the "continuity" that guarantees the efficacy of metaphor has been displaced by the "contiguity"
that implies metonymy, though the impulse toward metonymic
thinking will not, of course, take the form in Milton of, say, the
discontinuous imagery of "The Love Song of J. Alfred Prufrock."

Failing to keep "truth separate from truth" constitutes the "fiercest rent and disunion of all," for things "cannot be united into a continuity," they "can but be contiguous in this world"; and yet our aim in the "wars of truth" must be to unite the scattered limbs of the Virgin, to restore Her homogeneal and proportional unity. The two-fold task, "increasing under the very act of diminishing," produces the language of "brotherly dissimilitudes" in the great poems and implies an effort to achieve "continuity" in spite of the fact of "contiguity."

In Milton the desire for wholeness and the horror of dismemberment helps to explain the so-called "heresies" of his metaphysic. Early men presumably had other things on their minds than the philosophic differentiation of soul and body, self and nature; but Plato, among others, had leisure to distinguish, and certain strains in Christianity nurtured the cultures of dualism in Plato and the neo-Platonic thinkers—until it became commonplace to separate, even to oppose, body and soul, nature and grace, reason and faith, and time and eternity. Milton, whose tendency toward dualism seems obvious in the early tracts and in *A Mask*, moves later toward a kind of monism. In *Christian Doctrine* (*Works*, XIV, 35) he insists that man is created in the image of God "not only as to his soul, but also as to his outward form," and therefore Milton's doctrine of accommodation includes a sophisticated variety of anthropomorphism that has, it may be said, less "accommodating" to do (*Works*, XIV, 31–39). Man, created inwardly and outwardly in the image of God, forms an indivisible whole, for "it is said, as a consequence, that 'man became a living soul'; whence it may be inferred . . . that man is a living being, intrinsically and properly one and individual, not compound or separable, not, according to the common opinion, made and framed of two distinct natures, as of soul and body, but that the whole man is soul, and the soul man . . ." (*Works,* XV, 39–41).

From this formula for the integrity of man flow the other "heresies" of *Christian Doctrine* and the suspicions of heresy in *Paradise Lost*. Milton adopted the "mortalist" position that the "whole man," both soul and body, "dies" and is resurrected in his integrity (*Works*, XV, 219–51); even Jesus "was made flesh, without ceasing to be numerically the same as before" and died on the Cross in his divine as well as in his human nature (*Works*, XV, 263, 307–09). Similarly, Milton refused to accept the notion that Eternity is a "timeless" realm, entirely divorced from the world of Time, for there is "no sufficient foundation for the common opinion, that motion and time (which is the measure of motion) could not . . .

have existed before this world was made" (*CD, Works,* XV, 35), and in *Paradise Lost* the poet makes it explicit: "Time, though in Eternity, appli'd/ To motion. . ." (V, 580–81).[60] Similarly again, Milton denied creation *ex nihilo,* a world "formed from nothing," and proclaimed that "original matter" is "intrinsically good, and the chief productive stock of every subsequent good," for the prime matter was "of God and in God" (*Works,* XV, 17–27). It follows that the sociable angel of *Paradise Lost* digests his food with "real concoctive heat" and flushes the "proper hue" of excitation while discussing celestial intercourse; and if one is amused or irritated, perhaps one would make a good Cartesian . . . Although it may be doubted that the author of *A Mask* would have propounded such ideas, it seems clear that the idea of virgin wholeness has retained its importance in Milton's thinking; the notion of *integritas* has, however, been made to include not only the soul but the whole man, and it is finally extended to encompass Christ and the Creation.

From one perspective, the effort must be seen as an attempt to assert, or reassert, "continuity," to maintain a "metaphorical" or an "analogical" connection between man and God, the visible and the invisible worlds. Raphael in speaking to Adam, as Milton in speaking to us, must proceed by analogy, "by lik'ning spiritual to corporal forms"; but the method, "as may express them best," does not embarrass the angel in the way that it has discomfited some of Milton's critics. Since Raphael knows that all things are "of kind the same," he can permit himself to wonder whether the creation of the "one Almighty" does not possess more "continuity" than one might suppose, so that his analogies may be more apt than one might ordinarily assume:

> though what if Earth
> Be but the shadow of Heav'n, and things therein
> Each to the other like, more than on Earth is thought?
> (V, 574–76)

But finally the simile or analogy "can but be contiguous in this world." The "answerable style" used to convey the account of creation *ex Deo* may serve here as another case in point. Christ the "Omnific Word" may wield the "golden Compasses" in the manner of a human geometer "to circumscribe" the world and "all created things" (VII, 225 ff.), but since the matter is "of God and in God" and since God fills "infinitude, nor vacuous the space," the human analogy finally proves inadequate to this mystery and recourse must be made to a kind of "dissimilitude": God withdraws, as it were, from a part of himself but remains there as everywhere, proclaiming that "I uncircumscrib'd myself retire" (V, 179). Preeminently, perhaps, the poet must obtain an "answerable style" for the depiction of the ontological plant that in *Paradise Lost* represents the universe and "all created things."

> O *Adam*, one Almighty is, from whom
> All things proceed, and up to him return,
> If not deprav'd from good, created all
> Such to perfection, one first matter all,
> Indu'd with various forms, various degrees
> Of substance, and in things that live, of life;
> But more refin'd, more spiritous, and pure,
> As nearer to him plac't or nearer tending
> Each in thir several active Spheres assign'd,
> Till body up to spirit work, in bounds
> Proportion'd to each kind. So from the root
> Springs lighter the green stalk, from thence the leaves
> More aery, last the bright consummate flow'r
> Spirits odorous breathes: flow'rs and thir fruit
> Man's nourishment, by gradual scale sublim'd
> To vital spirits aspire, to animal,
> To intellectual, give both life and sense,
> Fancy and understanding, whence the Soul
> Reason receives, and reason is her being,
> Discursive, or Intuitive; discourse
> Is oftest yours, the latter most is ours,
> Differing but in degree, of kind the same.
>
> (V, 469–90)

Although the cosmogonic plant or tree is common enough in folklore and literature, Milton's version remains entirely his own.[61] For one thing, the emphasis on the pure being of the "one Almighty" and the "one first matter all" seems to assume if not creation *ex Deo* at least the goodness and the omnipresence of what is "of God and in God." For another thing, although the choice of words in "active Spheres assign'd" and "bounds" that are "proportion'd to each kind" seems to sanction the orthodox view of a rigid hierarchy in the chain of being, where the various degrees "can but be contiguous," this emphasis seems to run counter, at least in part, to the stress on "continuity" in the summary line: "Differing but in degree, of kind the same."

It is not merely that Milton, in accord with the direction of his other "heresies," wants to minimize the distance, while preserving the distinction, between human and angelic knowledge.[62] It is also that his description of the plant itself tends to assert "continuity" between the vegetable and animal kingdoms. Milton proceeds directly from the plant to man, carefully preserving the orthodox hierarchy of degree only in the doctrine of the spirits, those substances mysteriously mediating in triple gradation (vegetable, animal, intellectual) the extremes of body and soul. And then the poet, through verbal sleight, manages to slur the distinction between the plant itself and the higher degrees of being. Milton's concessive attitude toward gradation ("differing *but* in degree"), a consequence of his stress on "one first matter all," means that he will begin in traditional fashion "from the root"; but his ontological vegetable finally aspires beyond "the bounds proportion'd to each kind." Unlike the other cosmogonic plants of the period, which end in branches and fruits, Milton's enjambs the "bright consummate flow'r" and turns the line with a hint of human personification in "breathes" as well as a hazardous quibble on "spirits": "Spirits odorous breathes" enforces an almost magical sense of the interconnection, intimating that the plant and man may be "each to other like, more than on Earth is thought." The effect of all this is to grant degree and hierarchy, to recognize that "it cannot be united into a continuity, it can but be contiguous in this world"; and yet at the same time to assert a covert continuity underlying the various kinds that differ in degree, simultaneously preserving the "dissimilitudes" of being while whispering that the differences must be considered "neighborly" or "brotherly."[63]

Perhaps, after all, the "cunning resemblances" of the great contraries that arose "in the beginning" must be thought of "as two twins cleaving together"? If so, I do not think that these siblings leaped forth from Boyle's "Pregnant *Automaton*," which is "like a *Woman* with Twins in her Womb, or a Ship furnish'd with Pumps." Milton's understanding of the "frame of the World" depends, among many other things, on a view of Time that not only somehow resembles Eternity but derives its shape and power from Eternity. Boyle (and Hobbes, and others) knew, however, that

> many things are wont to be attributed to *Time*; as, when we say, that *Time* ripens some Fruits that are too early gather'd; that it makes many things moulder and decay, (*Tempus edax rerum*;) that 'tis the

Mother of Truth [*Veritas filia Temporis*]; that it produces great Alterations. . . . whereof really it is but an Adjunct.[64]

For Milton the eternal *logos*, which signifies reason, the word, and the Word, sanctifies "discourse," which means both reasoning and wording; language does not merely convey thought, it engenders and orders thought. But among the members of, say, the Royal Society, where thinking tends to follow the configurations of spatial and mechanical analogies, *verba* become subordinate to *res*; and temporal and verbal analogies become consequent to thought, illustrating it at best and, at worst, merely embellishing or even distorting it. In some ways Milton's view may be considered closer to commonsense, not to mention the researches of Merleau-Ponty, for it acknowledges that the name does not merely follow recognition but in a basic sense *is* the recognition.[65] But meanwhile the newer attitudes toward the word write an end to the close yet distant relation of Time to Eternity that had sustained a great poet in his life and that had enabled him to take down the dictation of the Holy Spirit in a language neither, quite, of metaphor nor of metonymy but of the "mysterious terms" of "brotherly dissimilitudes."

NOTES

1 "The Comings Forth of Christ" (London, 1650), A3ᵛ. Howard Nemerov, reviewing Harold Bloom in *Sewanee Review*, 83 (1975), explains:

> Thought proceeds to create the world by dividing it—what? the world, of course—into opposites, as in the initial Yin and Yang of the *Tao Te Ching,* the series of divisions in the first chapter of Genesis, the Love and Strife that Yeats took from Empedocles to be the base for the sequent complications of *A Vision,* and so on. Once there are opposites, a mere two tricks make game. The first is that the opposites will have to bear on one and the other hand the whole weight of the much and many of the world as experienced: every leaf and every star must join one team or the other. The second is that, since a world of opposites is impossible, intolerable, the opposites must be mediated and shown to be one; because, of course, in the world as experienced they *are* one....
>
> The opposites at first embody themselves in stories. How stories got started is as unknown and likely to remain so as how language did (they got together and talked it over among themselves?). With interpretation, whether exegesis or eisegesis, we are in a little better case: Edwin Honig tells us in his lovely book *Dark Conceit* that the behavior of the gods in Homer and in Hesiod was so scandalous it couldn't possibly mean what it plainly said it meant and had to be allegorized; hence scholiast, who begat rhapsode (like Ion) who begat exegete who begat theologian who begat literary critic who so far has begat nothing but more literary critic; an entire and respectable industry raised upon the strange mythological ordinance that things, in addition to being themselves, hence uninformative enough, had to mean something...else.

I have tried to allow Milton to mean what he said and not "something...else" while trying also to avoid Nemerov's third "melancholy

215

lesson or law" of modern criticism: "That the effort to render English unintelligible is proceeding vigorously at the highest levels of learning" (p. 169).

2 *Logic* (rev. ed.; New York, 1889), p. 54. Cf. the provocative use made of Bain by Freud in relation to the language of dreaming and waking in "The Antithetical Meaning of Primal Words," *Standard Edition of the Complete Psychological Works of Sigmund Freud,* tr. James Strachey with Anna Freud (24 vols.; London, 1953–74), XI (London, 1957), 155–61.

3 "Mower against Gardens," *Poems and Letters,* ed. H. M. Margoliouth (2 vols.; Oxford, 1952), I, 40.

4 *Of the Interchangeable Course, or Variety of Things in the Whole World,* tr. R[obert] A[shley] (London, 1594), p. 6. Cf. Lambert Daneau, *Wonderfull Woorkmanship of the World,* tr. T[homas] T[wyne] (London, 1578), pp. 85–86. The idea looks forward to Samuel Johnson on the "metaphysical poets," but the notion is itself very ancient; see Melissa C. Wanamaker, *Discordia Concors* (Port Washington, N. Y., 1975).

5 *Areopagitica, John Milton: Complete Poems and Major Prose,* ed. Merritt Y. Hughes (New York, 1957), pp. 728, 733. (Numbers in parentheses in my text will refer, unless otherwise indicated, to the Hughes' editon.) As Professor Enderby puts it drunkenly on a late-night talk show in Anthony Burgess' *The Clockwork Testament* (New York, 1975), p. 100: "A lot of simple (sinful?) bloody nonsense. You take the filament of human choice out of ethnical decisions. Men should be free to choose good. But theres no choice if theres only good. Stands to region there has to be evil as well."

6 See *Anthropologie Structurale* (Paris, 1958), *Le Totémisme* (Paris, 1962), and *La Pensée Sauvage* (Paris, 1962). Edmund Leach provides lucid exposition in *Claude Lévi-Strauss* (New York, 1970) and valuable analyses in *Genesis as Myth and Other Essays* (London, 1969).

7 Fr. Richard Simon was growing restive before the turn of the century in his *Critical History of the Old Testament,* tr. H. D. (London, 1682), p. 41:

> can any one believe that an Historian should write the History of the Creation of Man with so little order as there is in the first Chapter of Genesis. . . ? and moreover after the Man and the Woman were created in the first Chapter and 27th. Verse, the Woman is not supposed to be made, and in the following Chapter the manner how she was taken from *Adam's* side is described, nevertheless in the same Chapter it was before forbidden *him,* as he was her Husband, whom she accompanied in the Garden, to eat the fruit of a certain Tree.

Matthew Poole, *Annotations upon the Holy Bible,* 2 vols. (London, 1696; 3rd. ed., enlarged by Sam Clark and Edward Veale), representative of more orthodox opinion, simply glosses Genesis 1:27 in this fashion:

> Not both together, as some of the Jews have fabled, but successively, the Woman after and out of the Man, as is more particularly related, *Gen.*

2.21, &c. which is here mentioned by anticipation. Albeit the Woman also seems to have been made upon the sixth day, ... though the particular History of it is brought in afterwards Chap. 2. by way of recapitulation, or repetition.

Cf. Poole's *Synopsis Criticorum Aliorum Scriptae Interpretum,* 5 vols. in 4 (London, 1669–76); Andrew Willet, *Hexapla in Genesin* (Cambridge, 1605).

8 Sir Thomas Browne, *Religio Medici* ii.2, *Religio Medici and Other Works,* ed. L. C. Martin (Oxford, 1964), p. 58.

9 *The Confessions of Saint Augustine,* tr. Edward B. Pusey (New York, 1949), p. 253. Daniel Featley follows suit in *Clavis Mystica* (London, 1636), p. 401:

> Other things are with more ease described than understood; but *time* is easily understood, not described or defined so easily: there is no rusticke so rude who understandeth not what you meane when you speak of *time,* yet never any Philosopher to this day hath exactly defined or described it. ... I grant *time* is as it were a portion or cantle of eternity; yet I deny that this is a good description of *time,* because every description ought to be *per notius,* by something that is more known; whereas eternity is farre more obscure than *time* it selfe. ...

William Brent explains the fundamental difficulty in terms of the venerable "correspondence" theory of truth (to which Milton and Jonson acceded) in the preface to *A Discourse Upon the Nature of Eternitie* (London, 1655):

> Empedocles of Arigentum being demanded why 'twas so hard to finde out a wise man, gave this reason; because (said he) none can finde one out, who is not so himselfe; thereby inferring, that unlesse there bee a proportion between the object and the power, it will never bee able to produce the effects flowing from it. Upon this ground it may be well concluded, that t'is [sic] impossible for any to give a true description of Eternity, who hath no subsistence but in time. ...

Bacon, *Works,* edd. Spedding, Ellis, and Heath, VII (1892), 225–26, allows the usual tripartite division:

> there are three times (if times they may be called) or parts of eternity: The first, the time before beginnings, when the Godhead was only, without the being of any creature: The second, the time of the mystery, which continueth from the time of creation to the dissolution of the world: And the third, the time of the revelation of the sons of God; which time is the last, and is everlasting without change.

To go farther means to turn to hyperbole or paradox, which is the task of the poet.

10 *Religio* i.11, p. 11.

11 Thomas Blundeville, *His Exercises* (London, 1594), "The great yeare is a space of time in the which not onely all the Planets, but also all the fixed starres that are in the firmament, having ended all their revo-

lutions do returne againe to the selfe same places in the heavens, which they had at the first beginning of the world. . . ." (fol. 168). The *magnus annus* corresponds to God and has its microcosm in the annular composition of the stars. "One of the most convenient Hieroglyphicks of God," says Donne, on one of many occasions, in *Sermons,* edd. E. M. Simpson and G. R. Potter, VI (Berkeley and Los Angeles, 1953), 173, "is a Circle," and "His Sun, and Moone, and Starres, (Emblemes and Instruments of His Blessings) move circularly, and communicate themselves to all. His Church is his chariot; in that, he moves more gloriously, then in the Sun; as much more, as his begotten Son exceeds his created Sun, and his Son of glory, and of his right hand, the Sun of the firmament; and this Church, his chariot, moves in that communicable motion, circularly. . . ." Browne, *Religio* i.17, p. 18, explains that "the lives not onely of men, but of commonweales, and the whole World, run not upon an Helix that still enlargeth, but on a Circle. . . ." (Cf. Dante, *Inferno* viii; *Roman de la Rose* 16801 ff.)

12 12.13. Ed. Juan L. Vives, tr. J[ohn] H[ealey] (London, 1620), pp. 452–53. Paul Tillich (in common with many modern theologians) attacks "circular" views of time, which he casually (in common with many modern scholars) associates with the Greeks, in *The Interpretation of History,* tr. N. A. Rasetzke and Elsa Talmay (New York, 1936), esp. pp. 242 ff. But for the Renaissance commonplace, which is finally not incompatible with Augustine, see Joseph Fletcher's preface to *The Historie of the Perfect-Cursed-Blessed Man* (London, 1628): "God is Alpha and Omega, both first and last: the first of Causes, the last of Ends, that is, all in all: they being in him *simul,* as one individuall substance, or continued motion; He being in Him-selfe [in the famous definition from *The Book of the XXIV Philosophers* that caught the fancy of thinkers from Nicolas of Cusa to Sir Thomas Browne], *Eus cujus centrum est ubique & cujus circumferentia nullibi. . . .*" (Cf. Browne, *Pseudodoxia* 8.2.) As the Rev. Thomas Jackson declares, *Works,* ed. Barnabas Oley (3 vols.; London, 1673), II, 36, "Or, to speak as we think, it is impossible to conceive any duration to be without beginning, and ending, without conceiving it circular. . . ." And Augustine himself, when not agitated by polemical necessities, *On Music,* tr. Robert C. Taliaferro, "Fathers of the Church," II (New York, 1947), p. 355, can speak of the "times . . . imitating eternity as they do when the turn of the heavens comes back to the same state, and the heavenly bodies to the same place. . . . So terrestrial things are subject to celestial, and their time circuits (*circuitus)* join together in harmonious succession for a poem of the universe." So also Richard Hooker, *Works,* edd. John Keble, R. W. Church, and F. Paget, II (7th ed., rev.; Oxford, 1888), *Laws* V.lxix.2: "forasmuch as that motion is circular whereby we make our divisions of time, and the compass of that circuit such, that the heavens which are therein continually moved and keep in their motions uniform celerity

must needs touch often the same points, they cannot choose but bring unto us by equal distances frequent returns of the same times." The "two letters of Greece," Alpha and Omega, refer to Christ Himself because, says Tertullian, *On Monogamy,* edd. Alexander Roberts and James Donaldson (Michigan, 1956), IV, 62, He "figures the beginning and end which concur in Himself: so that, just as Alpha rolls on till it reaches Omega, and again Omega rolls back till it reaches Alpha, in the same way He might show that in Himself is both the downward course of the beginning on to the end, and the backward course of the end up to the beginning; so that every economy, ending in Him through whom it began . . . may have an end correspondent to the beginning." When Vaughan in "The World" envisages the rush of "Time in hours, days, years," it is "round beneath" the "great Ring" of Eternity. Thomas Granger, *Familiar Exposition . . . on Ecclesiastes* (London, 1621), speaks of "the restlesse revolution of time" by which "as all things come from his hand in their convenient seasons, so againe they returne into his hand . . . circularly for ever" (p. 86), but this "constant revolution of all things" applies not to the repetition of "individuall things," to which Augustine objected, but only to the circular return of the "kindes," which are the "same in substance but differenced by circumstances or individual properties." So runs Nature's argument in Spenser's *Cantos of Mutabilitie.*

13 I would place Oscar Cullmann, *Christ and Time,* tr. F. Filson (3rd. ed., rev.; London, 1962), somewhere in this category. John Briggs Curtis, in an article I chanced on after these pages were written, *Hebrew Union College Annual,* 34 (1963), 115–23, points out that the writers of the Old Testament lack the words "philosophy" and "history"; that straight-line patterns must be a matter of secondary inferences drawn from Yahweh's ordering of events; and that cyclical motifs of the return of time upon itself may be found throughout the Old Testament. James Barr, *Biblical Words for Time* (2nd ed., rev.; Edinburgh, 1969), exam-ines the claims for radical differences between the so-called "cyclic" views of the Greeks and the "straight-line" theories of the Hebrews in Ch. VI, and provides a learned, accurate survey of the distinction between *kairos* and *chronos* in Ch. II. Barr everywhere offers useful correctives to modern scholarship (from Bergson through Boman to Robinson), showing for example how Cullmann not only suffers from philological myopia but also betrays the Aristotelian bias that allows him to regard "eternity" as not other than "time": "This affords us," says Barr, "the delightful spectacle of Karl Barth being charged with Platonism for holding the contrary" (p. 158). Barr can be devastatingly right, but since Milton shared, along with the Fathers and Renaissance theologians, many of the same errors about *kairos* and *chronos,* Barr's caveats are only incidentally relevant in understanding the poet and his poetry. Ricardo Quinones' *The Renaissance Discovery of Time* (Cam-

bridge, Mass., 1972) is remarkable for range and learning, and a long section is devoted to Milton; but since Quinones' emphases fall elsewhere than my own, I have been unable to make direct use of his work. I have profited greatly, though at times indirectly, from Frank Kermode's brilliantly lucid *The Sense of an Ending* (New York, 1967).

14 Notes to "The Muse," *Literary Criticism of Seventeenth-Century England*, ed. Edward W. Tayler (New York, 1967), p. 314. I. B. [John Bullokar], *An English Expositor* (London, 1616), under "Hieroglyphikes": "Eternity, or everlastingnesse, they expressed by a round circle, which hath no end...." W[illiam] T[yping's] *A Discourse of Eternitie* (Oxford, 1633) offers this account (pp. 4-5), largely borrowed from Drexelius:

> Infinite are the descriptions of the Ancients, and divers their expressions, touching this Eternitie. The *Egyptians* conceiving that God was eternall, and his duration and being to bee properly tearmed Eternitie, represented the divine power by a Circle, which had neither beginning nor end. And hence it was that the Ancient Romans erected Temples which they dedicated to their Gods in circular figure.... Pythagoras the better to expresse that God was eternall, commanded his Schollers so oft as they accommodated themselves to the worship of God, they should turne themselves round.... Mercurius Trismegistus [actually the twelfth-century *Book of the XXIV Philosophers*], the most famous among the Philosophers, represented God the true Eternitie by an intellectual spheare, whose Center was every where, but without circumference, because he was the beginning and ende of all things....

A full compendium of commonplaces may be found in *The Considerations of Drexelius Upon Eternitie,* tr. Ralph Winterton (Cambridge, 1636), many of which are illustrated in the emblem books; see, for example, Henry Peacham, *Minerva Britanna* (London, 1612), p. 141, or George Wither, *A Collection of Emblemes* (London, 1635), fol. 102 (the plate from Rollenhagen's *Nucleus Emblematum*). Marjorie H. Nicolson documents the rise and decline of the idea in *The Breaking of the Circle* (Evanston, Ill., 1950).

15 So Luther in *Commentarie ... uppon Peter,* tr. Thomas Newton (London, 1581), p. 158[r]: "Seying therefore, that there is no Dinumeration of tyme with God, it followeth that ... the first manne Adam is as neere to God, as he that shalbe laste borne, the daie next afore the generall daie of Judgement."

16 *Religio* i.59 and i.11, pp. 54 and 11. Even a technical treatise on clock or "dead" time like Lilio Gregorio Giraldi's *De Annis et Mensibus* devotes its opening pages to preliminary definitions of *aeternitas, aevum, tempus,* and so on. Cf. the "theological" portion (pp. 289-303) of Joh. Garcaeus, *Primus Tractatus Brevis et Vtilis De Tempore* (Wittenberg, 1563) and the second tractate of Robert Fludd's *Utriusque cosmi* (Oppenheim, 1617).

17 *Five Bookes, Of Philosophicall Comfort*, tr. I. T. [John Thorie? Michael Walpole?] (London, 1609), p. 138. As "discourse is compared to vnderstanding; [and as] that, which is produced to that which is, [so] time to eternity, a circle to the Centre" (p. 110ᵛ). Although Christians often made use of the notion of "devouring time," which derives from Saturn's (Kronos, Chronos) having devoured his children and which has a kind of philosophic basis in *Physics* iv., Aristotle's ideas of time itself were in the main unacceptable in this context. (But even Aristotle, though only for the sake of analytical convenience, was ready to entertain the idea that there might be some relation between time and the "motion of the sphere," that here perhaps lies the origin of the common opinion that the affairs of men "form a circle," and that under certain circumstances we may therefore refer to the "circle of time.") For Aristotle time is what we confront when we contemplate change or motion. Since time has to be associated with motion in the specific sense that Aristotle gave to this basic concept, we may not with The Academy tend to identify time with the movement of the heavens but rather must relate it to "generation" and "corruption" (hence "devouring"). Time, "the number of motion with respect to before and after," becomes a line, continuous and uniform, in which "now" succeeds "now" succeeds "now," though this succession is not so much mathematical as metaphysical, for there would be no "time unless there were soul"—an intellect to measure and number motion. That this view is inadequate may be seen in Augustine or in, say, Donne's meditation, *Devotions*, ed. John Sparrow (Cambridge, 1923), p. 79, on what happens "if we consider *Tyme* to be but the *Measure of Motion*"; its "three *stations*"—past, present, future—are illusory and cannot account for the eternal, which is "not an everlasting flux of *Tyme*; but *Tyme* is a short *parenthesis* in a longe *period*; and *Eternity* had been the same, as it is, though time had never beene."

18 Tr. R. S. Pine-Coffin (London, 1961), p. 261.

19 Note 26, *Poems*, ed. A. R. Waller (Cambridge, 1905), p. 273. Explanations, even justifications, were growing increasingly necessary, for Hobbes was already entering the inevitable demurrals (*Questions Concerning Liberty, Necessity, and Chance*): "I know St. Thomas Aquinas calls *eternity*, *nunc stans*, an *ever-abiding now*; which is easy enough to say, but though I fain would, yet I could never conceive it: they that can, are more happy than I. . . . I understand as little how it can be true . . . that *eternity* is a *point indivisible*, and not a *succession*, nor in what sense it can be said, that an *infinite point*, and wherein is no *succession*, can comprehend all *time*, though time be *successive*." *Works*, ed. William Molesworth (11 vols.; London, 1839–42), IV, 271. For Eternity as known through Time, see Thomas, *Summa Theol.*, I, q. 10, a. 1; for Time as measure of motion (Aristotle), *S. T.*, I, q. 85, a. 1, and cf. I-II, q. 126, a. 2; for

things as impaired by Time, I-II, q. 48, a. 2; and for the virtuous act as properly occurring at due time or season (*kairos*), II-II, q. 55, a. 7. On the concept of *aevum*, which for Thomas occupies the metaphysical ground between *tempus* and *aeternitas*, see Ernst H. Kantorowicz, *The King's Two Bodies* (Princeton, N. J., 1957), esp. pp. 275–91.

20 Pine-Coffin, p. 262. Typing in his preface to *A Discourse of Eternitie* (see n. 14): "I doubt not but flashes of Eternitie, and transient thoughts thereof, doe often swimme in the braine, straggle about the heart of a sensuall worldling; but there they lodge not, they take not up their rest."

21 Winterton, *Considerations of Drexelius* (see n. 14).

CHAPTER I: Occasional Experiments

1 *Reason of Church Government,* Hughes, p. 668.

2 F. T. Prince, *The Italian Element in Milton's Verse* (Oxford, 1962), pp. 61–63. Ants Oras, less plausibly, suggests in *N & Q,* 197 (1952), 314–15, Tasso's *Beatissime Vergine.*

3 A catchphrase among the Scholastics and Renaissance thinkers. In Book I of the *Davideis* Cowley writes of the realm of deity where "Nothing is there *To come* and nothing *Past,/* But an *Eternal Now* does always last," and his note to the lines cites Boethius' *Consolation (Interminabilis vitae simul & perfecta possessio),* "Which *Definition* is followed by *Tho. Aquin.* and all the Schoolmen; who therefore call *Eternity Nunc stans,* a *standing Now. . . ." Poems,* ed. A. R. Waller (Cambridge, 1905), pp. 251 and 273. It seems probable to me that the idea of the *nunc stans* derives from Boethius' disquisition on *aeternitas* and *sempternitas* (itself deriving from Augustine, *Civ. Dei* 11.6 and 12.16) in *De Trinitate* iv, though the phrase itself does not occur in Boethius. Aquinas "quotes" Boethius (*Summa Theol.* 1, q. x, a. 2, obj. 1), *nunc fluens facit tempus, nunc stans aeternitatem;* and a number of modern scholars, among them S. G. F. Brandon, *History, Time and Deity* (Manchester, 1965), p. 103, simply follow the misattribution and make up a source for it in *Consolation* v. 6.

4 The rhetorical technique of allegory, whether used with calculation by the author or imposed from without by the critic, early became allied with Christian exegesis—with the "four-fold" method and its variations, and with typology or figuralism. Although the impetus for Christian allegorism lies in the Messianic prophecies, many of the techniques were drawn from the Greek grammarians and philosophers and from the *midrash* or hermeneutic of the Hellenistic Rabbis (especially as practiced by Philo of Alexandria); Philo died in 45 A. D., but as early as Plutarch, "On Reading Poetry," there are objections to those who distort Homer by finding concealed meanings "or, as they now are called, 'allegories'." The various methods are not easily distinguished,

and in certain contexts the terms are interchangeable, though clearly it will not do to confuse allegory as a way of writing, which offers its own satisfactions, with allegory as a mode of conscious or unconscious interpretation that "acculturates" the past, makes it presentable, by assuming for instance that Homer drew veils of indecency over the activities of the gods in order to conceal chaste truths; see Joseph A. Mazzeo, "Allegory and History," *Comparative Literature,* 30 (1978). "Allegory" (in Greek) was a rhetorical term signifying a succession of linked metaphors. Philo in *Allegory of the Laws* and *Questions on Exodus* was among the first to apply it in explicating Scripture (only later was it used in relation to the program of moral rehabilitation known as Homeric exegesis). John Marbeck, *A Booke of Notes* (London, 1581), pp. 22–24, provides the traditional definition from rhetoric ("an allegorie is that which is, one in words, and an other in sentence [*sententia*] and meaning") and then proceeds to equate allegory with typology: "as Christ is Jonas, who was in the heart of the earth three daies, as he was in the bellie of the Whale. Againe, that he is Salamon, or the serpent hanged up in the desert, or the Lambe: And that the two sonnes of Abraham are the two testaments." Similarly, George Wither, *A Preparation to the Psalter* (London, 1619), explains that allegory is the "continuance of any *Trope,*" then instances "Types, Figures." (In Prudentius' *Psychomachia* the personifications of abstract virtues and vices receive order and meaning from the typological method, and in Bale's *King Johan* the monarch has typological significance as "Verity" helps him thwart "Usurped Power" [Innocent III] and "Dissimulation" [Simon of Swynsett]. Such hybrids appear everywhere, to the discomfort of theologians and literary critics.) Marbeck's and Wither's conflation (or confusion) may be regretted but it is not unusual, for the exegetical writers naturally exerted a strong influence on what we have come to think of as the "allegorical habits" of mind that eventually issued in such works as the *Commedia* and *Paradise Lost.*

Edwin Honig, *Dark Conceit* (Evanston, 1959), remains perhaps the most helpful introduction to the study of literary allegory, though Angus Fletcher, *Allegory: The Theory of a Symbolic Mode* (Ithaca, N. Y., 1964), may be found more provocative in general; and Rosemond Tuve, *Allegorical Imagery* (Princeton, 1966), seems most useful for reading "allegories" of the Renaissance (even within chronological periods the term resists exact definition); see also Michael Murrin, *The Veil of Allegory* (Chicago, 1969). Two important articles, corrective in aim, are W. T. H. Jackson's "Allegory and Allegorization," *Research Studies,* 32 (1964), 161–75, and Robert W. Frank, Jr., "The Art of Reading Medieval Personification Allegory," *ELH,* 20 (1953), 237–50.

A learned, lucid account of Milton's attitude toward "allegory" may be found in H. R. MacCallum, "Milton and Figurative Interpretation of the Bible," *UTQ,* 21 (1962), 397–415, which emphasizes the "literalist" aspect of the poet's exegesis in order to moderate the "typologizing" of F. M. Krouse, *Milton's Samson* (Princeton, 1949), and the four-fold "allegorizing" of Rosemond Tuve, *Images and Themes in Five Poems by Milton* (Cambridge, Mass., 1957). I would only object that MacCallum does not always distinguish adequately the prose (of *Christian Doctrine*) from the poetry (the "literalist" Satan of *Paradise Regained*, after all, sees in the Descent of the Dove no more than a bird in the plummet) and that, in common with prevailing opinion, he seems too ready to assume a sharp distinction between "allegory" and "typology"; see in this last connection the incisive survey in Chapter IV of James Barr's *Old and New in Interpretation* (New York, 1966) and Henri de Lubac, "'Typologie' et 'Allegorisme'," *Recherches de Science religieuse,* 34 (1947), 180-226. (Daniélou in theology and Auerbach in criticism have good though not entirely historical reasons for maintaining a strong distinction between the two ways of transcending the literal sense.)

5 Fr. Henri de Lubac summarizes: "saint Thomas ne fait que reproduire un schème courant de son époque, fondé, suivant le principe déjà mis en oeuvre Origène, sur le texte même de la Bible. Là n'est pas son originalité, mais... elle est dans l'analyse plus fouillee...." *Exégèse médiévale: Les quatre sens de l'ecriture* (4 vols.: Paris, 1959-64), IV, 295. Fr. de Lubac shows (I, 309) that the antitype is not only "ahead" (within history) but also "above" (II, 621 ff.). And this "platonic aboveness" threatens, under the influence of the Areopagite, to obliterate the temporal, historical dimension basic to the theory of types. On typology, cf. I, 352f. Fr. de Lubac's books are extremely important, beginning with *Histoire et esprit* (1950), which deals with Origen's exegesis, and ending with *Pic de la Mirandole* (1974), which also has some relevance to the present topic; his researches supplement, and correct, those of Spicq and Smalley. George Wither provides a brief summary of the four-fold method in his *A Preparation to the Psalter,* p. 101:

> The *Literall* Sense is that which we barely vnderstand by the letters and words according to their ordinary significations: as, a meere relation of some things either done, to be done, or such like. The *Spirituall,* or mysticall sense, is when by those things done, or expressed, we vnderstand some other, whereof they are signes. And this *Spirituall* sense is threefold: For, Augustine saith, that as in the soule of Man there is a vegetatiue, a sensitiue, & a rationall facultie: so, in the *Letter* of the Scripture, there are three senses, to wit, *Morall, Allegoricall,* and *Anagogicall. Morall,* is that which tendeth to manners, & the duty of one man toward another. *Allegoricall,* Instructeth vs what is to be beleeued, *viz.* touching our faith in God. *Anagogicall,* is of those things which we are to hope for in the next life; and serueth to raise our thoughts from the base things of this world, to the high contemplation of heauenly felicities: and these three, with the *Literall* from whence they arise, are exprest in an olde *Disticke,* thus;

Litera, *Gesta docet; quod credas* Allegoria;
Moralis *quod agas; quò tendas* Anagogia.

Which I have turned in this manner;

The Letter *setteth downe the Storie:*
Our faith is in the Allegory:
The Morall *shewes our duties all:*
Our Hope, the Anagogicall.

See also Harrington's *Apologie* as prefixed to his *Orlando* (1634).

6 *Basic Writings,* ed. Anton C. Pegis (2 vols.; New York, 1944), I, 16–17. In Thomas, out of a theology derived partly from neo-Platonic speculations on Plato's Idea of the Good in the *Republic* and *Timaeus* 37C (together with the *locus theologicus* in Boethius, *Consolation* v. 6), *aeternitas* becomes the mode of being of God, for whom the creaturely world is *totum simul.* Time, a dim and mysterious reflection of the pure being of the Creator, is the medium in which things, against the recalcitrance of matter, come to be, then reach their final fulfillment outside both time and matter. See in this connection the Introduction, which first appeared as an essay in *The Hopkins Review,* 6 (1953), to Georges Poulet, *Studies in Human Time,* tr. Elliott Coleman (Baltimore, 1956); the concern with time and its literary manifestations recurs throughout Poulet's *oeuvre.*

7 *Looke from Adam,* tr. [Miles Coverdale] (London, 1624), p. 82. John 5:46 ff. is likewise explicit: "For had ye believed Moses, ye would have believed me: for he wrote of me." As Paul says in 1 Cor. 10:11, "Now all these things [in the Old Testament] happened unto them for ensamples [Vulgate: *haec autem omnia in figura contingebant illis*]." Hence all the prefigurative similes, as in Matthew 12:40: "Jonas was three days and three nights in the whale's belly; so shall the Son of Man be three days and three nights in the heart of the earth." Although these patterns may be considered distinctively Christian, the general habits of anticipating a fulfillment, either ironically in the manner of Greek oracles or through the myth of return as in Isaiah's vision of the future in terms of Eden, are of course common to all literatures. In Moses' Song at the Sea the future imperfect signifies not only the "redemption" from the Red Sea but also "redemptions" to come, such as Canaan, though most notably the grand "redemption" of the Messiah; see Judah Goldin, *The Song at the Sea* (New Haven, 1971), pp. 65–67, 150, 227–28. (I owe the reference to Dr. Alan Mintz.) But even the "types" of Hebrew thought are confined to the order of event; they do not involve persons, a development that, significantly, had to await the coming of Jesus the Christ. Out of the kerygmatic advertisement of the fulfillment of prophecy in Jesus the Christ—He, as the Son of Man, had been sacrificed as the Paschal Lamb, atoning for sin in the manner of Isaiah's Suffering Servant—comes the need for the peculiarly Christian theory of types. A modern reader may still inspect the fossil re-

mains of the typological method everywhere in the margins and headings of the King James, as for instance Psalm 71, where "Give the king thy judgements, O God" has the rubric, "David, praying for Solomon, sheweth the goodness and glory of his kingdom in type, and of Christ's in truth"; these headings appear most frequently, as might be expected, in connection with Isaiah II, Psalms, and Canticles.

8 Jean Daniélou, *The Bible and the Liturgy* (Notre Dame, Ind., 1956), pp. 5, 317-18, and throughout. Fr. Daniélou has written extensively on typology, perhaps most usefully in the collection of monographs first published together as *Sacramentum futuri: Etudes sur les origines de la typologie biblique* (Paris, 1950), translated as *From Shadows to Reality: Studies in the Biblical Typology of the Fathers* by Dom Wulstan Hibberd (London, 1960).

9 *A Disputation on Holy Scripture Against the Papists*, ed. William Fitzgerald, "Parker Society" (Cambridge, 1849), p. 407. A useful survey of the various positions may be found in Andrew Willet, *Synopsis Papismi* (London, 1600), esp. pp. 31-41.

10 *Citie of God*, tr. J[ohn] H[ealey] (London, 1620), p. 291. George Wither, *Preparation*, p. 99, is equally explicit:

> The *Patriarchs* oft received their promises in a double understanding: and the *Prophets* also in their prophecies spake oftentimes by a double Spirit: and all their *Promises* and *Prophecies* were doubly fulfilled; excepting some few, which immediately concerned the Kingdome of Christ, without respect of *Types*. Yea, and some of those, in regard they may have reference to the perfection of his kingdome in the world to come [i.e., at the end of time] may be also sayd to have in them a double Propheticall sense.

Robert W. Hanning, *The Vision of History in Early Britain* (New York, 1966), pp. 9-10, sees in Matthew's Gospel the usual process of fulfillment in Jesus the Christ; "the movement here is from the implications of the imperfect past to the explication of the perfected present." But Hanning remarks as well a "second progression ... from present to future," which is "apparent in the parables" of the return of the bridegroom and the master. These apocalyptic themes constitute a "second structural center ... vying with the crucifixion as the point toward which the gospel moves." The gospel text therefore "enshrines and illustrates the complex attitude of the early Christians toward time and history, perceived as a multiple system of movements synchronized by God in the person and message of Jesus"—movements "from past to present and present to future."

11 As the researches of Rosemond Tuve, *A Reading of George Herbert* (Chicago, 1952), and of other scholars have shown. In despite of Auerbach, p. 318: "Then, in the course of the sixteenth century, the Christian-figural schema lost its hold in almost all parts of Europe." See n. 15 of this chapter.

12 James S. Preuss, *From Shadow to Promise* (Cambridge, Mass., 1969), accounts for the way Luther's theology emerged from the medieval tradition of Augustine, Hugh of St. Victor, the Scholastics, and so on. Luther, in a sermon on John cited by W. Vischer, *The Witness of the Old Testament* (London, 1949), p. 7, flatly declares that the preaching of the Apostles "is based on the Old Testament, and there is no word in the New Testament that does not look back to the Old wherein it was already declared.... The Old Testament is thus the testament of Christ—a letter which he caused to be opened after his death and read ... in the light of the Gospel." Probably the best place to begin a study of the relevance of Luther's allegorizing to Renaissance thought is Jacobus Hertelius, *Allegoriarum, typorum, et Exemplorum Veteris & novi Testamenti* (Basil, 1561), which collects enough "allegories" from the Reformer's commentaries to fill 566 pages!

13 *Sermons of Maister John Caluin vpon the Booke of Iob,* tr. Arthur Golding (London, 1584), p. 733. In the *Institutes* 2.9.4 (ed. John T. McNeill, tr. Ford Lewis Battles [Philadelphia, 1960], p. 453) Calvin finds that the main difference "between the Old and New Testaments consists in figures," that the Old is "but an image and shadow." Calvin's dilemma, shared with the Reformers in general, stems from the need to maintain the divine authority of the entire Scriptures despite the unacceptability, on occasion, of the literal sense—hence recourse to forms of exegesis like "hypotyposis," "anthropatheia," and typology.

14 *Disputation on Holy Scripture,* p. 404. John Wolleb, whose work Milton knew (and appears to have used in *Christian Doctrine*), formulates it this way in *Abridgement of Christian Divinitie,* tr. Alexander Ross (London, 1650), p. 10: "The sense and meaning of each Scripture is but one; yet in the Prophesies of the Old-Testament it is composed of a history, and mysterie. For example, Hos. 11.1 In these words, *When Israel was a child, then I loved him, and called my sonne out of Egypt;* The sense is compounded: for literally and historically, they are to be understood of the delivery of the Isrealites out of Egypt; but typically and mystically, of Christs calling out of Egypt, Mat. 2.15." The position might be shared on occasion by Catholic expositors; Gregory the Great, for instance, in *Moralia* xx.1, says that Scripture in "one and the same word" speaks factually and sets forth mystery (*prodit mysterium*); referring to the past it can predict the future, and without changing language it can describe what has been done and declare what must be done.

15 *The Types or Figures* (Dublin, 1685), esp. pp. 66–77. In the second edition of 1705, published in London, Nathaniel Mather admits: "His making some of the old legal Ordinances Types of the instituted Church, and Ordinances under the New Testament and our Ordinances the Antitypes of theirs, it may be some may not assent to...." Milton was one of the many. Erich Auerbach in his influential *Mimesis,* tr. Willard Trask (New York, 1957), was apparently the first literary

critic to recognize the relevance of biblical typology to the study of a full range of literary works; and his essay "Figura," *Scenes from the Drama of European Literature,* tr. Ralph Manheim (New York, 1959), remains a model of philological inquiry, except for the erroneous assertion that *figura* was more widely used than *typus.* A concise, useful account appears in John Mulder's *Temple of the Mind* (New York, 1969), Chapter Six; see also J. M. Evans, *Paradise Lost and the Genesis Tradition* (Oxford, 1968), pp. 99–104; and Fr. Joseph A. Galdon, *Typology and Seventeenth-Century Literature* (The Hague, 1975). The best book on Milton and typology is William Madsen's *From Shadowy Types to Truth* (New Haven, 1968), which makes many valuable points but in my view misses something of the true literary significance of figuralism. I cannot agree that the types were "abolished" by Christ (p. 108), that *Lycidas* incorporates the theory of types for the first time in Milton, or even that in the major poems the poet uses typology in quite the way that Madsen suggests. I do agree with Madsen's polemic, passim, against the "platonizing" tendencies of a number of modern scholars; as John M. Steadman accurately observes (*MLR,* 64 [1969], 875–76), Madsen's book "should be read primarily as a corrective, rather than an alternative, to other interpretations." Theodore Long Huguelet's unpublished dissertation, "Milton's Hermeneutics: A Study of Scriptural Interpretation in the Divorce Tracts and in *De Doctrina Christiana*" (Chapel Hill, 1959), is thorough, informed, responsible. John C. Ulreich, Jr., "The Typological Structure of Milton's Imagery," *Milton Studies,* V (Pittsburgh, 1973), 67–85, attempts to apply Coleridge's distinction between the primary and secondary imaginations to typological imagery. From the theological rather than the literary point of view, there are fine essays in G. W. H. Lampe and K. J. Woollcombe, *Essays on Typology* (Napierville, Ill., 1957). The standard work doubtless remains Leonhard Goppelt's *Typos: Die typologische Deutung des alten Testaments im Neuen* (Gütersloh, 1939).

The primary and secondary literature on the subject is immense, but fortunately there now exists a splendid, though inevitably not exhaustive, bibliography compiled by Sacvan Bercovitch, "Annotated Bibliography," pp. 245–337, of *Typology and Early American Literature,* ed. Sacvan Bercovitch (Amherst, 1972), which also contains important essays by other hands. The subject has become fashionable, sometimes merely fashionable, and only rarely is it pursued with the nicety it requires— provoking caveats like those of Helen Gardner, *The Business of Criticism* (Oxford, 1959) or Robert Hollander's essay in *Literary Uses of Typology,* ed. Earl Miner (Princeton, 1957), which includes other items of interest in this connection. An interested reader of American literature might begin with Jasper Rosenmeier, "The Image of Christ" (diss., Harvard University, 1965), Ursula Brumm, *Religious Typology in American Thought,* tr. John Hoagland (New Brunswick, N. J., 1968), Emory

Elliott, *Power and the Pulpit in Puritan New England* (Princeton, 1975), and, most importantly, the works of Bercovitch, those cited in his bibliography as well as *The Puritan Origins of the American Self* (New Haven, 1975).

16 It is "allegory" but allegory securely based in actual time and history, therefore historical dogma. Benjamin Keach, the author in 1682 of *Tropologia: A Key to Open Scripture Metaphors and Types* (first published 1681), makes the crucial distinction in *Gospel Mysteries Unveil'd* (London, 1701), p. 2:

> Types suppose the Verity of some real History, as to Matter of Fact; as the *first Adam* was a *Type* or Figure of Jesus Christ. . . . *Types* are only *Historical*, as such, the *Truth* agreeing with the *Antitype* makes them up, and fulfils them as to the Design of God therein; as the *Brazen Serpent* [lifted up by Moses in the Desert] in its perfect Signification was fulfilled, when Jesus Christ was lifted up upon the Cross. . . ."

17 [Thomas Wilson], *Theological Rules* (London, 1615), p. 37. Cf. Augustine, *De Civ. Dei* 5, 18. The process is gradual, as Francis Roberts notes in *Clavis Bibliorum* (2nd edit.; London, 1649), for while God "makes known his gracious contrivances orderly," they are "too high & precious to be disclosed all at once" (p. 62); and the process involves a kind of reciprocal illumination as men "Parallel Types with Anti-types": "The *Types* more familiarly lead us to the understanding & apprehending of things typified" and the *"Anti-types* more evidently unfold and unveyl the *Types* unto us" (p. 64).

18 "Positions: Containing a Full Account of a Scripture-Line of Time" (London, n. d.), p. 2. Massively documented and lucidly presented research on Christian history may be found in C. A. Patrides, *The Phoenix and the Ladder* (Berkeley, 1964), abridged in Chapter VIII of his thorough *Milton and the Christian Tradition* (Oxford, 1966) and elaborated in *The Grand Design of God: The Literary Form of the Christian View of History* (London and Toronto, 1972). My own concerns are finally closer to those of William Kerrigan, "Prophetic Time," *The Prophetic Milton* (Charlottesville, Va., 1974).

19 "Sermon #6" (preached at Hamworth in 1622), *Sermons,* edd. George Potter and Evelyn Simpson, IV (Berkeley, 1959), 176.

20 [Thomas Beverley], "Positions," p. 1.

> The first Point is that First, and Perfect *Sabbatism* of the World, at the First Inviolate *Creation:* which was its Stasis, or the *First State* given it by God; and It is inclusive of the space to that Grand Oracle (*The Seed of the Woman shall break the Serpents Head*) Within which Space the first *Parents Fell,* and in them their Posterity. . . . The last Point is, *That Sabbatism* of the *Creation* Restor'd, or made New, sacred Scripture styles the *Apocatastasis,* or the *Restitution* of All things. . . .

21 Henry Church, *Miscellanea Philo-Theologica, or God & Man* (London, 1638), p. 25.

22 Peter Sterry, *A Discourse of the Freedom of the Will* (London, 1675), p. 231.
23 *Sermons*, edd. Potter and Simpson, VIII (Berkeley, 1956), 351. See also I, 291 and VII, 349. Theophilus Gale, *The Court of the Gentiles* (Oxford, 1669-77), relying on this view of history, was not the only one who sought to derive all languages and all literatures from Hebrew Scriptures.
24 *Commentarie Vpon . . . Romanes*, tr. Christopher Rosdell (London, 1583), p. 66ᵛ.
25 VIII. 12. Tr. R. S. Pine-Coffin (Baltimore, 1961), pp. 177-78.
26 *XCVI Sermons* (London, 1629), p. 28. Circumcision was perhaps more often a figure for Baptism, as it is for Milton himself in *Christian Doctrine*, though many writers, like William Guild in *Moses Unveiled* (rpt. in *The Christian Treasury*, ed. Rev. T. S. Memes [London, 1849], VIII, 6), treat it as a shadow of both Baptism and Passion. Thomas Washbourne, *Divine Poems* (London, 1654), pp. 105-06, prefers the Passion without passion in "A Soliloquy upon the Circumcision, commonly called New-Yeers-Day":

> Was't not enough that God himself became
> Man like to me, and in all things the same,
> Excepting sin alone; but he must be
> Under the Law, and circumciz'd for me?
> O extasie of Love! Which for my sake
> The Son of God the Son of Man did make;
> Make him, an infant, shed some drops of blood,
> As the first-fruits to that more liberal flood
> That flow'd in a ful tyde, from every part. . . .

I owe the reference to Dr. Paul Neuthaler.
27 But see Louis L. Martz, *The Poetry of Meditation* (New Haven, 1954), pp. 164 ff.
28 Arthur Barker, "The Pattern of Milton's Nativity Ode," *UTQ*, X (1941), 167-81; A. S. P. Woodhouse, "Notes on Milton's Early Development," *UTQ*, XIII (1943), 66-101. Cf. Laurence Stapleton, "Milton and the New Music," *UTQ*, XXIII (1954), 217-26; Don Cameron Allen, *The Harmonious Vision* (Baltimore, 1954); and Rosemond Tuve, *Images and Themes in Five Poems by Milton* (Cambridge, Mass., 1957). J. B. Broadbent attacks Tuve (whose emphasis falls on the Nativity as a typological event in time), the poet, and the poem in *The Living Milton*, ed. Frank Kermode (London, 1960), pp. 12-31.
29 David B. Morris, "Drama and Stasis in Milton's 'Ode on the Morning of Christ's Nativity'," *SP*, 68 (1971), 207-22, has anticipated me in print in his discussion of "two opposing views of time" (p. 214):

> The deliberate fixation in time ('This is the Month') seems at first to reflect the perspective of the poet Milton, who is writing his ode, as he tells Charles Diodati in 'Elegia Sexta' (11. 87-8), during the dawn of Christmas 1629. The perspective of the modern poet, however, soon

blends with that of an ancient bard who is sending his gift to the newborn Saviour. 'This is the Month,' then, refers both to December 1629 and to the historical moment of Nativity.

But I place a rather different construction on the "calculated ambiguity of the introductory stanzas." A. B. Chambers, "Christmas: The Liturgy of the Church and English Verse of the Renaissance," *Literary Monographs*, VI, edd. Eric Rothstein and Joseph Anthony Wittreich, Jr. (Madison, Wisc., 1975), 109–53, makes important observations, relevant in this context, on The Nativity Ode.

30 Lowry Nelson, *Baroque Lyric Poetry* (New Haven & London, 1961 [1962], pp. 32–34 and 41–52, provides an excellent analysis of the fluctuation in tenses, which he regards as "baroque." George Wither, *Preparation*, pp. 105–06, provides the more immediate context:

> For, it is very usual with him [one of the Prophets] to mention that which was not then come to passe, as if it had been alreadie fulfilled. . . . For, although the mysteries of the Gospell, of which [the Old Testament treats], were not then fulfilled in act: yet in regard of God, with whom all *Times* are present, they might be properly enough mentioned as things alreadie effected. . . .

31 David Dickson, in common with other exegetes, notes in *A Short Explanation of Hebrewes* (Aberdeen, 1635), pp. 306–07, the "terrible quaking of the Earth, and burning of Mount Sinai" and how God's anger "at the Daye of Iudgement, may be seene in that little Resemblance of Mount Sinai." That is, the "Resemblance" across time is typological.

32 Preface to *The Historie of the Perfect-Cursed-Blessed Man* (London, 1628). At its best the mind of man apprehends the "race of Time" but not without distinction of tense: "His Intellect a cleare Prospective glass / Attracts to Minde what shall be, is, and was" (p. 12). For Browne, see *Religio Medici* i.11, ed. L. C. Martin (Oxford, 1964), p. 11.

33 *Clavis Mystica* (London, 1636), p. 406.

34 More daringly, but Milton was by no means unique in plundering antiquity for types. Since the scope of typology was a matter for disagreement even among the theologians of the Cocceian School, there was a good deal of room for imaginative reconstructions; Thomas Worden, *The Types Unveiled, or The Gospel pick't out of the Legal Ceremonies* (London, 1664) exercises his ingenuity even on the "snuffers which did belong to the Lamps in the Tabernacle," and Edgar Wind, *Pagan Mysteries in the Renaissance* (New Haven, 1958), p. 32, n. 1, cites an amusing but not entirely uncommon instance:

> St. Gregory, *Moralia* III, xxviii, 55, extracted from the story of David and Bathsheba a prophetic allegory which rendered David innocent and Uriah culpable: 'Ille, per vitae culpam, in prophetia signat innocentiam; et iste, per vitae innocentiam, in prophetia exprimit culpam.' [The former, through the culpability of his way of life, signified his innocence through prophecy; the latter, by his blameless life, established his guilt in

prophecy.] And he was satisfied that this ingenious inversion followed the logic of biblical prefiguration.

Even the less ingenious Mather (see n. 15) sanctioned, in common with most exegetes, an element of disparity between type and antitype:

> As there is a Similitude, a Resemblance and Analogy between the Type and the Antitype in some things: so there is ever a dissimilitude and a disparity between them in other things. It is so in all similitudes.
> It is a Rule in Reason. There is a mixture of Consentaneity and Dissentaneity; or else instead of Similitude, there would be Identity.
> So here in these sacred Similies, it is not to be expected that the *Type* and the *Antitype* should *quadrare per omnia,* that they should agree in all things.

In Donne's succinct formulation: "It is a true, and an usefull Rule, that ill men have been Types of Christ, and ill actions figures of good." *Sermons,* edd. George Potter and Evelyn M. Simpson, III (Berkeley, 1957), 318. But given a situation in which Gregory could *in facto rem approbat, ut ei in mysterio contradicat,* or in which "Isaac" (i. e., "laughter") typifies Christ who brings joy, a syncretist like Reynolds could, in *Mythomystes,* find types everywhere, in the manner of Giles Fletcher, *Poetical Works,* ed. F. S. Boas, I (Cambridge, 1908), 59:

> Who doth not see drown'd in Deucalions name,
> (When earth his men, and sea had lost his shore)
> Old Noah; and in Nisus lock, the fame
> Of Sampson yet alive; and long before
> In Phaethons, mine owne fall I deplore:
>   But he that conquer'd hell, to fetch againe
>   His virgin widowe, by a serpent slaine,
> Another Orpheus was then, dreaming poets feigne.

John Owen, *An Exposition . . . on Hebrews* (London, 1674), separate title page and pagination of Vol. II of *Exercitations . . . on Hebrews* (London, 1674), discusses (esp. pp. 73–77) pagan history in relation to typology. John Swan, *Speculum Mundi* (2nd ed.; London, 1643), devotes his first twenty-eight pages to a "history" of the world that views pagan histories as corrupted versions of Scripture.

35 "Two Baroque Game Poems on Grace: Herbert's 'Paradise' and Milton's 'On Time'," *Criticism,* 12 (1970), 180–94. Cf. O.B. Hardison, Jr., "Milton's 'On Time' and its Scholastic Background," *Texas Studies in Literature and Language,* 3 (1961), 107–22.

36 H. R. Swardson, *Poetry and the Fountain of Light* (Columbia, Missouri, 1962), pp. 106–07, finds "evidence of Milton's uneasiness in his use of classical materials," citing the passage about Mulciber with ellipsis after "Erring." Cf. Douglas Bush, *Mythology and the Renaissance Tradition in English Poetry* (2nd ed.; New York, 1963), p. 287. Jonathan H. Collett, "Milton's Use of Classical Mythology in *Paradise Lost,*" *PMLA,* 85 (1970), 88–96, provides, I believe, a more accurate view.

CHAPTER II: *Lycidas* in Christian Time

1 Repr. in *Milton's "Lycidas": The Tradition and the Poem,* ed. C. A. Patrides (New York, 1961), pp. 27 and 55. (The situation seems particularly astonishing when we reflect that there has been so much sophisticated work on the pastoral genre since Empson's *Some Versions.*) The editor's preface to this useful collection acknowledges the "dissatisfaction still felt by readers" but "hopes, in part at least, to eliminate this fundamental difficulty by making available Professor Hanford's comprehensive study."

2 Patrides, *Milton's "Lycidas,"* p. 57. Johnson was of course aware that the "representation may be allegorical," but he has in mind the mixture of profane and religious elements, which, if anything, offends his religious sensibilities even more than the topical or personal allegory provokes his commonsensical ire. After making allowance for the note of deliberate excess in Johnson's judgments, it nevertheless seems clear that the genre, as understood by the greater Renaissance poets, is now to all intents dead: "its form is that of the pastoral, easy, vulgar, and therefore disgusting." Not only were its images "long ago exhausted" but from the first, Johnson implies, the form carried the defect of "inherent improbability" (p. 56).

3 I am drawing on the suggestive observations of E. H. Gombrich, as expressed in the title essay of *Meditations on a Hobbyhorse* (New York, 1963), pp. 1–11.

4 The game of biographical and topical allegory may involve almost infinite regress, deflecting attention from the poem into the details of Milton's life and times, so that the poem itself may become, to adapt the complaint of G. Wilson Knight, a "collection" of biographical and historical "fragments" in which Milton held the mirror up to himself and the minutiae of history. Who then is "old Damaetas"? Robert Gell, William Chappell, and Joseph Mede have all been candidates (see Patrides, p. 244), but certainty in such areas, while desirable, remains unconnected to the point at issue; Dr. Johnson would simply point out that Robert Gell was no shepherd . . .

5 Hughes, p. 668.

6 Although Hanford observes that the genre was "to a certain degree changed in essence by its contact with Christianity," he does not seek to define the (crucial) changes because he feels (with W. W. Greg and others) that medieval pastoral "need detain us but a moment" (see, however, my *Nature and Art in Renaissance Literature* [New York, 1964], esp. pp. 73–101); and although Hanford mentions the medieval "identification of the two kinds of 'pastor,'" he does not distinguish the traditions or appear to be aware that it is, crucially, identity with difference.

7 *The Arte of English Poesie,* ed. G. D. Willcock and A. Walker (Cambridge, 1936), p. 38. See also the previous note.

8 *"Lycidas:* Poet in a Landscape," *The Lyric and Dramatic Milton,* ed. Joseph H. Summers (New York, 1965), pp. 65–67.

9 David Dickson, *A Short Explanation of Hebrewes* (Aberdeen, 1635), pp. 306–07. Or see the compendious summaries in Matthew Poole, *Annotations Upon the Holy Bible,* 2 vols. (3rd edit., corrected and enlarged by Sam Clark and Edward Veale [London, 1696]), I, Kkkk2ᵛ—Kkkk3ʳ. Cf. John Pearson, *et. al., Critici Sacri* (9 vols.; London, 1660), VII, 4387. Thomas Wilson, *A Complete Christian Dictionary* (8th edit., additions by Bagwel and Sympson [London, 1678]; 1st edit. in 1612), under the heading "Shake Heaven and Earth," cites Hebrews, connects the passage with 2 Peter, and contrasts the two Dispensations; cf. William Gouge, *A Learned . . . Commentary . . . Hebrewes* (London, 1655), p. 369 of second pagination of second volume, and *A Commentarie on Hebrewes by M. Iohn Calvin,* tr. Clement Cotton (London, 1605), p. 313. David S. Berkeley, "A Possible Biblical Allusion in 'Lycidas'," *N&Q,* 206 (1961), 178, first identified the passage in print, but the allusion may have been turned to better uses by Louis Martz, "Who is Lycidas?," *Yale French Studies,* 47 (1972), 170–88; and by Joseph Anthony Wittreich, Jr., "A Poet Amongst Poets," *Milton and the Line of Vision,* ed. Wittreich (Madison, Wisc., 1975), pp. 97–117. More recently, Mother M. Christopher Pecheux, "The Dread Voice in *Lycidas*," *Milton Studies IX,* ed. James D. Simmonds (Pittsburgh, 1976), 221–41, has made use of the phrase in arguing that the "voice" is not exclusively that of St. Peter but a composite of Moses, Christ, and Peter. Although this kind of syncretism is of course common enough, I hope my argument makes clear that what counts in *Lycidas* is the *progression* from Apollo through St. Peter to Christ.

10 Arthur Barker, in a brilliant paragraph of his "The Pattern of Milton's Nativity Ode," *UTQ,* 10 (1941), 171ff., first drew attention to the three-part pattern that has since received wide acceptance. (L. G. Kelly, *Revue de l' Université d' Ottawa,* 38 (1968), 588–98, argues that the poem "falls into three parts: the first 131 lines are drawn mainly from Vergil X with heavy overtones of Theocritus; from 132 to 185 is based on key ideas from Vergil V; and the rest of the poem is modelled on the last section of Vergil X." But clusters of allusion ought not to be confused with the "three parts" that the poet himself demarcates.) I owe a less obvious debt to Josephine Miles, whose subtle observations about the way repeated words reveal the "motion from low to high" appear, revised, in Patrides as "The Primary Language of *Lycidas*"; see esp. pp. 96–97.

11 The "two-handed engine" refers to the "two massy Keys," though only one, that of iron, is fully relevant here. I make this identification in a note because my main argument does not require a specific meaning

for the "engine," because there exist in print at least sixty alternative
theories (many of them at least tangentially relevant), and because I
cannot explain *why* the keys were referred to by Milton's contemporaries as an "engine." But they were, and this fact has the artistic
advantage of preserving the imaginative continuity of the passage. As
G. W. Whiting has shown, *Milton and this Pendant World* (New York,
1969), pp. 29–58, "In Protestant and Puritan thought the Word of God
is both a *key* and a *sword*. . . ." Although Whiting cites most of the
proper texts—and there are many—he does not add that in the polemical controversies over the keys the power to bind and loose of Matthew
16:19 was understood as a cutting instrument or cleaving "engine"; it is
probably irrelevant that *key* means, etymologically, a cutting tool, but
nevertheless it appears that St. Peter's keys were themselves associated
with cutting "engines"—"the law" being the "keye that bindeth" and
the "Evangelion" being the "keye that looseth" (Tyndale, *Workes* [Lon-
don, 1572–73], as quoted in Whiting, p. 36). In *Of the Power of the Keyes*
(London, 1647), for example, Henry Hammond complains that this
"prime Act of Power entrusted by Christ" has degenerated into "an
empty piece of formality," or what is worse (among the Papists), into
"*an engine of State*," a "saecular contrivance" (A1^r). Hammond accordingly decries the use of the keys as "an engine in the shape of a spiritual
institution" for "secular advantage" (pp. 120–21), explaining that
Christ's "peculiar way" with the keys, the "power of *binding* and *loos-
ing*," ought never to be "look't on as a meer engine," for "he that can
take any *carnal* or *sensual* pleasure in the exercise of those Keyes, in the
using of that sharp engine of surgery, or ever draw it," except in
proper use, is one of the "sonnes of bloud" (A1^v-A1). At the end of
time the keys shall be wielded, and the iron, "that sharp engine," shall
"smite once, and smite no more," because then, to use Milton's words in
Animadversions, "thy Kingdom [shall be] at hand, and thou standing at
the dore." Cf. Kathleen Swaim, "Retributive Justice in *Lycidas:* The
Two-Handed Engine," *Milton Studies II* (1970), 119–29, who sees the
"engine" as glancing at both the keys and "th' abhorred shears"; W.
Arthur Turner, *JEGP*, 49 (1950), 562–65, who tries to make a case for
the keys in relation to the "engine" of the lock on St. Peter's "door"; J.
Milton French, *MLN*, 68 (1953), 229–31, who argues for the keys as in
accord with Milton's purpose in the poem; and Robert Fleissner, *Ang-
lia*, 91 (1973), 77–83, who supports French and Swaim, adding that we
may visualize the image as the crossed keys of Papal heraldry. Karl E.
Felsen, "The 'Two-Handed Engine'," *Milton Quarterly*, 9 (March,
1975), 7–14, argues for the scales of judgment in the hands of Michael,
but also describes a manuscript illumination (*Liber Vitae* of New Minster, presently MS. Stowe 944 in the B. M.) showing St. Peter locking a
door with one key (illustrations of the Last Judgment often depict an
actual door) and brandishing the other, smiting Satan with the keys

and using them to beckon the saved through the gates of heaven. There is of course no trouble with the verb used to describe the action, for as Milton himself says in *Tenure,* the "power of the Keyes" had been used to remove a king, "smiting him with a final excommunion."

12 It may be necessary to emphasize that the apotheosis of Lycidas as the "Genius of the shore" does not relegate King to the status of a local protective deity. A man's "genius" was allotted to him at birth: since it was associated with reproduction and fecundity, the figure "Genius" fittingly presides over nuptials, as in Spenser's *Epithalamium;* and since the same figure keeps the door of life (in the Garden of Adonis), "genius" also fittingly conducts man through the door of death, as when Shakespeare's Troilus says that "the Genius" cries "come" to "him that instantly must die." The "genius" of *Lycidas* ought therefore to be felt as a kind of saintly mediator, appropriately associated with the "unexpressive nuptial Song" and the massy "golden" key that "opes" the door to salvation.

13. Just as Vergil (*Sicelides Musae paulo maiora canamus*) had invoked his great predecessor to "take a higher flight" (so rendered by John Ogilby, *Works* [London, 1654], p. 19). Ogilby's annotation is standard: "alluding to *Theocritus* the Sicilian Poet, whose Imitatour our Author in these Eclogs professes himself to be."

14 *Mystagogvs Poeticvs* (London, 1648), pp. 16–17.

15 In annotating the Tenth Eclogue Ogilby observes that Vergil "invokes his Muse, *Arethusa* the Sicilian Nymph in relation (as more than once already) to *Theocritus.*"

16 Erich Auerbach in *Mimesis* (Princeton, 1953), but esp. in Ch. I of *Literary Language and its Public in Late Latin Antiquity and in the Middle Ages,* tr. Ralph Manheim (New York, 1965), shows how Christian writers modified the older principles of style. See also Joseph A. Mazzeo, "St. Augustine's Rhetoric of Silence," *JHI,* 23 (1962), 175–196.

17 *Complete Poetical Works,* ed. R. E. Neil Dodge (Cambridge, Mass., 1936), p. 5.

18 *Lyric and Dramatic Milton,* p. 192.

19 *Religio Medici* i.43, ed. L. C. Martin (Oxford, 1964), p. 41.

20 As in lines 169–70 where "his" refers exclusively to the "day-star" or sun. ("His" was the original genitive neuter, and while "its" was coming into general use during the early seventeenth century, it was apparently regarded as rather colloquial or newfangled, for it was avoided by the writers of the King James version of 1611. In his poetry Milton tends to avoid "its.") The "we" of line twenty-three also reveals functional ambiguity; although it refers, logically, to the pastoral singer and Lycidas, its (nearest grammatical) antecedent is "he" ("some gentle Muse"), which means that "we" includes past and future, as well as present, pastoral singers, emphasizing the continuities that are the subject of the passage and, ultimately, the poem as a whole.

CHAPTER III: *Paradise Lost:* From Shadows to Truth

1 *Discourse of the Freedom of the Will* (London, 1675), pp. 175 and 179. Northrop Frye makes suggestive observations on epic form in his introduction to *Paradise Lost and Selected Poetry and Prose* (New York, 1951); see also Arthur Barker, "Structural Pattern in *Paradise Lost,*" *PQ,* 28 (1949), 17–30; R. H. Perkinson, "The Epic in Five Acts," *SP,* 43(1946), 465–81; and John T. Shawcross, "The Balanced Structure of *Paradise Lost,*" *SP,* 62 (1965), 696–718. Michael Lieb, *The Dialectics of Creation* (Amherst, Mass., 1970), investigates the "structural" pattern of creation-from-destruction.

2 [John Fox], *Time and the End of Time* (London, 1669), p. 34.

3 Henry Church, *Miscellanea Philo-Theologica* (London, 1638), p. 25.

4 Sir Thomas Browne, *Religio Medici and Other Works,* ed. L. C. Martin (Oxford, 1964), pp. 43–44 and 41.

5 Lawrence Stapleton examines "Milton's Conception of Time in *The Christian Doctrine,*" *Harvard Theological Review,* 57 (1964), 9–21, and "Perspectives of Time in *Paradise Lost,*" *PQ,* 45 (1966), 734–48. More wide-ranging is the late Rosalie Colie's "Time and Eternity: Paradox and Structure in *Paradise Lost,*" *JWCI,* 23 (1960), 127–38.

    Albert R. Cirillo, "Noon-Midnight and the Temporal Structure of *Paradise Lost,*" *ELH,* 29 (1962), 372–95, and "'Hail Holy Light' and Divine Time in *Paradise Lost,*" *JEGP,* 68 (1969), 45–56, provocatively investigates a matter that deserves further attention: the way Milton has provided, throughout the epic, exact indications of the "time" of crucial events, most of which occur either at noon or midnight ("noon" or *meridies noctis* could still refer to midnight in the seventeenth century). See also Jackson I. Cope's brilliant *Metaphoric Structure of "Paradise Lost"* (Baltimore, 1962), pp. 130–37. The seminal studies include Roger Caillois, "Les démons de midi," *Revue de l'Histoire des Religions,* 115 (1937), 142–73; 116 (1937), 54–83 and 143 ff.; and Rudolph Arbesmann, "The 'Daemonium Meridianum',*" *Traditio,* 14 (1958), 17–31. Grant McColley, *Paradise Lost* (Chicago, 1940), p. 161, and Maurice Kelley, *This Great Argument* (Princeton, 1941), p. 148, offer alternative views. I am aware of only one editor who has taken due and accurate care with the chronology of the epic; see the imaginative, precise annotations (and introduction) of Alastair Fowler, *Poems of John Milton,* edd. John Carey and Alastair Fowler (London and Harlow, 1968).

6 *A Table Alphabeticall* (1604), facsimile edition by Robert A. Peters (Gainesville, Fla., 1966). John Bullokar's *English Expositor* (London, 1616) is equally imprecise—"a figure, forme or likenesse of any thing." Nicholas Ling, *Politeuphia* (London, 1598), can refer to "Truth" as the "tipe of eternity," and Milton (*PL,* I, 405) can call Gehenna the "Type of Hell." "Shadow" is of course susceptible of even greater ambiguities,

partly through its conventional opposition to "substance." Although Stapleton, "Perspectives," objects to William Madsen's thesis, "Earth the Shadow of Heaven," *PMLA*, 75 (1960), 519–26, that Milton is using the word in a typological rather than a "Platonic" sense, I think we must grant at least typological overtones to the passage; Madsen moderates his polemical thesis in *From Shadowy Types to Truth*.

7 *Garden of Cyrus* iv, ed. Martin, p. 167.

8 George (?) Puttenham, *Arte of English Poesie*, edd. Gladys Doidge Willcock and Alice Walker (Cambridge, 1936), pp. 167–68.

9 Exhaustively documented by Cope, *Metaphoric Structure*.

10 "Syntax and Music in *Paradise Lost*," *The Living Milton*, ed. Frank Kermode (London, 1960), p. 73.

11 Augustine Marlorat, *A Catholike exposition upon the Revelation of Sainct John*, tr. Arthur Golding (?) (London, 1574), p. 37. Christ is the "Apple wherewith the choosen faithfull are deyntely fed for evermore. For looke what was loste in Adam: the same is restored ageyn in Christ. . . ." See also Mother Mary Christopher Pecheux, "The Concept of the Second Eve in *Paradise Lost*," *PMLA*, 75 (1960), 359–66; "The Second Adam and the Church in *Paradise Lost*," *ELH*, 34 (1967), 173–87; and, also relevant, "Abraham, Adam, and the Theme of Exile in *Paradise Lost*, *PMLA*, 80 (1965), 365–71. For the closely-related traditon of the *hortus conclusus*, see Stanley Stewart's thorough *The Enclosed Garden* (Madison, Wisc., 1966).

12 *Devout Rhapsodies* (London, 1647), p. 64. Cf. Donne's "Hymne to God my God in my Sicknesse."

13 With the notable exceptions of Alastair Fowler and Scott Elledge, modern editors rarely bother themselves with the etymological quibbles that stand near the center of Milton's poetic understanding of language, though Patrick Hume, the first annotator of *Paradise Lost*, in Jacob Tonson's edition (London, 1695), seems everywhere alive, as he is in this instance, to the poet's ways with etymon. See also James Patterson, *A Complete Commentary with Etymological, Explanatory, Critical and Classical Notes on Milton's "Paradise Lost"* (London, 1744).

14 *Selections from The History of the World*, tr. Philemon Holland; ed. Paul Turner (Carbondale, Ill., 1962), p. 31. Cf. *Batman upon Bartholomew* VIII.xliiji. In IV, 776–77, Milton uses the "pyramis" as the hand of a "moon" clock to signify nine in the evening: "Now had night measur'd with her shadowy Cone/ Half way up Hill this vast Sublunar Vault." Alastair Fowler was, I believe, the first editor to annotate the astronomical clocks with comprehensive accuracy.

15 Vives' commentary on Augustine's *Citie of God* 13.21, englished by J[ohn] H[ealey] (2nd ed., rev.; London, 1620), p. 463.

16 R. G. Collingwood, *The Idea of History* (Oxford, 1946), p. 43: "Furneaux pointed out long ago [in 1896] that when Tacitus describes . . . the character of a man like Tiberius . . . he represents the process not as a

change in the structure or conformation of a personality but as the revelation of features in it which had hitherto been" concealed. Similarly, Livy's history of the "character" of Rome, as a result of what Collingwood labels "substantialistic metaphysics," treats the "essence" or "substance" of the city and ignores change and development.

17 *Ovid's Metamorphosis,* tr. G[eorge] S[andys] (Oxford, 1632), p. 89.

18 *The Club of Hercules* (Urbana, 1962), pp. 73–75.

19 *A Preface to Paradise Lost* (Oxford, 1942), p. 125. "Milton's talent temporarily failed him...."

20 John Donne, "Preached to the King... at White-hall, 18. Aprill 1626," *Sermons,* edd. G. Potter and E. Simpson (10 vols.; Berkeley, Calif., 1953–62), VII (1954), 138–39.

21 Henry Ainsworth, for example, simply assumes Augustine in *Annotations Upon the First Book of Moses* ([Amsterdam?], 1621) in discussing Genesis 2:31: "We may compare with these six dayes the six ages of the world, as they are manifestly distinguished in scripture."

22 Joseph Summers, *The Muse's Method* (Cambridge, Mass., 1962), p. 113, observes that the word "structure" functions "as a metaphor for our sense (or, more ideally, Milton's sense) of the organization and articulation of the whole, and it may dangerously imply that there is *one* principle of organization...." Summers concludes that it might be better to speak of "structures" (p. 114), and perhaps we should, providing that we do not suppose that our fragmentary and plural analyses preclude the poet's having envisioned a number of complementary "structures" that, co-existing perhaps in tension but not in conflict, make for a unified whole.

23 Andrew Willett, *Hexapla in Genesin: A Sixfold Commentarie* (Cambridge, 1605), p. 35. God had intimated as much to Adam earlier; see *Paradise Lost,* VIII, 331ff.; see also *The Common Places of the... Divine Doctor Peter Martyr,* tr. and compiled by Anthony Marten (London, 1583), p. 325.

24 Jean Bodin represents the opinion of the Renaissance commentators when, in the first section of the fourth book of *La Republique* (1576), he claims that the first form of a commonwealth is to be found in the Assyrian monarchy and that its first prince, sovereign by violence and force, was Nimrod. Cf. George Hakewill's *Apologie* (3rd. ed.; London, 1635), p. 368: "During this golden age, flourished *Camesis & Saturne,* & there is no doubt but by *Camesis* is understood *Cham* the son of Noah, & by *Saturne Nimrod*... a notorious Rebell... a great *Oppressour,* a Robber, as Aristotle numbers *robberie* among the severall kindes of hunting: And besides hee is thought to have beene the ring leader in that out-ragious attempt of building the *toure of Babel.*"

25 Stanley Eugene Fish, *Surprised by Sin: The Reader in Paradise Lost* (New York, 1967), p. 286, states flatly that the reader is "no longer a participant, he is here returned to the more conventional role of spectator,"

though he offers enough fine insights, especially in the discussion of Adam's "education" (pp. 308-31), to qualify—even to contradict—the generalization.

26 From his commentary on Genesis, as translated in Francis Roberts, *Mysterium & Medulla Bibliorum* (London, 1657), p. 209; Milton cites Paraeus a number of times, this particular commentary at least once (*Tetrachordon*). The preceding quotations are from Roberts himself (pp. 208-09). Cf. *Nowell's Catechism*, tr. Thomas Norton from the Latin of 1570 and ed. G. E. Corrie (London, 1853), pp. 150-51. H. R. Mac-Callum, "Milton and Sacred History," *Essays in English Literature*, edd. Millar MacLure and F. W. Watt (Toronto, 1964), pp. 149-68, chronicles the movement in the last books from despair to faith, the series of "graded steps" that proceed toward "full and spiritual understanding of the Son's prophecy concerning . . . the seed of the woman and the serpent" (p. 160).

27 In the *Adamus exul* of Grotius it is Adam who proposes suicide and Eve who dissuades, a division of roles that will not serve Milton's method of progressive illumination of the First Man's knowledge of the "greater Man."

28 See Anne Davidson Ferry, *Milton's Epic Voice* (Cambridge, Mass., 1963) and Fish, *Surprised by Sin, passim.*

29 *Davideis,* Book I, n. 31, *Poems,* ed. A. R. Waller (Cambridge, 1905), p. 274. Eve's "repetition" (IV, 641 ff.) is a rhetorical masterpiece rather than "epic repetition" in the sense applied to Homer.

30 In an essay that deserves to be better known, John E. Parish, "Milton and God's Curse on the Serpent," *JEGP,* 58 (1959), 241-47, suggestively describes Adam's gradual understanding as analogous to deciphering the "ambiguous oracle" of Greek literature. See also John M. Steadman's "Bitter Ashes: Protestant Exegesis and the Serpent's Doom," *SP,* 59 (1962), 201-10.

31 Summers, *Muse's Method,* p. 208, feels that Adam must acquire knowledge "in the way the [academic or epic?] reader has," through "narration rather than spectacle, inward rather than physical vision," for Adam and "we are among those 'that have not seen, and yet have believed' (John 20.29)." Barbara Kiefer Lewalski studies the problem in greater detail in "Structure and Symbolism of Vision in Michael's Prophecy," *PQ,* 42 (1963), 25-35. Other reasons, many of them as plausible as they are elaborate, have been advanced for the shift in technique. Perhaps the most persuasive is that of Raymond Waddington ("The Death of Adam," *MP,* 70 [1972], 9-21), who also provides what amounts to a critical bibliography of scholarship on the last books.

32 The effort to justify the ways of God to men lies somewhere near the center of Protestant experience, for it is involved, inevitably but uneasily, in the whole question of "justification by faith," though I am aware

of no Reformer other than Milton who had the inspiration (or the presumption) to confront the fact directly and draw out the full implications of its terrible paradoxes. Luther and Calvin had felt it blasphemous to inquire too closely into the question of God's ways with men, even though Luther had himself experienced the certainty that generally comes with conversion on the Pauline model. In the *Tischreden* Luther recurs to the insight of the tower at least three times, dwelling upon it with comparable intensity of feeling and the same lack of consistency as that displayed by Augustine in the varying accounts of his own *conversio*. Luther struggles with the idea of the *iustitia dei* until the words become lightnings (*fulmen in conscientia*), as though he still felt the psychic shock of the thunderstorm that drove him into monkhood on the wrong road to Damascus. "If God is just, He punishes," and Luther quakes with terror; but then *in hac turri* he is granted the grace to know that it is not through works or merit but through faith and mercy that we are saved. His soul becomes exalted—not through *scientia* but through the intervention of the Holy Ghost. Although Luther invariably mentions *hac turri*, only once does he specify *dieser cloaca*—about which there seems to be, thanks mainly to Erik Erikson's *Young Man Luther,* a good deal of scholarly squabbling, whether literal or figurative. But the point at issue is that Luther, after having fully assimilated Paul's words to the Romans about "righteousness" and "punishment," finds the release of new hope under the guidance of the Holy Ghost. Man is not just, though justly, a sinner; he is *simul iustus et peccator,* justified and yet a sinner. (My sense of Luther's "conversion" has been sharpened more than a little by Marilyn Harran.) But it was left to Milton to embody the Protestant paradox in great verse and to relate the contrary feelings of individual Christians to the grand paradox of history, the *felix culpa.*

Although the OED misquotes Milton's line about asserting Providence in defining "assert" as "to champion, protect, defend," the poet meant to redeem the time by demonstrating the existence of a primary attribute, setting free or liberating from prejudice the eternal workings of God's "mysterious terms"; when Samson trusts that God "will arise and his great name assert" (*assertus,* lay claim to, set free), Manoa agrees that He will "vindicate [*vindicatus,* lay claim to, set free] the glory of his name." As Matthew Poole was aware, in commenting upon Acts 17:26 in the second volume of *Annotations Upon the Holy Bible* (London, 1696), "The Apostle asserts the providence of God" to demonstrate "that nothing comes by chance, or through a fortuitous concourse of Atomes; but that God is in everything. . . . This doctrine was preached by Moses." Asserting Providence justifies God's ways, for Milton if not for Calvin. In *Sermons of Maister John Caluin vpon the Booke of Iob,* tr. Arthur Golding (London, 1584), we justify God, on the one hand, "by keeping our mouthes shut, according as St. Paul treateth thereof in the thirde to the Romanes" (p. 562); and, on the other hand, by demeaning man, "for God cannot be iust, and iudge also vntyll we be al damnable" (p. 720). But Milton's angel informs Adam that he should "be strong, live happy"—not that he should, like Job, suffer amathophobia, consider himself vile and abhor himself; and therefore "this wold iustifie, in the Latine mens eares" and in Milton's epic, "is as much to say, as to make iust: lyke as magnifie to make great," though Peter Martyr, *The Common Places,* pp. 570-71, goes on to argue that even Augustine has mistaken Paul's meaning by lending the word its Latinate signification. Milton took the word in its Latin sense, then pursued the paradoxical implications of the mysterious ways of God's Providence, refusing either to keep his mouth shut or to demean man.

33 *Discourse,* p. 179.

34 *Aristotle's Rhetoric* (London, 1686), iii. 9, p. 185.

35 *Milton's Paradise Lost* (London, 1732), p. 398. See also Bentley's sometime champion, William Empson, *Some Versions of Pastoral* (London, 1950), pp. 149-91.

36 Quoted from the edition (3 vols.; London, 1749-52) of Thomas Newton, who approves the "excellent note of Dr. Pearce," II, 428-29.

37 Although the full implications of Arthur O. Lovejoy's seminal study of the *felix culpa,* "Milton and the Paradox of the Fortunate Fall," *ELH,* 4 (1937), 161-79, remain even now to be assessed, readers since Summers, *The Muse's Method* (Cambridge, Mass., 1962), have become increasingly sensitive to "double motions and emotions" (p. 223), or to what Louis Martz, *The Paradise Within* (New Haven, 1964), pp. 143-45, aptly calls a "sense of immense loss subtly qualified by a sense of gain." See also John N. Morris, "Milton and the Imagination of Time," *SAQ,* 67 (1968), 649-58. The "twilight mood" of *Paradise Lost,* which does not take place at twilight, has its earliest counterpart in The Nativity Ode, where many readers and a few scholars tend to assume that it is evening when the Blessed Virgin "hath laid her Babe to rest." But the sun "pillows his chin upon an Orient [eastern] wave," so that the sun is rising as the Son is going down; this sensitivity to contrary motions, achieved by the poet at the age of twenty-one, never deserted him and may be thought to lie near the center of his most moving effects (think only of Adam's choice to fall with Eve).

38 See John R. Knott, Ch. III of *Milton's Pastoral Vision* (Chicago, 1971); and, more exactly and concisely, Mother M. Christopher Pecheux, "Their Place of Rest," *Milton Quarterly,* 6 (1972), 73-74, who concludes that in the last lines "Milton has miraculously united the human and the superhuman, the prosaic and the transcendent, time and eternity." A more ambitious study, with an exceptionally large number of useful citations, is Michael Lieb's "'Holy Rest': A Reading of Paradise Lost," *ELH,* 39 (1972), 238-53; Lieb investigates the notion of *sabbatismos* in its typological ramifications and attempts to extend its significance throughout the epic.

39 *Philosophical Works of Francis Bacon,* ed. J. M. Robertson (London, 1905), p. 268. The dichotomy, as old as Plato and at least as true, becomes pivotal in Hobbes on "wit" in *Human Nature* and in Locke on "fancy" and "judgment" in *Essay Concerning Humane Understanding;* Coleridge modifies and refines in distinguishing the primary and secondary imaginations.

40 *Rasselas,* ed. Gwin J. Kolb (New York, 1962), p. 24; "Preface to Shakespeare" [1765], *Johnson on Shakespeare,* ed. Arthur Sherbo (New Haven, 1968), p. 62. The break with the older view represented by Johnson appears forcibly in Blake: "To Generalize is to be an Idiot. To Particularize is the Alone Distinction of Merit—General Knowledges are those Knowledges that Idiots possess" (*The Poetry and Prose of William Blake,* ed. David V. Erdman, commentary by Harold Bloom [Garden City, N.Y., 1965], p. 630).

41 As quoted in Christopher Ricks, *Milton's Grand Style* (Oxford, 1963), p. 66. On pp. 109–17 Ricks discusses the fall of language, taking off from Arnold Stein's suggestive analysis of the river of Paradise that flows "with mazy error under pendant shades" (IV, 239) and arguing that "*error* here is not exactly a pun, since it means only 'wandering'—but the 'only' is a different thing from the absolutely simple use of the word, since the evil meaning is consciously and ominously excluded. . . . Certainly the word is a reminder of the Fall, in that it takes us back to a time when there were no infected words because there were no infected actions." Leslie Brisman discusses the "Snake with youthful Coat repaid" in *Milton Studies II,* ed. James D. Simmonds (Pittsburgh, 1970), pp. 27–35, from a similar point of view. The best and most extensive account of "Language in Paradise" is the third chapter of Stanley Fish's *Surprised by Sin* (New York, 1967); Fish deals with "wander" on pp. 130–41 and cites Isabel MacCaffrey (who discusses "wander" in her sensitive chapter on "Satan's Voyage," *Paradise Lost as 'Myth'* [Cambridge, Mass., 1959]) in order to disagree with her assertion (p. 188) that this "key word" has "almost always a pejorative, or melancholy connotation"; for Fish the word has a "neutral connotation" (p. 131), though he allows that in the last lines "wandering is now the movement of faith" (p. 141). It will be clear that I agree to some extent with both, though entirely with neither.

42 *Milton* (London, 1900), pp. 210–11.

43 Hughes, p. 728.

44 From a rather different perspective, John T. Shawcross has established the general importance of the theme of exodus to a reading of *Paradise Lost* in *Milton Studies II,* ed. James D. Simmonds (Pittsburgh, 1970), pp. 3–26. See also Mother Mary Christopher Pecheux, "Abraham, Adam, and the Theme of Exile in *Paradise Lost,*" *PMLA,* 80 (1965), 365–71.

45 *Glasse of Time in the Two First Ages* (London, 1620), pp. 67 (misnumbered "63") and 17.

46 Adam's spectacular vision of the kingdoms of the earth in Book XI is a

type for Milton of "our second Adam in the Wilderness" (381–84) when He is offered, as in *Paradise Regained,* a view of the kingdoms. Moses' Pisgah-Sight of Canaan prefigures both.

47 *Portraits,* ed. F. W. Hilles (New Haven, 1952), p. 135. See also Albert R. Cirillo, "Noon-Midnight and the Temporal Structure of Paradise Lost," *ELH,* 29 (1962), esp. p. 367; and, in the light of Jung as well as Nicolas of Cusa, Don Parry Norford, "'My Other Half': The Coincidence of Opposites in *Paradise Lost,*" *MLQ*, 36 (1975), 21–53.

48 Ed. John Sparrow (Cambridge, 1923), pp. 113–14.

CHAPTER IV: *Samson Agonistes:* Found in the Close

1 *True Intellectual System of the Universe* (London, 1678), p. 878. The emphasis on beginnings and endings is in part a consequence of the imaginative prestige of the circle (emblem of time, eternity, deity, the moral life, and so on). Samuel Gardiner, *Portraitvr of the prodigal Sonne* (London, 1599), pp. 41–42, is typical: "The Mathematicians doe esteeme the circular figure, as the perfect figure, because in a circle the beginning and the ende doe meete togither; therfore that we may bee made perfect, let vs in all actions, lay the beginning, and the ende togither. And let God who is the *Alpha* and beginning: be *Omega* vnto vs, and the ending likewise." See Marjorie H. Nicolson, *The Breaking of the Circle* (Evanston, Ill., 1950).

2 Thomas Heywood, *The Hierarchie of the Blessed Angells* (London, 1635), p. 30. Archibald MacLeish says it in "Seeing": "Men before us / thought in beginnings and ends, all of them."

3 Advanced most recently and precisely by French Fogle, "The Action of *Samson Agonistes,*" *Essays in American and English Literature,* ed. Max F. Schulz (Athens, Ohio, 1967), pp. 177–96. Fogle of course acknowledges the similar theses of a good many predecessors, seeing his own contribution as a closer reading of the play based securely on Milton's view of "regeneration" in *Christian Doctrine,* in this way providing a welcome theological corrective to the kind of "psychologizing" regeneration in Miss Una Ellis-Fermor's *Frontiers of Drama* (New York, 1946), p. 32: "steady psychological progression from despair through heroic conflict upwards to exultation and final assumption into beatitude." To confuse the hero's oscillation between hope and doubt with the "steady psychological progression" found in many novels is to misread Christian tragedy; see John M. Steadman, "'Faithful Champion': The Theological Basis of Milton's Hero of Faith," *Milton: Modern Essays in Criticism,* ed. Arthur E. Barker (New York, 1965), pp. 467–83, and Ann M. Gossman, "Samson, Job, and 'the Exercise of Saints,'" *English Studies,* 45 (1964), 212–24.

4 *Rambler* 139, *Works,* edd. W. J. Bate and Albrecht B. Strauss (New Haven, 1969), IV, 376.

5 "The Interpretation of *Samson Agonistes*," *HLQ*, 26 (1963), 377–78: "The way the 'intimat impulse' comes to him is consistent with the conception of grace as operating beyond human capacity and effort: moreover it comes to Samson while he is still uncomprehending and reverses the course of action on which he is bent. The facts of the play at this critical juncture deny such tempting interpretations as that Samson is now victorious in his drama of self conquest or that he here receives his reward for the trials undergone. The mode in which the divine impulsion is exerted—independent of Samson's volition and contrary to the course he proposed—demonstrates rather the sovereignty of providence, undistracted by man's errors and deserts, moving invincibly toward the objective proposed." Thomas Granger, *Familiar Exposition or Commentarie on Ecclesiastes* (London, 1621), knew well that God "in his secret providence hath prefixed a time unknowne, and unalterable by man. . . . To every thing that necessity urgeth us to doe there is a time, both of their beginnings and endings, ordained of God: So that wee cannot doe what we would, nor when we would, nor how long wee would, nor surcease when wee would, nor change when wee would" (p. 72), which leaves a predictable area for the exercise of free will: "For euen that which a man hath done by his free-will, was originally from the Vnchangeable decree of God's will, Act. 4.28." But for a view more in accord with most of the scholars see Albert C. Labriola, "Divine Urgency as a Motive for Conduct in *Samson Agonistes*," *PQ*, 50 (1971), pp. 99–107: Samson "exerts his free will in concert with Providence." On this issue Milton, I believe, stands closer to Boethius and Erasmus than to Occam or Granger.

6 Don Cameron Allen discusses the matter on pp. 83 f. of *The Harmonious Vision* (Baltimore, 1954).

7 John M. Steadman, "Milton's 'Summa Epitasis'," *MLR*, 69 (1974), 730–44, has shown that *Samson* does not "fit the three-episode, five-act scheme of the Renaissance critics, which was based on a misinterpretation of Aristotle as well as a misunderstanding of Greek tragedy" (p. 741).

8 The need to transcend such categories stems from the fact that we are reading Milton's Christian drama, which is to say the drama written as a species of prophecy; and the "Understandings of the Prophets," declares John Smith in "Of Prophecy," *Select Discourses* (2nd ed.; Cambridge, 1673), "were alwaies kept awake and strongly acted by God," so that in "Types and Shadows" they beheld "the intelligible Mysteries" of the "Antitypes themselves" (p. 172). The nature of the enterprise means that we may not expect a three- or five-part structure or indeed "any Methodical concatenation of things" in "Prophetical writ; it being a most usual thing with them many times . . . to knit the Beginning and End of Time together" (p. 271).

9 *Religio Medici* i.59 and i.11, ed. L. C. Martin (Oxford, 1964), pp. 54 and 11.

10 *Milton's Debt to Greek Tragedy in "Samson Agonistes"* (Baltimore, 1937), pp. 159–69 *et passim*. See also John T. Shawcross's fine "Irony as Tragic Effect: *Samson Agonistes* and the Tragedy of Hope," *Calm of Mind,* ed. Joseph Anthony Wittreich, Jr. (Cleveland, 1971), pp. 289–306; and the works by Anthony Low cited in note 21.

11 *Reason of Church Government,* Hughes, p. 668.

12 *Lectures and Notes on Shakespeare and Other English Poets,* ed. T. Ashe (London, 1904), p. 237.

13 My own distinction corresponds in important ways to Morgan's "suspense of plot" and "dramatic illusion," in "The Nature of Dramatic Illusion," *Transactions of the Royal Society of Literature,* N. S., 12 (1933), 61–77, repr. in *Reflections on Art,* ed. Suzanne K. Langer (New York, 1961), pp. 91–102; I am much indebted to the essay. The word "suspense" (L. *suspendere,* meaning "hang") may be ambiguous in this context. In its etymological signification it functions as an apt designation of Milton's methods; insofar as the word now connotes "surprise," it is misleading.

14 Tom F. Driver, *The Sense of History in Greek and Shakespearean Drama* (New York, 1960), illuminates *Oedipus* from this point of view, pp. 154–59.

15 Cf. Albert R. Cirillo, "Time, Light, and the Phoenix," *Calm of Mind,* ed. Wittreich, pp. 209–33, who finds the course of the drama and its fulfillment "incipient" in the opening lines (p. 219).

16 On the motif of ransom see T. S. K. Scott-Craig, "Concerning Milton's Samson," *Renaissance News,* 5 (1952), 45–53, and Ann Gossman, "Ransom in *Samson Agonistes,*" *Ren. News,* 13 (1960), 11–15.

17 John Carey's introductory material to his edition of *Samson* (*Poems of John Milton,* edd. Carey and Alastair Fowler [London, 1968], 330–43) includes a full, intelligent discussion of the imagery, though in neglecting the proleptic ironies it concludes oddly: "the imagery does not merely reinforce the drama's triumphant arc. On the contrary, it contributes meanings which threaten to invert this arc and bring the weak-minded, vengeful hero to the level of Dalila and the Philistines."

18 *Milton's Grand Style* (Oxford, 1963), p. 49.

19 *Works,* trans. Rhys Roberts *et al.,* ed. W. D. Ross (Oxford, 1924).

20 Milton's understanding of Aristotle would have been influenced by Augustine, as in *De Doctrina Christiana* 14.13, where God is at once the Physician and the Medicine, seeking to apply "Christian medicine operating either by contraries or by similar things": cold to hot, moist to dry—or a round bandage to a round wound. Trapped by the wisdom of the serpent, we become free through the foolishness of the Lord. The doctrine of cure by contrary relates to a universe based in *discordia concors* and to a poem founded in paradox. Francis Quarles, *Divine Poems* (London, 1674), p. 308, meditates on Samson and the Riddle of the Lion, which illustrates "the secret pleasure of his sacred will"; Christ

is the "wounded Lyon" in whose "dying body" may be found a "world of hony"—the "Mysteries" and "sacred Riddles" of Christ and of Christian poetry.

21 "Action and Suffering," *PMLA*, 84 (1969), 514; see also Low's full-length study, *The Blaze of Noon* (New York and London, 1974). Joseph Summers, "The Movement of the Drama," *The Lyric and Dramatic Milton*, ed. Joseph Summers (New York, 1965), p. 5, makes a number of useful observations on Milton's play with alternatives, especially with the word "or," a conjunction that appears more frequently in *Samson* than in any comparable work of which I am aware.

22 Hughes, p. 728.

23 As in W[illiam] Fenner, *Works* (London, 1657), I, 388, where "Redeeme the time" means to "yeild to the motions of Gods Spirit." See in this connection n. 22 of Chapter VI: "*Paradise Regained:* Waiting to Stand."

24 Stanley E. Fish, "Question and Answer in *Samson Agonistes*," *Critical Quarterly*, 11 (1969), 263: "The reader believes in God because to a certain extent he can play God."

CHAPTER V: The Tempestivity of Time

1 (Antwerp, 1605), Preface, and pp. 12, 135. (I owe the reference to Gwen Staniforth.) Edward Leigh, *Critica Sacra* (4th ed.; London, 1662), p. 130, glosses *kairos* as *tempus*, "often" signifying *opportunitas:* "The article and point of time that determines opportunitie.... It is put for mature and seasonable time, Mark 11:13. Mat. 13:20. Acts 14:7." Explaining that the "Greeks make a difference between" *chronos* and *kairos*, Leigh adds that "the word properly signifieth Opportunity, or present occasion, that present fit time...." Another common term is "season." Lancelot Andrewes, preaching on Ephesians 1:10 during Christmas of 1623, declares that "Time and season are two, and have in all tongues two different words to shew they differ. In Hebrew... ; in Greek... ; in Latin, *tempus* and *tempestivum*. And differ they do as much as a time, and a good time. It is time alway, all the year long; so is it not season, but when the good time is.... Now as 'the things,' *res*, have their autumn of maturity, so *tempora*, 'the seasons,' have their fulness, and when the things are ripe and ready to be gathered, then is the season full." *Ninety-Six Sermons*, ed. J. P. Wilson (Oxford, 1841), I, 267. Joseph Caryll, *et al.*, *An English-Greek Lexikon* (London, 1661), glosses "time appointed" as "prosthesmia" or "that which was laid down before"; *kairos* as "a certain and determined time. Luke 20:10. Rom.5:6."; and *chronos* as "time, the space of time in general, (but χαιρὸς is an opportunity wherein we may act something. Acts 2:7.) Iude 18. Job

12:12. Luke 4:5. Luke 20:9. Iohn 5:6. Iohn 7:33. Acts 15:33. Rom. 16:25." *Kairos* derives from Pythagorean epistemology.

2 *Time and the End of Time* [1669], pp. 4 and 53. "Time and opportunity differ," time being mere "duration or succession"; but "opportunity is the time apted and fitted" and "is called the season or tempestivity of time," for time must be "taken under a double notion: There is the space of time, and there is the opportunity of time. *Tempus longum,* and *tempus commodum*" (pp. 1–2). And our duty is clear; as Richard Corbett says in "Gods Providence" (London, 1642), preached before Commons 28 December 1642, "We must go along with Providence, and serve occasion and opportunities . . ." (p. 28).

3 *Reason of Church Government,* Hughes, pp. 667–68.

4 1 Cor. 7 includes Paul's wish that all were as he, though he understands that everyone has from God a particular gift or *charisma*. Milton by comparing 1 Cor. 1:7 with 12:4, 9, 28, 30 would know that the "gift" is tendered by the Holy Spirit in accord with the workings of Eternal Providence. Ernest Sirluck has argued persuasively that Milton had around 1637 conceived of himself as possessing the Pauline *charisma;* "Milton's Idle Right Hand," *JEGP,* 60 (1961), 749–85.

5 *Hughes,* pp. 830–31.

6 "Milton versus Time," *Milton's Unchanging Mind* (Port Washington, N.Y., 1973), pp. 17, 32, and 5. Paul Baumgartner, "Milton and Patience," *SP,* 60 (1963), 203–13, investigates an area deserving further attention.

7 *Works,* XII, 320–25. (As edited in the Yale Prose, these two distinct drafts are combined into one letter!) A. S. P. Woodhouse, "Notes on Milton's Early Development," *UTQ,* 13(1942), 66–101, makes use of Sonnet VII in arguing that Milton abandoned the priesthood for poetry around 1632; John T. Shawcross, "Milton's Decision to Become a Poet," *MLQ,* 24 (1963), 21–30, argues for 1637; and John Spencer Hill, "Poet-Priest," *Milton Studies VIII,* ed. James D. Simmonds (Pittsburgh, 1975), pp. 41–69, reviews the evidence, concluding that Milton thought of himself as both priest and poet until 1640 (the date of the Et Cetera Oath) and that the "tension" between the two vocations was not fully resolved until perhaps as late as 1641–42.

8 *The Redemption of Time* (London, 1608), p. 45. Whately's concern is that we may forget that "the vessell of time is not so full (as most men dreame) nay it will soone come to the bottome: it is then wisedome to spare betime, and not in the very dregs and lees." Since time, as we now say with less force, is running out, men would be well advised to avoid "immoderate following of worldly businesses and affaires, Play, Twatling, Sleeping, foolish thinking, excessive rooting in the earth." Sound advice. At the close of "that large voluminous Period of Providence, which, beginning with the first *Fiat Lux* in Genesis, ends not till the last *Thunder-clap* intimated in the Revelation" ("Franciscus Palaeo-

politanus" [Henry More?], *Divine Dialogues* [London, 1668], p. 287), we shall discover, according to Andreas de Soto, that "among other things that there be to accuse us" on the "day of doome," "one will be found to be that of time" (*The Ransome of Time Being Captive,* tr. John Hawkins [London, 1634], p. 43).

9 Daniel Featley, *Clavis Mystica* (London, 1636), pp. 401-02.

10 *Syntagma Logicum* (London, 1620), p. 75. The distinction between *aiōn,* or "sacred" time, and *chronos,* or "ordinary" time, seems to be very ancient. (Erwin Panofsky writes with his customary learning and acumen about time in *Studies in Iconology* [New York, 1962], pp. 69-94; see also Rudolph Wittkower, "Chance, Time and Virtue," *JWCI,* 1 (1938-40), 313-21, and G. L. Kittredge, "To Take Time by the Forelock," *MLN,* 8 (1893), 459-69; and there is much of interest in *The Philosophy of Time,* ed. Richard Gale [Garden City, N.Y., 1967], *Man and Time,* ed. Joseph Campbell [New York, 1957], and *The Voices of Time,* ed. J. T. Fraser [New York, 1966].) Yet it was only later, perhaps among the Orphic thinkers (see for example *Orphic Hymn* 13), that time comes to be conceived of as a first principle. When *chronos* became identified with (confused with?) that most elderly god, Kronos (see for example Macrobius, *Sat.* I. xxii. 8), it is almost as though a heightened awareness of time was leading some thinkers to attribute divinity to the idea, to legitimate it by finding a niche for it in the pantheon; Servius, commenting on Saturn in *Aeneid* 3. 104, calls him a god "*aeternitas et saeculorum.*" Personifications of time appear in Pindar, that time is Father of All; in Theognis, that time illumintes all things; in Solon, that time brings truth to light; and in Simonides, that the tooth of time devours all. Aristophanes affected to be amused by Euripides' allusion to the "foot" of time, which seems to imply that the process of personifying the idea was by no means complete, though it would not be long before time acquires wings and, from association with old Kronos, a scythe and hourglass. In *Timaeus* and the neo-Platonists, *aiōn* as the word usually translated "eternity" once more assumes metaphysical status and is again distinguished from *chronos.* Christian thinkers baptized the distinction.

11 *Paracelsus,* ed. and introd. Jolande Jacobi, tr. Norbert Guterman (2nd. edit.; New York, 1951), pp. 208-09. "Anyone who imagines that all fruits ripen at the same time as the strawberries knows nothing about grapes" (p. 117).

12 Thomas Granger, *Familiar Exposition or Commentarie on Ecclesiastes* (London, 1621), p. 207. Cf. "hour" in Thomas Wilson, *A Complete Christian Dictionary* (8th ed. with additions by Bagwel and Sympson; London, [1678]): "A special time prefixed of God in his counsel, for some particular work, which cannot prevent [come before] that time, nor be deferred, Joh. 2.4 Mat. 26.45."

13 *The Right Vnderstanding of the Times* (London, 1647; sermon preached at

Margaret Westminster, 30 December 1646), pp. 17–20. (I owe the reference to Boyd Berry.) Cf. Marshall's "God's Master-Piece" (London, 1645), p. 32, where the idea of delay, so important in *Paradise Regained,* receives theological justification: "But why doth he then so delay. . . ? I answere, the Lord is a God of judgment, he is a wise God, he knowes the fittest time: That he doth delay is neither because he is weary of the work, or because he is not able to doe it, or because the enemy is strong; No, no, the Holy One of Israel never fainted, neither is he weary, but it is onely because his best time is not yet come. . . ." And see "Why Divine Justice deferreth punishment" in Plutarch, *The Philosophy Commonly Called the Morals;* tr. Philemon Holland (rev. ed.; London, 1657), esp. pp. 448–51.

14 *Commentarie vpon . . . Romanes,* tr. Christopher Rosdell (London, 1583), p. 176ᵛ.

15 *Right Vnderstanding,* p. 20. Milton would doubtless concur with Edward Leigh's assertion that the "Parable of the Talents is the same in effect, with that of the Virgins" (*Annotations upon all the New Testament* [London, 1650], p. 68).

16 *Paracelsus,* ed. Jacobi, p. 186.

17 *Explicator,* VIII, 2 (1950), 10–11.

18 Marshall, *Right Vndestanding,* pp. 20–21.

19 *Paradise Lost,* ed. Scott Elledge (New York, 1975), p. xv.

20 Although I have of course consulted William Riley Parker's *Milton* (2 vols.; Oxford, 1968), my tendentious "biography" relies mainly on Sirluck, "Milton's Idle Right Hand," which I find brilliantly suggestive and carefully documented. The most thorough compilation of materials for a study of the labors of the left hand is John T. Shawcross, "A Survey of Milton's Prose Works," pp. 291–391, *Achievements of the Left Hand,* edd. Michael Lieb and John T. Shawcross (Amherst, Mass., 1974), which is notable for care and completeness, as well as suggestive comment; e.g., "a study of Milton the late bloomer, the servant constantly preparing himself for service but waiting for command, the contemplative whose self-regard and high ambition finally discharge his burden of thought and emotion might wisely" start with *An Apology* (p. 295). Arthur Barker's *Milton and the Puritan Dilemma* (Toronto, 1942) remains valuable; relevant to my argument are the observations about Milton's realignment of principle after the marriage.

21 Hughes, pp. 1031 and 1040.

22 Hughes, p. 708.

23 Davis P. Harding, *The Club of Hercules* (Urbana, 1962), p. 17, observes that Milton's *poscit opus* is a carefully designed reminiscence of the phrase in Ovid's "brutally frank passage."

24 See notes 20 and 4.

25 Georgia B. Christopher, "The Virginity of Faith," *ELH,* 43 (1976), 479–98, objects to Angus Fletcher's allegation in *The Transcendental*

Masque (Ithaca, 1971) that Milton exhibits "sublime emptyheadedness" and argues, with considerable learning and persuasiveness, that *Comus* is a unified "Reformation Conceit" based on *virginitas fidei*. If true, it adds a theological dimension to what I must persist in regarding as a psychological obsession.

26 The revisions may be conveniently examined in the first volume of Harris Francis Fletcher's facsimile edition, *John Milton's Complete Poetical Works* (4 vols.; Urbana, Ill., 1943–48). They are studied from the social point of view by Barbara Breasted, "Comus and the Castlehaven Scandal," *Milton Studies III,* ed. James D. Simmonds (Pittsburgh, 1971), esp. pp. 205–11, with full citation of those who have investigated the relation of the three versions.

27 *Poetry and Dogma* (New Brunswick, N. J., 1954), p. 196.

28 For the background to this kind of debate see my *Nature and Art in the English Renaissance* (New York, 1964).

29 Hughes, p. 825.

30 Ann Gossman and George Whiting, *RES,* N.S., 12 (1961), 364–72, gather up, and submit to scrutiny, most of the basic arguments (Fitzroy Pyle replies at some length). The *Variorum* contains summaries of what appears to be a history of special pleading; my own prejudices coincide with those of Douglas Bush in the *Variorum,* though I feel the force of John Shawcross's objections, made in a private communication, that blindness perhaps ought to be considered "a context, not a subject" and that in my assumptions about dating I am underestimating the evidence of the Trinity MS.

31 *Familiar Exposition,* p. 75.

32 Lt. Col. James L. Jackson and Capt. Walter E. Weese, *MLN,* 72 (1957), 91–93, cite Ephesians 6 (the armor of the Lord, "standing" against the Devil) to argue an active meaning for the verb. Boyd Berry, in Chapter XII (revised from *MLQ,* 35 [1974]) of *Process of Speech* (Baltimore and London, 1976), argues cogently that "Standing is the perfect verb to represent" the "Puritan mode of heroism" (p. 185). "Freely they stood who stood, and fell who fell" (*PL,* III, 102) describes the condition of all reasoning creatures, exhibited rightly and most grandly when the Jesus of *Paradise Regained* "stands" on the pinnacle to fulfill, as antitype to type, the "fall" of Adam.

33 This astonishing passage, together with ones quoted later, may be found on pp. 824–27 of Hughes.

34 *Areopagitica,* Hughes, p. 742. In the measured optimism of 1644 the images of dismemberment and virgin wholeness coalesce in the exalted language describing the body of Truth. One need not be Freud or Ferenczi to observe that blinding may symbolize dismemberment in the specific sense of castration. Sophocles' Oedipus, in his last "incestuous" gesture, blinds himself with Jocasta's brooches (used by Greek women to hold up the chiton at the shoulders).

CHAPTER VI: *Paradise Regained:* Waiting to Stand

1 *The Flight of Time* (London, 1634), p. 4.
2 *John Milton* (New York, 1963), pp. 329 and 328. More recent primary
   and secondary sources are cited in Walter MacKellar's *Variorum Commentary* (New York, 1975); and in Barbara Kiefer Lewalski's *Milton's
   Brief Epic* (Providence, R. I., 1966), which gathers up previous criticism, corrects much, and offers fresh perspectives based on extensive
   and original research; her "Time and History in *Paradise Regained,*"
   The Prison and the Pinnacle, ed. Balachandra Rajan (Toronto, 1973), pp.
   49–81, deals more directly with the thesis I advocate here.
      The difficulties with *Paradise Regained* are theological as well as
   aesthetic and may be expressed in the unequivocal strictures of an
   anonymous nineteenth-century editor who appears to have felt the
   force of earlier objections by Thyer and Warburton. Although the
   "Critique," *Poetical Works* (London, 1821), that precedes *Paradise Regained* is generally laudatory, the author finds it necessary to point out
   two defects that must be seen as "glaring and unpardonable in a Christian Poet." For one thing, "Poetical licence does not extend to the violation of divine truth. The *proper Divinity* of the Eternal Son, so unequivocally revealed in the Holy Scriptures, is kept entirely out of sight." As
   a result, the "Poet has injured himself no less than in excluding the
   scene of the Crucifixion from the action of his Poem. He has torn the
   sun from the firmament. . . ." The related problem finds its focus in
   the title, which seems patently impertinent. "If the Author had entitled
   his performance 'The Temptation of Christ,' the action of the Poem as
   it now stands at present would have been complete." But that "Paradise
   was regained, and human redemption effected, by the single act of our
   Saviour's temptation in the wilderness, is in open contradiction to the
   sacred Scriptures," which "plainly declare that he saved us by *his obedience unto death*" and that his "temptation was *initiatory* . . . and but a portion" of what He must endure. (*Paradise Regained* and the minor poems
   follow *Paradise Lost* and have separate signatures and pagination.)
   Joseph A. Wittreich draws my attention to a reprinting of the critique
   in *Paradise Regained* (New York, 1831), which in spite of Milton re-
   asserts the biblical proprieties by including a frontispiece of Christ on
   the Cross rather than a scene from the temptations. Both of the theological difficulties suggest that Milton's aim may be other than we have
   supposed.
3 Hughes, p. 1036.
4 "Temptation in *Paradise Regained,*" *JEGP,* 15 (1916), 603–04; "The
   Temptation Motive in Milton," *SP,* 15 (1918), 182; and "Theme and
   Pattern in *Paradise Regained,*" *UTQ,* 25 (1956), 170.
5 "Creating the Garden Anew," *PQ,* 50 (1971), 567–81. Hamilton begins
   by assuming that Jesus "is best understood when viewed as a dramatic

personage rather than as a static moral exemplar" (perhaps a false dichotomy?), then theorizes that criticism of the poem has moved in two main directions from assumptions like those of Arnold Stein, *Heroic Knowledge* (Minneapolis, Minn., 1957), p. 9, namely that Jesus undergoes a "soul-journey" or some other sort of "dramatic" development toward self-realization. (Such assumptions must always be open to challenge when predicated of the Son of God, but in any case it is hard to find full textual support for the "four stages" of evolving knowledge demarcated by Stein, pp. 104–05.) First, according to Hamilton, there are a number of theories based on Christ as Second Adam; these generally involve the use of the "triple equation" (Adam, Christ, Everyman) as described by Elizabeth Marie Pope, *"Paradise Regained": The Tradition and the Poem* (Baltimore, 1947), pp. 51–69, and cogently developed, despite Stein's suspicion of Pope's aims and methodology, by Barbara Kiefer Lewalski in her indispensable *Brief Epic*, pp. 182–92. (Although I cannot accept the "triple equation" as a principle of structure, I agree of course that Milton connects the temptations of Adam and Christ—and that we are intended to apply our knowledge to the trials of our own lives. (As Richard Guilpin [?] says in *Daemonologia Sacra: or, A Treatise of Satans Temptations* [London, 1677], p. 182, "This design . . . touched upon . . . Christ, as Mediator and second *Adam,* [for thus it became him to overcome the Enemy at the same Weapon, by which he overcame our first Parents . . .] yet was it wholly *for our sakes,*" for our instruction.) Second, Hamilton points to those theories that place a "dramatic" emphasis on the three aspects of Christ's mediatorial role, argued pre-eminently by Lewalski first in *SP,* 57 (1960) and utilized fully in *Brief Epic,* a theory that may be seen as modifying and redefining Northrop Frye's broadly-conceived reading based on Christ's Harrowing of Hell, "The Typology of *Paradise Regained,*" *MP,* 53 (1956), 227–38. Hamilton rightly praises Lewalski for her thorough and skilfull study of the Christology of *Christian Doctrine* in relation to the brief epic (*Brief Epic,* pp. 133–63), then notes that for her it is *kenosis* or the divine "emptying" that provides the opportunity for the Son's "growth" in knowledge: the Son reveals that he is Second Adam by resisting temptation, and by resisting temptation the Son grows in knowledge. Hamilton objects that Lewalski relates the two (*Brief Epic,* pp. 158–59, 213) only through "revelation," insufficiently a link; and accordingly proposes as a third approach his theory of Christ's acquiring, book-by-book, the virtues requisite for the "Paradise within." Although I cannot appreciate the force of Hamilton's objection to divine revelation as an inadequate connection between Christ as Second Adam and Christ as "growing" in knowledge, I fully concur with the notion of the Son's revealing, if not acquiring virtue-by-virtue, a "Paradise within" and with the contention (p. 569) that the Son is "not merely a man who refuses to do what Adam and Eve did; he also acts out Milton's vision of what Adam and Eve could have become" (citing *Paradise Lost,* V, 500–01 and VII, 157 ff., where Milton allows Raphael to propose a kind of moral and spiritual progress open to Adam and Eve, implying that they may, "improv'd by tract of time," scale the chain of being and dwell by choice in the paradises of heaven or earth).

6 The arithmetical gymnastics in this arena do not inspire confidence in our profession. Burton J. Weber, "The Schematic Structure of *Paradise Regained*," *PQ,* 50 (1971), pp. 553–56, cites, on the temptations of the second day, Barbara Lewalski's division into 3-3-1 (*Brief Epic*, pp. 219, 256, 281–82); Frye's, "Typology," pp. 230–34, into 2-2-3; Howard Schultz's, "Christ and Antichrist in *Paradise Regained*," *PMLA,* 67 (1952), footnote p. 797, into 1-4-2; and Woodhouse's, "Theme and Pattern," p. 176, into 1-5-1. Weber, p. 555, comes up with a "triple trial mirroring the three days' series: Abc, aBc, abC." Joseph Anthony Wittreich, Jr., "A Poet Amongst Poets," *Milton and the Line of Vision,* ed. Wittreich (Madison, 1975), p. 137, finds seven temptations to correspond to the seven-part structure of Revelation. James R. McAdams, "The Pattern of Temptation in *Paradise Regained*," *Milton Studies VI,* ed. James D. Simmonds (Pittsburgh, 1974), 177–93, observes that the temptations of the first and third days frame "nine distinguishable episodes" (II, 245-IV, 431) with the temptation of Israel at the center.

7 At the Baptism Jesus hears Psalm 2:7, "Thou art my beloved Son, in whom I am well pleased," which recalls for the exegete the covenant establishing the Davidic Kingship by constituting Israel the "son" of God (1 Cor. 10:2). Jesus, the New Israel, fulfils the Old Israel in his role as the Suffering Servant of Isaiah 52:4 whose humility shall overcome all worldly kingdoms. Thus the context for the temptations of *Paradise Regained:* the Suffering Servant rejects the kingdoms of the earth, while the temptations of the stones-into-bread and the pinnacle reveal that "Thou art my beloved Son."

8 See Michael Fixler, *Milton and the Kingdoms of God* (Evanston, Ill., 1964), esp. pp. 77–78. Although Fixler rightly observes that *Paradise Regained* "deals largely with the elusive reality of a metaphor, the Kingdom and Kingship of Christ" (p. 225), his emphasis, because of his stress on the "involvement of Jewish ideas," is finally different from my own.

9 In the witty formulation of Frank Kermode, *Sense of an Ending* (New York, 1967), p. 25: "No longer imminent, the End is immanent."

10 *Sermons of Maister Iohn Caluin, vpon the Book of Iob,* tr. Arthur Golding (London, 1584), p. 426.

11 *Pursuit of the Millennium* (rev. ed.; New York, 1970); Cohn focusses on the Middle Ages but could have followed his thesis through the twentieth century.

12 See Merritt Y. Hughes, "The Christ of *Paradise Regained* and Renaissance Heroic Tradition," *SP,* 35 (1938), pp. 254–77. Relevant primary

and secondary sources may be found in Burton O. Kurth, *Milton and Christian Heroism* (Berkeley, 1959) and in John M. Steadman's *Milton and the Renaissance Hero* (Oxford, 1967), a learned and accurate assessment; see also Steadman's *Milton's Epic Characters* (Chapel Hill, 1959).

13 As quoted in *Studies in Human Time*, tr. Elliott Coleman (Baltimore, 1956), pp. 12–13. More fully from *Dei Praedestinatione* (Geneva, 1551), *Calvini Opera*, VIII, 321 (Vol. 36 of *Corpus Ref.*): *Hic vero eum praevaricari dicas: nam quum probandum susceperit, non stare cum electione salutis fiduciam: eo nos ratiocinando deducit, ut hanc necessario in illa fundatam esse oporteat. Video me assidue fluctuari: nullum momentum praeterit, quo non obruendus videar. At, quia electos suos Deus sustinet, ne unquam mergantur, staturum me inter innumeras procellas certo confido.* Stuart Curran kindly provided the reference at a time when the *Opera* was unavailable to me.

14 Prologue, 11. 3891–95, *Works*, ed. F. N. Robinson (Cambridge, Mass., n. d.), p. 66.

15 "The First Anniversary," *Poems and Letters*, ed. H. M. Margoliouth (2 vols.; Oxford, 1952), I, 103.

16 Margoliouth, I, 5.

17 *Religio Medici* i. 43, ed. L. C. Martin (Oxford, 1964), p. 41.

18 *Ben Jonson*, ed. C. H. Herford, Percy and Evelyn Simpson, VIII (Oxford, 1947), 242–47.

19 "First Anniversary," Margoliouth, I, 103 and 106.

20 Ed. Henry A. Murray (New York, 1949), pp. 247–53 (subsequent quotations also from these pages).

21 *Works* (Cambridge, 1605), pp. 5–6.

22 Thomas Fuller, *A Comment on . . . S. Matthews Gospel, Concerning Christs Temptations* (London, 1652), pp. 5–6: "*The spirit driveth him;* but how? not as a ship is driven by a tempest . . . furiously: but, to joyn *Matthew* and *Mark* together, he was *led-driven,* by a mixt motion; *led,* there is willingness; *driven,* a kinde of violence; *led,* there is freedom; *driven,* there is force.

The sum is this: an efficacious impression from the spirit met in Christ with a voluntary condescention thereunto, and susception thereof."

Compare my discussion of the "mixt motion" that leads Samson finally to acquiesce in the command that he perform at the Feast of Dagon. Cf. Arthur Barker, "Structural and Doctrinal Pattern in Milton's Later Poems," *Essays in English Literature,* edd. Millar MacLure and F. W. Watt (Toronto, 1964), who concludes (p. 181) that in *Paradise Regained* "true self-dependence" and "waiting obediently" turn out to be the "same thing." See also n. 23 of Chapter IV.

23 *Comment,* pp. 19–20. "Because as Adam began mans ruine with eating, Christ would begin mans repairing with abstinence. Physicians commonly cure by the contraries. . . ." Cf. *Daemonologia Sacra,* "Thus was

Christ *evidenced* to be the *second Adam,* and the Seed of the Woman. His being tempted, and in such a manner, doth clearly satisfy us that he was *true man;* and that in *that nature* he it was that was promised *to break the Serpents head. . . .* This was a fair *preludium* and *earnest* of that *final conquest* over Satan . . . (pp. 16–17)." Perkins, *Works,* p. 17, says that the Devil "knew well, that if Christ were the true and proper sonne of God, then he must needs be the true *Messias;* and if he were that annointed of God, then also he it was that must accomplish that old and ancient promise made to our first Parents *for the bruising of the serpents head . . .*" It is "by the contraries," the inexorable march of type into antitype, intended from the beginning to be accomplished in the fullness of time: "And why did it please thee, O Saviour, to fast forty days and forty nights, unless as Moses fasted forty days at the delivery of the law, and Elias forty days at the restitution of the law, so thou thoughtest fit at the accomplishment of the law, and the promulgation of the gospel, to fulfil the time of both these types of thine, wherein thou intendest our wonder . . ." (Joseph Hall, *Contemplations on the Historical Passages of the Old & New Testaments* [4 vols; London, 1820], III, 339).

24 Laurie B. Zwicky, "Kairos in *Paradise Regained,*" *ELH,* 31 (1964), 271–77, was, I believe, the first to point out the importance of *chronos* and *kairos* in the brief epic. A fuller, and in some ways more accurate, discussion appears in A. B. Chambers, "Double Time Scheme in *Paradise Regained,*" *Milton Studies VII,* gen. ed. James D. Simmonds, edd. Albert C. Labriola and Michael Lieb (Pittsburgh, 1975), pp. 189–205. Chambers, following Cullmann, wants "Christian" or "linear" time to be identical with the succession of *kairoi,* so that the *kairoi* may be contrasted with *chronos,* which is assumed to be "cyclical" and "repetitive" or "liturgical"; for Chambers would like to argue that *Paradise Regained* "presents the devotional and moral meanings of Lent I in exaggerated form" (p. 196). Patrick Grant, "Time and Temptation in *Paradise Regained,*" *UTQ,* 43(1973), 32–47, argues that the background for the temptations may be sought in the "contemporary iconography of time," but Ira Clark, *MP,* 71 (1973), pp. 1–15, esp. pp. 13–14, finds more immediate inspiration in John's Gospel.

25 See Lewalski, *Brief Epic,* p. 218. It prefigures not only the Eucharist but also the nuptial banquet with the Lamb, which was to be celebrated in a city, The Heavenly Jerusalem, and on a mountain, the celestial Mount Sion; Milton exploits the full range of these types when he shows us the Temple in Jerusalem and makes it appear in the distance "like a Mount" (IV, 547). Jesus becomes, in effect, *deus in monte.*

26 As John Shower warns us in *A Discourse of Tempting Christ* (London, 1694), there are many who come to tempt "God, when he doth not . . . grant their Desires, at *that time*" they "expect it" (p. 43); and that "we Tempt God, when we would tie him to our Circumstances of Time. . ." (p. 72).

27 "Patience," tr. Sr. Emily J. Daly, "Fathers of the church," *Disciplinary, Moral and Ascetical Works* (New York, 1959), XL, 200, 195, and 195–96.

28 Interpreting 2 Thess. 1:4 in the second volume of *Annotations upon the Holy Bible* (3rd ed. enlarged by Sam Clark and Edward Veale; London, 1696).

29 Cartari, *Le Imagini* (Venice, 1556), fol. 96ᵛ: "This one, which the Latins called Occasion and Opportunity, and revered as a Goddess, was called Opportune Time by the Greeks. Therefore they worshipped him as a God, not a Goddess. His name for them was Caerus [i. e., "*nome Cero*," or *kairos*], for that word among the Greeks signifies opportunity of time. Thus for the Greeks, the God Caerus was the same as Occasion for the Latins." (I owe the reference to John Mulryan, whose complete translation of the *Imagini* will be published by *Renaissance Editions*.) The Son knows that "*Opportunities* and occasions do depend upon [God's] *Providence;* without which nothing comes to pass" (*Daemonologia Sacra*, p. 9).

30 Richard D. Jordan, "*Paradise Regained* and the Second Adam," *Milton Studies IX*, ed. James D. Simmonds (Pittsburgh, 1976), pp. 261–75, has recently taken a similar position, attacking (p. 263) Lewalski, *Brief Epic*, for her emphasis on "genuine dramatic action and real conflict," though Jordan himself wants to treat the "epic poem" as "a drama" (p. 272)—but not a naturalistic or psychological drama. The problems with the attempt to "psychologize" a Chronometer may be observed in one of those essays by J. B. Broadbent, "The Private Mythology of *Paradise Regained*," *Calm of Mind*, ed. Joseph Anthony Wittreich, Jr. (Cleveland, 1971), pp. 77–92, in which the brief epic becomes an "inadequately depersonalized expression" (p. 80) of Milton's anxieties and the "temptations are versions of hunger for love which is ultimately maternal (it feeds), and for a power which is incestuous" (p. 90). Probably there is no need to describe Broadbent's analysis of the "Oedipus" simile in Book IV? Stanley E. Fish, "Inaction and Silence: The Reader in *Paradise Regained*," also in *Calm of Mind* (pp. 25–47), is perhaps relevant here, esp. the observation (p. 31) that "waiting is the only action (or non-action) the characters in *Paradise Regained* ever take. . . ." And also Donald L. Guss, who deals with the idea of an "inactive heroism" in "A Brief Epic," *SP*, 68 (1970), 228: "Faith alone teaches Jesus to stand and wait." But Faith *alone*?

31 It appears "like a Mount" because in the apocalyptic vocabulary of the revolutionary Puritans King Jesus shall come for the second time to fulfil in judgment the moment prefigured in the "thunders and lightnings" on Mount Sinai. Edmund Calamy, preaching to the House of Lords at Westminster (25 December 1644), "An Indictment Against England" (London, 1645), asks that we "beseech the Lord Jesus Christ to come once more into the world by his Spirit of power! Let us not despaire of his coming. For he is *Deus in monte*. He is our peace now the

Assyrian is in the land, Mic. 5.5. And when he comes he will come as a Conqueror to subdue his enemies under his feet" (p. 40).

32 "Puritan Soldiers in *Paradise Lost*," *MLQ*, 35 (1974), 396; cf. Stanley E. Fish, "Standing Only: Christian Heriosm in *Paradise Lost*," *Critical Quarterly*, 9 (1967), 162–78. The verb has a long history in exegetical writings, as in Perkins, *Works*, p. 7: "here [on the Pinnacle] Christ stood in our roome and sted (as he did upon the Crosse) encountring with Satan for us, as if we in our owne persons had been tempted."

33 *PMLA*, 83 (1968), 1398.

34 (London, 1647), pp. 245 and 330 (the last passage is added only with the second edition of 1648).

35 George F. Sensabaugh, "Milton on Learning," *SP*, 43 (1946), 258–72, lucidly treats the difficulties; but see C. A. Patrides, *Milton and the Christian Tradition* (Oxford, 1966), esp. pp. 148–49.

36 "Of EI at Delphi," *The Philosophy Commonly Called the Morals*, tr. Philemon Holland (rev. ed.; London, 1657), pp. 1106–08, where these (and subsequent quotations) may be found spoken by "Ammonius," who uses "generation" and "corruption" in the manner of Aristotle to argue his Platonic thesis. My former colleague, the late Moses Hadas, suggested that I look at Plutarch in this connection. Cf. the Loeb *Moralia*, tr. F. C. Babbitt (Cambridge, Mass., 1936), V, 243–53; see also Plato's *Timaeus* 37D–38 and F. M. Cornford, *Plato's Cosmology* (New York, 1937), pp. 97–98.

37 *Mystagogus Poeticus* (London, 1647), p. 21.

38 My reading of the simile (and of Milton's ways with comparing small and great) derives from John Coolidge's learned and stimulating "Great Things and Small: The Virgilian Progression," *Comparative Literature*, 17 (1965), 1–23. The Vergilian formula may be used concessively even in theological discourse—for example in *Nowell's Catechism*, tr. Thomas Norton from the Latin of 1570, ed. G. E. Corrie for the Parker Society (London, 1853), p. 162: "If we may liken great things to small, Christ's body is so present to our faith, as the sun when we see it is present to our eye."

39 See Stanley E. Fish, *Surprised by Sin* (New York, 1967), esp. pp. 22–37; also Kingsley Widmer, "Iconography of Renunciation," *Critical Essays on Milton from ELH* (Baltimore, 1969), pp. 75–86.

40 *Literary Criticism of Seventeenth-Century England*, ed. Edward W. Tayler (New York, 1967), p. 310. For Coolidge see note 38.

41 *Looke from Adam*, [tr. Miles Coverdale] (London, 1624), p. 86.

42 *Types or Figures* (Dublin, 1685), p. 73. As Ralegh puts it more sweepingly in his Preface to the *History of the World*: God says, "I will destroy the wisedom of the wise," so that "in the end" men see "an effect ... directly contrary to all thir owne counsels." (Quoted in Helen Gardner, *The Business of Criticism* [Oxford, 1959], p. 43.)

43 *Religio* i.50, p. 48.

44 Henry Bunting, *Itinerarium Totius Sacrae Scripturae,* [tr. Richard Braith-waite] (London, 1682), offers the usual interpretation: "It is to be thought, that all these sharp temptations of the Devil were done in one day" (p. 328).

Some Conclusions

1 Documentation of the Italian experiments, begun with grace and learning by J. S. Smart in relation to the sonnets (1921), has been assembled most fully and sensitively by F. T. Prince, *The Italian Element in Milton's Verse* (Oxford, 1954). Wittgenstein's telling example of "games," which are so called not because of any element common to all but because of "familial" resemblances, suggests some of the problems in talking about concepts like "style" and "period." And yet it remains true that, say, the discovery of perspective, at a particular "period," made for large as well as small changes in artistic "style." Milton's style is not an amorphous family of procedures adopted by an anonymous practitioner at an undatable and indefinable moment: it appears, after a number of premonitory gestures, around 1637 in *Lycidas,* and it exhibits ever afterward highly characteristic, carefully integrated, relations between smaller and larger aspects of design. This style belongs first to Milton; second to a period that valued *discordia concors* according to "number, weight, and measure" (*Wisdom of Solomon* 11:21); and third to us.

2 "Three Academic Pieces," *The Necessary Angel* (New York, 1951), p. 81.

3 *De Augmentis,* tr. Spedding and Ellis, *Philosophical Works,* ed. J. M. Robertson (London, 1905), p. 634.

4 *A Commentarie or Exposition, vpon . . . Galatians* (Cambridge, 1604), p. 278.

5 *XCVI Sermons* (London, 1629), pp. 158 and 25. I am drawing on the sermon preached at Whitehall in 1623 on Ephesians 1:10 and on the one in 1609 on Galatians 4:4–5.

6 Roland Barthes, *S/Z* (Paris, 1970), tr. Richard Muller (London, 1975), p. 52. But in Milton's greater poems the end is also a beginning—in *Paradise Lost,* for example, the beginning of history as we know it.

7 *S/Z,* p. 76.

8 *Critique of Pure Reason,* tr. Norman Kemp Smith (London, 1950), p. 47, as quoted by Wayne C. Booth, "Preserving the 'Exemplar," *Critical Inquiry,* 3 (1977), 422, who observes that "we do not lose our freedom by molding our minds in shapes established by others. We find it there. As Kant says. . . ."

A. J. A. Waldock concluded in *"Paradise Lost" and its Critics* (Cambridge, 1964), which first appeared in 1947, that the poem is really

rather defective as a novel, and I do not mean that Waldock unconsciously assumes the relevance of an incompatible genre: "It is not
absurd to mention the novel in connection with *Paradise Lost,* for the
problems of such a poem and the characteristic problems of the novel
have elements in common" (p. 18), which leads Waldock, inevitably it
would seem, to contend that "the *Paradise Lost* that Milton meant is not
quite the *Paradise Lost* that Milton wrote, for the *Paradise Lost* that he
meant was, in a strict sense, unwritable" (p. 143). Unwritable for Defoe
or Flaubert. . . ?

In order to rescue *A Mask* Cleanth Brooks and John Edward Hardy,
Poems of Mr. John Milton (New York, 1951), similarly appeal, though for
more generous reasons, to an irrelevant genre. Rejecting "allegory"
apparently means that they must discard as well a perfectly viable, and
definable, genre—that of the masque—in favor of a form more amen-
able to the terminology of the two critics, that is, the drama. The
"superficial, mechanical form" (!) of the masque is dismissed (p. 186),
for the "essential form of the poem is dramatic" (p. 188). Therefore the
Elder Brother may be seen to display "too naive self-assurance of
virtue" (p. 200) whereas the Younger Brother exhibits a "more pleasing humility" (p. 205) and is "more realistically conscious of the fleshli-
ness of man" (p. 206); since the Elder Brother "reduces his sister to a
mere personification of Virtue" (p. 211), his utterances become part of
a dramatic situation that produces tension. Although Brooks and
Hardy admit, rather regretfully, that "one can find in [The Lady] no
positive *fault*" (p. 200) and confess that "there are flaws in [Comus's]
argument, of course" (p. 218), they feel that the Tempter must be
conceded "charm," even the "appearance of warmth and persuasiveness" in "contrast to the icy virtue of the Lady" (p. 219). She does not,
they feel, "really refute Comus's arguments" (p. 221), and he is to be
understood as a "satanic *personality*, not as a *personification* of evil" (p.
219). As usual, Brooks remains on the lookout for evidences of "irony"
and "tension," which he locates almost invariably in the paradigm of a
kind of a-temporal "drama" of human irresolution; and we therefore
find that this misguided attempt to rehabilitate *A Mask* by translating
its personages into the vocabulary of a foreign genre stems from the (circular) argument that the "characters must be humanized; for the drama
is earthly, human" (p. 193). Approaches such as these consign great
genres—the epic and the masque—to the same area of literary limbo
occupied by the pastoral, another great genre.

9 *S/Z,* pp. 75–76.
10 *Mirum in Modum, Complete Works,* ed. A. B. Grosart (2 vols.; rpt. New
York, 1967), I, 21.
11 *A Continuation of Morning-Exercise Questions* (London, 1683), pp. 1007
and 981. Boyd Berry provided me with the reference.

12 *Time, Cause and Eternity* (London, 1938), p. 2. Cf. Nelson Pike, *God and Timelessness* (London, 1972), who deals directly with the two main, and conflicting, interpretations of *eternity*—as infinite duration and as timelessness—in examining Augustine, Boethius, Anselm, Aquinas, and a number of more recent theologians.

13 *A Discourse of the Freedom of the Will* (London, 1675), p. 91.

14 *Works,* ed. Barnabas Oley (3 vols.; London, 1673), II, 31. Cf. Wallace Stevens, "Le Monocle de Mon Oncle": "The honey of heaven may or may not come,/ But that of earth both comes and goes at once."

15 In the anti-episcopal tracts, where Milton hopes to derive the "one right discipline" from Scripture, the emphasis falls on the way that the "understanding" has been clouded by the Fall and the way that "custom" and "error" have, in consequence, assumed their tyranny over the minds of men. In the divorce tracts, and in *Areopagitica,* the appeal is necessarily to (right) "reason" and "charity," which may be used to rectify error after its occurrence, for it has become apparent to Milton that the "one right discipline" is not enough and that Scripture is not invariably plain and perspicuous, at least on the question of divorce. There is correspondingly greater emphasis on that "intellectual ray," the candle of the Lord within that allows *ratio* to illuminate choice. But even the concept of *ratio recta* (see Robert Hoopes, *Right Reason in the English Renaissance* [Cambridge, Mass., 1962], so important in *Areopagitica* and *Paradise Lost,* assumes less significance in *Samson* and *Paradise Regained.* In *Paradise Lost* the first sin is, among other things, a sin against right reason, for Adam is "fondly overcome with female charm" and chooses "against his better knowledge, not deceiv'd." But though Samson chooses both badly and well, the faculty of reason itself receives little explicit emphasis; and in *Paradise Regained,* of course, the protagonist is nowhere "fondly overcome" and everywhere chooses not so much by "reason" but rather through the exercise of the rectified or "uninfected" will.

16 "Agon and Logos," *The Prison and the Pinnacle,* ed. Balachandra Rajan (Toronto, 1973), p. 151. Although Milton never abandoned the effort to call the English nation to its true role under God, it is almost as though he were coming more and more to agree with Frye's contention that "human life sets up a kind of perpetual Saturnalia or inversion of the providential order in which the wicked flourish and the good are persecuted or ridiculed" (p. 138). As the angelic pedagogue, historian turned prophet, tells Adam (XII, 537–38): "so shall the World go on,/ To good malignant, to bad men benign."

17 Hughes, p. 744.

18 Cited by Theodore L. Huguelet, "The Rule of Charity in Milton's Divorce Tracts," *Milton Studies VI,* ed. James D. Simmonds (Pittsburgh, 1974), p. 211. Huguelet cogently argues that in 1641–42 Milton, pro-

ceeding by way of Ramus' "method," refurbished the irenic principle of charity and turned it into the master rule of his exegesis.

19 Hughes, p. 381.

20 Hughes, p. 729. Ernest Sirluck, *MP*, 48 (1950), 90–96, first speculated on the meaning of the "misreading," though others, most notably and most brilliantly Harold Bloom, have continued the discussion.

21 Hughes, p. 728.

22 Ibid.

23 Hughes, p. 739.

24 Hughes, p. 747.

25 Hughes, p. 733.

26 In *Of Reformation* (*Works*, III, i, 66) Milton confidently attacks those who object to the Puritan tendency toward "sudden extreams," implying that the "two extreames" of *"Vice* and *Vertue, Falshood* and *Truth"* are easily distinguished by those not blinded by "degenerate and traditional corruption." (Arthur Barker, *Milton and the Puritan Dilemma* [Toronto, 1942], pp. 65–66, speculates wisely on what the author of *Comus* might have said, had he been presented with the hypothetical case of a man whose "marriage choices" [as Manoa phrases it to Samson] produced a series of divorce pamphlets.) In *Reason of Church-Government* (*Works*, III, i, 216) Milton's respect for the value of sect and schism had been qualified by his conviction that the reforms he contemplated would bring in a "unanimous multitude" rather than a "rabble of Sects"; but the divorce tracts threatened to isolate him even from the Presbyterians to whom he had committed his best endeavors, and he was now, as nearly a sect of one, compelled not only to tolerate but also to justify schism. It is often forgotten that *Areopagitica,* situated after the first two divorce tracts but before the last two, conveys an optimism necessarily modified by the exigencies of Milton's personal situation; Herbert Palmer, it will be recalled, had advocated before the Westminster Assembly that the "wicked" book on divorce (probably *Doctrine and Discipline*) be burned.

27 Today the oration is usually interpreted as a kind of clarion call to liberty, but W. Kendall, "How to Read Milton's *Areopagitica,*" *Journal of Politics,* 22 (1960), 439–73, and John Illo, "The Misreading of Milton," *Columbia University Forum,* 8 (1965), 38–42, emphasize (easily?) Milton's restrictions on license to such a degree that the great liberator emerges as a kind of tyrant. My argument explains, I believe, the reason for the divergent views.

28 First argued in depth by Wilbur Gilman, *Milton's Rhetoric* (Columbia, Miss., 1939) but later developed with greater accuracy by Ernest Sirluck in the Yale Prose.

29 Hughes, p. 742.

30 Hughes, p. 731.

31 Hughes, p. 742.

32 Hughes, p. 745.

33 Hughes, p. 742.

34 Hughes, pp. 741–42.

35 Hughes, p. 747.

36 Ibid.

37 *Dialogues,* tr. Benjamin Jowett (New York, 1937), II, 425.

38 Hughes, p. 733.

39 *Religio Medici* ii. 4, ed. L. C. Martin (Oxford, 1964), pp. 61 and 60.

40 The immensely moving story chronicled in the Book of Ruth was thought to have proceeded "from the Spirit of God, as well as the bookes of the Iudges, & Chronicles," and its author may have been "Samuel, or some other godly Prophet vnder the raigne of Saule," according to [Edward Topsell,] *The Reward of Religion: Deliuered in sundry Lectures Vpon the Booke of Ruth* (London, 1597), p. 1. The Breeches Bible of 1559—repeated in the Geneva of 1560—records that the House of David descends in part from a Moabite or "stranger from the people of God" to declare "that the Gentiles should be sanctified" by Christ and "ioyned with his people"; but the story of the marriage itself was not allegorized, for it served, in the words of Lewes [Ludwig] Lavater, *The Book of Ruth,* tr. (*anno aetatis* 11!) Ephraim Pagitt (London, 1586), pp. 142 f., to show that the "married life doth not displease God" and that we must "be opposed against the iudgement of those men which doe condemne, or forbid marriage. For Sathan settes him-selfe against marriage in all ages." The seventeenth volume of the unique "Kitto Bible," housed in The Huntington Library, contains a variety of illustrations (Dutch, English, German, Italian, French) of the Book of Ruth, mainly the gleaning but several of the moment at night; only one is from an emblem book, where the "calling of the Gentiles" is "Typifyd," and none of the illustrators seeks to allegorize the marriage itself.

41 Hughes, p. 728.

42 Englished by J[ohn] H[ealey] (2nd ed., rev.; London, 1620), p. 401.

43 "An Indictment Against England" (London, 1645), Epistle Dedicatory and pp. 6-7.

44 The philological validity of Abel's researches need not detain us, but Freud's remarkable review deserves more attention than I can give it here. See "The Antithetical Meaning of Primal Words," *Standard Edition,* tr. James Strachey, Anna Freud, Alix Strachey, and Alan Tyson, 24 vols. (London, 1953–74), 11 (London, 1957), 155–61. See also the late Rosalie Colie's *Paradoxia Epidemica* (Princeton, 1966), which documents the Renaissance obsession with paradox (a rhetorical expansion of primal word) and related forms of discourse.

45 *Logic: Deductive and Inductive* (rev. ed.; New York, 1889), pp. 54, 57, and 2-3.

46 Hughes, p. 744.

47 Of some relevance here is Harry R. Smallenburg's "Contiguities and Moving Limbs: Style as Argument in *Areopagitica*," *Milton Studies IX*, ed. James D. Simmonds (Pittsburgh, 1976), pp. 169–84.

48 See for example "Linguistics and Poetics," *Style in Language*, ed. Thomas A. Sebeok (New York, 1960); and cf. "Two Aspects of Language: Metaphor and Metonymy," *European Literary Theory and Practice*, ed. Vernon Gras (New York, 1973). Ever since Vico, who hazarded that civilizations pass through four stages (the Age of Gods or "metaphor," the Age of Heroes or "metonymy," the Age of Men or "synechdoche," and the Age of Decadence or "irony") before the *ricorso* or what Joyce calls the "commodius vicus of recirculation," the temptation to extend the relevance of master tropes has proven irresistible; see *The New Science*, tr. Thomas Bergin and Max Fisch (Ithaca, N. Y., 1968), particularly paragraphs 400–410 and 443–446, in relation to Kenneth Burke, "Four Master Tropes," *Grammar of Motives* (New York, 1945), pp. 503–517. The difficulty is, and always has been, the way the tropes dissolve into finer and finer distinctions and then merge into one another. Synechdoche is a figure that takes the part for the whole (a face that launches a thousand ships); the whole for a part (spent cask for empty glass); species (man) for genus (animal) or genus for species; material for the thing (irons for chains); and so on and on, until we can be sure only of how easy it is to mistake metonymy for synechdoche and of how both are metaphorical.

49 See for example "The Letter in the Unconscious," translated with verve by Jan Miel, *Structuralism*, ed. Jacques Ehrmann (New York, 1966).

50 *Critical Quarterly*, 17 (1975), 73–93; *PMLA*, 91 (1976), 101–14. They could of course both be "right," but we must nevertheless have a care for *le regard du démon embusqué dans les ténèbres*. Clifford Geertz, "Cerebral Savage," *Interpretation of Culture* (New York, 1973), 345–59, speaks usefully of the way "binary oppositions" may come to mean almost anything. (A "deep structure," similarly, "means" whatever meaning is attached to it.) Out of that "dialectical chasm between plus and minus which computer technology has rendered the *lingua franca* of modern science, " Claude Lévi-Strauss constructs "an infernal culture machine" that "annuls history, reduces sentiment to a shadow of the intellect, and replaces the particular minds of particular savages in particular jungles with the Savage Mind immanent in us all." But even Geertz's plea for particularity takes the form of a generalization, and the binary digit is here to stay.

51 *Critical Inquiry*, 2 (1975), 204. Meyer Abrams, "The Deconstructive Angel," *Critical Inquiry*, 3 (Spring, 1977), 431, is even less sanguine but much wittier on the contribution of Derrida and his disciples: for the "deconstructive" critic the "chamber of texts is a sealed echo-chamber in which meanings are reduced to a ceaseless echolalia, a vertical and

lateral reverberation from sign to sign of ghostly non-presences emanating from no voice, intended by no one, referring to nothing, bombinating in a void." Insofar as this assessment may prove valid, to that degree one would do well in trying hard to avoid committing a bombination; and yet I feel sure that, say, Professor J. Hillis Miller would not agree with the terms of the judgment.

52 *Religio Medici* ii.2, ed. L. C. Martin (Oxford, 1964), p. 57.

53 *Philosophical Works,* ed. John M. Robertson (London, 1905), p. 54.

54 *Works,* ed. Sir W. Molesworth (11 vols.; London, 1839–45), I, 17.

55 Michel Foucault's formulations, *The Order of Things,* no tr. (New York, 1973), are more complex—or at least more complicated—but come to much the same end. The habit of marking "similitudes" gives way to the tendency to find "identities" and "differences." Foucault notes (pp. 63–64) that when the *Logique de Port-Royal* defines the sign as compassing "*two* ideas, one of the thing representing, the other of the thing represented," the logicians in effect subvert the earlier theory of three elements: "that which was marked, that which did the marking, and that which made it possible to see in the first the mark of the second; and this last element was, of course, resemblance: the sign provided a mark exactly insofar as it was 'almost the same thing' as that which it designated." Thus the first example of a sign in the *Logique* is neither a cry nor a word but a drawing (map, figure, etc.) because a picture has no other "content" than what it represents; the older ternary relation has become binary, and this shift marks for Foucault the change from "commentary" on the Books of God and of Nature to "criticism," for "criticism would appear to contrast with commentary in the same way that an analysis of a visible form with the discovery of a hidden content. But since this form is that of representation, criticism can analyze language only in terms of truth, precision, appropriateness, or expressive value" (p. 80). In Dryden's prefaces we may observe the transition from "commentary" to (literary) "criticism."

56 As quoted in Hoopes, *Right Reason,* p. 5.

57 Hughes, p. 694.

58 *The History of the Royal Society* (1667), *Literary Criticism of Seventeenth-Century England,* ed. Edward W. Tayler (New York, 1967), pp. 316, 318. Swift accomplishes the final *reductio* in *Gulliver,* poking fun at the members of the Grand Academy of Lagado who tried to avoid the pratfalls of language by the complicated expedient of trucking about, for the purpose of conversation, large bundles of *things.*

59 *A Free Inquiry into the Vulgarly Receiv'd Notion of Nature* (London, 1686), pp. 88 and 441.

60 Patrick Hume, *Poetical Works* (London, 1695), makes it even more explicit in his annotation: "*For time, even in Eternity, being referr'd to Motion, measures the Duration and Continuance of all things, by what is present, past, and yet to come. Time, says Plato, is the Image of Eternity,*

Fluid and in Motion. *Aristotle* affirms . . . Time an *Instant* in Flux and Motion: But the Flux and Duration, the Constituents of Time, can no otherwise be reckoned but by applying it to Motion." Barbara Lewalski writes with her usual clarity and learning about this matter in "Time and History in *Paradise Regained,*" *The Prison and the Pinnacle,* ed. Balachandra Rajan (Toronto, 1973), esp. pp. 51–53.

61 Kester Svendsen, *Milton and Science* (Cambridge, Mass., 1956), pp. 114–16, cites a number of analogues from Renaissance literature, most notably Mercator's *Historia Mundi;* but even Mercator's elaborate tree of many gradations rises no higher than its "last branches and fruits."

62 The Angel speculates in the next lines that "time may come" when, "improv'd by tract of time," men may "turn all to spirit" and "wing'd ascend" to become "as we," transcending the "bounds proportion'd" to their "kind."

63 Browne, *Religio* ii.2, pp. 57–58, ever attentive to paradoxical implications, approaches the same question from a contrary angle. Although the "patterne or example of every thing is the perfectest in that kind," we "still come short" even if "wee transcend or goe beyond it. . . . Nor doth the similitude of creatures disparage the variety of nature, nor any way confound the workes of God. For even in things alike, there is diversitie, and those that doe seeme to accord, doe manifestly disagree. And thus is Man like God, for in the same things that wee resemble him, wee are utterly different from him."

64 *Free Inquiry,* pp. 81 and 262. When Robbe-Grillet inveighs against "temporality" in the "modern novel," time loses its status even as an adjunct; see "A Fiction outside Time," *TLS* (21 January 1965), p. 45.

65 See, for example, *Structure of Behavior,* tr. Alden Fisher (Boston, 1963), *Phenomenology of Perception,* tr. Colin Smith (New York and London, 1962), and *Signs,* tr. Richard McCleary (Evanston, Ill., 1964). Shifting attention from the axis of word and thing while modifying the relation of word to idea, Merleau-Ponty distinguishes *le mot,* the word, from *la parole,* the word as faculty of speech used subjectively, and argues that *la parole originaire* gives birth to ideas, brings thought into existence— that it is, in short, an act of meaning—whereas *parole secondaire* merely conveys through *mots* the thoughts originating in the primary motion of language. Erasmus, Ascham, and Renaissance schoolmasters like Brinsley would, I believe, appreciate instantly the power of *la parole originaire* to produce "thought"; they would say, Of course.

INDEX

Abbot, John, 65, 238
Abel, Karl, 201–02, 263
Abrams, Meyer, 264–65
Addison, Joseph, 45, 78, 90
Aesop, 22
Aeschylus, 186
Aldington, Richard, 94
Allegory (see Typology)
Allen, Don Cameron, 230, 245
Altieri, Charles, 204, 264
Andrewes, Lancelot, 32, 187–88, 230
Annesley, Samuel, 191, 250
Ainsworth, Henry, 239
Anonymous, biographer of Milton, 134, 250
Anonymous, ed. of *Paradise Regained*, 252
Anselm, 15, 261
Aquinas, St. Thomas (see Thomas Aquinas, St.)
Arbesmann, Rudolph, 237
Aristotle, 1, 3, 15, 37, 43, 62, 88, 89, 105, 107–08, 116, 168–69, 188, 192, 206, 207, 221, 242, 246, 258
Ascham, Roger, 206, 266
Auerbach, Erich, 26, 186, 224, 226, 227–28, 236
Auden, W. H., 185
Augustine, St., 8, 11–17, 23–24, 26, 28, 30–31, 55, 60, 71–72, 76, 78, 181, 200, 203, 206, 217, 218, 221, 222. 226, 227, 229, 230, 238, 241, 246, 261
Augustus, Caesar, 37, 39
Marcus Aurelius, 8, 9

Bacon, Sir Francis, 11, 94, 157, 187, 206, 217, 243, 259, 265

Bain, Alexander, 2, 202, 216, 263
Baldwin, William, 21
Bale, John, 223
Barker, Arthur, 34–35, 230, 234, 237, 244, 250, 255, 262
Barr, James, 219, 224
Bartas, G. Salluste du, see Sylvester, Joshua
Barth, Karl, 219
Barthes, Roland, 188–190, 259
Bateman, Stephen, 238
Baumgartner, Paul, 248
Beckett, Samuel, 22
Bellarmine, Robert Cardinal, 27
Bentley, Richard, 90–1, 93, 94, 95, 98, 99, 102, 242
Bercovitch, Sacvan, 228, 229
Bergson, Henri, 13, 34, 94
Berkeley, David S., 234
Berry, Boyd M., 170, 251, 258, 260
Beverley, Thomas, 28–9, 229
Blake, William, 243
Bloom, Harold, 215, 262
Blundeville, Thomas, 217
Bodin, Jean, 239
Boethius, 15, 16, 220, 222, 225, 245, 261
The Book of the XXIV Philosophers, 14, 218, 220
Boman, Thorleif, 219
Booth, Wayne C., 259
Boyle, Robert, 208, 212, 265, 266
Brandon, S. G. F., 222
Breasted, Barbara, 251
Brent, William, 217
Bridgewater Ms. (of *A Mask*), 137
Bridgit, St., 58
Brinsley, John, 267
Broadbent, J. B., 230, 257

Brooks, Cleanth, 190, 260
Brisman, Leslie, 243
Browne, Sir Thomas, 1, 8, 36, 57, 62,
  63, 108, 156, 183, 197, 205, 217, 218,
  220, 231, 236, 237, 238, 245, 255,
  258, 263, 265, 266
Brumm, Ursula, 228
Buckhurst, Thomas Sackville, Lord
  (later first Earl of Dorset), 21
Bullinger, Heinrich, 24–25, 180, 225,
  258
Bullokar, John, 237
Bunting, Henry, 259
Bunyan, John, 23, 141
Burgess, Anthony, 216
Burke, Kenneth, 264
Bush, Douglas, 173, 232, 251

Caillois, Roger, 237
Calamy, Edmund, 200, 257–58, 263
Calvin, Jean, 26–27, 30, 81, 106, 132,
  153, 155, 195, 227, 230, 234, 241–42,
  254, 255
Carey, John, 246
Carlyle, Thomas, 157
Cartari, Vincenzo, 257
Cary, Lucius, Lord Falkland, 156
Caryll, Joseph, 247
Cassian, 23
Cawdrey, Robert, 63, 237
Chambers, A. B., 231, 256
Chappell, William, 233
Chatman, Seymour, 170–71, 258
Chaucer, Geoffrey, 56, 155, 255
Christopher, Georgia B., 250–51
chronos (see *kairos*)
Church, Henry, 29, 61–62, 229, 237
Cicero, 178, 190
Ciceronians, 181
Cirillo, Albert R., 237, 244, 246
Clark, Ira, 256
Cleveland, John, 34, 185
Cocceian School, 231
Cohn, Norman, 153, 254
Coleridge, Samuel Taylor, 111, 189,
  228, 243, 246
Colie, Rosalie L., 237, 263
Collett, Jonathan H., 232
Collingwood, R. G., 238
Condillac, Etienne Bonnot de, 207
Coolidge, John, 178, 258
Cope, Jackson I., 237–238
Corbett, Richard, 248
Cornford, F. M., 258
Corpus Reformatorum, 255

Cowley, Abraham, 14, 16–17, 178–79,
  221, 222, 240, 258
Crane, Hart, 13
Crashaw, Richard, 35
Cromwell, Oliver, 144–45, 157
crypsis, 190–91
Cudworth, Ralph, 105, 114, 121, 244
Cullmann, Oscar, 219, 256
Curran, Stuart, 255
Curtis, John Briggs, 219
Cusanus, Nicolas, see Nicolas of Cusa

Daneau, Lambert, 216
Daniel, Samuel, 71
Daniélou, Fr. Jean, 25, 224, 226
Dante, 23, 24, 32, 218, 223
David, Fr. Joannes, 123–24, 247
Davie, Donald, 65, 238
Davies, John, of Hereford, 191, 260
Defoe, Daniel, 260
Demosthenes, 126
Derrida, Jacques, 264
Descartes, René, 3, 7, 206, 207, 210
Dickson, David, 231, 234
Diodati, Charles, 37, 125, 136, 230
Dionysius the Areopagite, 15, 24, 25
discordia concors, 3, 102–03, 200–03, 216,
  246, 259
Donatus, 179
Donne, John, 8, 18, 28, 29, 42, 71,
  103–04, 177, 187, 218, 221, 229, 230,
  232, 238, 239, 244
Doolittle, Hilda, 94
Dorian, Donald, 132–33, 250
Drexelius [Drexel, Hiermias], 220, 222
Driver, Tom F., 246
Dryden, John, 265

Elias, Norbert, 206
Eliot, T. S., 2, 93, 97, 169, 171, 199, 208
Elledge, Scott, 133, 238
Elliott, Emory, 229
Ellis-Fermor, Una, 244
Empedocles, 215, 217
Empson, William, 233, 242
Erasmus, 97, 245, 266
Erikson, Erik, 241
Euripides, 110, 117, 249
Evans, J. M., 228

Featley, Daniel, 39, 217, 231, 249
felix culpa, 87, 91–92, 102, 205–06, 241,
  242
Felsen, Karl E., 235
Fenner, William, 247

Ferry, Anne Davidson, 240
figuralism (see typology)
Fish, Stanley E., 239–40, 243, 247, 257, 258
Fixler, Michael, 254
Flaubert, Gustave, 260
Fleissner, Robert, 235
Fletcher, Angus, 223, 250-51
Fletcher, Giles, 21, 33, 185, 232
Fletcher, Joseph, 36, 218, 231
Fletcher, Phineas, 21, 33, 185
Fludd, Robert, 220
Fogle, French, 244
Foucault, Michel, 265
four-fold method, 23–24, 222, 224-25
Fowler, Alastair, 238
Fox, John, 61, 124, 237, 248
Frank, Robert W., Jr., 223
French, J. Milton, 235
Freud, Sigmund, 137, 200-02, 216, 263
Frye, Northrop, 20, 60, 171, 192–93, 204, 253, 254, 261, 264
Fulgentius, 31
Fuller, Thomas, 159, 255
Furneaux, Henry, 238

Galdon, Fr. Joseph A., 228
Gale, Theophilus, 230
Garcaeus, Joh., 220
Gardiner, Samuel, 244
Gardner, Helen, 228, 258
Geertz, Clifford, 264
Gell, Robert, 233
Gide, André, 134
Gilbert, Allan H., 149–50, 252
Gilman, Wilbur, 262
Giraldi, Lilio Gregorio, 220
Goldin, Judah, 225
Gombrich, E. H., 46, 233
Goppelt, Leonhard, 228
Gossman, Ann M., 244, 246, 251
Gouge, William, 234
Granger, Thomas, 129–30, 131, 133, 142, 219, 245, 249
Grant, Patrick, 256
Greek Anthology, 42, 123
Greg, W. W., 233
Gregory the Great, St., 227, 231
Greville, Fulke, Lord Brooke, 25
Greville, Robert, Second Lord Brooke, 207, 265
Grotius, Hugo, 233
Guild, William, 230
Guilpin, Richard, 253, 255-56, 257
Guss, Donald L., 257

Hadas, Moses, 258
Hakewill, George, 239
Hall, Joseph, 256
Hamilton, Gary D., 149–50, 252, 253
Hammond, Henry, 235
Hanford, James Holly, 45–46, 149, 233, 252
Hanning, Robert W., 226
Harding, Davis P., 71, 239, 250
Hardison, O. B., Jr., 232
Hardy, John Edward, 190, 260
Harnack, Adolph, 155
Harington, Sir John, 225
Harran, Marilyn, 241
Harvey, Gabriel, 56
Henley, William Ernest, 132
Herbert, George, 42, 181
heresies, 125, 208–09, 212
Herodotus, 89, 178
Hertelius, Jacobus, 227
Hesiod, 186, 215
Heywood, Thomas, 244
Hill, John Spencer, 248
Hippocrates, 188
Hobbes, Thomas, 89, 205, 206, 208, 212-13, 221, 265
Hollander, Robert, 228
Homer, 4, 15, 22, 31, 61, 83, 84, 136, 186, 215, 240
Honig, Edwin, 223
Hooker, Richard, 218
Hoopes, Robert, 261, 265
Hugh of St. Victor, 227
Hughes, Merritt Y., 37, 254
Huguelet, Theodore Long, 228, 261
Hume, Patrick, 69, 265

Ignatius, St., 34
Illo, John, 262
Imagist Manifesto, 94
Isidore of Seville, 22

Jackson, Lt. Col. James L., 251
Jackson, Thomas, 192, 218, 261
Jackson, W. T. H., 223
Jakobson, Roman, 203–04, 264
Jerome, St., 74
Joachim de Fiore, 71
John, St., Apostle, 137
Johnson, Samuel, 46, 55, 94, 106-07, 109, 113, 114, 116, 149, 177, 216, 233, 243, 244
Jones, Inigo, 138
Jonson, Ben, 18, 115, 156, 178, 185, 255
Jordan, Richard D., 257

Joyce, James, 138, 264
Jung, Carl, 244
justification, 240–41
Juvenal, 97

Kafka, Franz, 23
kairos (and *chronos*), 9, 17, 123–47, 156, 169, 187–88, 219–20, 247–48, 256, 257
Kant, Immanuel, 189, 206, 259
Kantorowicz, Ernst H., 222
Keach, Benjamin, 229
Keats, John, 207
Kelley, Maurice, 237
Kelly, L. G., 234
Kendall, W., 262
Kermode, Frank, 220, 238, 254
Kerrigan, William, 229
King, Edward, 46, 53
Kittredge, G. L., 249
Knight, G. Wilson, 233
Knott, John R., 242
Krouse, F. M., 224
Kurth, Burton O., 255
Kyd, Thomas, 19

Labriola, Albert C., 245, 256
Lacan, Jacques, 203–04, 264
Lampe, G. W. H., 228
Landor, Walter Savage, 97
Langland, William, 23, 68
Lavater, Lewis [Ludwig], 263
Lawes, Henry, 138
Lawrence, D. H., 206–07
Leach, Edmund, 4, 216
Leavis, F. R., 1
LeComte, Edward, 126, 248
Leibniz, Gottfried Wilhelm von, 206
Leigh, Edward, 247, 250
Lévi-Strauss, Claude, 3, 203, 216, 264
Lewalski, Barbara, 240, 252, 253, 254, 256, 257, 266
Lewis, C. S., 71, 78, 239
Liber Vitae of New Minster, 235
Lieb, Michael, 237, 242
Ling, Nicholas, 237
Livy, 239
Locke, Johne, 206, 264
Lodge, David, 204, 264
Logique de Port-Royal, 265
logos, 188, 213
Lovejoy, Arthur O., 242
Low, Anthony, 121, 246, 247
de Lubac, Fr. Henri, 224

Luther, Martin, 26–27, 155, 220, 227, 241
Lycurgus, 9

McAdams, James R., 254
MacCaffrey, Isabel, 48, 56, 234, 236, 243
MacCallum, H. R., 223–24, 240
McColley, Grant, 237
MacLeish, Archibald, 244
Macrobius, 249
Madsen, William, 228, 238
magnus annus, 9, 16, 217–18
Marbeck, John, 223
Marlorat, Augustine, 238
Marshall, Stephen, 133, 134, 135, 249–50
Marten, Anthony, 239
Martz, Louis L., 230, 234, 242
Marvell, Andrew, 3, 45, 199, 216, 255
Mather, Nathaniel, 227
Mather, Samuel, 27–28, 181, 227, 232, 258
Matthew, Roger, 148, 252
Mazzeo, Joseph A., 223, 235
Mede, Joseph, 233
Melville, Herman, 43, 157–58, 174–76, 182, 255
Mercator, Gerardus [Gerhard Kremer], 266
Merleau-Ponty, Maurice, 213, 266
Michelangelo, 174
Miel, Jan, 264
Migne, Abbé Jacques Paul, 25
Miles, Josephine, 234
Miller, J. Hillis, 265
Milton, John, *Animadversions,* 134, 148, 154, 235; *Apology for Smectymnuus,* 134, 194, 207; *Areopagitica,* 3, 98, 117, 119, 173, 176, 193, 194, 195, 199, 200, 202–03, 204–05, 216, 243, 247, 251, 261, 262, 263; "At a Solemn Music," 37, 186; *Art of Logic,* 119, 190–91, 192; *Christian Doctrine,* 27, 63, 80, 92, 134, 142, 144, 158, 163, 172, 207, 209, 210–11, 224, 227, 230, 244, 253; Divorce tracts, 127–28, 135, 136, 140, 193–94, 202, 204, 250, 261, 262; "Elegia Prima," 136; "Elegia Quinta," 136; "Elegia Sexta," 37, 230; "Epitaph on the Marchioness of Winchester," 18; *History of Britain,* 208; "Il Penseroso," 18; "L' Allegro," 18; Letter to an Unidentified Friend, 128–

30, 132, 248; Letter to Leonard
Philaris, 110, 140–42; Lycidas, 18–20,
44, 45–59, 179, 186, 191, 228, 234,
236, 259; A Mask, 47, 124, 125, 134,
135–37, 185, 193, 195, 199, 209, 210,
260, 262; Of Education, 188–89, 190–
91; Of Reformation, 14, 134, 262; "On
the Death of a Fair Infant Dying of a
Cough," 18–20, 21, 33, 43, 44, 47, 52;
"On the Morning of Christ's Nativity,"
21, 34–40, 43, 44, 45, 47, 49, 135, 177,
185, 230, 242; "On Time," 41–42,
184; "On the University Carrier,"
185; Paradise Lost, 23, 43–44, 57, 60–
104, 105, 109, 110, 115, 120, 121,
124, 143, 144, 147, 158, 162, 165,
167, 168, 169, 171, 174, 176, 177–78,
179, 180, 181, 182, 193, 197, 200,
201, 203–04, 207, 208, 223, 237, 238,
239, 242, 250, 254, 259–60, 263;
Paradise Regained, 21, 34, 39, 57, 82,
89, 103, 123, 124, 132, 143, 145,
146–82, 185, 187, 193, 224, 244, 250,
251, 252, 254, 263; "The Passion," 21,
33–34, 43, 124, 135, 185; Pro Populo
Anglico Defensio, 107, 121; "Paraphrase of Ps. CXIV," 18; Reason of
Church Government, 47, 124, 134, 222,
246, 248, 262; Samson Agonistes, 89,
96, 103, 105–22, 134, 146, 148–49,
185, 193, 263; Second Defense, 125,
128, 130, 140–41, 144, 145, 248, 253;
"Seventh Prolusion," 60; Sonnet VII,
122, 127, 130–33, 167–68, 169, 184,
248; Sonnet IX, 198–99; Sonnet XVI,
142; Sonnet XIX, 141–44, 147; Son-
nett XXII, 110, 125, 143–44; Tenure
of Kings and Magistrates, 236; Tetra-
chordon, 240; "Upon the Circumcision," 21–22, 32–33, 35, 43, 45, 186
Mintz, Alan, 225
Montaigne, Michel de, 174
More, Thomas, St., 97
Morgan, Charles, 109, 246
Morison, Sir Henry, 156–57
Morris, David B., 230–31
Morris, John N., 242
Mulder, John, 228
Mulryan, John, 257
Murrin, Michael, 223

Nelson, Lowry, 231
Nemerov, Howard, 204, 215
Neuthaler, Paul, 230

Nicholas of Lyra, 27
Nicolas of Cusa, 14, 218, 244
Nicolson, Marjorie Hope, 148–49, 220,
252
Norford, Don Parry, 244
Nowell, Alexander, 240
nunc stans, 17, 22, 32–33, 35, 221, 222

Occam, William of, 245
occasion (see kairos)
Ogilby, John, 236
opportunitas (see kairos)
Oras, Ants, 222
Origen, 23, 224
Ovid, 4, 18, 21, 22, 54, 70–71, 136, 178,
185, 239
Owen, John, 232

Palmer, Herbert, 262
Panofsky, Erwin, 248
Paracelsus, 131, 132, 249, 250
Paraeus, David, 81
Parish, John E., 240
Parker, William Riley, 250
Parker, William S., 109, 246
Patrides, C. A., 229, 233, 258
Patterson, James, 238
Paul, St., Apostle, 27, 29–30, 31–32,
48–49, 125, 137, 140, 151, 167, 180–
81, 248
Peacham, Henry, 220
Pearce, Zachary, 90–91, 102, 242
Pearson, John, 234
Pecheux, Mother M. Christopher, 234,
238. 242, 243
Perkins, William, 158–59, 187, 255, 256,
258, 259
Perkinson, R. H., 237
Peter Martyr, 239, 242
Petrarch, 21–22, 130, 141
Peyton, Thomas, 100, 243
Phillips, Edward, 134, 149
Philo of Alexandria, 29, 222, 223
Pindar, 249
Pike, Nelson, 261
Plato, 9, 10, 12, 15, 16, 22, 23, 62, 63,
71, 77, 137, 189, 191, 196–97, 205,
207, 209, 225, 243, 249, 258, 263
Pliny, 9, 66–67, 238
Plotinus, 15, 16
Plutarch, 31–32, 157, 174, 176, 222,
250, 258
Polybius, 67

Poole, Matthew, 167, 216–17, 234, 241, 257
Pope, Alexander, 178
Pope, Elizabeth Marie, 253
Posidippus, 123
Poulet, Georges, 155, 225, 255
Pound, Ezra, 93, 94, 95
Powell, Mary, 126, 134–35, 140, 144, 193
Preuss, James S., 227
primal words, 2–3, 200–03, 216
Prince, F. T., 222, 259
prolepsis, 64, 109, 191
Prudentius, 22, 223
punning, 96–97
Puttenham, George (?), 48, 64, 156–57, 191, 234, 238
Pyle, Fitzroy, 251
Pythagoras, 220

Quarles, Francis, 246–47
Quinones, Ricardo, 219–20

Ralegh, Sir Walter, 258
Raleigh, Sir Walter, 97, 243
Ramus, Peter, 262
Randolph, Thomas, 185
ratio recta, 192, 194–95, 261
Reynolds, Henry, 232
Reynolds, Sir Joshua, 102, 104, 244
Ricks, Christopher, 113, 243, 246
Robbe-Grillet, Alain, 266
Roberts, Francis, 229, 240
Rollenhagen, Gabriel, 220
Roman de la Rose, 218
Rosenmeier, Jasper, 228
Ross, Alexander, 54, 172–73, 236, 258
Ross, M. M., 138
le Roy, Louis, 3, 216
Royal Society, 208, 213

de Saussure, Ferdinand, 203
Schleiermacher, Friedrich, 15
Schultz, Howard, 254
Scott-Craig, T. S. K., 246
Sensabaugh, George F., 258
Servius, 179
Shakespeare, William, 18, 45, 94. 102, 109, 112, 131, 132, 136–37, 185, 189, 236
Shawcross, John T., 237, 243, 246, 248, 250, 251
Shower, John, 256
Sidney, Sir Philip, 36–37, 98, 110

signatures, 205–08
Simon, Fr. Richard, 216
Simonides, 249
Sirluck, Ernest, 134, 137, 248, 250, 262
Smallenburg, Harry R., 264
Smalley, Beryl, 224
Smart, J. S., 259
Smith, John, 245
Solon, 9, 249
Sophocles, 79, 88, 106, 109, 110, 120, 186, 207, 246, 250
de Soto, Andreas, 249
Spencer, Herbert, 13
Spenser, Edmund, 18, 19, 21, 23, 29, 33, 45, 52, 56, 68, 110, 139, 179, 185, 194, 200, 219, 236
Spicq, Fr. Ceslaus, 224
Sprat, Thomas, 208, 265
Stapleton, Thomas, 27
Stapleton, Laurence, 230, 237, 238
Statius, Publius Papinius, 178
Steadman, John M., 228, 240, 244, 245, 255
Stein, Arnold, 243, 253
Sterry, Peter, 2, 29, 60, 61, 88, 104, 191–92, 215, 230, 237, 242, 261
Stevens, Wallace, 3, 19, 52, 173, 186, 259, 261
Stewart, Stanley, 240
Stocks, J. L., 191, 261
Strabo, 54
Summers, Joseph, 239, 240, 242, 247
Svendsen, Kester, 266
Swaim, Kathleen, 235
Swan, John, 232
Swardson, H. R., 232
Swift, Jonathan, 265
Sylvester, Joshua, 18, 19, 185

Tacitus, 68, 238–39
Tasso, Torquato, 222
Tayler, E. W., 233, 251
"tempestivity" (see kairos)
Tertullian, 167, 219, 257
Theocritus, 48, 53–55, 56–58, 234, 236
Theognis, 249
Thomas Aquinas, St., 17, 22, 23–24, 25, 27, 220–21, 224
Thucydides, 178
Thyer, Robert, 250
Tiberius, 68
Tillich, Paul, 218
Topsell, Edward, 263
Trinity Ms., 21, 42, 137, 138, 251

Trismegistus, Mercurius, 220
Turner, W. Arthur, 235
Tuve, Rosemond, 223, 224, 226, 230
Tyndale, William, 26, 97, 235
W[illiam] T[yping], 220, 222
typology, 17, 22–32, 45, 46, 88–89,
  103–04, 123–24, 180–81, 187–88,
  222–32, 234

Ulreich, John C. Jr., 228

Vaughan, Henry, 219
Vergil, 18, 22, 31, 47, 48, 53–55, 56–58
  61, 136, 179, 181–82, 185, 186, 190,
  234, 236, 249
Vico, Giambattista, 264
Vischer, Wilhelm, 227
Vives, Juan Luis, 12, 26, 198, 238, 263

Waddington, Raymond, 240
Waldock, A. J. A., 189–90, 259–60
Waller, A. R., 221
Wanamaker, Melissa C., 216
Warburton, William, 252
Washbourne, Thomas, 230
Weber, Burton J., 254
Weese, Capt. Walter E., 251
Whately, William, 129, 248

Whitaker, William, 26, 27, 226, 227
Whiting, G. W., 235
Whiting, George, 251
Widmer, Kingsley, 258
Wilkes, G. A., 106, 121, 245
Willett, Andrew, 74. 217, 226, 239
Williams, R. Darby, 42, 232
Wilson, Edmund, 136
Wilson, Thomas, 229, 234, 249
Wind, Edgar, 231–32
Wither, George, 220–23, 224–25, 226,
  231
Wittgenstein, Ludwig, 8, 259
Wittkower, Rudolf, 249
Wittreich, Joseph Anthony, Jr., 234, 252
Wolleb, John, 227
Woodhouse, A. S. P., 34, 149, 230, 248,
  254
Woollcombe, K. J., 228
Worden, Thomas, 231
Wordsworth, William, 178

Yeats, William Butler, 215
Young, Thomas, 133

Zwicky, Laurie B., 256
Zwinglius, 195